Sociology
GCSE for AQA

SOCIOLOGY ②

Pauline Wilson and Allan Kidd

William Collins's dream of knowledge for all began with the publication of his first book in 1819. A self-educated mill worker, he not only enriched millions of lives, but also founded a flourishing publishing house. Today, staying true to this spirit, Collins books are packed with inspiration, innovation and practical expertise. They place you at the centre of a world of possibility and give you exactly what you need to explore it.

Collins. Freedom to teach.

Published by Collins
An imprint of HarperCollinsPublishers
77-85 Fulham Palace Road
Hammersmith
London
W6 8JB

Browse the complete Collins catalogue at
www.collinseducation.com

© HarperCollinsPublishers Limited 2010

10 9 8 7 6

ISBN 978-0-00-731070-8

British Library Cataloguing in Publication Data. A Catalogue record for this publication is available from the British Library.

Commissioned by Charles Evans
Original concept design by Jordan Publishing Design
Page layout and cover design by Thomson Digital
Illustrations by Jerry Fowler and Thomson Digital
Photos sourced by Suzanne Williams/Pictureresearch.co.uk
Index by Indexing Specialists (UK) Ltd
Production by Simon Moore
Printed and bound by Printing Express, Hong Kong

Sociology
GCSE for AQA

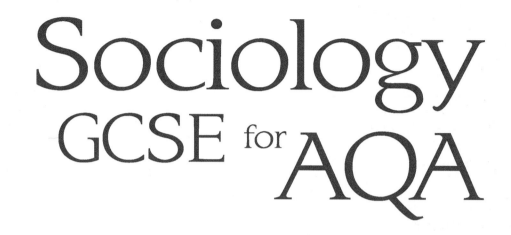

Pauline Wilson and Allan Kidd

Contents

This book has been written to cover the AQA GCSE specification in Sociology. It provides a student-centred and activity-based introduction to the subject at GCSE level. The contents cover the material that you will need to know and understand. However, studying Sociology is not just about acquiring knowledge. It is also about developing important skills such as being able to interpret and evaluate information, so you will find lots of activities in this book to help you develop these skills. You will also have opportunities to participate in discussions and undertake your own research.

The AQA GCSE specification in Sociology has two Units.

If you are doing the Short Course, you will study Unit 1.

If you are doing the Full Course, you will study Unit 2 as well as Unit 1.

Unit 1:

Studying Society

Education

Families

Unit 2:

Crime and Deviance

Mass Media

Power

Social Inequality

Text features

Each of the chapters in this book covers one area of the AQA specification. Chapters 2 to 4 cover Unit 1 and Chapters 5 to 8 cover Unit 2. Each chapter consists of a number of Topics to make it easier for you to work through it. The topic title (1) tells you what key question will be addressed, while the objectives (2) focus on what you should be able to do once you have worked through the material and activities.

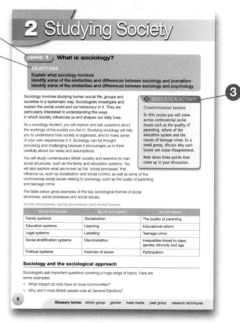

Activities

Within each topic you will find a range of activities that are designed to get you thinking about the material you are studying. There are four types of activity in each chapter: discussion activities, written activities, stretch and challenge activities and research activities.

Discussion activities

Discussion activities (3) are designed to stimulate discussion and debate on sociological issues. They may be used as the basis of a whole-class or a small-group discussion. You may be asked to note down the main points of your discussion or to feed your ideas back to the rest of the class. In this way, you will deepen your understanding of an issue and develop your skills when it comes to evaluation. It is important to appreciate that there may be no 'right' answer to a discussion activity. Everyone's views should be considered equally. This can lead to lively and interesting debates.

Written activities

Written activities (4) may present you with some statistical data or an extract from a book or newspaper article and you will be asked to answer questions based on this source. This will help you to develop your skills in interpreting and making sense of information.

Stretch and challenge activities

Some stretch and challenge activities (5) follow on from written activities and others are stand-alone activities. They may ask you to assess arguments and respond using your own ideas or drawing on your experiences. As their name suggests, these activities are designed to encourage you to consider carefully a particular issue or question.

Research activities

Research tasks (6) provide you with the opportunity to explore more fully a particular aspect of the topic you are covering by undertaking activities such as carrying out opinion polls, piloting surveys or conducting internet-based research.

Eye on the exam

Each chapter includes some tips and advice to help you to prepare for the written examination in sociology. You will find these under the heading Eye on the exam (7).

Glossary terms

As you read through each topic, you are likely to come across some new terms and concepts. Many of these terms are explained in the text when they first appear. The more complex terms and concepts also appear in the glossary towards the end of the book, where they are defined for you. The first time a glossary term (8) appears in the book, it will be shown in the ribbon at the bottom of the page.

Check your understanding

These questions (9) appear towards the end of each Topic. They are designed to enable you to check that you have understood the key ideas in the topic you have been studying.

Key points

Each topic finishes with a short section on Key points (10) which summarize the contents of the topic.

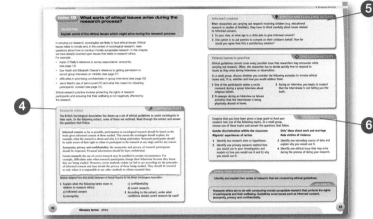

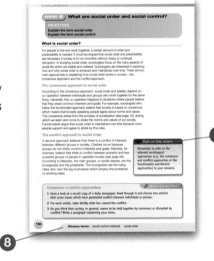

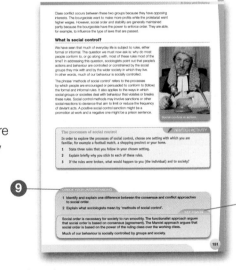

Examination practice questions and answers

Examination practice questions and answers can be found towards the end of the book. These questions resemble those that could come up in the examination. The answers have been written by students and have been marked and commented on by an experienced sociology examiner. It is worth spending time on this section so that you understand why each student has been awarded their marks, the point the examiner is making in the comments and what the student needs to do to develop and improve their answer.

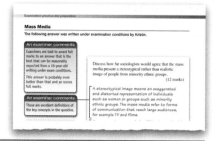

Sociological skills

This book is designed to help you develop the skills you need to be a competent sociologist at this level. The examination assesses a number of different skills. These skills can be summarized as follows:

- **Knowledge and understanding** – Put simply, can you show that you know and understand the subject matter (for example, the different methods of research or the various explanations of the effects of the media on the audience) that you have been studying?

- **Application of knowledge and understanding** – Can you apply your knowledge to the set question? In other words, can you use what you know about an issue in order to address the question being asked?

- **Interpretation, analysis and evaluation** – Can you make sense of material such as tables of statistics or extracts from newspapers? Can you select or pick out the relevant data from this material? Can you assess an explanation or idea by identifying its strengths and weaknesses? Can you evaluate one approach to a question or issue by comparing and contrasting it to other relevant approaches? After weighing up the evidence, can you reach a balanced conclusion?

Do not worry if this looks like a tall order! As you work through the material and activities in this book, you will have lots of opportunities to develop and hone these skills.

Study skills

In addition to the sociological skills outlined above, you should aim to develop a range of other skills to help maximize your chances of success. These are usually referred to as 'study skills'.

Time management

Have you ever felt that you have too much to do and too little time in which to do it? This is a common problem for students. One way to help ease this situation is to think about your time management; in other words, try to make maximum use of the time that you have available.

The first step is to identify how much time you have available for study in the given week and establish when exactly this is. You will need to consider all of your other commitments and then, in theory, the time left over can be used as study time.

The next step is to prioritize the tasks you have to complete – perhaps according to when they have to be done by.

Once you have done this you can produce a study plan for the week.

This identifies what you will do and when you will do it. All you then have to do is to stick to your plan!

Time	Monday	Tuesday	Wednesday	Thursday	Friday	Saturday	Sunday
9 a.m.							
10 a.m.							
11 a.m.							
12 noon							
6 p.m.							
evening							

An example of how you might organize a weekly study plan.

Note taking

In order to develop your sociological knowledge and understanding further, it is often a good idea to read around a topic. You might look at other books or at newspaper articles related to a particular topic you are studying.

As a result of your reading, you may wish to make some notes to use later. While students often have their own approach to taking notes, you may find it useful to read these suggestions for effective note taking.

- Do not simply produce a slightly shorter version of the material you are taking notes on.
- Do skim read the information to get a general understanding first.
- Do use headings and sub-headings to identify key areas.
- Do use numbers or letters to identify key points.
- Do use underlining or indentation to help make notes clearer.
- Do use abbreviations if you prefer – for example, '+' for 'and'.

Making sense of statistical information

You will come across many examples of statistical tables and charts in this book and throughout your study of sociology. It is important for you to be able to interpret these tables accurately.

The following example is included to give you an idea of what you should be looking for in a table of statistical information.

❶ Table heading – What general subject is referred to? In the table on page 5 it is size of households in Great Britain.

❷ Relationships in the table – What is being referred to in particular and what is it being related to? Here, the table refers to households according to the number of people in them at five different points in time. We can see, for example, that 18 per cent of households in 1971 contained one person.

4

Households: by size, Great Britain ①

	Percentages ④				
	1971	**1981**	**1991**	**2001**	**2007** ③
One person	18 ②	22	27	29	29
Two people	32	32	34	35	35
Three people	19	17	16	16	16
Four people	17	18	16	14	13
Five people	8	7	5	5	5
Six or more people	6	4	2	2	2

Source: : *Social Trends* ⑤ (2008) ⑥

③ Timescale – Are any dates or years shown? Here, we are looking at household size in 1971, 1981, 1991 and so on.

④ Units of measurements – Are the figures shown in percentages? If they are in numbers, is it thousands or millions? Or is it numbers per thousand of the population? Here, the unit of measurement is percentages.

⑤ Source of the statistics – Where are the statistics from? Can this source be relied upon? Is it likely to be biased in any way? Here, the table is from *Social Trends*, which is a major source of government statistics, published annually.

⑥ Date – When were the statistics produced? How up to date are they? Here, the statistics are from 2008.

Identifying trends and changes

In some cases, you will be asked to identify or pick out trends in statistics. A trend refers to the general direction in which statistics on something (such as household size) move over time. In the case of this table, we can find several trends. For example, we could identify the trend in the percentage of households containing one person between 1971 and 2001. The trend shown is an increase in the percentage of households containing one person from 1971 to 2001.

Some statistics present a change between just two points in time, for example between 2001 and 2007. In this case, you may be asked to identify the percentage change between these two points in time.

Statistics may be presented in a variety of other forms including bar charts (where columns or rows are used to represent percentages or numbers) or graphs where the rise and fall of a line represents a trend. Pie charts can also be used to represent statistics in the form of percentages in a highly visual way.

The main thing to remember about statistics is not to be afraid of them. Consider them carefully, using the advice given here.

2 Studying Society

What is sociology?

OBJECTIVES

Explain what sociology involves
Identify some of the similarities and differences between sociology and journalism
Identify some of the similarities and differences between sociology and psychology

Sociology involves studying human social life, groups and societies in a systematic way. Sociologists investigate and explain the social world and our behaviour in it. They are particularly interested in understanding the ways in which society influences us and shapes our daily lives.

As a sociology student, you will explore and ask questions about the workings of the society you live in. Studying sociology will help you to understand how society is organized, and to make sense of your own experiences in it. Sociology can be thought provoking and challenging because it encourages us to think carefully about our views and assumptions.

You will study contemporary British society and examine its main social structures, such as the family and education systems. You will also explore what are known as the 'social processes' that influence us, such as socialization and social control, as well as some of the controversial social issues relating to sociology, such as the quality of parenting and teenage crime.

The table below gives examples of the key sociological themes of social structures, social processes and social issues.

> ✦ **DISCUSSION ACTIVITY**
>
> **Controversial issues**
>
> In this course you will come across controversial social issues such as the quality of parenting, reform of the education system and the causes of teenage crime. In a small group, discuss why such issues can cause disagreement.
>
> Note down three points that come up in your discussion.

Social structures, social processes and social issues

Social structures	Social processes	Social issues
Family systems	Socialization	The quality of parenting
Education systems	Learning	Educational reform
Legal systems	Labelling	Teenage crime
Social stratification systems	Discrimination	Inequalities linked to class, gender, ethnicity and age
Political systems	Exercise of power	Participation

Sociology and the sociological approach

Sociologists ask important questions covering a huge range of topics. Here are some examples:

- What impact do riots have on local communities?
- Why don't more British people vote at General Elections?

Glossary terms: ethnic group   gender   mass media   peer group   research techniques

- How do women of South Asian heritage experience university?
- What do people in Britain believe in nowadays?
- How have families changed since the 1960s?

When addressing such questions, sociologists use:

- a body of terms (specialized vocabulary) and concepts (key ideas) that they have built up
- a 'tool kit' of research techniques such as questionnaires and interviews.

Journalists, like sociologists, undertake research as part of their work.

Sociology and journalism

News journalists working in the mass media (for example, the press and television) ask similar questions to those listed above. Television news broadcasts, for instance, examine why there is low turnout at elections. Like sociologists, journalists carry out research in order to try to answer these questions, but it is important to understand what makes sociology different from journalism.

- Journalists' research is less systematic and thorough than that of sociologists. This is partly because journalists often have tight deadlines to meet.
- Journalists may side with one political party over another, or use evidence in a biased or one-sided way in their reports. Sociologists, however, should be balanced in their use of evidence.
- Sociological research is subject to peer review (see "Evaluation" on page 17). This means that other sociologists (peers) check and evaluate research reports and articles.

Sociology and psychology

If you have studied psychology, you will know that psychologists also study people, drawing on key concepts such as personality or aggression, and using research techniques such as experiments. However, while psychology focuses on the behaviour of individuals, sociology focuses on group behaviour, social structures and the social processes that influence us. For instance, psychologists might explain racial prejudice in terms of factors related to the individual who is being racist. However, sociologists emphasize the role of social structures such as families, and social processes such as socialization.

CHECK YOUR UNDERSTANDING

1 Identify one similarity and one difference between sociology and journalism.

2 Identify one similarity and one difference between sociology and psychology.

KEY POINTS

Sociology is the systematic study of human social life, groups and societies. Sociologists examine social structures such as families, and social processes such as socialization.

Sociologists ask questions about the workings of society, for example, how families have changed since the 1960s.

The sociological approach is based on the use of key concepts, terms and research techniques.

social issues   social processes   social structures   socialization   stratification

TOPIC 2 · What key concepts are used in sociology?

OBJECTIVE

Explain the terms culture, values and norms

In Topic 1, you learned that sociologists draw on key concepts (ideas)
in their work. These key concepts include culture, values and norms.

Living with the British — ❖ DISCUSSION ACTIVITY

The following information is for international students studying at university in England.
It aims to help these students become familiar with the British culture or way of life.
Read through the extract, then answer the questions that follow.

Personal Space
British people like a lot of space around them. They tend not to make physical contact of any
kind with strangers. They will instinctively draw away if anyone comes too close.

Shaking Hands
One example of the British 'keeping their distance' is the infrequency with which people shake
hands with one another. British people do not shake hands very often at all.

Making Polite Requests
In making polite requests, British people tend to use very indirect language. For instance, 'I
don't suppose you could open the window, could you?' rather than 'Please open the window.'

Topics of Conversation
It is not usually considered polite to ask someone their age or income. Otherwise, most topics
can be discussed openly and frankly.

Source: http://www.shef.ac.uk/welcome/index.html

1 Which two of the four pieces of information
do you think are most helpful in describing
aspects of British culture? Why have you
chosen these two?

2 In small groups, compare your answers and
explain your reasons for choosing these
two pieces of information.

3 In your group, think of two more pieces
of information to help overseas visitors
become familiar with the British culture
and way of life. Make a note of these.

Culture

The word 'culture' refers to the whole way of life of a particular society. It
includes the values, norms, customs, beliefs and language of a society.
Sociologists understand that culture is not the same everywhere around the
world. It varies according to place (where you are) and time (when). You can
see this by looking at food and diet:

* Whole roasted guinea pig is enjoyed as a traditional delicacy in Ecuador, while
guinea pigs are often kept as family pets in the UK.

Glossary terms: culture   negative sanctions   norms   positive sanctions   taboo   values

- Traditionally, the Apache of North America did not eat fish, snakes or frogs as reptiles were considered a cultural taboo.

Values

Values are ideas and beliefs that people have about what is desirable and worth striving for. For example, privacy and respect for human life are highly valued by most people in Britain. Values give us general guidelines for conduct.

Not all societies or groups value the same things. Values vary cross-culturally, which means that they differ from one culture to another. In Western societies, for example, wealth and material possessions are often valued and considered worth striving for. In contrast, the Apache of North America gave away the property of relatives who had died rather than inherit it. They believed that keeping this property might encourage the relatives who inherited it to feel glad when a person died.

Norms

Values provide us with general guidelines for conduct; norms are more specific to particular situations. For example, we value privacy, and the norms related to this include not reading other people's e-mails or text messages without permission. Norms tells us what is appropriate and expected behaviour in different contexts (settings) such as classrooms, cinemas, restaurants or aeroplanes. They provide order in society and allow it to function smoothly.

Norms are enforced by positive and negative 'sanctions'. This means that people are rewarded for conforming to (or following) the norms (e.g. being given a present), and punished for deviating from (or acting against) the norms (e.g. being told off). Norms and sanctions vary depending on place and time (where you are and when). For example, among the Apache of North America, people who broke the rules were banished from the group.

Norms — WRITTEN ACTIVITY

Consider the following social settings: a cinema, an aeroplane.
Identify two norms related to each setting.

CHECK YOUR UNDERSTANDING

Explain what sociologists mean by:

a) culture   b) values   c) norms.

KEY POINTS

The term 'culture' refers to the whole way of life of a particular society, including its values and norms. Values provide general guidelines for conduct and norms define expected behaviour in particular contexts, such as at school or in the cinema.

TOPIC 3 · What do sociologists mean by 'socialization'?

OBJECTIVE
Explain the term socialization

You have learned that culture – and its values and norms – varies according to place and time; that is to say, between societies and historically. Because of this, sociologists argue that culture is based on learning rather than on instinct – it is not inborn or natural. So, although we are born into a particular culture, we still have to learn how to fit into it and become a member of it.

Sociologists use the term 'socialization' to describe the way we learn the culture and appropriate behaviour (the norms and values) of the society we are born into.

Learning to hunt | WRITTEN ACTIVITY

The extract below describes an aspect of the socialization of boys of the Hidatsa native people of North America. It shows that the socialization process varies from one group to another according to the group's culture.

Read through the extract, then answer the questions that follow.

> Widespread was the practice of boys being taught how to hunt and trap by their fathers, older relatives or a trusted family friend; their roles as hunters were thus conditioned from an early age. Typical are the experiences of the Hidatsa men, Wolf Chief and Goodbird...Wolf Chief told of his early use of the bow and arrow: "I began using a bow, I think, when I was four years of age...I very often went out to hunt birds for so my father bade me do". Armed with blunt arrows and snares, the Hidatsa boys learned skills they would need as hunters and warriors.

Source: Taylor (1996) p. 87

1 How were the boys taught to hunt and trap?

2 Why do you think such skills were important among the Hidatsa people?

STRETCH AND CHALLENGE ACTIVITY

Using the Hidatsa native people as an example, explain the idea that the socialization process varies from one group to another according to the group's culture.

Primary and secondary socialization

Sociologists distinguish between primary and secondary socialization. Primary socialization refers to learning during early childhood when, as babies and infants, we learn the basic behaviour patterns, language and skills that we will need in later life.

The term 'agencies of primary socialization' refers to the groups or institutions responsible for primary socialization. These are usually families and parents.

Glossary terms: agencies of socialization   primary socialization   secondary socialization

Secondary socialization begins later in childhood and continues throughout our adult lives. Through this process, we learn society's norms and values. The 'agencies of secondary socialization' are the groups or institutions that contribute to this process. Examples include:

- the mass media
- peer groups
- schools
- workplaces
- religions.

👁 Eye on the exam

Remember to use the relevant key concepts and terms (such as 'culture' and 'socialization') in your answers.

Wolf children

✎ WRITTEN ACTIVITY

Case studies of feral children (children found in the wild) illustrate the idea that human behaviour is linked to the socialization process rather than being based on instinct. The following extract is about two girls thought by some to have been reared by wolves in India. They were discovered in a wolf's lair in the Bengali jungle in 1920. Read the extract and answer the questions that follow.

Their bodies were encrusted with dirt, smelt strongly of the wolves' den and appeared to be full of fleas...The children reacted violently to being touched or to any contact with water. What dirt could be removed revealed many small scars and scratches covering their bodies, and on their elbows, knees and hands, heavy calluses – presumably from going on all fours.

All attempts to make them eat failed until one afternoon they were taken into the courtyard when the orphanage dogs were being fed...Showing no fear...the girl ...lowered her face to the dog bowl, seized her food and bolted it with compulsive shakes of her upper body, keeping her head close to the ground. She secured a large bone and carried it in her mouth to a corner away from the others. She soon settled down, holding it under her hands as if they were paws, and began to gnaw at it, occasionally rubbing it along the ground to separate meat from the bone.

They slept little, either by day or night, though they would lie down for a while around midday and were often caught dozing while sitting in a corner...When they did sleep, it was usually lying one on top of the other, like puppies in a litter...They were noisy sleepers, snoring, grinding their teeth and giving little cries, but they slept lightly and the least sound awoke them...

After midnight, the children never slept and were constantly on the move, prowling around, pacing to and fro. Sometimes they howled at night.

Source: Maclean (1979) pp. 69–70, 79

1 Give four examples of behaviour the children may have learned from the wolves.

2 Give four examples of human behaviour they have not learned.

3 Note down three points from this case study which support the view that human behaviour is linked to the process of socialization rather than instinct.

CHECK YOUR UNDERSTANDING

Explain what sociologists mean by the term socialization.

KEY POINTS

In studying society, sociologists draw on the concept of socialization. This term refers to the process by which we learn the culture, norms and values of the society or group we are born into.

TOPIC 4 How do sociologists go about their research?

OBJECTIVES

Identify the steps involved in the research process

Explain the role of aims, hypotheses and pilot studies in the research process

We have seen that sociologists draw on a body of key concepts and terms in trying to make sense of society. Sociologists also carry out research and have developed a 'tool kit' of research techniques – systematic methods of collecting data (information), such as questionnaires, interviews and observation.

The research process

Sociologists carry out research in order to collect data (information) in a systematic and organized way. This data provides them with evidence to help them explain the social world. Sociological research involves several steps or stages. In broad terms, these are:

1 developing the aims or hypotheses of the research

2 carrying out pilot studies

3 selecting samples

4 collecting data

5 analysing the data

6 evaluating the project.

In practice, a researcher may not stick rigidly to these steps. However, they provide a general guide to the research process and how a study progresses over time.

Research aims and hypotheses

Sociologists ask questions about the social world. When they carry out research, they put these questions in the form of research aims or hypotheses. Research aims set out what the researcher is planning to investigate and give a clear focus to the study. A hypothesis is a hunch or informed guess. It is usually written as a statement that can be tested and then either supported by the evidence or refuted (proved wrong).

Researchers may develop their research questions, aims and hypotheses from a study they carried out previously. Something may have struck them as interesting, unexpected or puzzling and so they go on to explore this in more detail. Researchers may also develop research questions that are linked to social problems such as poverty or racism. Alternatively, they may develop questions, aims or hypotheses from their background reading of other sociological research studies published in journals or books.

Research questions may emerge from background reading.

Pilot studies

A pilot study is a small-scale trial run carried out before the main research. It may save time, money and effort in the long run because the researcher can check whether the chosen research method is likely to be appropriate and to give them the sort of data they need to address their aims. It helps to

Glossary terms: anonymity of research participants   hypothesis   pilot study   poverty

overcome potential problems, for example with the wording of questions, so that they get them right in the main research. Carrying out a pilot interview may, for instance, show that some questions are repetitive. Piloting a questionnaire may reveal that it takes so long to complete that most people simply give up on it.

Piloting a questionnaire on the Costa del Sol — WRITTEN ACTIVITY

A pilot study can be valuable in any type of research, including questionnaire-based research. In the following extract, O'Reilly, who studied the lifestyles and experiences of British migrants to Spain's Costa del Sol, discusses the use of a pilot study. Read this extract and answer the questions that follow.

Since I had hoped the survey would reach a large sample, I decided that questionnaires would be quicker, cheaper and less time consuming than interviewing respondents. I designed a questionnaire that asked for background details on household size, age, income, work, class background, and length of stay in Spain. The questionnaire also had questions on lifestyle, attitudes, health and language learning. Replies were to be anonymous (those replying did not have to give their names).

I conducted a pilot study, requesting seven individuals of various ages, both men and women, to complete the questionnaire for me so that mistakes or problems might be revealed before it was distributed more widely. Each respondent was pleased to do this, but some were not happy about the idea of a survey in general. They worried that people would not want to 'be bothered' or would not want to answer personal questions.

One of the men in the pilot study commented: 'Why do you have to ask questions on income? As soon as people see questions like that, they are going to think you are from the tax. They think you're a tax inspector or something'. He recommended that I ask no questions on name, address, date of birth, income or work as he thought these could make the questionnaire's anonymity doubtful.

As a result of these concerns, I adapted the questionnaire and added a cover note to make it clear that respondents would remain anonymous.

Source: adapted from O'Reilly (2000) pp. 154–155, 170

1 Why did O'Reilly use a questionnaire?
2 Why did she undertake a pilot study?
3 Identify two concerns raised by those who took part in the pilot study.
4 What changes did O'Reilly make to her questionnaire after doing the pilot study?

CHECK YOUR UNDERSTANDING

1 What is a pilot study?
2 Identify and explain two reasons why researchers use pilot studies.

KEY POINTS

Sociologists undertake research in order to find answers to the questions they ask. The research process involves several stages, from formulating research aims and hypotheses to evaluation. Research aims and hypotheses provide focus. Pilot studies enable researchers to trial the chosen research methods and ensure that these are cost effective.

racism   research process   respondent   sample   social problems

TOPIC 5 How do sociologists select samples?

OBJECTIVE
Explain the different sampling procedures used within the research process

Before carrying out interviews or surveys, the researcher must identify the population or group they want to study. The population may be made up of people (such as househusbands or students) or institutions (such as families or schools), depending on what the research is for.

If it is too expensive or time consuming to question the whole population, a sample or subgroup of the population will be studied. A sample is usually selected from a sampling frame. This is a list of members of the population, for example membership lists, school registers or the Royal Mail's list of postcode addresses.

If the sampling frame is inaccurate it may make the sample unrepresentative (not typical of the population in general). For example, if it includes too many females, it will be difficult to generalize from the findings. Generalizations are general statements and conclusions that apply to the whole population, not just the sample.

Sociologists can choose between several sampling techniques in order to select a sample. May (2001) divides sampling into two categories:

- Probability (or random) sampling: simple random sampling; systematic random sampling; stratified random sampling.
- Non-probability sampling: snowball sampling; quota sampling; purposive sampling.

With a probability or random sample, each member of the sampling frame has a known chance of being selected. If the sample is selected randomly, it is likely that it will mirror the population, so general conclusions can be drawn. Non-probability sampling is used where a sampling frame is unavailable.

Probability sampling

With **simple random sampling**, each member of the population has an equal chance of being included in the sample. Researchers use computers to select simple random samples.

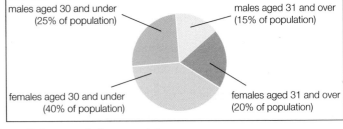

males aged 30 and under (25% of population) | males aged 31 and over (15% of population) | females aged 30 and under (40% of population) | females aged 31 and over (20% of population)

Systematic sampling involves taking every 'nth' item from the sampling frame, for example every tenth name from a college register. If the population consists of 1000 people and a sample of 100 is required, the researcher will randomly select a number between 1 and 10. If this was 5, then the 5th, 15th and 25th names – and so on up to the 995th name – would be selected.

Stratified random sampling might be used if, for example, a sociologist wants the sample to reflect the age and gender characteristics of the population. Stratified random sampling would involve dividing the population into strata (layers or subgroups), in this case according to age and gender, as shown in the pie chart. The sociologist then randomly draws a sample from each subgroup in proportion to the numbers in the population. She would, for example, select 15% of her sample from males aged 31 and over.

Glossary terms: generalizations population probability (or random) sample

Non-probability sampling

A sociologist may be interested in studying a population for which there is no sampling frame, for example, members of youth subcultures or homeless people. In this case, **snowball sampling** may be the only option. Using this technique, the researcher would contact one member of the population, gradually gaining his or her confidence until they are willing to identify others in the same population who might co-operate. In this way, the researcher can obtain a sample, although it is unlikely to be representative.

Quota sampling is often used by market researchers who interview people on the street. Each interviewer has to interview an exact quota (number) of people from categories such as females or teenagers, in proportion to their numbers in the wider population. So, if the population has 10 per cent white females aged 40 to 49, the interviewer must interview enough white women from this age group to make up 10 per cent of the sample.

With **purposive sampling**, the sample is selected according to a known characteristic (such as being a managing director, head teacher or MP).

Sampling techniques 🖊 WRITTEN ACTIVITY

Imagine that you are investigating students' views on equal opportunities in your school or college. The population consists of 1000 students and you need a sample of 200 students. Study the pie chart and answer the questions below.

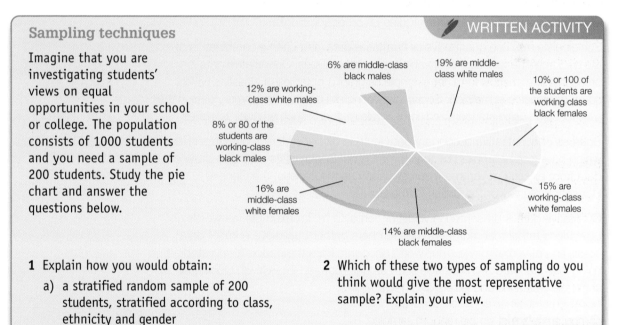

- 6% are middle-class black males
- 19% are middle-class white males
- 10% or 100 of the students are working class black females
- 12% are working-class white males
- 8% or 80 of the students are working-class black males
- 16% are middle-class white females
- 14% are middle-class black females
- 15% are working-class white females

1 Explain how you would obtain:
   a) a stratified random sample of 200 students, stratified according to class, ethnicity and gender
   b) a systematic sample of 200 students.

2 Which of these two types of sampling do you think would give the most representative sample? Explain your view.

CHECK YOUR UNDERSTANDING

1 Explain briefly what sociologists mean by the following terms:
   a) representative sample b) generalizations.
2 Identify and explain two reasons why researchers might find it difficult to obtain a representative sample.

KEY POINT

As part of the research process, researchers select a sample (or subgroup) of the population using either probability or non-probability sampling.

representative sample sampling frame sampling procedures subcultures

TOPIC 6 — How do sociologists collect and analyse data and evaluate their research?

OBJECTIVE

Explain the role of data collection, analysis and evaluation in the research process

Data collection

Once a researcher has carried out a pilot study, made any necessary changes to it and selected a sample, he or she is ready to begin the process of gathering data. Data can be collected by using one or more methods from a range of research techniques such as questionnaires, interviews and observation. When data is collected by doing research in this way, it is known as primary data. When data already exists and was collected by other people, it is known as secondary data.

- Sources of primary data include: questionnaires; structured interviews; unstructured interviews; observation.

- Sources of secondary data include: official statistics; the mass media; letters; diaries; photographs; studies by other sociologists.

Sociologists may use quantitative or qualitative data (and often a combination of the two) from the various primary and secondary sources. Quantitative data is presented in numerical form, for example as graphs or tables of statistics which count or measure something. Sociologists generate quantitative primary data in their own research using standardized, large-scale methods such as questionnaires.

Sources of quantitative secondary data include official statistics on crime rates which have been compiled by the Home Office. Sociologists may also draw on data from existing government surveys such as the census, the General Household Survey or the British Crime Survey.

Qualitative data is presented in visual or verbal form, for example, as words or quotations rather than numbers. Researchers gather qualitative primary data consisting of verbatim (word-for-word) accounts from the people being studied, using less standardized methods such as unstructured interviews. Qualitative secondary data include letters and newspapers.

Data analysis

Research can produce vast quantities of data in the form of, for example, interview transcripts and completed questionnaires. The researcher then analyses the data by interpreting it and presenting the main findings or results.

With questionnaires, the researcher presents the responses as statistics and then looks for patterns in the data. These patterns may take the form of relationships between different factors, for instance links between students' career aspirations and their parents' occupations. With qualitative data from interviews, the researcher may analyse the data by indexing (or coding) the interview transcripts. One section of a transcript may be coded 'peer pressure', for example, and another 'homework', depending on the focus and aims of the research.

Sociologists publish their findings in journals and books.

Glossary terms: analysis   official statistics   primary data   qualitative data

The use of computers and software packages speeds up the process of analysis. Statistical software packages such as SPSS (Statistical Package for the Social Sciences) can summarize data, examine relationships between factors and present results in the form of graphs and bar charts.

Evaluation

While they are carrying out studies, sociologists present conference papers on their work to their peers (other sociologists). The British Sociological Association's annual conference, for example, provides opportunities for sociologists to present their work and discuss their ideas. Sociologists also submit articles on work in progress to journals such as the British Journal of Sociology of Education.

Once their studies are complete, sociologists discuss their research and findings in conference papers and journal articles. At this stage, they are also expected to provide the organization that funded the study (such as the Economic and Social Research Council) with a report on the research.

Sociological research outputs (for example, journal articles, conference papers and final reports) are all evaluated by peer review. This means that, before papers are accepted for presentation at conferences or before articles are published in journals, they are assessed by experienced sociologists.

The research process — WRITTEN ACTIVITY

Copy out the following table and, for each stage of the research process, write one or two sentences to summarize what is involved.

The research process

Developing research aims or hypotheses	
Carrying out a pilot study	
Selecting a sample	
Collecting data	
Analysing the data	
Evaluating the project	

CHECK YOUR UNDERSTANDING

1 Explain, with examples, one difference between primary and secondary sources of data.

2 Identify and explain one difference between quantitative and qualitative data.

KEY POINTS

As part of the research process, researchers collect and analyse data. Sources of data are either primary (collected first hand through methods such as surveys) or secondary (already generated in the form of, for example, official statistics or newspapers).

Data may be either quantitative (presented in numerical form) or qualitative (presented in words).

Peer review, an important part of the research process, operates as a form of quality control.

quantitative data   secondary data   transcript

What are social surveys?

OBJECTIVES

Describe the use of social surveys in sociological research
Outline the main ways of delivering questionnaires

When sociologists carry out research, they can use one or more methods from a range of research techniques to collect primary data. They may also use a variety of sources of secondary data. A research design is a particular combination of techniques and sources. It is possible to combine techniques and sources in a wide variety of ways. Eden and Roker (2002), for example, wanted to explore young people's participation in and experiences of social action groups such as environmental and community groups. In their research design, they combined individual and group interviews, observation and self-completion questionnaires.

Finding out through social surveys

Social surveys involve collecting information from a large number of people, usually through questionnaires or structured interviews. They are used by opinion pollsters (see page 231), market researchers and government departments as well as sociological researchers.

Asking questions through questionnaires

A questionnaire consists of a list of pre-set questions to which the respondent supplies the answers. The questions are standardized so each respondent answers an identical set of questions, presented in exactly the same order.

There are three main ways of delivering questionnaires.

1 **Postal questionnaires:** the self-completion questionnaire is mailed (or e-mailed) to the respondent, who completes it and sends it back to the researcher.

2 **Hand-delivered questionnaires:** a second possibility is that the researcher hands the questionnaire to the respondent and returns to collect the completed questionnaire.

3 **Formal or structured interviews:** the interviewer reads the standard questions from the interview schedule and the respondent gives his or her answers there and then. This is a formal question and answer session. Structured interviews are carried out either face to face or by telephone.

Within a questionnaire, two types of questions may be used: closed questions and open-ended questions.

Closed or fixed-choice questions

These require respondents to choose between a number of given answers, often by just ticking the appropriate box in response to a set question so it can be answered quite quickly. The question, for example, might be "Did you vote in the last General Election?" and the given answers could simply be "yes" or "no". The responses to closed questions are relatively easy to add up and present in numerical form.

However, closed questions would be unsuitable if the researcher was interested in obtaining in-depth, detailed accounts of the reasons for voting in a particular way. Also, it is essential that all possible answers are anticipated and included in the questionnaire and that the questions and answers are carefully worded so that their meaning is perfectly clear.

Open-ended questions

These enable respondents to put forward their own answers to the set questions, rather than choose a response from several pre-set answers. An example of an open-ended question is: "What are your views on the results of the last general election?" Responses to this type of question are likely to be very varied and so are more difficult to convert into statistics. Open-ended questions, therefore, would be unsuitable if the researcher was only interested in obtaining quantitative data.

> **STRETCH AND CHALLENGE ACTIVITY**
>
> Write a paragraph explaining why the answers to closed questions would be easier and less time consuming for the researcher to make use of than open-ended questions.

Using questionnaires WRITTEN ACTIVITY

Here are some examples of questions taken from a questionnaire on the topic of "work, leisure and family life". Study the questionnaire and answer the question that follows.

1) How long have you been employed in your current post?

Less than 1 year [ ]   1–5 years [ ]   6–10 years [ ]   11+ years [ ]

2) Please rate the opportunities for promotion within this company:

Excellent [ ]   Good [ ]   Fair [ ]   Poor [ ]   Very poor [ ]

3) In your view, does your job affect your family life outside work?

Yes [ ]   No [ ]   Don't know [ ]

4) If yes, please give some examples of how your job affects your family life.

_____

Which of the above questions are open-ended and which are closed?

CHECK YOUR UNDERSTANDING

1 Identify two different ways of delivering questionnaires.

2 Explain one difference between open-ended and closed questions.

KEY POINTS

Sociologists use one or more research methods to find answers to the questions they ask.

Questionnaires are a popular way of undertaking social research. Questions can be open-ended or closed.

Questionnaires may be delivered as self-completion postal questionnaires or as structured (or formal) interviews.

TOPIC 8 What are the pros and cons of postal questionnaires?

OBJECTIVE

Discuss the strengths and limitations of postal questionnaires in sociological research

All research methods, including postal questionnaires, have strengths and limitations. Postal questionnaires can be difficult and time consuming to design.

Questionnaire design ♣ DISCUSSION ACTIVITY

The following draft postal questionnaire was designed to find out whether domestic tasks are shared equally between partners with children. Study the questionnaire and, in a small group, answer the questions that follow.

---

1 WHAT IS YOUR NAME? _____   **2** AGE _____

3 GENDER Male/Female   **4** OCCUPATION (please state) _____

5 Are you: **6** How many children do you have?

   Married   Cohabiting   0   1–3   3–4   4 or more

7 How much housework does your partner do each week?

   none   not much   a lot   a bit   quite a bit   quite a lot

8 How strongly do you agree with the following statement?

   In general, married women do more housework and childcare than their husbands.

   Strongly agree   Agree   Unsure   Strongly disagree

9 Explain in detail your views on this topic.

In your group:

1 Identify the questions that are clear and straightforward.

2 Identify the questions that need revising and rewrite them in a more appropriate way.

3 Identify any questions that you might not want to include in questionnaires.

4 Provide three tips for other students on designing postal questionnaires.

The advantages of postal questionnaires

- Postal questionnaires are a relatively cheap, quick and efficient way of obtaining large amounts of information from large numbers of people.

- As the researcher is not present, respondents may be more willing to answer potentially embarrassing, personal or sensitive questions, for example about smoking or drinking alcohol during pregnancy.

- Closed questions provide quantitative data. With such statistical data, it is possible to examine patterns between different factors. Respondents' answers can be compared and any differences highlighted.

Glossary terms: reliability   replication   response rate

- Postal questionnaires ask standardized questions and each respondent answers an identical set of questions. If respondents answer the questions differently, this is seen as showing real differences of opinion between respondents.

- As the questions are standardized, a postal questionnaire can be replicated or repeated by other researchers to check that the research findings are reliable. If a second researcher repeats the questionnaire and gets the same results, then these can be seen as reliable.

The limitations of postal questionnaires

- As the interviewer is not present to clarify, questions may be misunderstood by respondents and answered incorrectly.

- The respondent may not fully complete the questionnaire.

- You can never be sure that the right person completed the questionnaire. For instance, a group of people may work on it together.

- Postal questionnaires would be unsuitable for some populations, such as homeless people and people with literacy problems.

- Postal questionnaires consist of pre-set questions, at least some of which are fixed-choice or closed. In this case, the researcher has already decided the questions and the possible answers in advance.

- Closed questions do not allow respondents to develop their answers. They have no opportunity to explain why they ticked one box rather than another.

- The response rate, that is the number of replies received in proportion to the total number of questionnaires distributed, is usually low. Those who do respond may not be representative or typical of the population under study. It will be impossible, therefore, to generalize from the sample of respondents surveyed to the population as a whole.

CHECK YOUR UNDERSTANDING

1 Imagine that you are investigating how much time women and men spend on housework and childcare. You are going to use a self-completion postal questionnaire.

   a) Explain one problem you may face.

   b) Explain two advantages of using postal questionnaires when carrying out this research.

2 Identify and explain one advantage and one disadvantage of using open-ended questions in questionnaires.

3 Identify and explain one advantage and one disadvantage of using closed (or fixed-choice) questions in questionnaires.

KEY POINTS

Postal questionnaires are a cost-effective way of reaching large samples of people. They ask standardized questions and provide statistical data on differences between respondents. They can be replicated to check the reliability of findings; getting the same or similar results a second time round confirms reliability.

Postal questionnaires, however, tend to have a low response rate. Respondents cannot develop their answers and may misunderstand or skip questions.

What are the uses, advantages and limitations of structured interviews?

OBJECTIVES

Describe the use of structured interviews in sociological research
Discuss the strengths and limitations of structured interviews

Interviews may be structured, semi-structured or unstructured depending on how far the questions are standardized in advance. Structured (or formal) interviews are questionnaires that are delivered face to face or by telephone. As with any other method of research, they have both advantages and disadvantages.

The advantages of structured or formal interviews

Structured interviews and postal questionnaires are both examples of social surveys and so it is not surprising that they have some advantages in common.

- As with postal questionnaires, interview questions are standardized. Each interviewee responds to the same set of questions, asked in exactly the same way. As a result, any differences between interviewees' answers are seen as revealing real differences in their attitudes or opinions.

- The researcher is able to compare interviewees' responses and measure the strength of a connection between different factors. This provides the researcher with statistical data.

- The questions are standardized and so other researchers can replicate or repeat a structured interview to check the reliability of the findings. As in the case of postal questionnaires, if another researcher carries out the interview a second time and finds the same or consistent results, then these can be seen as reliable.

Structured interviews may be undertaken by telephone.

- Interviewers are trained in interviewing techniques and are familiar with the interview schedule. Consequently, they will be able to clarify the meaning of questions and clear up any misunderstandings. The interviewer can also ensure that all relevant questions and sections are fully completed.

The limitations of structured or formal interviews

- Structured interviews, as we have seen, are delivered face to face. As such, problems can arise from the interaction between the interviewer and interviewee. The interview situation itself may influence the interviewees to give answers which they think are socially acceptable or which show them in a positive light. In this way, interviewees might not reveal their true thoughts or behaviour. They may lie, try to shock or impress the interviewer. When this occurs, it is known as 'interview bias' or the 'interview effect'.

- Additionally, the age, gender, ethnicity, accent or appearance of the interviewer may influence the interviewee's responses. When this occurs, it is referred to as 'interviewer bias' or the 'interviewer effect'. In cases of

Glossary terms: interview bias   interviewer bias

interview and interviewer bias, the results will be invalid in that they do not provide a true or authentic picture of the topic being studied.

- Structured interviews (and postal questionnaires) are based on a pre-set list of standardized questions. The wording, order and focus of the questions are all predetermined by the researcher. This assumes that the researcher knows, in advance, exactly what the important and relevant questions are. Critics argue that these techniques impose the researcher's prior assumptions about the topic being researched. They also limit opportunities for respondents to express their own views and opinions. In this sense, structured interviews (and postal questionnaires) close off rather than open up new and interesting issues and areas.

Comparing structured interviews and postal questionnaires

✎ WRITTEN ACTIVITY

Copy out and complete the following table. Try to include at least two similarities and two differences between structured interviews and postal questionnaires.

Structured interviews and postal questionnaires

Similarities	Differences
• •	• •

💡 STRETCH AND CHALLENGE ACTIVITY

Give one reason why a researcher might carry out structured interviews by telephone rather than face to face. Explain your answer.

CHECK YOUR UNDERSTANDING

Explain one advantage and one disadvantage that structured interviews have when compared with postal or e-mailed questionnaires.

KEY POINTS

Structured (or formal) interviews are based on a standardized interview schedule. Differences between interviewees' answers are seen as reflecting real differences in attitudes or opinions. Interviewers are able to clarify questions.

Disadvantages include the potential for interview and interviewer bias.

TOPIC 10 What are the uses, advantages and limitations of unstructured interviews?

OBJECTIVES

Describe the use of unstructured interviews in sociological research
Discuss the strengths and limitations of unstructured interviews

An unstructured (or in-depth) interview is like an informal, guided conversation, so no two interviews will be identical. In an in-depth interview, instead of following a standardized interview schedule (pre-set list of questions), the researcher may simply work with a list of points or prompts covering the topics of interest.

The advantages of unstructured interviews

- Unstructured interviews are much more flexible than standardized methods. The interviewer can clarify questions, rephrase them and clear up any misunderstandings. Interviewers can also prompt, probe and ask additional questions in response to what interviewees tell them.

- Interviewees have the opportunity to talk at length in their own words. They can develop their answers fully and introduce issues that they consider important but which the interviewer might not have thought of. So, informal interviews provide a more in-depth account of the topic through which sociologists can obtain detailed data. Consequently, informal interviews allow you to explore more complex issues than standardized methods do.

The limitations of unstructured interviews

- Unstructured interviews are relatively time consuming and expensive to conduct. For example, interviewers may need to be trained, and their salary and travel expenses paid.

- Even with trained interviewers, informal interviews are not necessarily easy to conduct successfully. They require a skilled interviewer who is able to keep the conversation flowing smoothly and encourage interviewees to open up. Where interviewees are unresponsive, the quality and quantity of the data will be affected.

- Unstructured interviews may be affected by interview bias. As we saw with structured interviews, the interviewee may give answers that they think the researcher wants to hear or that present them in a positive light.

- There is also the potential for interviewer bias if the interviewer asks leading questions or unconsciously influences the interviewee. If interview or interviewer bias occurs, the findings are likely to be invalid.

- Each unstructured interview is unique. With no standardized schedule of questions to follow, it would be difficult to replicate or repeat an informal interview in order to check the reliability of the findings.

- Compared with survey research, fewer interviews can be undertaken, making for a relatively small sample size. With a small sample, it is more difficult to claim that the findings apply to the wider population.

Violent night

WRITTEN ACTIVITY

Winlow and Hall (2006) studied night-time leisure in city-centre pubs and alcohol-related violence among young people. In this extract they discuss interviews with male victims of violence. Study the extract, then answer the questions that follow.

> There were a number of rather awkward moments during interviews with the victims of violence. They were keenly aware of the impact of being a victim upon their reputations and their masculine identities. All those who spoke about being victims were men and we felt that, in what was basically a conversation between two men, much was left unsaid. Some, for example, gave the impression that they might be playing down the impact of being a victim on their social status. Others seemed to be searching for ways to brush off the incident as unimportant.

Source: adapted from Winlow and Hall (2006) p. 15

1 What do you think the authors mean by "much was left unsaid"?
2 Drawing on this study, explain one problem in using interviews as a research method.

The interviewer effect

STRETCH AND CHALLENGE ACTIVITY

Factors affecting the quantity and quality of interview data include the style and presentation of the interviewer, for example, their dress, age, gender, ethnicity or accent. In this extract, Beth comments on the interview styles of two researchers involved on a project interviewing young people. Read through the extract, then answer the questions that follow.

> Beth on researcher one, a 30-something female:
>
> "I think young people feel quite comfortable with her because of how she's quite young in feeling, and she dresses quite young, so I think she gets a good response…[and] she sounds more down to earth. She talks more – I won't say common – but like down to earth."
>
> Beth on researcher two, a 50-something male:
>
> "He's very soft when he speaks and he sounds quite caring towards them. But I don't think he gets as good responses. I think he's very well spoken and they may feel threatened by that…I don't know if they feel under pressure to explain things but as they explain, it comes out not completely as they intended. So he's re-explaining it for them and they're going 'yes, that's what I mean'."

Source: Robson, E. (2001) p. 48

1 Identify three factors which help to explain why one researcher gets a better response.

2 Explain what is meant by the term 'interviewer effect'.

CHECK YOUR UNDERSTANDING

Explain fully one advantage and one disadvantage of unstructured (or informal) interviews.

KEY POINTS

Unstructured interviews offer flexibility. Interviewers can clarify questions and probe answers. Interviewees have more scope to discuss topics. However, they are time consuming, expensive and need a skilled interviewer. Possible problems include interview and interviewer bias.

TOPIC 11 What are the uses, advantages and limitations of group interviews?

OBJECTIVES

Describe the use of group interviews in sociological research

Discuss the strengths and limitations of group interviews

Group interviews usually take the form of small group discussions. They may be used together with other methods such as individual interviews.

Advantages of group interviews

- Group interviews enable researchers to access a wide range of views and experiences and so provide a rich source of information on a topic.
- Individuals from the group interviews may be recruited to take part in follow-up individual interviews.
- Individuals may feel more comfortable putting their experiences forward in a group setting because they are supported by other members of the group.

Limitations of group interviews

- Group interviews need to be managed carefully by the researcher, particularly when the topic is potentially sensitive.
- One thing to bear in mind is that in a group setting, the interviewees may influence each other. Some individuals may dominate the discussion and, in this case, not everyone's voice will be heard. Others may be less open in a group interview than in a one-to-one setting.
- While researchers can promise that the contents of an individual interview will remain confidential (that is, what the particular interviewee said will not be revealed beyond the interview), they are unable to guarantee confidentiality in a group interview setting.

WRITTEN ACTIVITY

Using group interviews

Group interviews have been used to study topics such as:

- house sharers' experiences of living in shared households
- young peoples' participation in groups such as environmental groups or youth councils.

Choose one of these topics and explain why group interviews would be a good method to use in this situation.

Young, free and single?

Sue Heath and Elizabeth Cleaver (2003) studied young adult house sharers and their experiences of living in shared households. As part of their research design, they used group interviews. Read through the following extract and answer the questions that follow.

Our sample consisted of 25 shared households, containing a total of 81 individuals. The way shared living routinely worked was explored partly through group interviews with 75 household members, 61 of whom later agreed to be interviewed individually. The group interviews lasted an average of 95 minutes and most were held in a communal space in each household.

The group interviews covered a number of areas including: a discussion of the household's history, its ground rules, different expectations of acceptable behaviour, how shared spaces and private spaces are organized, who does what tasks, household finances, how conflict is addressed, and the pros and cons of shared living. In most of these interviews, each major theme was introduced by a video clip from *Friends*, *This Life* or *Shallow Grave* as a way of breaking the ice and stimulating discussion.

Permission was given to record the group interview on minidisc. All but one of these interviews were conducted jointly by both of us, partly for safety reasons, but also as a means of keeping track of the order of speech for later transcription*. This was particularly important in single-sex households where it was very difficult otherwise to recognize different voices on the recording.

Source: adapted from Heath and Cleaver (2003) pp. 7, 195–6
* Transcription involves producing a written copy of the full contents of an interview.

1 Why did the researchers show video clips during the group interviews?

2 Why were most of the group interviews conducted jointly by both researchers?

3 Why do you think it is necessary to transcribe interviews such as these?

Themes were introduced by video clips.

Identify and explain one advantage and one disadvantage of group interviews.

Group interviews are like small group discussions covering a number of relevant areas or themes. They can access wide-ranging views and experiences, and so provide rich data. Interviewees may feel supported in a group setting and so open up more. However, participants may influence each other; some may dominate the discussion, others may say very little. Confidentiality cannot be guaranteed.

TOPIC 12 What are longitudinal studies?

OBJECTIVES

Describe the use of longitudinal studies in sociological research

Discuss the advantages and limitations of longitudinal studies

In designing and carrying out research based on interviews or questionnaires, researchers may use either 'one-shot' surveys or longitudinal studies. A one-shot survey questions a sample of the population on the relevant issues only once. This is a one-off, quick approach but only gives us a 'snapshot' view. This means that it only tells us about individuals at one particular point in time and does not allow researchers to measure changes in values, opinions or attitudes over time.

Longitudinal studies

Longitudinal studies are studies of the same group of people (often a cohort, such as people of the same age) conducted over a period of time. After the initial survey or interview has taken place, follow-up surveys or interviews are carried out at intervals over a number of years.

Some longitudinal studies have been running for several decades. The 1970 British Cohort Study, for example, began by collecting information about the births and families of around 17 200 babies born in the UK during one particular week in April 1970. Since then, the respondents have been followed up and surveyed at intervals (aged 5, 10, 16, 26, 30 and 34) to monitor their health, physical development, education and social and economic circumstances.

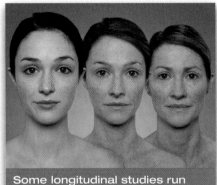

Some longitudinal studies run for several decades.

The millennium cohort study

WRITTEN ACTIVITY

Read through the information below, then answer the questions that follow.

> The Millennium Cohort Study (MCS), based at the University of London, is an example of a longitudinal study. The first survey was undertaken between June 2001 and January 2003. It gathered information from the parents of 18 818 babies born over a 12-month period and living in selected areas of the UK when aged 9 months.
>
> The second survey was undertaken between September 2003 and April 2005 when the children were around 3 years old. The third survey took place between early 2006 and early 2007 when the children were starting school. Future surveys will provide information on issues such as the respondents' education, employment and health experiences as these unfold over time, as well as changes in the family and gender roles.

1 Identify two research questions that the MCS researchers could address by using a longitudinal study rather than a one-shot survey.

2 Identify two possible disadvantages of longitudinal studies such as the MCS.

Glossary terms: cohort   longitudinal studies

Longitudinal studies may involve interviews rather than surveys. In their research on young people's post-16 choices in south London, for example, Stephen Ball et al (2000) carried out a longitudinal study which interviewed students at intervals over a period of four years (1995–9). In Ball et al's words: "They were interviewed once in each of the Spring and Summer terms of Year 11 (1996) and at some point in their first year post-16 (1996–7) and again at two or three points in the second and thirds years (1997–9)" (Ball et al, 2000, p.14).

Advantages and limitations of longitudinal studies

Longitudinal surveys allow researchers to examine social changes over time. Changes, for example, in individuals' daily lives, experiences, behaviour, values, opinions, attitudes and expectations can be identified.

However, longitudinal studies have several limitations. In particular:

1 The timescale involved means that longitudinal studies are relatively expensive.

2 Involvement in a longitudinal study may affect the behaviour of participants. They might behave differently from the way they would have behaved if they had not been involved in the study.

3 There are problems in maintaining contact with the original sample over time. Ball and his colleagues found it difficult to stay in contact with some of the young people who moved, left home or otherwise disappeared for periods of time. Other researchers experience similar difficulties in tracing and contacting people who have moved and whose landlines or mobile telephones have been disconnected.

4 People may change their minds and decide not to continue participating in the study.

💡 STRETCH AND CHALLENGE ACTIVITY

Generalizing from longitudinal studies

Over time, as more and more people withdraw from the study or become untraceable, the sample becomes less representative of the population. Explain why this would make it more difficult to generalize from the findings.

CHECK YOUR UNDERSTANDING

1 What is a longitudinal study?

2 Explain one advantage and one disadvantage of a longitudinal study.

KEY POINTS

Longitudinal studies are studies of a group of people over time. Changes over time, for example in people's social attitudes and experiences, can be examined. However, they are expensive to conduct and there are practical problems in retaining the original sample.

TOPIC 13 How is participant observation used in sociological research?

OBJECTIVE
Discuss the use of participant observation in sociological research

We have seen that much sociological research involves asking questions, either formally or informally. Sociologists may also conduct research by using observation techniques, which involve watching and listening to the group under study and recording what is observed over time. There are two types of observation: participant observation (either overt or covert) and non-participant observation.

In a participant observation (PO) study, the researcher joins a group and participates in its activities as a full member on a daily basis in order to investigate it. The researcher has to decide whether to carry out the study overtly or covertly.

With **overt PO**, the researcher 'comes clean' and so the group is aware of his or her research activities. The potential problem with overt PO, however, is that the researcher's presence may influence and change the behaviour of the group under study. When this occurs, it is known as the 'observer effect'.

With **covert PO**, the researcher joins the group without informing its members about his or her research activities. A potential difficulty with covert PO is that researchers may be reluctant to ask too many questions in case they 'blow their cover'. Another problem with covert PO is that the people under observation have not been informed that they are involved in a study and so they do not have the opportunity to consent (or otherwise) to taking part in it. This is considered unacceptable research practice by some because it involves deception and invasion of privacy.

Overt PO was used by Barker to study why people joined the Moonies (the Unification Church).

Supporters of covert PO, however, argue that it may sometimes be the only way to study and develop sociological knowledge about topics related to illegal activity. Additionally, if group members are unaware that they are being observed for research purposes, then they will not change their behaviour. In other words, covert PO avoids any observer effect. Supporters argue, furthermore, that covert methods are acceptable so long as research participants are not harmed as a result of taking part in the research.

Researching drug sellers

Jenni Ward (2008) studied drug use and drug selling within the London rave dance culture during the 1990s. Semi-covert participant observation was used as the main study method. By blending in among her friends, she was able to examine drug use and selling activities as they occurred in their natural settings. In doing so, she generated in-depth, rich data. Jenni Ward suggests that sitting down with a drug seller, pen poised ready to record illegal activities, could have closed down a study before it even began. In the following extract, she discusses her use of PO. Read through the extract and answer the questions that follow.

I located myself over a five-year period in London nightclubs, dance parties, bars and pubs and people's houses. I was already a member of the rave dance drugs culture when my study began. I was friends with people whose social and leisure lives were embedded within the 'clubbing' scene. These people became a focus of my study. Rather than people being systematically recruited to my study, they were drawn in, as part of the friendship circle to which I belonged.

I used a semi-covert style of observation, as while many of the people I was socialising with knew I was undertaking a study of drug selling, over time they often forgot that I was a researcher. They simply viewed me as a member of the friendship group to which we belonged. The problem with this was that many observations were made in situations where people were not fully aware that their actions were the focus of my research. In my desire not to upset naturally occurring activities, I generally did not announce my research.

Source: adapted from Ward (2008)

1 What role did Jenni Ward adopt in order to access the world of the rave dance drugs culture?

2 Why was she, in particular, able to adopt this role successfully?

STRETCH AND CHALLENGE ACTIVITY

1 What does Jenni Ward mean by "semi-covert" PO?

2 How far do you agree that interviews would have been less successful as a method of researching the rave dance drugs culture? Explain your reasons.

3 Give one reason why Jenni Ward's use of semi-covert PO could be seen as unacceptable research practice.

CHECK YOUR UNDERSTANDING

1 What is meant by the term 'participant observation'?

2 What is the difference between overt and covert participant observation?

KEY POINTS

Participant observation may be conducted overtly or covertly.

While covert PO may be seen as unacceptable, supporters argue that it may be the only way to study some topics.

TOPIC 14   What are the strengths and limitations of participant observation?

OBJECTIVE
Discuss the strengths and limitations of participant observation

The advantages of participant observation

Participant observation has several advantages.

- It allows the researcher to study a group in its natural everyday settings and observe its activities as they occur. PO is seen, therefore, as less artificial than standardized methods such as questionnaires.

- By participating in its activities, the researcher can see things from the group's perspective and develop a deeper understanding of the group, its behaviour and activities, at first hand. This enables the researcher to obtain a more valid or truthful picture of the group.

- Some groups such as religious cults, violent football supporters or users of illegal drugs may not agree to be interviewed. In this case, PO may be the only method available.

The limitations of participant observation

PO throws up a number of problems.

- At the outset it may be difficult to gain entry to the group under study.

- Once entry has been achieved, it may be hard to gain group members' acceptance and trust.

- Researchers may not find it easy to take notes and record activities as they happen; often, they will have to make notes after the event, relying on memory. This is particularly an issue with the use of covert PO, where the group is not aware of the true identity of the researcher. In this case, producing a notepad or digital recorder would probably arouse suspicion.

- PO tends to be a relatively time consuming and therefore expensive research method. Some researchers have spent over two years collecting data for a particular PO study, so by the time the results are published, they may be out of date!

Dr Smith, I think our research into football hooliganism is starting to get to you!

Over-involvement may lead to bias.

- With overt PO, the very presence of the researcher may influence the group and its activities and so the group may behave differently. If this observer effect occurs, then the validity of the findings will be affected.

- There is also a danger with PO that a researcher may become too involved with a group and its activities. Such over-involvement may invalidate the findings and results of the research if they are biased or one-sided.

- Each PO study is unique and so it would be virtually impossible to replicate (repeat) a study based on PO. This means that a second sociologist would find it difficult to check the reliability of the results of the first sociologist's work.

Glossary terms: validity

Consequently, it is difficult to generalize or draw general conclusions about other similar groups.

Strengths and limitations of PO

Copy out and complete the following table. Try to include two or more points under each heading.

Strengths of overt PO	Limitations of overt PO
• •	• •
Strengths of covert PO	**Limitations of covert PO**
• •	• •

CHECK YOUR UNDERSTANDING

Imagine that you are undertaking research on the levels of sexism in a local college or school using participant observation.

a) Identify and explain one advantage of using participant observation when carrying out this investigation.

b) Identify and explain one problem you may encounter when carrying out this research.

KEY POINTS

PO enables the researcher to observe naturally occurring events and to gather rich data. However, the researcher may face difficulties in gaining entry to the group, and then in gaining acceptance and trust. Recording data may be a problem, particularly with covert PO.

PO tends to be relatively time consuming and expensive. The researcher may become too involved in the group, leading to bias. Each PO study is unique and so it would be virtually impossible to replicate a study to check its results, making generalizations difficult.

TOPIC 15 How is non-participant observation used in sociological research?

OBJECTIVES

Describe the use of non-participant observation in sociological research

Discuss the strengths and limitations of non-participant observation

With non-participant observation, the researcher is like a 'fly on the wall', observing the group's activities without taking part in them. Studies of teachers' behaviour in classrooms, for example, may involve non-participant observation of lessons.

The main advantages of non-participant observation are that:

- Non-participant observers are less likely than participant observers to be drawn into the group's activities.

- Non-participant observers may be more objective than participant observers. In other words, they may be less influenced by their personal feelings or opinions about the group, its members and activities.

Studies of teachers' behaviour in classrooms often involve non-participant observation of lessons.

The main limitations of non-participant observation are that:

- It is more difficult for the non-participant observer to see the world through the eyes of group members. The researcher is less likely to understand things in the same way as group members.

- As we have seen with overt PO, the observer effect may come into play with non-participant observation. This means that group members may change their behaviour if they are aware that they are being observed.

PO or non-PO?   ❖ DISCUSSION ACTIVITY

Simon Winlow and Steve Hall undertook a year-long study based partly on detailed observation of young people, night-time leisure and alcohol-related violence (see page 25).

Imagine that you are part of a research team studying young people, night-time leisure and alcohol-related violence in a city centre near your home. You have decided to use observation but you have yet to decide whether to use participant observation or non-participant observation.

In a small group:

1 Discuss the advantages and disadvantages of using participant observation and non-participant observation in your study.

2 Reach a decision about whether to use participant observation or non-participant observation. Note down your decision and your reasons for reaching this decision.

Looking at data

For each of the following research techniques, state whether the data would be mainly qualitative or quantitative:

a) structured interview

b) unstructured interview

c) questionnaire

d) participant observation.

Factors affecting choice of methods

Several factors influence sociologists' choice of research methods, including:

- how much time is available
- how much money is available.

Take each factor in turn and explain how it could influence a researcher to choose one method rather than another.

Other factors affecting choice of methods

Other factors influencing sociologists' choice of methods include:

- the research topic and aims
- whether the researcher is interested in measurement (e.g. of attitudes) or in seeing the world through other people's eyes
- the researcher's views on what is acceptable (or ethical) practice in research.

Taking each factor in turn, explain how it could influence a researcher's choice of methods.

CHECK YOUR UNDERSTANDING

Imagine that you are undertaking research on students' behaviour in classrooms in a local primary school using non-participant observation.

a) Identify and explain one advantage of using non-participant observation when carrying out this investigation.

b) Identify and explain one problem you may encounter when carrying out this research.

KEY POINTS

With non-participant observation, the researcher observes the group's activities without participating in them and is, therefore, less likely to be drawn into these activities. As a result, non-participant observers may be more objective than participant observers. On the other hand, it is more difficult for the non-participant observer to see the world through group members' eyes. Additionally, the observer effect may come into play and group members may change their behaviour.

TOPIC 16 What sources of quantitative secondary data are available to sociologists?

OBJECTIVE
Describe sources of quantitative secondary data that are available to sociologists

So far, we have examined sources of primary data such as questionnaires, interviews and observation. Secondary data is information which has been collected by other people or organizations such as government agencies. It is available to the sociologist second-hand.

Secondary data may be either quantitative or qualitative. Quantitative data is presented in statistical form, for example as percentages. Examples of quantitative secondary data include official statistics such as:

- birth rates
- marriage rates
- death rates
- suicide rates
- unemployment rates
- crime rates.

Official statistics, compiled by government agencies, are an important source of quantitative secondary data. The census, for example, is conducted every 10 years and collects information on the full population. The information collected allows central and local governments to plan housing, education, health and transport services.

The census involves delivering a self-completion questionnaire survey to every household in Britain during a census year. Although we are legally required to complete the questionnaire, not everyone does so. The 2001 census had a response rate of 94 per cent in England, 96 per cent in Scotland and 95 per cent in Northern Ireland. However, the response rate varied regionally and, for example, in Inner London as a whole it was estimated at 78 per cent. Particular groups within the population, such as people living in inner city areas, students and other young people, are considered less likely to respond.

For the first time in official statistics, the 1991 census asked a direct question on ethnic group origin, so providing detailed information on the ethnic composition of the population. The 2001 census in England, Wales and Scotland included questions on religion for the first time.

Inevitably, given the massive scale of the census, errors do occur. Incorrect information may be provided on the census forms, for example, or coding errors may be introduced during the stage when the responses are processed.

Another source of quantitative secondary data is the registration of births, marriages and deaths. All births, marriages and deaths must be registered with the registrar at the local council offices.

Questions asked by the 2001 census for England and Wales

The census questions asked for specific information on the household, such as:

- the type of tenure (e.g. rented or owned)
- the number of rooms
- whether amenities such as a bath, WC or central heating are available
- availability of cars or vans.

There were also questions on each person in the household regarding:

- their sex
- their date of birth
- their marital status
- their country of birth
- their ethnic group
- their religion (to be answered voluntarily)
- whether they are a school child or student
- whether they have had any long-term illness.

There were also work-related questions for household members over the age of 16 on their:

- qualifications
- employment status
- occupation
- place of work
- usual means of travel to work
- number of hours worked per week.

Glossary terms: ethnic group

Your birth will be documented on your birth certificate and officially recorded as a statistic. In this sense, each of us is recorded as an official statistic!

Other important sources of official statistics used by sociologists include nationwide surveys such as the Family Resources Survey, the General Household Survey, the Labour Force Survey and the British Crime Survey. Up-to-date official statistics can be found in *Social Trends*, published every year by the Office for National Statistics. It contains a wide range of statistical data, for example on birth, marriage, divorce and death rates, education, crime and employment.

All marriages are officially recorded as statistics.

Sources of official statistics: major surveys

Survey:	Family Resources Survey	General Household Survey	Labour Force Survey	British Crime Survey
Frequency:	continuous	continuous	continuous	annual
Sampling frame:	Postcode Address File	Postcode Address File	Postcode Address File	Postcode Address File
Type of respondent:	all members in household	all adults in household	all adults in household	adult in household
Location:	UK	GB	UK	England and Wales
Sample size:	44 973 households	9731 households	52 000 households	47 138 addresses
Response rate:	63%	73%	69%	75%

Source: adapted from *Social Trends* (2008) pp. 204–205

Researching official statistics
RESEARCH ACTIVITY

The following surveys are all important sources of official statistics:

- the Family Resources Survey
- the General Household Survey
- the Labour Force Survey
- the British Crime Survey.

Choose one of these surveys and find out what topics are covered by it and what sorts of information it provides. You could begin by looking at the latest version of *Social Trends,* which is published annually by the Office for National Statistics and is available online at http://www.statistics.gov.uk. Your school or college library may also have recent copies of *Social Trends*.

When you have done your research, write a paragraph to explain what topics are covered by the survey and the information provided by it.

CHECK YOUR UNDERSTANDING

1 Explain, with examples from major surveys, what is meant by the term 'response rate'.

2 Identify and explain one possible problem arising from a low response rate.

KEY POINTS

Secondary data is information collected by other people or organizations. It may be quantitative or qualitative. Official statistics are complied by government agencies.

TOPIC 17 — What are the advantages and limitations of official statistics?

OBJECTIVE
Discuss the value and limitations of official statistics

The advantages of official statistics

Official statistics have several advantages.

- Official statistics are relatively cheap, readily available and cover many aspects of social life.

- They may be the only source of data on a topic – on the suicide rate 100 years ago, for instance.

- They allow sociologists to do 'before and after' studies. Researchers could study, for example, the impact of the Divorce Reform Act (1969) by examining official statistics on divorce before and after the Act came into effect. In this way, official statistics allow sociologists to investigate trends in the divorce rate over time. It is possible to study trends in a range of areas such as crime, unemployment, abortion, births and deaths by looking at official statistics.

- Official statistics may be used as part of a research design which combines primary and secondary sources. If the researcher was investigating educational achievement and gender, for instance, then official statistics on gender, subject choice and examination results would provide useful quantitative secondary data. Qualitative primary data could be generated through participant observation in lessons and unstructured interviews with teachers and students in order to understand social processes (such as labelling) in the school and classroom.

The limitations of official statistics

Many sociologists are wary of official statistics and tend to handle them with caution.

- Official statistics are collected by officials, so the definitions used may not be acceptable to sociologists. Statistics on the divorce rate, for example, obviously provide us with useful information on the number of divorces recorded each year. Such data, however, tell us nothing about the important question of the strength of marriage in society. This is because divorce statistics exclude 'empty shell' marriages (couples remaining in unhappy marriages) and separations that are arranged informally without going through the courts.

- It is not possible for sociologists to check the validity of official statistics. Some statistics, such as the number of births recorded, are likely to give us a valid or true picture of how many babies are born. Statistics on crime, domestic violence or violence in classrooms, however, may be invalid. In other words, they may not actually measure what they are supposed to measure. They may reflect the process of collecting data itself rather than levels of crime, domestic or classroom violence.

- Official statistics on unemployment, divorce or crime, for instance, tell us nothing about what it means to the individuals involved to be unemployed, divorced or the victim of a crime.

- Sociologists argue that official statistics are 'socially constructed'. By this, they mean that the statistics are the outcome of the decisions and choices made by the various people involved in their construction. Crime statistics, for example, are published as statements of fact. They are, however, the outcome of decisions made by people such as victims and police officers. A victim of assault, for example, has to decide whether to report this to the police. Research by Winlow and Hall (2006) suggests that male victims of violence in urban centres tend not to report the assault to the police. Domestic violence, rape and vandalism are also likely to be under-reported to the police.

Male victims of violence tend not to report the assault to the police.

Under-reporting of crime

DISCUSSION ACTIVITY

In a small group, discuss the possible reasons why crimes such as assault, domestic violence and vandalism are likely to be under-reported to the police.

Make a note of three possible reasons.

STRETCH AND CHALLENGE ACTIVITY

Explain why some official statistics (such as birth rates) are more likely to give a true picture of what they are supposed to be measuring than others (such as crime rates).

👁 Eye on the exam

Look out for the cue or prompt words and phrases in exam questions. These are important because they tell you exactly what to do. Such words and phrases include: 'Identify...', 'Explain what is meant by...' and 'Discuss how far...' .

CHECK YOUR UNDERSTANDING

Identify one advantage and one disadvantage of official statistics.

KEY POINTS

Official statistics are relatively cheap, readily available and cover many topics. In some cases, official statistics are the only source of information. Sociologists can study trends, for example in divorce or crime. However, official statistics have disadvantages. Crime statistics, for example, do not provide a true measurement of criminal activity.

TOPIC 18 What sources of qualitative secondary data are available to sociologists?

OBJECTIVES

Describe sources of qualitative secondary data that are available to sociologists
Discuss the value and limitations of qualitative secondary data

We have seen that official statistics are an important source of quantitative data. Qualitative secondary data, presented in words rather than numbers, may also be used by sociologists.

Qualitative secondary data

WRITTEN ACTIVITY

Read through the following information about two sociological studies that draw on qualitative secondary data, then answer the questions that follow.

In her study of British migrants living in the Costa del Sol, Karen O'Reilly (2000) used newspapers as sources of data. She writes:

> The English-language newspapers, many of which are written by expatriates (British people living in Spain) for both tourist and expatriate readers, were invaluable sources of data, reflecting topics and issues of general importance. What they chose to report I could safely decide were matters of common interest. I could learn a lot from their tone and from their advertising.

Source: adapted from O'Reilly (2000) p. 11

Charles et al (2008) studied families and how they have changed since 1960. Their research was inspired by, and took the form of, a restudy of earlier work by the sociologists Rosser and Harris. In this instance, Rosser and Harris's study provided a source of qualitative secondary data. Charles et al describe their study as follows:

> This is a book about families and how they have changed since 1960. It is based on the findings of two studies of the family in Swansea (in industrial South Wales), one carried out in 1960 by Rosser and Harris, the other carried out [by the authors] in the first few years of the 21st century. The book draws on two sets of research findings: those of the original family study by Rosser and Harris and those of the restudy which was carried out between 2001 and 2004. It therefore provides a unique perspective on how families in a particular place have been affected by the massive social changes of recent decades.

Source: adapted from Charles et al (2008) pp. 1–2

1 Explain, using these two studies as examples, what is meant by qualitative secondary data.

2 With reference to the two studies, explain two advantages of using qualitative secondary data.

3 In small groups, compare your answers.

Glossary terms: ethos

Sources of qualitative secondary data

Examples of sources of qualitative secondary data include:

- documentary sources such as diaries and letters
- autobiographies (an individual's account of their own life, usually written for publication)
- biographies (a written account of someone else's life)
- photographs
- novels
- mass-media products such as newspaper articles, television documentaries and the internet
- studies carried out by other sociologists.

The advantages and limitations of qualitative secondary data

Qualitative secondary data in the form of written documents may provide useful background information about the organizations, experiences or events which they refer to. In researching different school cultures, for example, existing documentary sources may be a valuable resource. Documents such as school prospectuses and newsletters could provide information on a school's curriculum and the subjects on offer, the school rules and discipline, and provision of careers education guidance. These, in turn, may help the researcher to build up a picture of a school's culture and ethos. Additionally, inspection reports from bodies such as the Office for Standards in Education and the Independent Schools Inspectorate may help a researcher to get a feel for a particular school. Information from documentary sources such as these could supplement primary data gathered through participant observation in schools, and interviews with staff and students.

Qualitative secondary sources, along with official statistics, have to be treated with caution, however. Written documents such as diaries, letters or autobiographies may have been forged, in which case they are not genuine. If the documents are genuine, the contents may not actually be true. The experiences or events described may have been misinterpreted, for example, due to the writer's prejudices. Autobiographies are likely to be one-sided and written for an audience of readers. Similarly, letters are written to a particular person and the contents are likely to be influenced by the writer's views of the recipient.

CHECK YOUR UNDERSTANDING

1 Identify and explain one similarity and one difference between quantitative and qualitative secondary data.

2 Identify one advantage and one disadvantage of using written documents as sources of qualitative secondary data.

KEY POINTS

Qualitative secondary data include documentary sources which may provide useful background information on a topic.

Letters and diaries, however, may have been forged, the contents may be untrue or the author may have misinterpreted the events described. Autobiographies may have been written with publication in mind and this may have distorted the contents.

TOPIC 19 What sorts of ethical issues arise during the research process?

In carrying out research, sociologists are likely to face ethical issues. Ethical issues relate to morals and, in the context of sociological research, raise questions about how to conduct morally acceptable research. In this chapter, we have already touched upon issues that relate to research ethics.
For example:

- Karen O'Reilly's reference to survey respondents' anonymity (see page 13)
- Sue Heath and Elizabeth Cleaver's reference to getting permission to record group interviews on minidisc (see page 27)
- difficulties in promising confidentiality in group interviews (see page 26)
- Jenni Ward's use of semi-covert PO and what this meant for obtaining participants' consent (see page 31).

Ethical research practice involves protecting the rights of research participants and ensuring that their wellbeing is not negatively affected by the research.

Research ethics
WRITTEN ACTIVITY

The British Sociological Association has drawn up a set of ethical guidelines to assist sociologists in their work. In the following extract, some of these are outlined. Read through the extract and answer the questions that follow.

Informed consent: as far as possible, participation in sociological research should be based on the freely given informed consent of those studied. This means the sociologist should explain, for example, what the research is about and why it is being undertaken. Research participants should be made aware of their right to refuse to participate in the research at any stage and for any reason.

Anonymity, privacy and confidentiality: the anonymity and privacy of research participants should be respected. Personal information should be kept confidential.

Covert research: the use of covert research may be justified in certain circumstances. For example, difficulties arise when research participants change their behaviour because they know they are being studied. However, covert methods violate (or fail to act according to) the principles of informed consent and may invade the privacy of those being studied. They should be resorted to only where it is impossible to use other methods to obtain essential data.

Source: adapted from BSA (2002) *Statement of Ethical Practice for the British Sociological Association*

1 Explain what the following terms mean in relation to research ethics:
   a) informed consent
   b) anonymity
   c) confidentiality
   d) covert research.

2 According to the extract, under what conditions should covert research be used?

Glossary terms: ethics

Informed consent

When researchers are carrying out research involving children (e.g. educational research or studies of families), they have to think carefully about issues related to informed consent.

1 In your view, at what age is a child able to give informed consent?

2 One option is to ask parents to consent on their children's behalf. How far would you agree that this a satisfactory solution?

Ethical issues in practice

Ethical guidelines cannot cover every possible issue that researchers may encounter while carrying out research. Often, the researcher has to decide quickly how to respond to issues as they arise during interviews or observation.

In a small group, discuss whether you consider the following examples to involve ethical issues and, if so, whether and how you would address them.

1 One of the participants makes a racist comment during a group interview about religious beliefs.

2 It emerges during an interview on leisure activities that the interviewee is being physically abused at home.

3 During an interview, you begin to suspect that the interviewee is not telling you the truth.

Imagine that you have been given a large grant to fund your research into one of the following topics. In a small group, choose one of these topics and answer the questions that follow.

Gender discrimination within the classroom

Migrants' experiences of racism

Girls' ideas about work and marriage

Male victims of violence

1 Identify two research aims or hypotheses.

2 Identify one primary research method that you would use in your investigation and explain a) how you would use it and b) why you would use it.

3 Identify one secondary source of data and explain why you would use it.

4 Identify one ethical issue that may arise during the process of doing your research.

CHECK YOUR UNDERSTANDING

Identify and explain two areas of research that are covered by ethical guidelines.

KEY POINTS

Research ethics are to do with conducting morally acceptable research that protects the rights of participants and their wellbeing. Guidelines cover issues such as informed consent, anonymity, privacy and confidentiality.

TOPIC 20 What are the links between sociology, social policies and social problems?

OBJECTIVES
Identify ways in which sociology addresses social problems
Explain ways in which sociology contributes to social policy

Social policies are sets of plans and actions put into place by governments, local authorities or other organizations in order to address particular social problems such as poverty, sex discrimination or racism. Sociological concepts and research results may be useful to governments or local authorities in designing and implementing social policies in the fields of, for example, welfare, criminal justice and education. In this way, sociology has practical uses in addressing social problems and proposing changes in social policy to alleviate the problems.

Jane Pilcher (2004) points out that through investigations into poverty, sociological studies in the late 19th and early 20th centuries played a significant role in the creation of the welfare state. Pilcher also highlights sociology's practical uses in dealing with today's social problems. The inquiry into the murder of Stephen Lawrence (discussed opposite), for instance, is an important example of how sociology is useful in addressing social problems such as racism.

Sociology has also made an important contribution to policy debates within the field of education. Paul Bagguley and Yasmin Hussain (2007), for example, explored young South Asian women's experiences of going to university and barriers to higher education. One of their findings was that some students, particularly those in universities or on courses without large numbers of Asian students, experienced racism from staff and students.

In writing up their research, Bagguley and Hussain discussed the policy implications of their findings and produced recommendations for changes in policy. They suggest that, in order to improve the university experience for South Asian women, some schools, colleges and universities need to ensure that unacceptable behaviour from staff and students is challenged.

The sociological approach

DISCUSSION ACTIVITY

In pairs, discuss what you think the main features of the 'sociological approach' are. Note down two main features of the sociological approach.

Eye on the exam

As part of your preparation for the exam, you could check whether you can explain in your own words what the glossary terms mean.

Glossary terms: institutional racism   poverty   race   social policies   welfare state

The uses of sociology

Read through the following extract, then answer the questions that follow.

The family of Stephen Lawrence.

> Stephen Lawrence, a young man of African-Caribbean descent, was killed in 1993 by a group of white men in South London. There was a failure to convict anyone of Stephen's murder and, in 1997, a public enquiry was held into the police handling of the investigation. This resulted in the Macpherson Report, published in 1999. One of the key conclusions of the report was that the police's handling of the investigation into Stephen's murder was hindered by 'institutional racism'. Sociologists played a key part in this aspect of the report.
>
> Individual sociologists submitted evidence to the inquiry in areas such as policing, 'race' and community relations. These sociologists were also involved in defining the key term: 'institutional racism'. This concept refers to a process that produces racist outcomes, even when individuals themselves act without racist intent. In other words, unintentional prejudice and discrimination can lead to institutional racism. The inquiry into Stephen Lawrence's death is a good example of the ways in which sociologists contribute to public debates and to social policy initiatives.

Source: adapted from Pilcher (2004) pp. 2–4

1 Explain the following terms:
  a) prejudice
  b) discrimination.

2 Explain two ways in which sociologists have contributed to public debates or social policy initiatives.

Identify two questions that sociologists might ask about:
- poverty
- racism.

CHECK YOUR UNDERSTANDING

1 Explain two ways in which sociology has been useful in addressing social problems such as racism or poverty.

2 Explain one way in which sociological research might help universities to design policies to tackle racism among staff and students.

KEY POINTS

Sociological research may be useful to governments and local authorities in formulating social policies in fields such as education and welfare. Sociology has a practical use today in addressing social problems such as racism.

3 Families

What is a family?

OBJECTIVE
Explain what is meant by a 'family'

At some stage in our lives, most of us live as part of a family unit, and the family is very important in our society. However, even though we are likely to have some experience of family life, this does not necessarily mean that it is an easy topic to study. One problem is that it can be difficult to separate the facts about families from our own experiences of them and beliefs about them.

Happy families!

Here are just a few examples of people's beliefs about families, family life and parenting:

1 There is nothing wrong with an unmarried woman who lives on her own choosing to have a baby.

2 Dangerously overweight children are victims of parental neglect and should be taken away from their parents and put into care.

3 It is OK for gay men or lesbian women to adopt children.

4 Children need firm discipline from their parents. An occasional clip round the ear does them no harm at all.

5 It should be easier for couples with young children to divorce if they no longer get along.

6 Mothers with children under the age of 11 should not work in full-time, paid employment.

7 Free abortion should be available to all women on demand.

8 Marriage is still the best form of relationship for partnering and parenting.

Issues such as these can arouse strong feelings because they involve judgements not only about how we live but also about how other people think we should live. These issues are hotly debated by politicians and the media. Through their research, sociologists aim to inform these debates.

> **❖ DISCUSSION ACTIVITY**
>
> **Beliefs about families, family life and parenting**
>
> Working on your own, decide whether you agree or disagree with each of the statements on the left.
>
> Then, in pairs, compare your responses and discuss any differences you may have.

What do we mean by 'family'?

Initially, answering the question of what we actually mean by 'family' might seem fairly straightforward, as we probably all use this word on a regular basis.

Glossary terms: civil partnership   cohabitation

However, the problem is that we tend to use it to mean a range of different things. This is illustrated in the extract below:

> At times, 'my family' can mean my partner and children; at other times, it may include my grandchildren too. Alternatively, it may refer to my own family of birth, that is my parents, brothers and sisters, or it may mean a wider range of relatives including, for instance, aunts and uncles. It may also mean a much smaller group, for example just a married or cohabiting couple living alone. Often, the meaning intended is clear enough from the context in which the term is being used. However, when sociologists study the family, there is a need for greater precision in the use of terms.

Source: adapted from Allan and Crow (2001)

Defining family

🍀 DISCUSSION ACTIVITY

One possible, but very narrow, definition of a family is that it refers to a group consisting of a married couple and their dependent children who all live together. This definition implies that a family is a group based on marriage and blood ties and also on shared residence. It can be criticized because it is not broad enough to include all of the types of family that exist in Britain today.

In a small group, discuss and note down:

a) any examples of types of family that are excluded from this definition

b) your own definition of a family, which includes all the possible family types.

When we begin to look more closely at the idea of the family, the picture becomes complicated. It is difficult to come up with a definition which manages to capture the growing diversity (or variety) of families that exists in Britain today. One approach is to define 'family' broadly in terms of: *a couple whose relationship is based on marriage, civil partnership or cohabitation, with or without dependent children, or a lone parent and their child or children.*

Some sociologists prefer to use the term 'families' rather than 'the family'. This is because they recognize that there are more and more different types of families, relationships and household arrangements in contemporary Britain.

💡 STRETCH AND CHALLENGE ACTIVITY

Explain in your own words what Allan and Crow might mean by: "when sociologists study the family, there is a need for greater precision in the use of terms".

CHECK YOUR UNDERSTANDING

Identify two different ways in which people use the term 'family'.

KEY POINT

It is difficult to produce an adequate definition of a 'family' that captures the variety of families in Britain.

What different types of households and families are there in Britain today?

OBJECTIVE
Describe the different forms a family can take

When discussing the different types of family in contemporary British society, sociologists distinguish between nuclear, extended, lone-parent families and stepfamilies. They also recognize that many people do not live with their families. Instead, people might live alone or with friends. We are now going to examine these different types of households and families.

Households

A household consists of either one person who lives alone or a group of people who live at the same address and who share at least one meal a day or facilities such as a living room. For example, a household could consist of an individual who lives alone in a flat. It could also comprise (be made up of) a group of students, young professionals or friends who live together in a shared house. People living together in shared households are not necessarily related to one another by blood ties or marriage. A 'family household', however, is one in which family members live together in the same home.

Nuclear families

A nuclear family consists of a father, mother and their dependent child or children. It contains just two generations and the family members live together in the same household. The parents may be married to each other or they may be cohabiting before, or instead of, getting married.

Gay and lesbian families

A gay or lesbian family, in which a same-sex couple live together with their child or children, can be seen as one alternative to the traditional, heterosexual nuclear family. The rise of gay and lesbian families marks a shift towards greater freedom for individuals to make choices about their domestic situations and personal relationships.

The 'cereal packet' nuclear family: mum, dad and their two children.

Extended families

An extended family includes relatives beyond the nuclear family. The classic extended family contains three generations who live together under the same roof (Charles et al, 2008a) or who live nearby. In this case, the family is extended vertically. Families may also be extended horizontally, for example with the addition of the husband's brother or the wife's cousin. In this case, the family would consist of just two generations who live together under the same roof or nearby. The term 'modified extended family' is used in relation to extended-family groupings whose members live apart geographically but who nonetheless maintain regular contact and provide support for each other. One example is children who leave home to work or study elsewhere but stay in regular contact with their parents.

Glossary terms: extended family   gay or lesbian family   household

Lone-parent families

A lone-parent family consists of one parent and a dependent child or children who live together. The majority of lone-parent families are headed by women who may, for example, be divorced, separated or widowed.

Stepfamilies

Stepfamilies – or 'reconstituted families' as they are also known – are families in which one or both partners have a child or children from a previous relationship living with them. Most stepfamilies comprise a stepfather and a biological mother and her child or children who live together. This family form might come about as a result of, for example, a previously divorced woman with children marrying a single childless man. In this case, while the man is the children's social father, in that he helps bring them up, he is not their biological father. However, the couple may go on to have a child or children together.

Most lone-parent families are headed by females.

Family and household types

Most of us live in households but not all of us live in family units. Select five of your relatives or friends, but only include one person from any one household.

1 For each relative or friend, state what type of family or household they live in.

2 Which family or household type occurs most often in your list?

	Relative or friend	Family or household type
1		
2		
3		
4		
5		

Family types
STRETCH AND CHALLENGE ACTIVITY

What do you think the idea of the 'cereal packet' nuclear family is getting at?

Have you noticed many advertisements on television or in magazines, for products such as breakfast cereals, that show the nuclear family? Have you noticed any advertisements that show family types other than the nuclear family?

CHECK YOUR UNDERSTANDING

1 What do sociologists mean by the terms
   a) household   b) nuclear family   c) reconstituted family   d) lone-parent family?

2 Identify and explain two other family types found in contemporary Britain.

KEY POINT

Several different types of households and families exist in Britain today.

lone-parent family   nuclear family   stepfamily

TOPIC 3

How might an individual's family and household settings change over the course of their life?

OBJECTIVE

Understand that an individual's family and household settings change over the course of their life

At any one time, an individual will live in a particular household setting. Individuals are likely to move between different family and household settings during their lifetime as their relationships and situations change. This idea of changing family and household settings is illustrated in the following pictures, which focus on one female passing through the stages of childhood, youth and adulthood into older age.

1 A nuclear family

2 A lone-parent family

3 A reconstituted family

4 A student household

5 Solo living

6 A married couple

7 A nuclear family

8 A retired couple

The individual, families and households over time

WRITTEN ACTIVITY

Examine the pictures above.

1 Describe the changes shown in the female's family and household settings over the course of her life, starting from when she is a baby in picture 1.

2 In each case, note down what may have triggered the change in her family or household setting.

When an individual is born, for example, she may live with her parents and older siblings in a nuclear family. Her parents may later separate, marking a turning point in family life. After the separation, the girl may live with her mother in a lone-parent family. Her mother may later meet a new partner who comes to live with them. This marks another turning point as the girl now lives in a stepfamily.

As a young adult, she may leave home to go to university or take up a job in a different city. During this period, she is likely to live alone or in a shared house with friends. After three years at university, she may return to live at home temporarily until she pays off her bank loan and saves to buy a flat. By this time, her mother may have remarried and had a baby daughter.

Significant events such as the birth of a child, marriage, separation, divorce and remarriage may mark important turning points in a person's life. Such turning points may lead to changes in an individual's family and household settings. It is likely that such changes will continue over the course of people's lives.

RESEARCH ACTIVITY

Interview an older relative to find out what different family and household settings they have lived in over the course of their live.

Write a paragraph to summarize what you have learned from this.

STRETCH AND CHALLENGE ACTIVITY

Why do you think it is important for sociologists to look at an individual's movement between different family and household settings over time?

Eye on the exam

As a sociology student, it is important to reflect on your experiences of the social world. In the exam, however, you need to base your answers on your knowledge of the relevant sociological ideas, arguments and evidence.

CHECK YOUR UNDERSTANDING

Identify one turning point in an individual's life and explain why this might lead to change in their family or household situation.

KEY POINT

Individuals will live in many different family and household situations during their lifetime.

How do functionalist approaches view families and family life?

OBJECTIVE

Explain the functionalist approach to the study of families and family life

There are a number of different sociological approaches to the study of families and family life. These include the functionalist, New Right, Marxist and feminist approaches. During the 1940s and 1950s, the nuclear family was viewed by many functionalists in very positive terms as a necessary and important part of society. We will now look in more detail at the functionalist approach.

The functionalist approach to the study of families

Some sociologists believe that the nuclear family is a key institution in society. This is because it performs a number of essential functions for individuals and for society as a whole. This view, known as the 'functionalist approach', starts off from the assumption that individuals and society have basic needs which must be met if society is to function smoothly.

The needs of individuals

DISCUSSION ACTIVITY

1 In a small group, discuss what sorts of things individuals need in order to survive. You could, for example, consider people's physical, emotional or financial needs. Note down three things that people need to survive.

2 Does the nuclear family meet any of the

needs you have identified? If so, make a note of how the nuclear family meets them.

3 If the needs you listed are not met by the nuclear family, discuss and note down how they are met in ways other than through the nuclear family.

Functionalists identify four main functions of the nuclear family in meeting the needs of individuals and society. These are: reproduction, primary socialization, emotional support and economic provision. We will consider each of these in turn.

Reproduction

Society obviously needs new members if it is to survive over time. The nuclear family has an important role in this through procreation and childbearing. The family reproduces the human race and the future workforce. It also helps to regulate adult sexual behaviour. This is because the nuclear family is based on monogamy (a relationship between one man and one woman). Consequently, married couples are expected to have only one sexual partner, and extra-marital sex (sex with someone outside the marriage) is viewed with disapproval.

Primary socialization

Society needs a way of ensuring that, from an early age, new members support its norms and values. Through the primary socialization process which takes place within the nuclear family (see page 10), we become familiar with

Glossary terms: agencies of social control   functionalism

the culture and way of life of the society we are born into. Through this we learn how to fit in and conform to the rules. By ensuring that we behave according to the rules, the family also acts as an agency of social control. The effects of not going through the process of primary socialization can be seen in case studies of feral children such as the wolf children (see page 11).

Emotional support and nurture

Most of us need stable relationships with, and support from, other people. The nuclear family provides us with emotional and psychological support and comfort. It is a place of safety and security and provides for our wellbeing.

Economic provision

We all need financial support, food and shelter, particularly when we are young, elderly or in poor health. The nuclear family meets these needs. For example, it does this by providing children – who are economically dependent on their parents – with a home and three meals a day.

Critics of the functionalist approach point to the amount of domestic violence and abuse within the home to highlight the negative side of families. They argue that family life may be linked to emotional conflict between family members. This, in turn, can lead to stress, frustration and mental health problems.

> ### ◉ Eye on the exam
>
> Remember to refer to the relevant sociological approaches (e.g. functionalism, feminism) in your answers.

How realistic is this image of the nuclear family?   ❖ DISCUSSION ACTIVITY

Since the 1950s, the rosy image of the nuclear family associated with the functionalist approach has been heavily criticized as unrealistic and outdated. For example, in practice, the four functions outlined above are not necessarily carried out adequately or effectively by all families. Also, by focusing on the nuclear family, this approach ignores family diversity. In other words, it does not take into account the variety of families that are found in society today.

1 In a small group, discuss the four functions and, for each, suggest two reasons why the ideas presented could be seen as unrealistic or outdated.

2 Make a note of your reasons.

CHECK YOUR UNDERSTANDING

1 Explain what sociologists mean by the term 'primary socialization'.

2 Explain two ways, other than through socialization, in which families may contribute to the wellbeing of their members.

KEY POINTS

There are different sociological approaches to the study of families.

Functionalists believe that the nuclear family performs important functions for individuals and society.

How do New Right approaches view families and family life?

OBJECTIVE

Explain the New Right approach to the study of families and family life

The New Right approach to the study of families

The New Right approach of the 1980s and 1990s can be seen as a more recent version of the functionalist approach. Like the functionalist approach, it believes that the nuclear family is the type of family that works best. It suggests that children are more likely to develop into stable adults if they are brought up by both parents, who are married to each other. This is because children brought up by both parents are thought to do better educationally, physically, psychologically and socially than the children of single parents. Because of this, the New Right approach is seen by some as an attack on gay and lesbian rights, single parenthood and fatherless families.

The New Right approach believes that family values are important. Jewson (1994) identifies four main aspects of family values:

- Family values are based on the view that there is a normal family type, made up of a married couple bringing up their own natural (that is, biological) children.
- Supporters of family values believe that the woman should be the carer and nurturer within the family, while the man should be the breadwinner (the one who goes out to work) and protector.
- Family members have a duty to provide for each other and to look after older, sick, unemployed or homeless members of the family.
- Supporters of family values tend to oppose gay and lesbian rights, sexual freedom, certain types of sex education and (especially in the USA) abortion.

The New Right warns us that family values are declining and that this has put the family in crisis.

The New Right approach   **DISCUSSION ACTIVITY**

In a small group, discuss how far you agree with the following statements:

- The woman should be the carer within the family and the man should be the breadwinner.
- Family members have a duty to provide for each other and look after older, sick, unemployed or homeless family members.

Make a note of four main points arising from your discussion.

Glossary terms: New Right approach

Family values

1 Which family type do you think supporters of family values would see as the ideal?

2 How do you think supporters of family values might view:

   a) an increase in divorce?

   b) an increase in lone-parent families?

   c) mothers who work in full-time paid employment?

3 Do you think supporters of family values want the welfare state (for example, provision of the National Health Service and state benefits) to have a larger or a smaller role?

Families without fatherhood

Although not part of the New Right, Halsey (1992) shares its concerns about fatherless families. Read through the extract, then answer the questions that follow.

Divorce, separation, birth outside marriage and one-parent families as well as cohabitation and sex outside marriage have increased rapidly. Children whose parents do not follow the traditional norm (i.e. taking on personal, active and long-term responsibility for their children's social upbringing) are thereby disadvantaged. On the evidence available, such children tend to die earlier, to have more illness, to do less well at school, to suffer more unemployment, to be more prone to crime, and finally to repeat the cycle of unstable parenting from which they themselves have suffered.

Dennis and Erdos highlight one consequence of family breakdown – the emergence of a new type of young male, who is weakly socialized regarding the responsibilities of being a husband and father. He no longer feels the pressure felt by previous generations of males to be a responsible adult in a functioning community.

Source: adapted from Halsey (1993)

1 Explain in your own words what is meant by "the traditional norm".

2 State three ways in which children whose parents do not follow the traditional norm may be disadvantaged.

3 Explain briefly how family breakdown may affect some young men.

CHECK YOUR UNDERSTANDING

Identify one similarity between the functionalist and the New Right approaches to the study of families.

KEY POINT

The New Right approach argues that family values are declining and, as a result, the family is in crisis.

TOPIC 6

How do critical approaches view families and family life?

OBJECTIVES

Explain the Marxist approach to the study of families and family life

Explain the feminist approach to the study of families and family life

So far, we have examined views of families and family life which suggest that the nuclear family is a good thing for individuals and society alike. However, a second view sees things rather differently. A number of sociologists, including those from the Marxist and feminist approaches, take a critical view of the modern family.

The Marxist approach

Sociologists who adopt the Marxist approach apply the ideas of Karl Marx (1818–83) to contemporary society. Unlike functionalism, the Marxist approach is critical of the family as an institution and the role it plays in society.

Sociologists with a Marxist perspective think that capitalist societies (societies in which private owners invest money in businesses to make a profit) are based on conflict between two social classes: the bourgeoisie (the people who own the big businesses) and the proletariat (the working class). The key difference between these two groups is the ownership and non-ownership of property and wealth. The bourgeoisie own the means of production (for example, the factories, businesses or land), which enables them to make huge profits. The proletariat, on the other hand, own nothing and are forced to work for the bourgeoisie in order to survive.

Marxists argue that the set up of the nuclear family enables social inequalities to continue from one generation to the next. For example, the rich are able to pass on huge amounts of money and property to their family members. In this way, the social class system is repeated from one generation to the next.

> **STRETCH AND CHALLENGE ACTIVITY**
>
> Identify the differences between functionalist (see pages 52–3) and Marxist views on the family.

Educational advantages are also passed down through families. For instance, people from wealthy backgrounds can afford to pay the high fees to send their children to public schools. In addition, Marxist approaches argue that through the socialization processes within the family (see page 10), working-class people may learn to accept their lower position in an unequal society.

The feminist approach

Feminist approaches are also critical of the family as an institution and its role in society. In particular, they see families as having a negative impact on the lives of women. While feminist sociologists accept that biological differences exist between women and men, they argue that many differences are actually socially constructed, which means that they are created by society. Families actively contribute to the creation of these differences through primary socialization processes. We can see this, for instance, in the ways that girls and boys tend to be dressed and the toys they are given.

Glossary terms: feminism   Marxism   patriarchy   social construction

Within families, young children learn how they are expected to behave not only as individuals but also as males and females. A girl who sees her mother doing the cleaning and ironing may assume that such tasks are part of a woman's role. A boy who is encouraged to help his father with home improvements or to wash the car may think that this is part of a man's role. In this way, families can be seen as preparing their members for their roles in a male-dominated society.

Feminists argue that families are patriarchal, which means that they are based on male power and dominance over women. The males within families (husbands, fathers, sons and brothers) benefit while the females (wives, mothers, daughters and sisters) lose out.

Gender socialization in families.

Jessie Bernard (1982) suggested that in the 1970s and early 1980s there were really two marriages in every marital union, his and hers, and that his was better than hers. Marriage was good for men and they needed marriage more than women did. The mental health of married men, for example, was far better than that of men who had never married. The wife's marriage, on the other hand, was not only different from, but much worse than, that of her husband. More wives than husbands, for example, considered their marriages unhappy and had regretted getting married. (See pages 58–63 for a discussion of the domestic division of labour.)

(See pages 58–63 for a discussion of the domestic division of labour.)

Parents' expectations of daughters and sons

DISCUSSION ACTIVITY

1 Many people, including parents, often treat female and male babies differently, for instance in the ways they are dressed and in the toys they are given. In small groups, discuss and note down the possible reasons why baby girls and boys tend to be treated differently.

2 In your group, discuss whether parents have different expectations of daughters and sons, for example regarding how much housework they do, how much freedom they have and what time they have to be home in the evenings. Make a note of the main points raised during your discussion.

CHECK YOUR UNDERSTANDING

1 Identify and explain one criticism of the nuclear family put forward by the Marxist approach.

2 Identify one similarity and one difference between the Marxist and feminist approaches to the study of families.

KEY POINTS

Some sociological approaches are critical of modern families and their role in society.

Marxist approaches link families to social class inequalities.

Feminist approaches link families to gender inequalities.

TOPIC 7 What were gender roles and relationships between adult partners like in the past?

OBJECTIVE
Describe gender roles and relationships between adult partners in the past

Sociologists are interested in examining changing family relationships in the home. In particular, they are keen to explore role and authority relationships between family members. These include:

- gender roles and relationships between adult partners

- authority relationships between parents and their dependent children.

When examining such issues, sociologists focus on gender and age divisions within families and how these have changed over time.

There is evidence to suggest that family relationships have changed over the last 100 years and that they are continuing to change in the early 21st century. For example, it is argued that family life has become more democratic, or fair and equal, as men's control over women and parents' dominance over their children have declined. Here, we will examine changing role relationships between men and women.

Segregated conjugal roles during the early 20th century.

Some sociologists argue that one important change within families is the move towards greater gender equality. It has been suggested that the domestic division of labour – who does what within the home – is more equal today as men are now much more involved in household tasks and childcare than they were in the past. According to this view, conjugal roles within the home, that is the domestic roles of married or cohabiting partners, have become increasingly joint or shared and equal.

Conjugal roles in the past

During the early part of the 20th century, conjugal roles were segregated, in other words they were separate and unequal. In general, married women were expected to take the main responsibility for housework and childcare. Their husbands were expected to be the main breadwinner (wage earner).

However, women's roles differed according to their social class. In addition to housework and childcare, many working-class women also had to go out to work to earn money, or take on paid work from home, such as taking in laundry in order to survive. Among the middle class, on the other hand, the wife was not expected to undertake paid employment. She supervised the work of the household employees such as the maid, the governess and the nanny. Families were male dominated and both working-class and middle-class husbands were expected to provide for their family.

> ### ❖ DISCUSSION ACTIVITY
>
> **Men as 'househusbands'**
>
> Consider the following view:
>
> "Men are clearly less suited to childcare and other caring tasks than women."
>
> In small groups, discuss how far you agree or disagree with this view. Give three reasons to support your view.

Glossary terms: conjugal roles   democratic relationships   division of domestic labour

Planning research on housework and childcare

Imagine that you are part of a small research team that has been awarded a research grant to investigate the division of housework and childcare amongst married and cohabiting couples today. Address the following issues and questions that your research team would face:

1 Identify two research aims or hypotheses.

2 Who would your population consist of (e.g. couples or female/male partners only) and why?

3 a) What sampling technique would you use?

   b) Why would you use this sampling technique?

4 Identify one method of research that you would use and explain why you would use it.

5 Identify one secondary source of data and explain how it might help you.

6 Identify one ethical issue that could arise during the research process.

STRETCH AND CHALLENGE ACTIVITY

Some sociologists have strong views on the social issues they are researching.

1 How far do you think that it is possible for sociologists to set aside their own views when undertaking research on issues such as gender relationships?

2 How far do you think that they need to do so?

Eye on the exam

While reading through the material in this topic, you are likely to have come across several new terms. These are all included in the 'glossary terms' below. When answering questions for homework, try to get into the habit of using these key terms.

As part of your revision, it is useful to check whether you understand what these terms mean. You could do this by working in pairs and testing each other to see whether you can explain terms such as 'conjugal roles'. Can you explain what the different terms mean? Can you do so clearly and briefly in your own words?

Alternatively, working in pairs, one of you could write down your definition of a particular term such as 'gender'. Without telling your partner which term you have in mind, read out your definition and ask them to identify it. They then take a turn to write a definition and you guess what term it is for.

CHECK YOUR UNDERSTANDING

What do sociologists mean by the following terms?

a) the domestic division of labour

b) joint domestic roles

c) segregated domestic roles

KEY POINTS

Sociologists study roles and relationships between married and cohabiting partners.

It is argued that, in the early part of the 20th century, conjugal roles were segregated, or separate and unequal.

gender   joint conjugal roles   role   segregated conjugal roles

TOPIC 8 # What is the symmetrical family and why has it emerged?

OBJECTIVES

Understand what is meant by the term 'symmetrical family'
Explain the move to symmetry

The symmetrical family

Young and Willmott (1973) published research findings which suggested that the 'symmetrical family' had become the typical family form in Britain. One key characteristic of this family was that the roles of husband and wife were less segregated than in the past. While some segregation in roles still existed within the symmetrical family, there was a greater degree of equality between the spouses. Young and Willmott described symmetrical relationships as being opposite but similar. In other words, although the husband and wife might carry out different (opposite) tasks, they each made a similar contribution to the home. So while women still took the main responsibility for housework and childcare, men were spending an equivalent amount of time on home-related tasks and were more likely to help with housework and childcare.

Another aspect of the symmetrical family was the growth of a financial partnership between husband and wife. Decision-making, including decisions on how money was spent, was more of a shared activity. A further characteristic of the symmetrical family was that the couple and their children were more home centred than in the past. This could be seen, for example, in the growing interest in DIY. Family members also spent much of their leisure time together and, with developments in technology, more of their entertainment was home based. Additionally, relationships between spouses were warmer and more caring.

RESEARCH ACTIVITY

Who does the housework and childcare?

1 Design a short questionnaire to find out whether childcare and housework tasks are equally shared between partners today. Think carefully about how you word the questions. Is your population made up of couples or one partner only?

2 Pilot your questionnaire on a sample of 10 people.

3 Make a note of the three most significant results from your pilot questionnaire.

STRETCH AND CHALLENGE ACTIVITY

Identify one advantage and one limitation of using a questionnaire to find out whether childcare and housework tasks are equally shared between partners today.

Explaining the move to symmetry

Let us assume for the moment that Young and Willmott were correct in identifying the move to more symmetrical gender roles within families, even if they did not necessarily get the details right. We now need to identify possible reasons for this change. Some sociologists think that wider social changes explain the move towards more equal gender relationships identified by Young and Willmott. In particular, they highlight the following:

- The rise of feminism since the 1960s has had an impact on gender roles generally. Feminists have fought for equal rights for women and men, for example in the workplace and in education. Feminism has influenced many women's attitudes and has led them to reject the traditional housewife role.

Glossary terms: spouse   symmetrical family

- More effective forms of contraception have meant that women have fewer children. Families can now be planned, so women can combine motherhood with paid employment and a career.

- As a result of their participation in paid employment, many women are financially independent and have more freedom, equality and status, both inside and outside the home, than in the past.

- There has been an increased interest in home life generally, for example in DIY and home improvements. Technological developments have created opportunities for home-based leisure pursuits linked, for example, to computer games, DVDs and satellite television. As a result, men are now more likely to spend time at home and to become more involved with their family.

STRETCH AND CHALLENGE ACTIVITY

Drawing on examples from the information in the written activity, write a short paragraph to show how far men's and women's attitudes to females' employment changed between 1989 and 2006.

WRITTEN ACTIVITY

Changing attitudes to women's employment

Study the following information, then answer the questions that follow.

Attitudes to women's employment, by sex, 1989–2006

	1989		2006	
	% agree		% agree	
	Men	Women	Men	Women
A man's job is to earn money; a woman's job is to look after the home and family.	32	26	17	15
A pre-school child is likely to suffer if his or her mother works.	53	42	41	29

Source: adapted from *British Social Attitudes* (Crompton and Lyonette, 2008)

1 What percentage of men said that "a man's job is to earn money; a woman's job is to look after the home and family" in 1989?

2 Did this figure increase or decrease over the period shown?

3 What percentage of women said that "a pre-school child is likely to suffer if his or her mother works" in 1989?

4 Did this figure increase or decrease over the period shown?

CHECK YOUR UNDERSTANDING

1 What do sociologists mean by the 'symmetrical family'?

2 Identify and explain two possible reasons for the rise of the symmetrical family.

KEY POINTS

There is some evidence that roles and relationships between married and cohabiting partners are becoming more equal.

Young and Willmott (1973) suggested that the symmetrical family – in which there is greater equality between spouses – was typical in Britain.

The rise of the symmetrical family is linked to feminism, effective contraception, changes in the social position of women and increased interest in home life.

TOPIC 9   Is the symmetrical family reality or a myth?

OBJECTIVE

Evaluate the idea of the 'symmetrical family'

Feminists reject the idea of symmetry. Ann Oakley (1974) is critical of Young and Willmott's *Symmetrical Family* study and is not convinced by their evidence. For example, Young and Willmott regard a husband who washes up at least once a week as 'helpful in the home'. Furthermore, they regard occasional help from a husband, such as ironing his own trousers on a Saturday, as a sign of a 'good' husband. In her own research on housework, Oakley found little evidence of symmetry. In fact, even women in paid employment still had the major responsibility for housework.

Crompton and Lyonette (2008) note that more women are in paid employment today. In addition, there are far more dual-earner households in Britain now than old-style, male-breadwinner households. However, despite such social changes, gender differences in the home persist. Crompton and Lyonette argue that men's involvement in household work has not increased to the same extent as women's involvement in paid work. They also argue that the main reason why the gap between men's and women's contribution to domestic labour narrowed between the 1960s and 1980s was that women spent less time on domestic work. The main reason was not linked to men increasing their hours.

Crompton and Lyonette (2008) accept that attitudes to gender roles have changed a lot since the late 1980s, but that men's actual participation in

---

WRITTEN ACTIVITY

Changing attitudes to household tasks

The information in the table below is from a survey that asked respondents who had partners to report on their partner's contribution to laundry and grocery shopping. The results for 1994 show, for example, that 77 per cent of men and 84 per cent of women with partners said that laundry was always or usually done by the woman.

Study this information, then answer the questions that follow.

Allocation of household tasks, 1994 and 2006 (percentages)

	1994		2006	
'Always' or 'usually' done by the woman	Men	Women	Men	Women
Laundry	77	84	71	80
Shopping for groceries	39	45	38	45

Source: adapted from *British Social Attitudes* (Crompton and Lyonette, 2008)

1 What percentage of men with partners in 2006 reported that laundry was always or usually done by the woman?

2 In 2006, were men or women with partners more likely to report that grocery shopping was usually or always done by the woman?

3 From the information in the table, is it possible to tell:

   a) whether men are over-reporting their share of household work?

   b) whether women are under-reporting the domestic work done by their partners?

Glossary terms: dual-earner household   male-breadwinner household   new man

household tasks has not. For example, in most cases, women usually still do the laundry. Women's responsibilities for domestic work and caring mean that, in practice, many of them do not compete on equal terms with men in paid employment.

The role of fathers in families

Research suggests that the role of fathers within families has changed. Caroline Gatrell (2008) studied heterosexual dual-worker couples and found that many fathers today play a greater role in the lives of their children than fathers did in the past. In some instances, these men had fathers who were not involved as parents and so they want to do things differently with their own children.

However, Gatrell notes that among some married or cohabiting couples, the idea of the increased involvement of fathers in childcare causes tension. Some women do not want to see their traditional maternal role being eroded. Other women are unenthusiastic about father–child relationships because they think fathers tend to 'cherry pick' the most rewarding jobs and manage to avoid boring domestic tasks such as ironing. Gatrell concludes that mothers' resistance to the enhanced role of fathers might be linked to the idea that, if men want to divide 'parenting time' more equally, then they should also be expected to divide housework equally.

It's A Chore!

Since the 1990s, numerous commentators have reported on the emergence of the 'new man', a caring, sharing man who gets fully involved in the housework and childcare. However, Charter (2007) suggests that the 'new man' is nowhere to be seen when the cleaning needs to be done! Findings from a detailed survey funded by the European Union show that ironing is still "overwhelmingly women's work".

1 In small groups, discuss the possible reasons why men with female partners tend not to do the ironing or cleaning.

2 Note down three points raised during your discussion.

CHECK YOUR UNDERSTANDING

1 Identify one way in which the role of fathers in families has changed since the 1970s.

2 Discuss how far sociologists would agree that the roles of men and women in the family have changed since the 1970s.

KEY POINTS

Feminists reject the idea that conjugal roles and relationships are equal. Between the 1960s and 1980s, women reduced their time spent on domestic work but men did not significantly increase theirs.

Attitudes to gender roles may have changed and there is some evidence that fathers are becoming more involved as parents. This may, however, lead to tension between partners.

TOPIC 10 How is power distributed between partners in relationships?

OBJECTIVE
Understand the distribution of power in relationships between partners

Sociologists are interested in the issue of who holds power in family relationships. One way of studying power is to look at decision-making and, in particular, who makes the decisions on how money is spent.

Power and money in marriage

One aspect of the symmetrical family identified by Young and Willmott was the growth of a financial partnership between husband and wife. Decision-making, including decisions on how money was spent, was becoming more of a shared activity. Some feminists, however, argue that family life is still patriarchal. In other words, family life is still based on male power and dominance over women.

Jan Pahl (1989), in her study of power and money in marriages, interviewed 102 married couples with dependent children in Kent. She found that husbands are more likely than wives to be dominant in decision-making. As such, they can be seen as wielding more power in the relationship. Pahl argues that, compared with 30 years ago, more couples share decisions concerning the spending of the household income. She points out, however, that there are still many marriages in which the husband controls the finances and the wife's access to money is very limited. Women and children can live in poverty, even though the man with whom they live has a good income.

Power and domestic violence within families

Domestic violence can be seen as a form of power and control in which one family member attempts to dominate others. Domestic violence includes violence by men against women within the home and violence by women against their male partners. It also includes the physical, psychological or sexual abuse of children, violence between brothers and sisters and the neglect and abuse of the elderly (Clarke, 1997).

There is some disagreement about the extent of domestic violence. Victim surveys such as the British Crime Survey indicate that domestic violence is often not reported to the police. Some male victims, for example, may be very reluctant to report that their female partners have been violent towards them. Victims may also not report domestic violence because they consider it to be a private matter or they believe that the police can do nothing about it. An increase in the recorded incidence of domestic violence may be due to increased reporting of it rather than to an actual increase in its occurrence.

Awareness of domestic violence is increasing

Some critical approaches highlight the apparent increase in violence within the home in order to show that families are not necessarily safe havens for their members. Such approaches argue that family life does not always function in ways that contribute to members' wellbeing. Domestic violence among married and cohabiting couples can be seen as a form of control in which one partner, often the male, attempts to coerce and dominate the other.

Domestic violence is a crime society ignores

Read through this extract from a newspaper article about domestic violence, then answer the questions that follow.

The figures are horrifying: almost 60 murders so far this year, and on average a victim calls the police every single minute. Families are devastated, children orphaned, and the damage continues into the next generation; it's an epidemic of crime but you'll rarely read about it or see the victims' photographs.

I'm talking about domestic violence, which affects one woman in four, according to the Home Office, which also says that two women a week are killed by their current or former male partner. Why don't we see their pictures? Why isn't there a public outcry about our fractured society which is failing to protect vulnerable women and children?

If we care about young men being stabbed on the streets of Manchester or London, as we should, why aren't we also up in arms about a crime which accounts for 15 per cent of all violent incidents and leaves hundreds of thousands of women in fear for their lives?

I'm not saying it doesn't happen to men as well, but the Home Office says quite clearly that this type of crime 'consists mainly of violence by men against women'. Children who witness their mothers being beaten or murdered are severely traumatized, and there is a strong connection between domestic violence, sexual violence and child abuse.

Source: adapted from Joan Smith, *The Independent*, 18 July 2008

1 What proportion of women are affected by domestic violence?
2 What percentage of all violent incidents involve domestic violence?

💡 STRETCH AND CHALLENGE ACTIVITY

1 Identify one crime which receives more media coverage than domestic violence.
2 According to the extract, how does domestic violence affect children?
3 We have seen that early sociological approaches focused on the functions of the family, such as emotional support and nurturing. Using the information in the extract, write a paragraph to show that these functions are not always fulfilled.

CHECK YOUR UNDERSTANDING

To what extent would sociologists agree that living in a family tends to benefit women less than men?

KEY POINTS

Sociologists are interested in studying the distribution of power in relationships between partners. They focus on financial decision-making and domestic violence.

TOPIC 11

How have relationships between parents and their children changed over time?

OBJECTIVE

Outline changes in authority relationships between parents and children

Relationships between parents and their children have changed over time. During the 19th century, children's experiences and the opportunities available to them varied significantly according to their age, gender and social class. Middle-class children, for example, were often looked after by a paid employee such as a nanny. Working-class children, especially boys, were expected to work in paid employment from an early age.

Parent–child relationships in the past

Details from the 1841 census show that in towns around Lancaster, more boys than girls aged 10 to 14 were employed in paid work. The textile industry in Lancashire provided the greatest number of jobs for children, who were, for example, employed as cotton mill workers, spinners and weavers. There was a wider range of jobs for boys than for girls.

Few children under the age of 10 worked in paid employment. According to census figures for England and Wales, in 1851, 36.6 per cent of boys and 19.9 per cent of girls aged 10 to 14 worked. By 1911, these figures stood at 18.3 per cent for boys and 10.4 per cent for girls. Many girls were involved in unpaid work at home, for example in housework and child minding, but this was not officially recorded in the statistics.

It is possible that poverty prevented many parents from sending their children to school. Well into the 20th century, many working-class parents seem to have viewed education as a barrier to their children's paid employment. Many sent their children out to work as soon as they could and relied on the children's income.

Following the introduction of the Education Act (1918), however, all children had to attend school until the age of 14. Young and Willmott argue that only then did childhood come to be officially recognized as a separate stage in human life.

Children at work in the 19th century.

Contemporary parent–child relationships

Some sociologists argue that relationships between parents and children are becoming less authoritarian. In other words, there is less emphasis on discipline, obedience and parental authority over children and more emphasis on individual freedom. Children are regarded as important members of the family household. They are listened to and their views on family issues and decisions are not only sought but also taken seriously. It is increasingly recognized that children have rights and are able to contribute to decisions to do with parental separation and divorce, for example.

The rights of children in families

In a small group, discuss how far you agree with the view that children do have rights in families today. Should their rights be extended?

Make a note of three points raised during your discussion.

Pryor and Trinder (2004), however, note that there are class differences in the relationships between parents and children. Middle-class families, for example, are more likely to have 'democratic' parenting where children are consulted and involved in decision-making within the family.

Today, relationships between parents and children are generally more child centred in that they focus on the interests and needs of the child. Parent–child relationships are emotionally closer and warmer. The average family size is smaller than at the beginning of the 20th century, so individual children are likely to get more attention from their parents. At the same time, for many parents full-time parenting is not seen as an option, due to either financial necessity or choice. As a result, many young children are regularly separated from their parents, sometimes for most of the working week.

Childrearing is no longer dominated by economic factors. The minimum school-leaving age was raised to 16 in 1976 and, although young people today may obtain part-time paid employment before they are 16, the number of hours they can work is restricted by law. This means that young people are financially dependent on their family for longer, particularly if they continue into further and higher education. Youth unemployment can also make it more difficult for young people to become independent from their families. This can potentially lead to conflict and stress within families.

Sociologists such as Scott (2004), however, question how far children should be seen as dependent. Children may contribute to childcare and domestic labour within the home as well as helping out in family businesses. They may also provide emotional support to their parents at quite a young age. Additionally, children of immigrant parents may be asked to act as translators for their parents. As a result, it is misleading to see children solely as dependants who contribute nothing within families.

STRETCH AND CHALLENGE ACTIVITY

1 Identify one way in which children can be seen as dependent on their families.
2 Identify two ways in which children may make a contribution to their families.

CHECK YOUR UNDERSTANDING

Identify and explain two changes that have occurred in the relationships between parents and children over the last hundred years.

KEY POINTS

Relationships between parents and their children have changed over time. One view is that there is now less emphasis on discipline and more emphasis on individual freedom.

Children may contribute to childcare and domestic tasks within families.

TOPIC 12 How have people's relationships with members of their wider family changed over time?

OBJECTIVE

Describe changes in people's relationships with members of their wider families

Young and Willmott (1957) studied family life in Bethnal Green in the East End of London, during the mid-1950s. Among their working-class sample, they found that the extended family flourished. For example, many young couples began their married life living with one set of parents. Family ties were strong and 43 per cent of daughters had seen their mothers within the last 24 hours.

More recently, it has been suggested that increasing geographical mobility (moving to live in another area, region or country) and women's involvement in full-time work have meant that family members see each other less often. Some sociologists think that because of this, the wider family is becoming less important in our lives and family ties are weakening.

Other approaches, however, believe that family members continue to depend on each other. In their study of changing families in Swansea between 1960 and 2002, Charles et al (2008b) found that mothers and their daughters were still central to kinship groupings. High rates of face-to-face contact between family members were found. For example:

Grandparents may be involved in caring for their grandchildren.

- Grandmothers and sometimes grandfathers were regularly involved in caring for their grandchildren, which enabled younger women to return to work after maternity leave.

- Fathers often provided practical support with home improvements for their adult children.

- Adult children were involved in caring for their parents.

- Older grandchildren were sometimes involved in caring for their grandparents.

In 2002, over two-thirds of married children lived close enough to their parents to see them every week or more regularly than this. Frequency of contact between siblings (brothers and sisters), however, fell significantly between 1960 and 2002.

Geographical distance, according to Charles et al (2008a), affects the type of support between family members. For example, support at a distance took the form of visits, telephone contact, financial help and the exchange of gifts. Geographical distance, however, does not eliminate family support altogether. Several other studies have found that middle-aged parents may provide financial support to their children, for example loans or gifts of money when they are buying a house. However, this transfer of money may not be possible among families on low incomes who do not have savings.

Glossary terms: geographical mobility   kinship relationships

Grown-up offspring cost parents £21 500

Read through the following newspaper extract, then answer the questions that follow.

Going to university

The first car

The first house

The first wedding

Total   £ 21 540

Parents know their children cost a fortune to bring up, but it seems the financial commitment lasts well past young adulthood. Not only are parents contributing towards the cost of going to university, the first car, the first house and the first wedding, but many are forking out for their children's children too, according to a survey today.

An adult child over 18 costs parents, on average, a grand total of £21,540, not counting day-to-day living expenses, says the insurance and investment group LV. The survey involved nearly 1,200 adults aged 40 and over with at least one adult child. Of these, 94 per cent claimed to have contributed financially to the younger generation. Under a third said they had received similar financial help from their parents after leaving school.

Eight in 10 parents with grandchildren find themselves supporting these too, nearly half helping the youngest generation start savings and investments, and a third paying for some travelling.

Source: adapted from James Meikle, *The Guardian*, 5 September 2008

1 According to this information, how are parents and grandparents helping family members in the younger generations?

2 Does this information seem to suggest that parents are more likely or less likely to give financial help to the younger generation today?

3 Which social groups may not be giving money between the generations?

Using this information, write a short paragraph to show that family ties have not necessarily become weaker over time.

Eye on the exam

Make sure you use the relevant key concepts and terms in your answers.

Discuss how far sociologists would agree that the wider family is becoming less important in people's lives.

Some approaches suggest that the wider family is becoming less important in our lives. Others emphasize the continuing importance of family ties.

TOPIC 13 · What are the current trends in families and households?

OBJECTIVES

Describe the increase in one-person households

Describe the apparent decline in the nuclear family

We have already identified the diverse forms of households and families that exist in Britain today. Examples include one-person households, nuclear families, lone-parent families and stepfamilies. Since the mid-1970s, there have been important changes in these families and households.

The increase in one-person households

Over the last 30 years, there has been a significant increase in the number of one-person households in Britain. This increase can be explained partly by the changing age structure of the population. People are living longer so there are more elderly, one-person households. These households typically comprise older women who have outlived their partners.

However, the growth in one-person households is also linked to the increase in solo living among younger people. Between 1971 and 2007, the proportion of households consisting of one person under retirement age (60 for women and 65 for men) increased from 6 per cent to 14 per cent. These households may consist, for example, of people who:

- remain single and childless throughout their lives
- are divorced
- are international migrants, including students who have moved to Britain from abroad
- live alone before marrying or cohabiting
- have partners but choose to live apart from them.

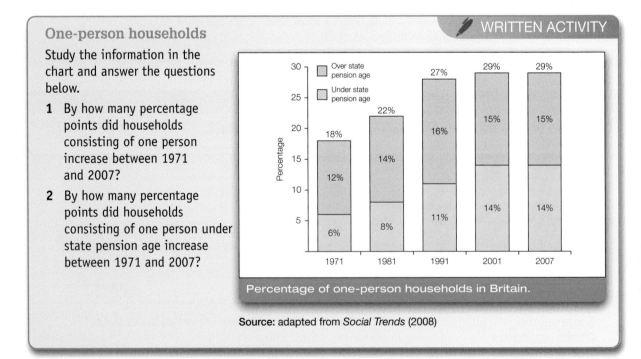

One-person households

WRITTEN ACTIVITY

Study the information in the chart and answer the questions below.

1 By how many percentage points did households consisting of one person increase between 1971 and 2007?

2 By how many percentage points did households consisting of one person under state pension age increase between 1971 and 2007?

Percentage of one-person households in Britain.

Source: adapted from *Social Trends* (2008)

The apparent decline in the traditional nuclear family

If we look at official statistics, we can see that the percentage of households in Britain that are made up of nuclear families (two adults and dependent children) is declining. This marks a decline in the 'traditional' or the 'cereal packet' family.

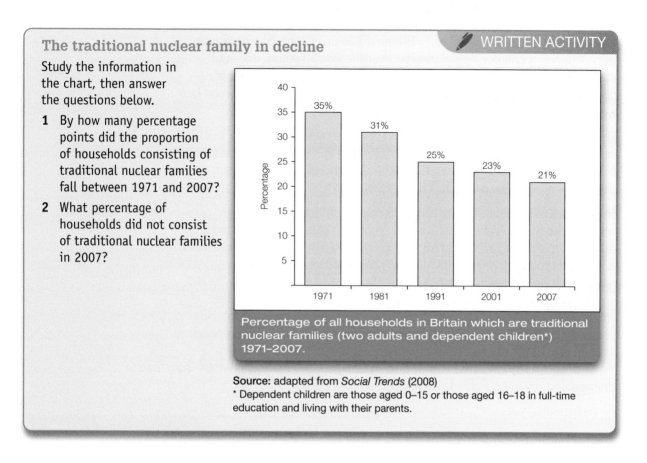

WRITTEN ACTIVITY

The traditional nuclear family in decline

Study the information in the chart, then answer the questions below.

1 By how many percentage points did the proportion of households consisting of traditional nuclear families fall between 1971 and 2007?

2 What percentage of households did not consist of traditional nuclear families in 2007?

Percentage of all households in Britain which are traditional nuclear families (two adults and dependent children*) 1971–2007.

Source: adapted from *Social Trends* (2008)
* Dependent children are those aged 0–15 or those aged 16–18 in full-time education and living with their parents.

STRETCH AND CHALLENGE ACTIVITY

Write a paragraph to summarize the trends in households containing one person and traditional nuclear families that are shown in the bar charts in the written activities.

CHECK YOUR UNDERSTANDING

Outline two reasons for the increase in one-person households.

KEY POINTS

Since the mid-1970s, there have been significant changes in families and households. These changes include an increase in one-person households and a decline in the traditional nuclear family.

TOPIC 14 What are the current trends in lone-parent families?

OBJECTIVES

Describe the increase in the number of lone-parent families

The proportion of all households in Britain made up of lone-parent families with dependent children has increased over the last 30 years. Some of these lone-parent families come about because a couple separates or divorces, or one of the partners dies. Others form when a single woman has a baby and chooses to bring up the child on her own.

The proportion of dependent children living with one parent rose from 7 per cent in 1972 to 23 per cent in 2007. The vast majority of these children live with their mothers rather than their fathers. Between 1972 and 2007, the proportion of dependent children living with their mothers rose from 6 per cent to 21 per cent.

Jewson (1994) indicates that there is evidence that African-Caribbean communities have a higher than average proportion of lone-parent families, and Asian communities a lower than average proportion. He warns, however, that it is important to avoid stereotyping: the majority of African-Caribbean households with children contain two parents. More recently, Williams (2008) notes that Black Caribbeans and Black Africans are more likely than other ethnic groups to head lone-parent households with dependent children. He points out, however, that these numbers appear to have been falling between the 1991 and 2001 censuses. By contrast, lone-parent households with dependent children increased slightly among Bangladeshi, Pakistani, White, Chinese and Indian households between 1991 and 2001.

Households containing lone-parent families

Study the information in the chart, then answer the questions below.

1 What percentage of households in 2007 consisted of lone parents with dependent children?

2 Between 1971 and 2007, what was the percentage increase in households consisting of lone-parent families with dependent children?

3 Identify the overall trend in the proportion of households containing lone-parent families between 1971 and 2001.

WRITTEN ACTIVITY

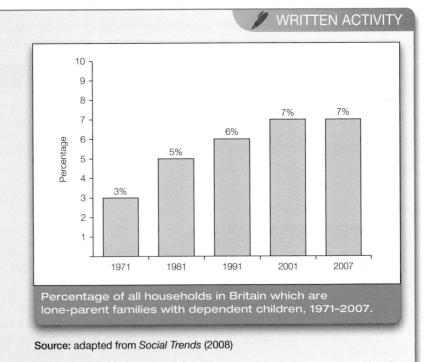

Percentage of all households in Britain which are lone-parent families with dependent children, 1971–2007.

Source: adapted from *Social Trends* (2008)

One reason for the increase in the number of lone-parent families is that attitudes have changed. As a result, it is now more socially acceptable for single women to have children. A second reason is the growth in divorce which has resulted in an increase in families headed by divorced mothers. Each year, however, many lone mothers will form new partnerships and stop being lone parents.

The consequences of lone-parent families   ❖ DISCUSSION ACTIVITY

As we have seen, the number of lone-parent families has increased.

1 In a small group, discuss the possible consequences of this increase for:
   a) marriage
   b) family life
   c) demands on the welfare state.
2 Note down three of the possible consequences that you identified during your discussion.

💡 STRETCH AND CHALLENGE ACTIVITY

We have seen that the British Social Attitudes Survey examines changing attitudes over time (see pages 61 and 62). Devise a closed question that could be used in a survey to investigate changing social attitudes to extra-marital births (births outside marriage). Remember to supply all of the possible answers.

👁 Eye on the exam

In the Sociology exam, you may be given information in the form of a bar chart like the one in the written activity opposite. Some of the questions will require you to interpret or make sense of the information provided. When studying a bar chart, look out for the heading as this will tell you what the general subject is. The bar chart opposite, for example, is looking at the proportion of all households in Britain containing lone-parent families with dependent children. Another thing to look out for is the timescale. Here, the timescale runs from 1971 to 2007. Also, check whether any trends are shown. In this bar chart, it shows an upward trend between 1971 and 2001 in the proportion of all households containing lone-parent families with dependent children. However, no change is shown between 2001 and 2007. Check what unit of measurement is being used. Here, it is percentages.

CHECK YOUR UNDERSTANDING

1 Outline two reasons for the increase in lone-parent families.
2 Identify one reason for the increase since the 1970s in the number of lone-parent families headed by women.

KEY POINTS

The proportion of households containing lone-parent families increased from 3 per cent to 7 per cent between 1971 and 2007. This is linked to changing attitudes and the increase in divorce.

What other changes are taking place in families and households?

OBJECTIVES

Describe the increases in stepfamilies and dual-worker families
Outline the view that the wider family is increasingly being replaced by friends

The increase in significance of stepfamilies and dual-worker families

The significance of stepfamilies (or reconstituted families) has increased over the last 30 years. Stepfamilies may come about as a result of remarriage or cohabitation. When parents separate, children often stay with their mother and so the majority of stepfamilies comprise a biological mother and stepfather.

As a result of the increasing proportion of married or cohabiting women now working, there has been an increase in dual-worker families, in other words, families in which both partners are in paid employment. In 2007, 72 per cent of married and cohabiting mothers of working age in the UK were in employment.

Stepfamilies in Britain, 2006 — WRITTEN ACTIVITY

1 In 2006, what percentage of stepfamilies contained children from both partners' previous relationships?

2 What percentage had a biological mother, her child or children, and a stepfather?

6 per cent comprise children from both partners' previous marriage or cohabitation

10 per cent comprise a stepmother, a biological father and his child or children

84 per cent of stepfamilies comprise a stepfather, a biological mother and her child or children

Source: *Social Trends* (2008)

Working mothers — DISCUSSION ACTIVITY

1 Some people believe that women with young children should not work in paid employment. In a small group, discuss what evidence would be needed to identify the effects on young children of their mothers going out to work.

2 Note down three important points that were raised during your discussion.

Glossary terms: dual-worker families

Are friends becoming the new family?

One view is that the wider family is less central in our lives and is increasingly being replaced by friends. For example, our friends rather than our family may provide us with emotional support and nurture (see page 53). In their research, Sasha Roseneil and Shelley Budgeon (2006) found that, among people who did not live with a partner, it was friends more than biological kin who offered support to those who suffered mental health problems or emotional distress. Friends more than kin were also there to pick up the pieces when love relationships came to an end.

Friends rather than family may be providing emotional support today.

However, not everyone agrees that friends may be replacing families. Some researchers argue that many people turn first to their family rather than to friends when they need help or support with a problem. According to the British Social Attitudes Survey (Duncan and Phillips, 2008), only 29 per cent of respondents saw friends as more dependable than family in times of crisis. Furthermore, many people have a sense of obligation to family members. For instance, 68 per cent of respondents agreed that people should make time for close family members, even if they have nothing in common (Duncan and Phillips, 2008). It may be that friends are becoming more like family, rather than replacing them, and family members are becoming more like friends.

STRETCH AND CHALLENGE ACTIVITY

1 Identify and explain one piece of evidence from research which suggests that friends are replacing families.

2 Identify and explain one piece of evidence from research which suggests that friends are not replacing families.

CHECK YOUR UNDERSTANDING

1 Identify one reason why the majority of stepfamilies have a biological mother and a stepfather.

2 Outline one reason for the increase in dual-worker families.

KEY POINTS

Changes in families and households since the mid-1970s include an increase in the significance of stepfamilies and dual-worker families.

Some approaches suggest that the wider family is becoming less important in our lives. Others emphasize the continuing importance of family ties.

TOPIC 16 **What are the links between families, households, ethnicity and social class?**

OBJECTIVE

Describe the links between families, households, social class and ethnicity

Families, households and ethnicity

As a culturally diverse society, Britain is home to a rich mix of cultural, ethnic and religious groups. For instance, in London today a total of over 300 languages are spoken. People have been migrating to Britain for many centuries. In the 19th century, for example, migrants came from Ireland, and after the Second World War there was migration from former colonies such as India, Pakistan and parts of the Caribbean.

Charles et al (2008a) note that the cultural diversity in Britain is associated with different patterns of family formation. For example, among people of African-Caribbean heritage, becoming a mother is not necessarily associated with stopping full-time paid work. By contrast, among Asian heritage families there is still some emphasis on being a full-time mother. However, this does appear to be changing among second-generation migrants.

We have seen that lone-parent households with dependent children are increasing in some groups in Britain (such as Pakistani and white households) and decreasing among other groups (such as black Caribbean households – see page 72). Data from the 2001 census provide additional information on variations in households by ethnic group. For instance, household size varies: in 2001, Bangladeshi and Pakistani households, on average, contained more people than households from other ethnic backgrounds in Britain. White Irish households, which have an older age structure than other ethnic groups, were the smallest. Census data on one-person households in Britain reveal that 18 per cent of white Irish households contained a pensioner living alone in 2001, compared with only 2 per cent of Bangladeshi households.

One-person households by ethnic group

WRITTEN ACTIVITY

The chart on page 77 focuses on one-person households in Britain. It shows them according to the ethnicity of the person living alone and whether or not that person was a pensioner in 2001.

We can see from the first column, for example, that 15 per cent of white British households contained a pensioner living alone and 15 per cent contained a person below pension age living alone.

Study the information, then answer the questions below.

1 Which households were most likely to be one-person households in 2001 in Britain?

2 Which households were least likely to be one-person households?

3 Which households were most likely to contain a person below pension age living alone?

4 What percentage of Chinese households contained a pensioner living alone?

Glossary terms: cultural diversity   ethnic group   migration

Data on households containing three or more generations in England and Wales in 2001 show that 10 per cent of Bangladeshi and Pakistani households contained a multigenerational extended family compared with 2 per cent of white British and mixed households and 3 per cent of black Caribbean households.

Family relationships, ethnicity and social class

Popular beliefs suggest that British Asian families are based on unequal, male-dominated relationships. Westwood and Bhachu (1988) challenge such beliefs, suggesting that popular images of 'the Asian family' are often based on prejudice or prejudgments. In reality, there are ethnic differences among people of Asian heritage in Britain, for example according to religion and social class. This makes it very difficult to generalize about 'the Asian family'. Westwood and Bhachu point out that 'Asian families' are, in fact, British families and are a major source of strength and resistance against the racism of British society.

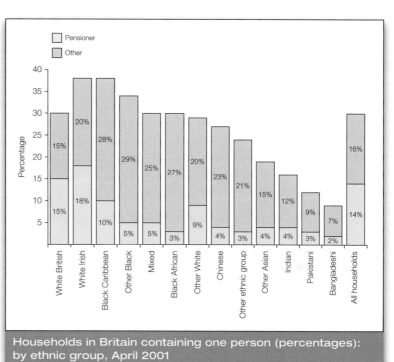

Households in Britain containing one person (percentages): by ethnic group, April 2001

Source: adapted from *Focus on Ethnicity and Religion* (ONS, 2006)

Some sociologists argue that relationships within families vary according to social class. Popular images suggest that working-class families are male dominated. There is some evidence to suggest that, in general terms, middle-class role relationships are more equal than working-class ones. But other evidence seems to suggest that working-class fathers are more involved in childcare than middle-class ones.

💡 STRETCH AND CHALLENGE ACTIVITY

Identify one reason why the size of a household might be linked to the age of the person or people living in it.

CHECK YOUR UNDERSTANDING

What do sociologists mean by 'cultural diversity'?

KEY POINTS

Britain is a culturally diverse society and immigration has been taking place for centuries.

Migration has added to the overall diversity of families and households in Britain.

TOPIC 17 How have changing patterns of fertility affected families and households?

OBJECTIVE
Outline and explain changing patterns of fertility

We have seen that important changes are taking place in families and households. Some types of households, such as one-person households, are increasing. Others, such as those containing traditional nuclear families with dependent children, are declining (getting smaller in number). There are also important demographic changes taking place which have an impact on individuals, families and society.

Demography involves the statistical study of the population, examining things like the number of people in the population (its size), birth rates, fertility rates, death rates, life expectancy and so on. Two factors that have a particular impact on society, households, families and individuals are changing fertility and life expectancy rates. We will look at changing patterns of fertility now, before moving on to examine life expectancy in the next topic.

Falling fertility, smaller family size and having children later

The term 'fertility' refers to the average number of children that women of childbearing age (usually 15–44) have in a society. Women born in the UK are having fewer children than 30 years ago and so there is a trend towards a smaller family size. Among women born in 1920 in the UK, the average number of children was 2.07 per woman. This peaked at 2.46 children for women born in 1934 and contributed to the 'baby boom' of the 1960s. Since then, however, family size has been declining. Among women born in 1961 in the UK, the average number of children is 1.96.

Changes in the fertility rates

WRITTEN ACTIVITY

The fertility rate is the number of live births per 1000 women of childbearing age (usually aged 15–44) in a given year. The information in the table shows fertility rates among women in different age groups. For example, we can see that in 1971, UK fertility rates were highest for women in their late twenties at 155.6 births per 1000 women. Study this information, then answer the questions below.

1 In 1971, UK fertility rates were highest for women in their late twenties. Which age group were they lowest for?

2 In 2006, which age group had the highest fertility?

3 What was the fertility rate for teenagers in 2006?

Fertility rates: by age of mother at childbirth

Age	Live births per 1000 women in the UK	
	1971	2006
15–19	50.1	26.4
20–24	153.9	72.0
25–29	155.6	100.1
30–34	79.4	104.6
35–39	33.9	53.4
40 and over	9.1	11.1

Source: adapted from *Social Trends* (2008)

Glossary terms: birth rate   death rate   demography   fertility   fertility rate

Women born in the UK are not only having fewer children, they are also having them at an older age. In 1971, the average age of mothers at childbirth in England and Wales was 26.2; in 2006, it was 29.5.

DISCUSSION ACTIVITY

Before you read on, work in a small group and discuss the possible reasons why UK-born women are having children at an older age than they were in the 1970s.

Note down two reasons for this.

These changes in patterns of fertility are linked to:

STRETCH AND CHALLENGE ACTIVITY

Write a paragraph to describe changes in the pattern of fertility between 1971 and 2006.

- Changing attitudes towards family sizes. During the 19th century, part of the reason why poor families wanted to have large families was to do with economic factors. Children tended to start work when they were still young, and many parents relied on their children's income. Having larger families therefore meant having a larger income. By the 1920s, laws about children working in factories, and the raising of the school-leaving age to 14, made it more difficult for children to contribute to the family income through paid employment. Today, there is little financial incentive in having children. On the contrary, bringing up children is expensive!

- The trend since the 1970s for people to get married at a later age, which means that some women will delay having children.

- Women's increased participation in education and paid employment. One impact of the feminist movement is that many women no longer feel that an adult female's main social role should centre on motherhood and childcare. There have been more opportunities for women in education and employment over the last 35 years, backed by laws on equal pay and sex discrimination. These have given women a wider range of options.

- The increased availability and use of effective birth control methods. The introduction of the contraceptive pill in the 1960s has meant that women have much greater control over their fertility, including whether and when to conceive (become pregnant). Additionally, the availability of legal abortion means that women can choose whether to continue with a pregnancy.

CHECK YOUR UNDERSTANDING

1 What is meant by the term 'fertility rate'?
2 Identify and explain two changes in patterns of fertility in the UK over the last 30 years.

KEY POINTS

Demographic changes are having an impact on families and households. Changing patterns of fertility mean that women are not only having fewer children, they are having them later in life.

There is also a trend towards a smaller family size.

TOPIC 18   What are the changing patterns of life expectancy and infant mortality?

OBJECTIVE

Describe and explain changing patterns of life expectancy and infant mortality

Life expectancy

Life expectancy at birth is the average number of years a newly born baby may be expected to live. People are, on average, living longer. Denscombe (1997) states that the UK life expectancy in the 5th century was around 33 years for men and 27 years for women. By 1901, this had increased to 45.5 for men and 49 for women. At that time, many people died during what we would regard today as middle age. Data from *Social Trends* (2008) shows that life expectancy was 76.6 years for men and 81 years for women in 2005. In the future, life expectancy is expected to increase further.

Increased life expectancy is linked to a number of factors, including welfare state provisions, developments in public health and medicine, and improvements in diet and nutrition.

The provisions of the welfare state

When the welfare state was established after the Second World War, living standards improved considerably (see page 260). The welfare state means that the state (through government departments such as the Department for Work and Pensions) plays an important role in looking after people's health and welfare. Today, the state, along with voluntary organizations and private businesses, provides help to those in need. For example, people have access to damp-free housing through their local authority, free health care through the National Health Service and state benefit payments (such as income support and pensions) when in financial need.

Developments in public health and medicine

During the 19th and early 20th centuries, life expectancy rose as a result of government improvements in public health services. Services such as clean water supplies, sewerage and drainage systems, and refuse disposal meant that fewer people died from contagious waterborne diseases.

Most of the increase in life expectancy, especially among children, results from improvements in preventive measures (preventing people becoming ill in the first place). Since 1945 there has been a lot of progress in controlling major infectious diseases by taking preventive steps, for example by vaccinating children against diseases such as diphtheria, polio, tetanus, measles, mumps and rubella. The development of immunization programmes has been an important factor in increasing life expectancy. Also, for

> ### ❖ DISCUSSION ACTIVITY
>
> ### The increase in life expectancy
>
> Before you read on, work in a small group and think of possible reasons why people are living longer today than they were at the start of the 20th century. Note down the two most likely reasons.

An example of a vaccination campaign.

Glossary terms: infant mortality   infant mortality rate   life expectancy at birth

women there are national screening programmes for breast cancer and cervical cancer. In 2008, the government launched a campaign to vaccinate young girls against a virus that causes cervical cancer.

Increased life expectancy can also be linked to important advances in medicine and surgery during the 20th century. Advanced medical developments such as open-heart surgery, kidney dialysis and chemotherapy in the treatment of cancer, help people to live longer.

Improvements in diet and nutrition

Over the last 30 years, there have been changes in our diet which suggest that people are taking more notice of messages about healthy eating from health organizations and the media. For example, household purchases of fruit (measured in grams per person per week) in the UK increased by 77 per cent between 1974 and 2005/06.

STRETCH AND CHALLENGE ACTIVITY

How far do you think our diet and eating habits are private matters? How far do you think the government should introduce policies (such as getting supermarkets to identify healthy and less healthy products on food packaging) to improve the nation's diet?

Write a paragraph to explain your views.

Decrease in infant mortality rates

Increased life expectancy can be partly explained by the reduction in infant mortality (the number of children dying in the first year of life) since the beginning of the 20th century. The infant mortality rate refers to the number of infant deaths (under one year) per 1000 live births per year. In 1930, the rate of infant mortality in England and Wales was 60.0 infant deaths per 1000 live births. In 2006, the infant mortality rate fell to 5.0 deaths per 1000 live births.

Many of the factors that have contributed to the increase in life expectancy (such as improvements in sanitation and diet and the development of immunization programmes) also help to explain the improved infant mortality rates. In addition, the introduction of a midwifery service in the early part of the 20th century meant that more babies were delivered by qualified midwives. More recent improvements in care provided during pregnancy (known as antenatal care) and after childbirth (post-natal care) have also helped to improve infant mortality rates.

CHECK YOUR UNDERSTANDING

1 What is meant by the following terms?

   a) life expectancy   b) infant mortality   c) infant mortality rate

2 Men and women in Britain tend to live longer today than they did 100 years ago. Identify and explain two reasons for this.

3 Outline one reason for the improved infant mortality rates over the last 100 years.

KEY POINTS

Life expectancy has increased. This is linked to welfare state provisions, developments in public health and medicine, and improvements in diet and nutrition.

The infant mortality rate has fallen.

TOPIC 19 # How has the age structure of the population changed and what are the consequences of this?

OBJECTIVES
Describe the changing age structure of the population
Outline the social consequences of an ageing population

The changing age structure of the population

Declining fertility rates combined with longer life expectancy mean that there is a smaller proportion of children and young people in the population and an increasing proportion of older people. This means that the UK has got an ageing population. In 2006, 19.1 per cent of the population was aged under 16, 64.9 per cent was aged 16–64 and 16 per cent was aged 65 and over. It is estimated that by 2026, 19 per cent of the population will be aged under 16, 61 per cent will be aged 16–64 and 20 per cent will be aged 65 and over.

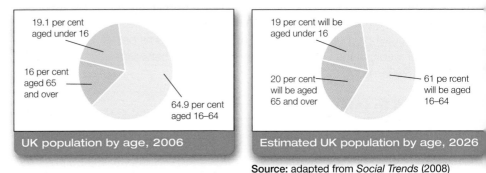

UK population by age, 2006

19.1 per cent aged under 16
16 per cent aged 65 and over
64.9 per cent aged 16–64

Estimated UK population by age, 2026

19 per cent will be aged under 16
20 per cent will be aged 65 and over
61 per cent will be aged 16–64

Source: adapted from *Social Trends* (2008)

The social consequences of an ageing population

An ageing population has consequences for individuals, families and society. In an ageing population, an increasing proportion of the population comprises retired people. As a result, there will be a growing financial burden on the working population to meet the demand from older people for facilities such as social services, medical services and hospitals. There may be insufficient money to fund state pensions unless changes (such as increasing taxation or raising the retirement age) are made. For some individuals, retirement may mean a loss of income, reduced standard of living and the risk of poverty.

Longer life expectancy and an ageing population may result in changes to household and family structures, such as a growth in one-person households (see page 70). They may also lead to an increase in families with three or more generations. In four-generation families, children have parents, grandparents and great grandparents alive at the same time. The term 'beanpole families' is sometimes used to describe these multigenerational families, which are long and thin in shape.

Within multigenerational families, women such as Ann* in the diagram on page 83 who are daughters, mothers and grandmothers are likely to be under the most pressure, having the burden of care for family members from different generations. Brannen (2003) uses the term 'pivot generation' to refer to Ann's* generation,

DISCUSSION ACTIVITY

Meeting people's needs in later life

In a small group, discuss the likely social and economic effects of increasing numbers of elderly people in the UK. What changes might be required in order for society to meet the needs of older people?

Make a note of three significant points raised during your discussion.

Glossary terms: ageing population   beanpole families   pivot generation

WRITTEN ACTIVITY

The age of beanpole families

Read through the information below, then answer the questions that follow.

There is a rise in the number of four-generation families and these are changing shape. Many multigenerational families are now long and thin – typically described as 'beanpole families'. They have fewer horizontal 'intragenerational' ties (ties within a generation) because of high divorce rates, falling fertility and smaller family size. They have more vertical 'intergenerational' ties (ties between the generations) because of increased longevity (longer life).

1 What is meant by the term 'beanpole families'?

2 Explain the difference between intragenerational and intergenerational ties.

3 Identify three reasons why multigenerational families have fewer intragenerational ties.

4 Identify one reason why multigenerational families have more intergenerational ties.

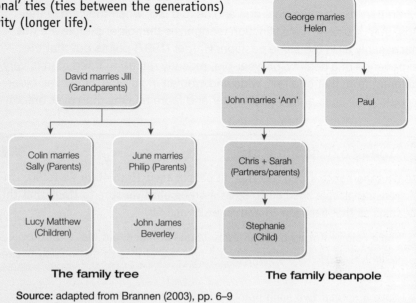

The family tree

The family beanpole

Source: adapted from Brannen (2003), pp. 6–9

sandwiched between younger and older family generations. Some grandmothers in the pivot generation may, for example, provide childcare for their grandchildren as well as looking after their frail elderly parents.

Some people, however, do not have kin in the older generations and, therefore, they do not receive intergenerational support. Some minority ethnic groups, for example, may miss out on informal care because they frequently have fewer older kin to call on due to patterns of migration and early mortality. Some older people without family or friends to provide care and without the financial resources to pay for it themselves are left to manage their situations as best they can.

STRETCH AND CHALLENGE ACTIVITY

Explain the difference between a 'family tree' and a 'family beanpole'.

CHECK YOUR UNDERSTANDING

1 What is meant by the term 'ageing population'?

2 Explain two social consequences of an ageing population.

KEY POINTS

Britain has an ageing population.

Multigenerational families are associated with longer life expectancy and an ageing population.

TOPIC 20 # How do older people experience retirement?

OBJECTIVE

Explain how older people experience retirement

Older people's experiences of retirement differ according to whether they are 'young old' or 'old old'. A person could be described as 'young old' when they reach retirement age and as 'old old' when they are in their 80s, 90s or older. This distinction recognizes that older people are not necessarily all in the same position. Harper (1997) points out that the experience of a healthy, 65-year-old, recently retired married man is very different from that of a frail, widowed woman in her 90s. However, older people of all ages are generally fitter and more healthy than ever before.

'Young old' and 'old old'

DISCUSSION ACTIVITY

We tend not to group together all people aged 15 to 40 or 25 to 50. It is more common, however, to consider people aged 60 to 85 as a group until we stop to think that this span of 25 years is the same as that between 15 and 40 or 25 and 50.

Some commentators use the terms 'young old' and 'old old' to acknowledge that older age can cover a span of 25 years or more. Discuss how useful it is to distinguish between the 'young old' and 'old old' in this way.

Make a note of two main points arising from your discussion.

People in later life are not only on the receiving end of services – they also provide services and unpaid care. Older people may provide care informally within their families, for example by babysitting or child minding (see page 68). Furthermore, much of the work within organizations such as Age Concern is done by volunteers, the majority of whom are retired. Some commentators suggest that we should try to encourage more part-time paid work beyond current retirement ages.

Living independently in later life

Social and medical advances mean that the quality of later life is improving. Most people are able to maintain reasonably healthy and independent lives into their 70s and 80s. A relatively small proportion of older people in Britain live in communal establishments such as nursing homes. Most older people continue to live in the community well into later life. For example, in 2001, around three-quarters of people aged 90 and over were living in private households. In addition, a relatively small proportion receive personal social services such as local authority home help. For instance, only 1 per cent of people aged 65–69 and 18 per cent of people aged 85 and over in Britain received local authority home help in 2001/02 (Evandrou, 2005).

Retired people may provide services as well as receiving them.

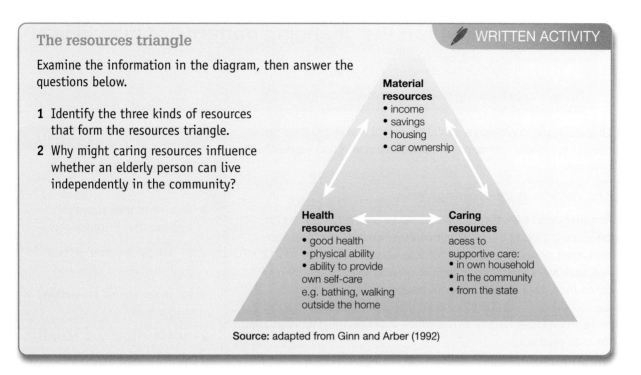

The resources triangle

Examine the information in the diagram, then answer the questions below.

1 Identify the three kinds of resources that form the resources triangle.

2 Why might caring resources influence whether an elderly person can live independently in the community?

Material resources
• income
• savings
• housing
• car ownership

Health resources
• good health
• physical ability
• ability to provide own self-care
e.g. bathing, walking outside the home

Caring resources
acess to supportive care:
• in own household
• in the community
• from the state

Source: adapted from Ginn and Arber (1992)

Ginn and Arber (1992) note that elderly people want to maintain their independence for as long as possible. They do not wish to depend on others because, in so doing, they may lose their self-respect. Ginn and Arber identify three key resources that influence whether an elderly person can live independently in the community. These are material, health and caring resources. The three kinds of resources interlock to form a resource triangle.

Ginn and Arber make the important point that an individual's social class, gender and ethnicity influence his or her chance of having each type of resource. As a result, class, gender and ethnicity affect an individual's independence, wellbeing and opportunities for full participation in social life. In their research, Ginn and Arber found gender differences, with older women being less well off than men in each of the three areas. In this way, some people are worse placed than others in later life depending on their gender, ethnicity and social class.

CHECK YOUR UNDERSTANDING

Identify and explain two resources that influence whether an elderly person can live independently in the community.

KEY POINTS

Older people's experiences of retirement differ according to their age.

People in later life may provide services in the community and unpaid care within families.

Elderly people's access to material, health and caring resources influence whether they can live independently in the community.

What are the changing patterns of marriage?

OBJECTIVE

Outline the changing patterns of marriage in Britain

Official statistics provide a useful source of numerical data about changing patterns of marriage, cohabitation and non-marital births in Britain.

The decline in the marriage rate

The marriage rate refers to the number of marriages per 1000 people per year. In the UK, the marriage rate has declined from 7.1 marriages per 1000 people in 1981 to 5.2 per 1000 people in 2005. The number of marriages in the UK peaked in 1972 at 480 000. Since then, the overall number of people getting married has decreased, and in 2005 there were just under 284 000 marriages. More than 60 per cent of all marriages in 2005 were first marriages for both partners.

Civil partnerships

Since the Civil Partnership Act came into effect in the UK in December 2005, same-sex couples aged 16 and over can have their relationships legally recognized in the form of a civil partnership. Between December 2005 and September 2006, 15 700 civil partnerships were formed in the UK, and in 2007, 8728 civil partnerships (3958 female and 4770 male) were formed. Eleven per cent of men and 23 per cent of women who formed a civil partnership in 2007 had been in a previous civil partnership or marriage.

People are getting married at a later age

Compared with the early 1970s, people are now postponing (putting off) marriage until they are older. Consequently, the average age of first marriage for men and women in England and Wales has risen over the last 30 years (see opposite). This is linked to increased educational and employment opportunities, particularly for women. It is also related to changing attitudes towards premarital sex, which in general is now considered more acceptable.

The increase in cohabitation

Official statistics show that the proportion of people cohabiting (living with a partner outside marriage or civil partnership) in Britain has more or less doubled over the last 20 years. Cohabiting couples with children tend to be much younger than married couples with children. Ethnicity provides another way of examining variations in cohabitation in Britain. In 2001, cohabiting-couple families were more common in households headed by someone from a mixed ethnic group or a white ethnic group.

✦ DISCUSSION ACTIVITY

Changing patterns in marriage

1 In a small group, suggest two possible reasons why:

   a) people are now getting married at a later age

   b) fewer people are getting married.

2 Make a note of your reasons.

Average age of first marriage (England and Wales)

	1971	2004
Men	24.6	31.4
Women	22.6	29.1

Source: adapted from *Social Trends* (2008)

✎ WRITTEN ACTIVITY

Extra-marital births

Identify two possible reasons why more couples are having children outside marriage.

Glossary terms: civil partnership   cohabitation   marriage rate

Some people may cohabit without expecting the relationship to develop into a long-term one. Alternatively, cohabitation may lead to marriage and, for example, an engaged couple may live together while saving up money to get married. For other couples, cohabitation may be a long-term alternative to marriage.

The increase in cohabitation is linked partly to changes in social attitudes towards sex outside marriage since the mid-1960s. Before the 1960s, it was considered unacceptable for unmarried women to be sexually active.

The increase in births outside marriage

During the 1960s and 1970s in the UK, births outside marriage became more commonplace. In 1988, 25.2 per cent of all births in the UK were outside marriage, and by 2006 this proportion stood at 43.7 per cent. Compared with the situation before and during the 1950s, births outside marriage are no longer stigmatized or disapproved of. This is reflected in the use of language around non-marital births. Allan and Crow (2001) note, for example, that terms such as 'shot-gun wedding' and 'illegitimacy' are no longer common.

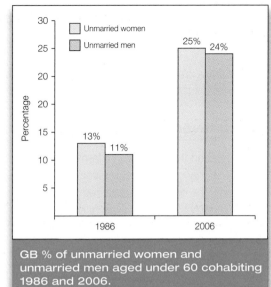

GB % of unmarried women and unmarried men aged under 60 cohabiting 1986 and 2006.

Source: adapted from *Social Trends* (2008)

Much of the increase in births outside marriage results from rising numbers of babies born to cohabiting partners. In other words, a high proportion of unmarried mothers are living with their child's father at the time of birth. In 1988, 17.4 per cent of births outside marriage were registered jointly. This means that, while the parents were not married, both of their names were entered on the baby's birth certificate. In 2006, the proportion of jointly registered births rose to 36.9 per cent.

Changing patterns in cohabitation

💠 DISCUSSION ACTIVITY

1 In a small group, discuss the possible reasons why more people are choosing to cohabit rather than marry.

2 Make a note of three possible reasons for the increase in cohabitation.

CHECK YOUR UNDERSTANDING

1 Identify and explain one reason why the average age at which people get married has increased in the last 30 years.

2 Outline one reason why cohabitation has increased in Britain over the last 20 years.

KEY POINTS

The marriage rate is declining, people are getting married at a later age, cohabitation has increased and the proportion of births outside marriage has increased.

Civil partnerships were introduced in the UK in 2005.

TOPIC 22 # What are the changing patterns of divorce?

OBJECTIVES
Outline changes in the divorce rate over the last 30 years
Explain the increase in divorce in Britain

Rising divorce rates

We have seen that patterns of family life are currently changing. One of the most significant changes relates to divorce. A divorce is the legal ending of a marriage. In general, the number of divorces per year is going up, although there have also been decreases. The numbers of divorces in the UK in 1970, 1993 and 2005 are shown below.

1970	63 000 divorces
1993	180 000 divorces
2005	155 000 divorces

The term 'divorce rate' refers to the number of divorces per 1000 married people per year. The divorce rate in the UK doubled between 1971 and 1981, increased again in the 1990s, and has declined recently, as shown below.

1971	around 6.0 divorces per 1000 married people
1981–86	12.0 divorces per 1000 married people
1995	13.6 divorces per 1000 married people
2005	13.1 divorces per 1000 married people
2007	11.9 divorces per 1000 married people

Explaining the increase in divorce rates

A number of factors have been identified to explain the increase in divorce in Britain since 1945. These factors are examined below.

Changing social attitudes and values

The 1960s can be seen as marking a shift towards more liberal attitudes to issues such as divorce. As a result of changing attitudes, divorce has become less stigmatized and more socially acceptable. Some members of the Royal Family, for example, have divorced and we regularly hear about celebrity divorces in the media.

Changes in the law

Legal changes have made divorce easier, quicker and cheaper to obtain than in the past. The Divorce Reform Act (1969) in England and Wales came into effect in 1971. Following this, an individual could petition for divorce on the grounds of 'irretrievable breakdown of marriage' as a result of separation, desertion, adultery or unreasonable behaviour.

Further legislation in 1984 allowed couples to request or petition for divorce after only one year of marriage, rather than three years as previously. Legal aid facilities became available, which made divorce cheaper to obtain. By contrast, in the Republic of Ireland people have

> ### ✿ DISCUSSION ACTIVITY
>
> **The effects of divorce**
>
> 1 In a small group, discuss the possible consequences of divorce for the individuals involved and for society as a whole. You could include in your discussion the effects of divorce on the number of single-parent families, the remarriage rate and the incidence of poverty.
>
> 2 Note down three significant consequences of divorce that you identified during your discussion.

Glossary terms: divorce rate   secularization

only been able to petition for divorce since 1997, and in Malta people are unable to divorce.

Changes in the social position of women

Women in unhappy marriages are less tied to their husbands through economic dependence than in the past as more women are able to work to earn their own living. There are now more employment opportunities for females and more women are in the workforce than in the 1960s. This means that married women are less economically dependent on their husbands and have more financial security than before. Additionally, with the availability of welfare benefits, women with children will not be destitute (left without any money) as a result of divorce. They may be able to apply for a number of state benefits with which to support their family.

Despite these social changes, however, women with young children and few qualifications may still experience financial problems after divorce. In addition, it is still much easier for the male partner to walk away from his marriage and family than it is for the female.

Secularization

The term 'secularization' refers to the idea that religion is losing its influence and importance in society. Statistics suggest that the Christian churches, in particular, are attracting fewer members today compared with 20 years ago. Rather than a Church wedding, many people now choose to have a civil ceremony in a registry office or elsewhere. This means that fewer people take sacred vows before God to stay together "till death us do part". Consequently, the religious barrier to divorce is weaker today than it was in the past.

Media influence

The popular media (such as pop music, magazines and soap operas) tend to emphasize the importance of mutual attraction and 'romantic love' in relationships between couples. As a result, individuals getting married may have high expectations of what marriage should be like. These expectations may not match the realities of married life. As an increasing number of marriages do not fulfil such hopes over the long term, more people are getting divorced.

> **STRETCH AND CHALLENGE ACTIVITY**
>
> Which approach to studying families is likely to view the increase in the divorce rate as problematic for individuals and for society?

Media representations of romance.

CHECK YOUR UNDERSTANDING

How far would sociologists agree that changes in the position of women have been responsible for the increase in the divorce rate since the 1960s?

KEY POINTS

The divorce rate in the UK doubled between 1971 and 1981, increased again in the 1990s, and has declined more recently.

Several factors explain the increase in divorce in the UK. These include changing social attitudes, legal changes, changes in the social position of women, secularization and the influence of the media.

TOPIC 23 What are the consequences of divorce?

OBJECTIVE

Explain the consequences of divorce

Divorce has consequences not only for the individuals involved but also for society. Rising divorce rates have contributed to greater variety in families and households such as lone-parent families, stepfamilies and one-person households.

As a result of rising rates of divorce, for example, there are now more stepfamilies. Some children may have full siblings (brothers and sisters), half siblings and stepsiblings. Full siblings share both biological parents and half siblings share just one. Stepsiblings are unrelated by blood but each has a biological parent in a relationship together. Living in a stepfamily may cause problems for family members who have to adjust to different expectations of behaviour. On the other hand, it may result in more people being there to provide attention, support and love.

Pressure groups such as F4J believe that fathers receive unfair treatment from the divorce courts.

After their parents divorce, most children live with their mother and visit their father. However, it is common for children to lose daily contact with their father and estimates suggest that between one-third and one half of divorced fathers lose contact with their children over time.

Conflict between the former husband and wife may continue after divorce due to disputes over issues such as parenting and property (houses, money and so on). Pressure groups such as Fathers 4 Justice (F4J) aim to draw attention to the cause of fathers who believe they have been treated unjustly by the divorce courts.

Divorce can lead to loss of income for the former partners after property, money and other belongings are divided. Lone-parent families with dependent children are at risk of poverty and, after divorce, single parents may experience financial hardship. They can also face difficulty in juggling the demands of paid employment and home life.

Men in particular may experience loss of emotional support after divorce as their friends and kinship networks may change. Women, on the other hand, are more likely to have their own support networks (Pryor and Trinder, 2004).

Remarriage

Marriage in Britain is based on monogamy, which means that people can only be married to one person at a time. After divorcing, the former spouses may remarry. Serial monogamy occurs when a divorced person marries for a second time, then divorces, remarries, divorces, remarries and so on. The number of remarriages in the UK has remained fairly stable over the last 30 years. In 1976, there were approximately 124 000 remarriages and in 2005 there were almost 113 000 remarriages. However, the remarriage rate (the number of divorced women and men marrying per 1000 divorced people) has decreased markedly.

Glossary terms: monogamy   serial monogamy

In 1976, the remarriage rate was 122.2 for women and 178.8 for men. By 2005, the remarriage rate had fallen to 29.5 for women and 40.2 for men.

Divorced people remarry for a number of reasons:

- It is argued that people who divorce are not rejecting the institution of marriage itself. Rather, they are rejecting one particular partner. In other words, they are not against marriage in general but just do not want to be married to that particular person. People still value a happy marriage and hope to succeed in a relationship the second time round.

- Divorced people with young children may want a partner to help them bring up their children.

- People may remarry for companionship and love.

- In the past, marriage was a source of status, particularly for women. While this is not so true today, in many ways marriage remains the norm.

Changing patterns in households, families, marriage and divorce

WRITTEN ACTIVITY

We have examined changing patterns in households, families, marriage and divorce, such as the increasing number of one-person households and the declining birth rate.

Summarize these changes by copying and completing the table below. Two examples are included to give you a start. Add at least another three changes under each heading.

Changing patterns in families and households

Increase in	Decrease in
Number of one-person households	The birth rate

👁 Eye on the exam

When answering an exam question that requires a piece of continuous writing, it is well worth spending a few minutes planning your response. This will help you to show that you can organize what you know and communicate it clearly.

CHECK YOUR UNDERSTANDING

1 Identify and explain two possible consequences of the increase in divorce for the people involved.

2 Discuss how far sociologists would agree that it is realistic to talk of a 'typical British family' today.

KEY POINTS

Divorce has consequences for individuals and society. One consequence is an increase in stepfamilies. Other possible consequences are loss of contact between children and one parent, conflict between former spouses over parenting and property issues, loss of income for former spouses and loss of emotional support, particularly for divorced men.

TOPIC 24 · What is the difference between arranged and forced marriages?

OBJECTIVE
Understand the difference between arranged and forced marriages

We have seen that marriage may be based on romantic love and mutual attraction between the partners. Marriage may also be arranged. Garrod (2005b) notes that arranged marriages are traditional in many communities. It is important, however, not to confuse arranged marriage and forced marriage.

The difference between arranged and forced marriages

WRITTEN ACTIVITY

In the following extract, Garrod (2005b) makes the important distinction between an arranged marriage and a forced marriage. Read the extract, then answer the question that follows.

> The essential difference between arranged and forced marriages concerns the right to choose. In arranged marriages, the families of the prospective spouses take a leading role in finding a partner and making arrangements. However, the choice of whether to accept the proposed partner rests with the individuals concerned. In forced marriages, one or both parties do not consent to the marriage and some element of duress is involved.

Source: adapted from Garrod (2005b)

According to this information, what is the main difference between arranged and forced marriages?

Forced marriage

WRITTEN ACTIVITY

In the following extract, the possible reasons behind forced marriage are explored.

Read the extract, then answer the questions that follow.

> Although forced marriages are sometimes seen as a religious issue, all major faiths condemn them and base marriage on freely given consent. However, the preservation of religious or cultural traditions is sometimes given as a reason by parents who force their children into marriage. Arvinder Lall, from the Ashiana Project, says: "First-generation immigrants fought for their culture to be accepted in Britain. Now they're watching as their achievements are whittled away by their own, increasingly westernized children. They're desperate to protect their culture and this is an extreme way in which they try to do that."

Source: adapted from Garrod (2005b)

According to this information:

1 Are there any religions that support the practice of forced marriage?

2 What reason do parents sometimes give to defend forced marriage?

Arranged marriage among British Asians

In this extract from a newspaper article, Ziauddin Sardar discusses arranged marriage among British Asians and how the process has changed. Read the extract, then answer the questions that follow.

So what is an arranged marriage? How is the man deemed an appropriate life partner for that woman and vice versa? The process involves a lot of to and fro and both partners are free to reject or accept. Arranged marriage never involves just two people. Marriage is much too important to be based on the dreams of a would-be bride and groom. Arranged marriage is not just a marriage between two individuals, but two families.

The newest generation of British Asians have reinvented the whole concept of arranged marriage. The process now involves finding a partner first and then getting the family to arrange the marriage. And if education, work, membership of clubs or the network of family gatherings does not offer opportunities to meet who is out there in need of a wife or husband, there is always speed dating. At an Asian speed-dating event, where the whole family is welcome, you can check people out without being lumbered with the greatest bore for an entire evening.

To those who scoff at arranged marriages, I only have this to say: look at your own dilemmas of family breakdowns, divorce and human despair. And if you want ongoing continuity of love, comfort and support in your old age, go for an arranged marriage.

Source: adapted from Ziauddin Sardar, *The Guardian*, 13 September 2008

1   In a small group, discuss what an arranged marriage is. Note down what an arranged marriage involves.

2   Discuss the possible advantages and disadvantages of arranged marriage. You should focus in particular on social and economic factors. Make a list of these advantages and disadvantages.

CHECK YOUR UNDERSTANDING

Identify and explain one difference between an arranged and a forced marriage.

KEY POINT

In arranged marriages, the partners consent to the marriage. In forced marriages, either one or both of the partners do not consent to the marriage and some degree of force is involved.

TOPIC 25 What sort of family-related issues are currently causing concern?

OBJECTIVES

Outline some of the social problems often associated with families and family life

Outline the role of sociology in contributing to policies that address these problems

In Chapter 2, we looked at the links between sociology, social problems and social policies. We saw that sociological research may be useful to governments or local authorities in influencing social policies. Now we will examine some of the social problems often associated with families and family life and the role of sociology in contributing to policy to address these problems.

Jacqueline Scott (2004) identifies several areas of policy concerns about children and families. These include concerns about:

- growing levels of child poverty
- parental responsibilities when children are born outside marriage
- the rights of children and how these should be put into practice
- long working hours that have increased the pressures on family care
- changes that have altered the ratio of children to the elderly, and what this means for welfare provision.

Issues related to families and children, such as teenage motherhood and forced marriage, cause concern in the media and among politicians and policy makers. Teenage motherhood, for example, is often seen as a serious problem not only for the young mothers and their children but also for society. However, sociologists do not simply accept such judgements at face value. Instead, they undertake research and gather evidence in order to explore what is really going on. Ideally, such research evidence should inform the debates and contribute to social policy.

RESEARCH ACTIVITY

Researching Sure Start

The Sure Start programme is an example of one way in which the government has attempted to help families in recent years. The Sure Start programme:

"aims to deliver the best start in life for children and to achieve better outcomes for children, parents and communities by:

- increasing the availability of childcare for all children
- improving health and emotional development for young children
- supporting parents as parents and in their aspirations towards employment."

Source: http://www.surestart.gov.uk/

In small groups, identify three services (such as Children's Centres or Sure Start Maternity Grants) currently available under the Sure Start programme and, for each, explain briefly what it involves and how it seeks to help children, parents or communities. Present your findings in the form of a written report.

You will find relevant information about the Sure Start programme at http://www.surestart.gov.uk.

Simon Duncan (2006), for example, has researched teenage parenthood and found that having a baby is usually not a disaster for young mothers. On the contrary, the research evidence suggests that becoming a teenage parent can be more of an opportunity than a disaster. For example, having a baby could make young mothers feel stronger and more responsible or encourage them to take up education, training and employment.

Duncan's work provides a good example of the ways in which social research can inform debates on issues that are viewed as social problems. It also highlights an area in which research on families might contribute to social policy.

One way in which governments have tried to tackle child poverty is through providing payments such as Child Tax Credits to help parents or guardians with the cost of looking after children. Additionally, most parents with children under 16 (or older if in relevant education or training) qualify for Child Benefit payments.

The quality of parenting

DISCUSSION ACTIVITY

Childhood obesity has been seen by some people as evidence of poor parenting. The extract below focuses on childhood obesity and considers one way to tackle it. Read through the article, then answer the questions that follow.

> Dangerously overweight children will have to be removed from their parents and put into care because of Britain's worsening 'obesity epidemic', council leaders have warned. The Local Government Association (LGA), which represents 400 councils in England and Wales, predicted that social services teams would have to take drastic action to improve the health of seriously overweight children. Social workers have only become involved very rarely in such cases, considering the issue best tackled by parents. But the LGA warned that social services might have to treat very overweight children as victims of 'parental neglect' – just as malnourished children are.
>
> The LGA said the increasing weight of the average citizen was pushing up council tax bills. The costs come from the need for bigger furniture in classrooms, canteens and gyms to cope with larger pupils.
>
> The LGA spokesperson on public health commented: "There needs to be a national debate about the extent to which it is acceptable for local authorities to take action where children's welfare is in jeopardy."

Source: adapted from N. Morris, *The Independent*, 16 August 2008

In small groups, discuss how far you agree with the suggestion that is being proposed here. Consider whether it is acceptable for local authorities to take action. Whose rights and responsibilities are involved here? Can you think of other ways to deal with this issue that might be more effective?

Make a note of the main points raised during your discussion.

CHECK YOUR UNDERSTANDING

Describe one way in which governments have attempted to help families in recent years.

KEY POINTS

Issues related to families and children cause concern in the media and among politicians and policy makers. Sociological research can inform the debates on these issues and influence social policy.

Governments try to help families, for example by providing payments such as Tax Credits and through programmes such as Sure Start.

4 Education

What are the economic and selective roles of education?

OBJECTIVE

Describe the role that education plays in society: economic and selective roles

Initially, we need to examine the role that education plays in society. There is a lot of disagreement among sociologists over this question.

Functionalist perspectives examine institutions in terms of the positive role they play in society as a whole. So, for functionalists, education is seen as performing a beneficial role in society.

Marxist perspectives, on the other hand, examine society in terms of the struggle between powerful and less powerful groups. They argue that the powerful groups in society (the ruling classes) use the education system to impose their own beliefs and values on the rest of society. From this point of view, education would be seen as having a beneficial role only for certain groups.

So according to these different viewpoints, what is the role of education?

Is this what education is for?

The economic role – teaching skills for work

For functionalists, schools and colleges teach the skills and knowledge necessary for work in a modern, technical, industrial society, for example literacy, numeracy and computer technology. Vocational courses aim to train young people for the world of work. So education prepares young people for their future occupational roles.

For Marxists, education is seen as reinforcing the class system. Thus, children from less powerful groups (the working classes) learn the skills necessary for lower-status occupations, while the children from more powerful groups (the middle and upper classes) gain the qualifications needed for higher-status occupations.

The selective role – choosing the most able people for the most important jobs

Functionalists see the education system as a sieve, grading students according to their ability and placing individuals in occupational roles best suited to their talents and abilities. This process is based on the functionalist belief that all individuals have equal opportunities in their school career. In this way, those who achieve high qualifications are seen as the most

✤ DISCUSSION ACTIVITY

Thinking about the future

Think about all the subjects you are studying.

1 For each subject, explain how it could be useful in preparing you for your future working life.

2 Do you think the education system teaches the skills and knowledge necessary for work in a modern industrial society? Explain your answer.

Glossary terms: meritocratic   social mobility

able and are therefore rewarded with higher pay and higher status in society. This is known as a meritocratic system.

One result of this process is social mobility. By receiving qualifications through the education system, students can progress to a higher position in society than they started from.

Marxists, on the other hand, do not believe that the education system provides equal opportunities for everyone. They argue that it is designed to benefit the powerful groups. They claim that both teachers and schools reject working-class children and that working-class children therefore under-perform.

From the Marxist point of view, the education system is not seen as meritocratic because it does not offer an equal opportunity to all groups in society.

RESEARCH ACTIVITY

Looking at occupations

The list of occupations below has been ranked in terms of qualifications required.

1 doctor
2 lawyer
3 bank manager
4 teacher
5 nurse
6 typist
7 supermarket cashier
8 pop singer
9 refuse collector

Carry out research to answer the following questions.

1 Identify what qualifications each of these occupations would require. Do the jobs requiring more qualifications pay more than those requiring fewer qualifications?
2 How else could we rank occupations, other than by qualifications needed? Rewrite the list using another method. Explain which you think is the best method of deciding on the importance of occupations.
3 Do you think people who get high qualifications always gain the more skilled, better-paid jobs?

Eye on the exam

Although you will be encouraged to consider your own views on the role of education, written answers in the exam should contain the relevant sociological knowledge, evidence and arguments.

CHECK YOUR UNDERSTANDING

Identify and explain one function of schools in Britain today.

KEY POINTS

Education can be seen to play an economic and selective role in society. Functionalist perspectives see these as positive and of benefit to the whole society. Marxist perspectives see education as having a beneficial role for privileged groups in society and reinforcing existing inequalities.

TOPIC 2 What are the socialization, social control and political roles of education?

OBJECTIVE

Describe the role that education plays in society: socialization, social control and political roles

The socialization role – teaching norms and values

For functionalists, education also plays a role in teaching the values and norms of society to each new generation. School is seen as an agency of socialization, through which young people learn a common culture, beliefs and expectations. The education system 'knits' children from different backgrounds into a flexible whole.

Marxists, on the other hand, see education as socializing individuals into accepting the values of the powerful groups. For example, the stress placed on the importance of hard work in schools and colleges is seen as preparing the future workforce for accepting hard work as normal when it enters the workplace.

Values and beliefs   DISCUSSION ACTIVITY

1 Decide what values or norms are being learned in the situations shown in the photographs.
2 To what extent do you think that we exit the education system with a set of shared values and beliefs?

Social control – teaching acceptance of rules and authority

Functionalists argue that for society to run smoothly there must be some means of regulating people's behaviour and activities. Schools act as an agency of social control by teaching rules such as obedience and punctuality.

Social control operates at two levels: the formal and the informal. In this way, people learn to conform to rules and authority in later life.

Glossary terms: agency of social control   socialization

Social control

Formal	Informal
• discipline of staff (e.g. during lessons)	• through general school life (e.g. peer-group pressure)
• punishments	• learning to live and work with others
• school rules	

For Marxists, social control in schools and colleges is seen as reflecting social control in the wider society, which benefits the powerful groups. For example, the importance of obeying a teacher in school is seen as preparation for obeying a boss in the workplace.

The political role – teaching people to be effective citizens and creating social cohesion

The development of Citizenship as a subject in schools and as an examined subject at GCSE and A-level has been linked to the belief that it is important to create social cohesion in society. This relates to the idea that education has a role in teaching the norms and values of British culture as well as helping individuals to identify themselves as part of that wider culture. This is sometimes called developing a sense of 'Britishness'. This may involve teaching students about the voting system in Britain and the legal system, or asking them to consider what it means to be 'British'.

According to functionalists, people learn about society through education. In this way, they accept the political system and, for example, are able to exercise their voting rights wisely at election time.

Marxists disagree, suggesting that only certain political opinions and ideas are tolerated in education – radical ideas are rejected or ridiculed. In this way, the political ideas of the powerful groups come to be accepted by individuals.

Fuctionalist v Marxist
STRETCH AND CHALLENGE ACTIVITY

Consider functionalist and Marxist views of the education system.

Make a list of arguments for and against each point of view.

CHECK YOUR UNDERSTANDING

Identify one way in which schools teach children to become part of society.
Explain with one example how this is done.

KEY POINTS

The education system has a role in socializing, controlling and politically educating people in society. Functionalist perspectives see these roles as positive and of benefit to the whole society. Marxist perspectives see education as having a beneficial role for privileged groups in society and reinforcing existing inequalities.

TOPIC 3 What is learned through formal and informal education?

OBJECTIVES

Understand the differences between formal and informal education

Identify the role of the 'hidden curriculum' in schools and colleges

It is important to note that the education system, consisting of schools, colleges and universities, is not the only source of learning. Learning also takes place informally through the socialization process.

The education system provides students with formal learning through the official curriculum, which includes all those subjects studied in lessons, for example maths, history, and so on. But students also learn through the 'hidden curriculum', which refers to the learning that takes place outside particular subjects or lessons as part of general school or college life. The hidden curriculum of a school may be very different from that of a college, but it will generally involve learning rules, routines and regulations. Students may learn such things without explicit teaching and without necessarily realizing they are learning them. This is known as informal learning.

The hidden curriculum reflects society's values and prepares students for their place in society and their future work role in the following ways.

Hierarchy

Schools are hierarchical institutions. Any hierarchy can be illustrated in the shape of a pyramid: each layer of the pyramid is smaller than and has more power than the one below it, with the layer at the top having the most power of all. So, in a school, the head teacher is at the very top of the pyramid and the students are at the bottom. Students may also see themselves in a hierarchy with older students at the top. Teachers may also see themselves in a hierarchy based on which subjects are seen as most important.

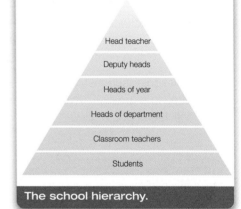

The school hierarchy.

The hierarchy in school can be seen to reflect the hierarchical structure of society at large. In the workplace, for example, a hierarchy may exist between a manager and a trainee.

Competition

Schools encourage competition between students, for example in sport or exam results. Society is also based on competition, for jobs, material possessions or status, for example. So schools reflect the value that society places on competition and prepare students for their place in a competitive society.

Social control

The hidden curriculum – of rules, regulations, obedience and respect for authority – is one mechanism of social control that reflects those social controls operating in society at large. In effect, students learn to accept society's social controls while they are in the education system.

The importance of competition is learned through the exam system.

Glossary terms: hidden curriculum   official curriculum   power

Gender role allocation

There is a link between expectations, subject choice and gender in school and gender role allocation in the wider society. Job segregation begins at school. For example, teachers may still expect girls to be less good at science than boys. This may discourage girls from entering science-based careers. Equally, girls may learn that the playground is a space that boys tend to dominate, for example, through taking up space with football games. This may prepare girls for the idea that men may seek to dominate other aspects of the social world as adults.

Lack of satisfaction

Critics of schools claim that much of the school day is taken up with boring and meaningless activities. Students have little say in the content of the subjects they study or in the overall organization of the day. Equally, following the same timetable, week in, week out, may lead to a sense of boredom and powerlessness.

The playground is a space that boys tend to dominate.

Schools, it is argued, prepare students for boring, meaningless and repetitive jobs. In this way, there is a link between students' experience of school and many employees' experience of work.

The hidden curriculum
WRITTEN ACTIVITY

For each aspect of the hidden curriculum described (hierarchy, competition, social control, gender role allocation, lack of satisfaction):

1 Note down whether this happens in your school or college and give an example.
2 Note down two other things that students may learn through the hidden curriculum.
3 Identify two ways in which the hidden curriculum in a college may be different from that of a school.

Researching the hidden curriculum
WRITTEN ACTIVITY

Informal learning, which takes place through the hidden curriculum, is often thought to take place without people realizing it is happening to them.

1   What problems might this create for researching the hidden curriculum?
2   What method(s) might you use to research the effects of the hidden curriculum?

CHECK YOUR UNDERSTANDING

1 Explain what sociologists mean by the 'hidden curriculum'.
2 Explain what part the hidden curriculum plays in the socialization of a child.
3 Identify and explain three ways in which the hidden curriculum may reflect society's values.

KEY POINTS

The education system provides both formal and informal learning to students. This learning takes place through the official curriculum and the hidden curriculum.

What changes took place in Britain's education system up to 1965?

OBJECTIVES

Describe reforms made by Education Acts up to 1965
Assess the impact of the tripartite system

There have been a number of major changes and developments in Britain's education system over the years. We will look here at the most significant ones.

The 1870 Education Act

Before 1870, the education system was not formally organized in the way it is now. People's access to educational provision depended to a large extent on their position in society. For example, church-run charity schools were available to the poor, while the rich could afford private tutors or could send their children to private school.

The 1870 Education Act tried to ensure that some basic education became available to all children from the ages of 5 to 11. It led to the general acceptance of the idea that revenue from state taxation should be used to pay for schooling. This was the start of the link between the state and education that exists today. Between 1870 and 1944, the education system was firmly based on social class. Three types of school were available:

- elementary schools for the working classes up to the age of 14
- fee-paying grammar schools for the middle classes, with a limited number of scholarships available to working-class boys
- expensive fee-paying public schools for the upper classes.

The 1944 Butler Education Act

During and after the Second World War there was widespread debate over what sort of society Britain should be. It was felt that the

A classroom in the 1900s.

talents of the nation were not being fully used and that the education system should be reformed in order to allow individual talent to flourish. It was also felt that Britain needed a better-educated workforce in order for its economy to be competitive. (This desire to educate a workforce to meet the needs of the economy has also influenced some of the changes in the education system in recent years.)

The 1944 Act aimed to give all students an equal chance to develop their talents and abilities in a system of free, state-run education. A new, three-stage structure was created:

1 Primary – up to the age of 11, including infant and junior stages
2 Secondary – from 11 to 15 (school-leaving age was raised to 16 in 1976)
3 Further/higher – education beyond the school-leaving age.

The main changes were in the organization of the secondary sector. The aim here was to introduce a meritocratic system where children would receive an education based on their own academic ability, rather than on the ability of their parents to pay. The result was the tripartite system.

Glossary terms: 11-plus exam   tripartite system

The tripartite system

Children's ability was tested at the age of 11 by the '11-plus' exam. Based on the results of this exam, children went to one of three types of school, each of which was designed to meet their needs. The 11-plus still exists in some areas of the country and much of the private sector uses entry tests at age 13 (the Common Entry Exam).

The tripartite system

11-plus exam (taken at age 11; designed to test ability and potential of student) Based on this, students were placed in either:		
SECONDARY MODERN	SECONDARY TECHNICAL	GRAMMAR
General education for the less academic (approximately 75% of all students)	Practical education, e.g. crafts, skills (approximately 5% of all students)	Academic education for more academic (approximately 20% of all students)

♣ DISCUSSION ACTIVITY

Testing ability

In the tripartite system, school allocation was based on the 11-plus exam.

1 What arguments can you make to suggest that students may not have shown their true abilities in the 11-plus exam?

2 Does this raise any issues for the use of testing in schools today, for example, the SATs tests or Common Entrance Exam in the private sector?

🔍 RESEARCH ACTIVITY

What was it like?

Think of a relative or friend who might have experienced the tripartite system.

Try to carry out an unstructured or informal interview with them. You might like to ask about which type of school they attended; how it felt to do an 11-plus exam; whether they became separated from friends as a result of the exam and so on.

💡 STRETCH AND CHALLENGE ACTIVITY

Views on the tripartite system

How might functionalist and Marxist perspectives view the tripartite system?

CHECK YOUR UNDERSTANDING

1 What types of school were introduced by the tripartite system?
2 What determined which type of school a student attended?

KEY POINTS

A formal education system began in Britain in 1870, linking the state to educational provision. This was developed further by the tripartite system, which aimed to allocate students to schools based on their academic ability.

TOPIC 5   What is the comprehensive system?

OBJECTIVE
Describe the comprehensive system and assess its impact

1965: the start of the comprehensive system

In 1965 the Labour government decided to ask Local Education Authorities (LEAs) to reorganize secondary education so that all students, regardless of academic ability, attended the same type of school. This became known as a 'comprehensive' school, and still exists in this form today. This policy was continued by the Conservative Government and, by 1986, approximately 90 per cent of secondary school students were attending comprehensives.

Students at a comprehensive school.

Why are comprehensives thought to be a good idea?

Comprehensive schools were introduced in response to what some saw as the failings of the tripartite system, which often simply reflected social class backgrounds, with more middle-class children in grammar schools. Instead, comprehensives are based on the principle of one type of school for everyone.

- **Social reasons** – as children of all abilities and from different social classes attend the same school and mix, so social barriers are broken down.

- **Educational reasons** – they are designed to cater for children of all abilities. There is no entrance examination or selection such as there was in the 11-plus, so no child is labelled as a 'failure'. This is seen to be fairer to many, and particularly to late developers. Comprehensives are said to provide students with more opportunity to achieve success according to their ability.

- **Economic reasons** – comprehensives are larger, so more subjects and more facilities are available. They are seen as cheaper to fund and run.

- **Geographical reasons** – each school has a specific 'catchment area' – a particular area or neighbourhood from which students are drawn. This has established the principle of local schools enrolling local children of all abilities and providing them with the same opportunities.

What are the problems with the comprehensive system?

It is argued that in practice comprehensives limit parental choice. Each student is expected to go to the nearest school in the area, no matter how good or bad that school's reputation.

It is also argued that the more academically able students are held back by the less able, particularly in mixed-ability groups (that is, where children of all abilities are taught in the same classroom). Teachers' attention and time might be torn between meeting the needs of the very bright as well as of less able

Glossary term: comprehensive system

students. However, it may also be that the understanding of less able students is helped by the presence of more able students in the class.

Some people believe that the education of bright working-class children may suffer if they go to the local comprehensive rather than to the local grammar school.

There is also a criticism that comprehensives accept lower standards. This criticism is related to social class, as comprehensives contain a mixture of classes with a range of values and attitudes. The grammar school, on the other hand, was largely middle class and so would reflect middle-class standards only.

Assessing the comprehensive system   ✥ DISCUSSION ACTIVITY

In a small group, discuss your views on the comprehensive system and its strengths and weaknesses. Be prepared to share your group's views on what its key strengths and weaknesses may be.

Do comprehensives break down class barriers?

Comprehensives are not really of mixed social class as they are based on a local neighbourhood; for example, inner-city comprehensives are usually working class and suburban ones are usually middle class.

Some argue that most comprehensives are not really comprehensive at all because, for instance, they stream or band students within the school according to ability. Critics claim that streams reflect social class differences. In other words, the comprehensive system simply reproduces the old tripartite system, but in one school.

One school for all?   💡 STRETCH AND CHALLENGE ACTIVITY

Having read about the tripartite and comprehensive systems, write a brief paragraph to explain your views on which system you feel could be fairer.

CHECK YOUR UNDERSTANDING

1 Explain what is meant by the 'comprehensive system'.
2 Identify and explain two reasons for the introduction of comprehensive schools.
3 Give two disadvantages of the comprehensive system.

KEY POINTS

The comprehensive system was introduced to allow all students, regardless of academic ability, equality of opportunity by attending the same type of school. However, whether this has happened in every case has been questioned.

How is the education system organized in contemporary Britain?

OBJECTIVE

Describe the general structure of education in contemporary Britain

There is a range of different types of schools and colleges in Britain. Some are provided through Local Authorities (LAs), while others are financed by charging attendance fees and others are directly funded by government. However, we can broadly describe educational provision in the following ways.

Pre-school and primary education

Pre-school education refers to the care and education of children under the age of 5. This includes:

- day nurseries, which may be provided through the local authority or by voluntary or private means
- playgroups, which provide care and learning experiences mainly for 3–5-year-olds
- nursery education, which may be provided in nursery schools or in nursery classes attached to primary schools for children up to 5 years old.

Primary education refers to infant and junior schools, which tend to take any student from a particular area from age 5 to 11. Most primary education is provided by the state (or public sector) through the LA. However, some schools at this level are private and fees must be paid.

Secondary education

This refers to schools that take students from the ages of 11 to 16, although many may also provide sixth-form education up to the age of 18. In some areas, middle schools provide a bridge from primary to secondary education, taking children from 8 to 12, 9 to 13 or 10 to 13 years old. Most secondary education is provided by the state in comprehensive schools where no fees are paid. However, some secondary education is provided by private fee-paying schools, grammar schools and independent faith schools.

The independent sector

These are schools that charge fees. This sector is made up of:

- private schools – all schools that charge fees
- public schools – the older and more famous independent secondary schools, such as Eton, Harrow and Rugby.

Around 7 per cent of all schoolchildren attend independent schools. These are not subject to the same rules as state schools. For example, they do not have to teach the National Curriculum. Because of the high tuition fees paid (for example, £26 000 at Eton in 2007/8), critics have claimed that independent

RESEARCH ACTIVITY

Secondary provision in my area

Find out about the range of secondary schools in your area. Are there only comprehensives? Are there any fee-paying schools, faith schools or other types of secondary provision?

You could: look on your Local Authority's website; ask your school's careers advisers; contact Connexions in your area or even go and visit the schools to identify what types they are.

Glossary terms: independent sector   private schools   public schools

schooling allows the children of the rich to receive an education that gives them certain advantages over state-educated children. For example, ex-independent school students made up 44.5 per cent of places at Oxford university in 2007, compared with 26.8 per cent coming from state sector comprehensives, sixth-form centres and grammar schools.

Further and higher education

This refers to education outside schools beyond the compulsory age of 16. From 16 to 18, students can study for a range of qualifications (e.g. A-levels and Scottish Highers) at sixth-form colleges or further education colleges, or go on to skills training courses and apprenticeships. At 18, students may then be qualified to go on to higher education and study at higher levels, including at universities. Many adults choose to return to education, taking courses at further education colleges or universities.

More students from independent schools get a place at Oxford University than from state schools.

Developments in further education

At 16, young people must decide whether to remain in full-time education, go into apprenticeships or seek employment, with or without training.

In recent years there has been a trend to remain in full-time education. The government is committed to raising the number of young people remaining in full-time education or training after the age of 16 (78 per cent of 16-year-olds were in full-time education in 2006). This is because, in order for Britain to remain competitive and prosperous in a global economy, it needs a highly educated and well-trained workforce. However, the figures for Britain are still lower than other countries. One response to this has been to consider raising the school-leaving age to 18 in order to try to ensure 16–18-year-olds are receiving some form of education and training.

All further and higher education colleges are funded by government. In effect, colleges are separate businesses, in competition with each other for students to increase their funding. The funding councils monitor colleges' performance against targets set for recruitment, exam performance, and so on. Supporters hope that these measures will result in improved quality of provision in the sector.

> ### STRETCH AND CHALLENGE ACTIVITY
>
> ### Views on tuition fees
>
> How might functionalist and Marxist perspectives view the high tuition fees charged by schools in the independent sector?

CHECK YOUR UNDERSTANDING

1 Identify one form of pre-school educational provision.
2 Explain what is meant by the 'independent sector'.
3 Explain what is meant by a 'public school'.

KEY POINTS

In Britain, most primary education is provided by the state through LAs. Most secondary education comes through state comprehensive schools. There is also provision through the independent sector where fees are paid. A range of provision exists beyond compulsory education and there is an emphasis on remaining in education or training after the age of 16.

TOPIC 7 — Should education be provided by the state or by the independent sector?

OBJECTIVE
Assess the advantages and disadvantages of state and private education

Why are independent schools favoured by some?

- They have a lower teacher-student ratio than state schools, which means that classes are smaller and students receive more attention from the teacher.

- Resources and facilities are often better than in some state comprehensive schools.

- Many independent schools have an academic culture, in which academic achievement is emphasized and examination results are good. Students are said to be highly motivated and most go on to university.

- Parental input is high in terms of fees, support and expectations.

- Independent boarding schools are said to benefit from the full immersion of staff and students in school life.

Why are state schools favoured by others?

- State schools are free – they are not based on the ability of parents to pay the high fees of private schools. Some critics argue that it is not morally right to have a private education system to which only the rich have access as this reinforces inequalities in society based on wealth.

A state school and an independent school.

The pros and cons of the independent sector

DISCUSSION ACTIVITY

Read the following summaries of the main arguments for and against the independent sector.

> Independent schooling maintains privilege based on social class position; that is, it can only be afforded by the rich. It is used by the rich to give their children a head start. Education should only be provided through a properly funded state system to ensure that everyone has access to the same levels and quality of education.

> Independent schooling is similar to private health care in that people should be able to spend their money however they choose. If they can afford to send their children to an independent school, then, in a free society, this option should be available to them.

Using these summaries and other information in this section, discuss arguments for and against the following statement: 'Education should be provided only by the state.'

- State schools are more socially mixed. Independent schools are seen as elitist and socially divisive.

- State schools may provide a route for upward social mobility for students from poor families. Fee-paying schools are less likely to do so.

- Students do not have to travel so far on a daily basis if they attend a local state school. Private school students may have to travel relatively long distances, or live away from home altogether at a boarding school.

Private schools still best route to top jobs

WRITTEN ACTIVITY

Examine the table, then answer the questions.

1 People from which of the professions in the table are most likely to have gone to a private school?

2 For which profession has there been a rise in the proportion of people in top jobs from private schools?

3 Which professions have seen the biggest reduction in the proportions of people from private schools occupying the top jobs?

4 To what extent do you think this information suggests that those who are privately educated have an advantage?

Percentage of leading people at different types of school

		Private	Grammar	Comprehensive
Judges	Now	70	28	2
	1980s	74	20	6
Politicians	Now	38	27	36
	1980s	46	32	22
Journalists	Now	54	33	12
	1980s	49	44	6
Medics	Now	51	32	17
	1980s	51	32	17
CEOs	Now	54	26	20
	1980s	70	20	10
Overall	Now	53	29	17
	1980s	58	32	12

Source: adapted from a report by The Sutton Trust, 2007

Applying theories

STRETCH AND CHALLENGE ACTIVITY

Having read the material on state and private sector education, write a brief paragraph to explain how a functionalist might view the availability of private education. Do the same from a Marxist viewpoint.

CHECK YOUR UNDERSTANDING

1 Identify and explain three arguments in favour of private education.
2 Identify and explain three arguments in favour of state schools.

KEY POINTS

Currently, Britain has a mixture of state and independent provision, with the majority of children attending state schools. Both forms of provision can be seen to have advantages and disadvantages.

TOPIC 8 What are vocational education and alternative forms of provision?

OBJECTIVES

Explain the role of vocational education

Describe and assess some alternative forms of educational provision

Vocational education and training

In recent years, governments have placed much more emphasis on providing vocational (or work-related) qualifications and training for students aged 14 to 18. Although this policy has been developing since the mid-1970s, it is still sometimes known as 'the new vocationalism'.

This development reflects the view that the education system has to provide the skills and expertise needed by industry and the economy in the modern world, and to engage a wider range of learners, more effectively than in the past.

In addition to compulsory work-related and enterprise learning at Key Stage 4, a range of qualifications have been brought in, including work-based National Vocational Qualifications (NVQs), which train students in specific jobs, and GCSEs and A-levels which provide a broad introduction to sectors such as Health and Social Care, Applied Business and Applied Science. The most recent development is the Diplomas, of which the first five were introduced in 2008, with 12 more to follow in subjects such as Engineering, Hair and Beauty Services, and Travel and Tourism.

By 2015, it is intended that all students aged up to 18 must be involved in some form of full or part-time education or training, at school, college or in employment.

Supporters of these changes argue that they will lead to a more skilled, better-qualified workforce that will allow Britain to be more competitive. However, some see vocational qualifications as being similar to the ideas of the tripartite system in that students who are not seen to be academic are considered failures and are pushed into what some see as lower-status vocational training.

Alternative forms of educational provision

There are a number of alternatives to mainstream, formal education, such as home education (also called home schooling or home learning). This involves teaching children at home rather than in a school. Home education is usually carried out by parents or professional tutors. It is a legal option for people who wish to provide a different learning environment from local schools.

An alternative form of education.

Another form of alternative provision comes in the way a school is organized and the types of values it teaches. A.S. Neill's Summerhill school is one example. This co-educational (for boys and girls) boarding school, set up in 1921 in Suffolk, has been seen by some as a model for progressive education.

Glossary terms: home education   vocational education

Home schooling

1 Discuss the pros and cons of home education.
2 Explain your view on home education as an alternative to mainstream, formal education.

Sands School – an alternative approach

Read the following details about Sands School, then answer the questions that follow.

> We value people as individuals. Students are free to be themselves and to explore their own paths through education. There are no uniforms, no petty rules resulting in detention and everyone is on first name terms.
>
> No-one has more power than anyone else, the teachers and students are equal and there is no headteacher. The school is democratic with everyone having their say and an equal vote in the weekly school meetings. It is the students who have the real power and this encourages a real sense of responsibility.
>
> Sands has timetabled lessons… if a student chooses not to study a subject, leaving a gap in their timetable, they are encouraged to find a constructive activity to fill that time… It seems foolhardy to put every child through the same programme of study hoping that at the end individuals will surface… (as in other schools)… (it is) better to teach children how to make wise choices relative to their own needs and interests.

Source: adapted from www.sands-school.co.uk

1 Make a list of the ways in which you think Sands School might be different from your school or college.
2 Outline the advantages and disadvantages that there might be in attending a school like this.

Sands School, students and teachers.

CHECK YOUR UNDERSTANDING

1 Identify and explain two criticisms of vocational education.
2 Identify one alternative approach to education.

KEY POINTS

Over the years, vocational education has been seen by governments as an increasingly important way of ensuring a more effective workforce to meet the needs of the economy.

Some alternative forms of educational provision do exist in Britain.

TOPIC 9 # What have been the effects of marketisation, the National Curriculum and testing?

OBJECTIVES

Describe and assess the impact of marketisation in education
Describe and assess the impact of the National Curriculum and testing

The 1988 Education Act brought in by the Conservative Government introduced many changes that are still fundamental to the contemporary education system.

Marketisation in education

This refers to the idea that the forces of the market, such as consumer choice and competition, have been introduced into education. The focus on parental choice, funding based on student numbers and more freedom for schools have reflected this process.

The National Curriculum and testing

The National Curriculum was introduced in September 1989 in all state schools in England and Wales. It established a number of core subjects (English, maths, sciences), which all students aged 5–16 must study, and also a number of foundation subjects (for example history and geography), which must be studied to Key Stage 3.

In addition, students' progress was to be assessed formally by their teachers and by national tests in the core subjects at the end of key stages, at the age

---

Marketisation in education

WRITTEN ACTIVITY

Read the extract below, then answer the questions that follow.

> Schools need to create an 'image' that is attractive to parents and students. They do this through school policy, documentation, the building, name and their students. Newly developed schools need to create instant 'traditions' through logos and uniforms. School documentation had to fit with 'school style'. School prospectuses were better produced and glossy.
>
> The concern was to give schools a more middle-class flavour in order to attract the high-achieving child of ambitious parents. The term 'able' had become code for students who were 'middle class', female, white or Indian. Unattractive intakes consisted of less able, emotionally damaged children with learning disabilities. Integration was resisted for children with special educational needs in some schools because of the possible perceptions of parents. Image making is turning schools into organizations that value certain children above others. The market does not ensure equality of access for all if schools only desire the custom of certain groups at the expense of others.

Source: adapted from Gewirtz et al (1995)

1 Identify two effects of marketisation in schools.
2 Which social groups may face inequality as a result of marketisation in schools?

Glossary terms: marketisation

of 7, 11 and 14. Sixteen-year-olds are assessed by means of the GCSE examination.

The aim is to measure students' performance against national targets so that parents and schools can see how a child is performing for their age. Measures can then be taken to improve the performance of children who are below the expected level, as well as the performance of schools whose students fall below the national targets.

In 2008 the government decided to remove testing at Key Stage 3 (age 14). This has led to further debate about the amount and usefulness of formal testing. The Independent Review of the Primary Curriculum carried out in 2008 recommended further changes to testing partly based on the effects on the curriculum of using time for preparing children for testing.

Science is compulsory for all students up to GCSE level.

One aim of the National Curriculum has been to provide greater equality of education for all by ensuring that all students take the same subjects. Science, for example, has traditionally been a boys' subject but it is now compulsory for *all* students up to GCSE level.

Assessing students' progress

WRITTEN ACTIVITY

Read the extract, then answer the questions that follow.

> I think we're now trapped in an education system driven by testing... we have too much testing now. Assessment actually goes on all the time in school. Teachers will say: 'Well done', 'That's right', every day to their pupils – but 99% of this school assessment is low stakes and informal. Only 1% of assessment is high stakes and formal, and it is this 1% – SATs, GCSEs, A-levels, AS-levels – on which everything rests.

Source: adapted from Wragg (2003)

1 Make a list of the possible benefits and problems of testing 7-year-olds and using the results as a measure of their ability.
2 What might be better ways of assessing students' progress?
3 Note down your views on the usefulness of testing as a way of assessing progress.

CHECK YOUR UNDERSTANDING

1 Explain what is meant by 'marketisation' in education.
2 Identify and explain two effects of the introduction of the National Curriculum.

KEY POINTS

Market forces have become part of the education system through parental choice and competition. The National Curriculum has resulted in compulsory core subjects for all and testing at different key stages.

TOPIC 10   How have freedom and choice increased?

OBJECTIVE

Examine increases in freedom and choice in educational provision

Increased competition and choice

The 1988 Act introduced the principles of choice and diversity in educational provision linked to the idea of marketisation. The idea here is that parents should be able to choose the type of school they prefer for their children from a range of options. Schools must now produce a prospectus and publish exam results and National Curriculum test results, as well as a comparison between the school and national results. Increased parental choice has led to schools having to compete with each other for students.

Parental choice?   ✎ WRITTEN ACTIVITY

Read extracts, then answer the questions that follow.

> The aim of introducing market forces into education was justified in two ways: as an extension of personal freedom and also to improve schools as they compete to attract parents – who are effectively 'customers' for education.

> The researchers have identified parents as belonging to broad categories of choice-making:
>
> Privileged/skilled choosers were generally middle class… These parents arrange for their children to attend the correct primaries and then use negotiating skills and training of their children to ensure that they are accepted by the selected schools.
>
> Semi-skilled choosers were a mixed class group of aspirant working-class parents. They were highly motivated for their children, but were less aware of some of the … insider knowledge of the system necessary in order to privilege their children. They were more open to media reports of the schools and they relied on the judgements of others. Many did not fully understand the significance of the open evenings and brochures and so they relied on reputation and rumour in their selection processes.
>
> Disconnected choosers who were less able to make choices, often viewed parental choice as being of little significance and viewed all schools as being 'much the same'. They usually made their selections on geography or on the current 'happiness' of the child rather than in terms of job prospects…

Source: adapted from Gewirtz et al (1995)

1 Explain why the idea of schools competing for parents would lead to them improving their standards.
2 According to the research, what factors may affect parents' ability to make choices about which school to send their children to?
3 How might some parents be more able to get their children into the 'correct' primary schools for the secondary school of their choice?
4 Note down two arguments for the idea of parental choice in education and two arguments against this.

STRETCH AND CHALLENGE ACTIVITY

The ideal school?

Identify the features you might expect of an 'ideal' school. How likely is it that the state education system can meet the expectations of all parents?

Local Management of Schools (LMS)

Under LMS, the governors of all state sector schools were given responsibility for managing their school budgets and staff. This has had the effect of weakening the role of the LAs, which had traditionally had more control over budgets and staffing arrangements in schools.

City technology colleges (CTCs)

These began in 1993 and were designed to meet the increasing emphasis on developing the skills needed for industry and the economy. They are part state and part privately funded and offer a curriculum that specializes in technical, vocational and scientific education.

Open days allow schools and colleges to market themselves.

Grant-maintained schools (GMSs)

This development has allowed any LA school to apply for self-governing grant-maintained status and to receive direct grants from the government rather than being funded through LA budgets. This process is sometimes known as 'opting out'. This allowed the school to have almost total control over the management of its budget, staffing decisions, priorities for spending, and so on. These schools also had the right to introduce the selection of some students through entry exams. More recently, these schools have become known as Foundation schools.

Eye on the exam

To broaden your sociological awareness of education, and to find contemporary examples, it can be useful to read broadsheet newspapers, such as *The Guardian*, or to look through the *Times Educational Supplement*.

CHECK YOUR UNDERSTANDING

1. Identify and briefly explain two ways in which freedom and choice have been introduced into the education system.
2. Explain one way in which parental choice might have increased opportunities and one way in which it might not have.

KEY POINTS

Schools and colleges must now publish a prospectus and results, providing parents with more information on which to base choices. A greater diversity of school provision includes CTCs and Foundation schools. Governing bodies have been given greater freedom through Local Management of Schools.

TOPIC 11 — What are school league tables?

OBJECTIVE

Assess the impact of league tables in education

School league tables

School league tables were introduced to provide information about the performance of schools. They allowed parents to make comparisons between schools more easily. The aim was to create more competition between schools, with the assumption that this would lead to higher standards. Schools that appear successful in league tables become oversubscribed, with many parents wanting to send their children there. The tables can take various forms, with some providing details of raw results only (actual grades achieved). Other tables use a value-added measure. This allows parents to see how well the school does in improving the performance of students while they are at the school. For some schools, their raw results may be average but they can demonstrate that they have significantly improved the performance of the students from when they first started at the school.

Parents can study school league tables published in newspapers.

In all these ways, the forces of the market have been applied to education. This has been seen as leading to improvements by some, but as creating more inequality by others.

Influences on league tables

WRITTEN ACTIVITY

Read the extract, then answer the questions that follow.

> Schools have become dominated by a need to appear in a good position in league tables, of which the principle measure of success is the number of pupils achieving five A–C passes... [a school's] position in these tables can attract parents to send their children to certain schools. Income is generated by pupil numbers. This creates an ethos...which the research team call *the A–C economy*.
>
> Schools are also pressured into tackling that small group of pupils who are on the borderline between achieving five A–Cs and failing to gain that target. Already teachers focus on those who will improve the A–C rate for the whole school by gaining more than five passes, but now the borderliners are brought into policy planning. This leaves those who are not entered or predicted to fail in a position of increasing inequality of provision and attention.

Source: adapted from Gillborn and Youdell (2000)

1 Explain, in your own words, the importance of league tables for a school.
2 Which groups of students do schools focus on to gain a good position in league tables?
3 How might this lead to inequality for students in the school?
4 Suggest three benefits of having league tables.
5 Suggest three reasons why league tables may not be an accurate measure of how good a school is.

Looking at league tables

RESEARCH ACTIVITY

Try to find details of league tables for schools in your area. You could examine the local press or relevant websites. How useful are these tables? Do they provide value-added data?

More equality

STRETCH AND CHALLENGE ACTIVITY

Using the information on the 1988 Education Act, make two lists: one of ways in which you think these changes have improved education for everyone and one of ways in which they may have created more inequalities.

Eye on the exam

Remember that although your sociological knowledge is key, it is also important to demonstrate that you are able to be critical of sociological ideas and to assess different points of view.

DISCUSSION ACTIVITY

What makes a good school?

Consider what makes a good school and how this might be measured. What might a parent, a teacher and a student be looking for? Note down three points arising from your discussion.

You can find league tables online at www.dcsf.gov.uk/cgi-bin/performancetables.

School	Number of 15 year old pupils on Roll in 2007/08	% of 15 year old pupils achieving 5+A*-C (and equivalent) including English and maths GCSEs				% of 15 old pupils 5+A*-C (and	
		2005	2006	2007	2008	2005	2006
Local Authority Average		45.0%	48.7%	46.3%	50.7%	58.8%	61.7%
England Average		44.3%	45.3%	46.0%	47.3%	56.3%	58.5%
Ashington Community High School	270	29%	35%	33%	40%	41%	43%
Astley Community High School	233	46%	48%	44%	49%	58%	57%
Bedlingtonshire Community High School	220	36%	37%	41%	40%	43%	44%
Berwick Community High School	193	34%	33%	35%	53%	62%	69%
Blyth Community College	337	28%	28%	26%	34%	32%	36%
Coquet High School	160	37%	42%	41%	40%	49%	45%
Cramlington Learning Village	420	51%	64%	56%	65%	76%	83%
The Duchess's Community High School	292	52%	54%	45%	51%	59%	62%
Haydon Bridge Community High School and Sports College	190	45%	52%	55%	41%	65%	62%
Hirst High School	177	24%	23%	22%	29%	44%	44%
The King Edward VI School	325	60%	68%	70%	74%	77%	80%
Longridge Towers	34	88%	90%	88%	94%	91%	96%

CHECK YOUR UNDERSTANDING

Identify and briefly explain one positive and one negative effect of the introduction of league tables.

KEY POINTS

The introduction of league tables has created more competition and provided more information to parents. However, critics suggest they may have led to a reduction in educational opportunities for some.

TOPIC 12 How has educational policy developed since 1997?

OBJECTIVE

Describe and assess educational policies since 1997

Since 1997, Labour governments have viewed education as a key area of policy. A number of themes have been addressed.

Raising standards

This has involved a range of policies such as:

- providing nursery places for all 3–4-year-olds
- reducing class sizes in primary schools
- national literacy and numeracy schemes
- looking at league tables as a measure of how well a child has progressed in a school academically, rather than simply relying on their final results
- placing failing schools in 'special measures'
- identifying 'Beacon schools' to pass on good practice to other schools or colleges in a local area.

There are nursery places for all 3–4-year-olds.

Reducing inequality

This has involved bringing in policies aimed at reducing inequalities in achievement and widening the range of people participating in post-16 education. These policies have been aimed, in particular, at disadvantaged groups in society with the aim of combating social exclusion (see page 319).

Policies include:

- Educational Maintenance Allowances (EMAs) – payments for students from disadvantaged backgrounds designed to encourage them to carry on into post-16 education.
- Excellence in cities, which has led to the development of the use of learning mentors and a focus on helping students designated as gifted and talented, regardless of social background.
- The Aim Higher programme, designed to raise aspirations for students from disadvantaged backgrounds and to encourage them to go on to higher education.
- The Sure Start programme to support families with pre-school children.
- The Connexions service, introduced to offer personal support to young people, particularly those at risk of social exclusion. It brings together a range of services such as careers and youth services.

Critics of these policies have argued that although they were designed to support students from disadvantaged backgrounds, they have, in fact, been used by a range of students and thus have also been beneficial to the middle classes.

Promoting diversity and choice

This has been linked to the idea of moving education into the 'post-comprehensive era'. So, rather than having one type of school for everyone, we

Glossary terms: academy   Beacon school   social exclusion   specialist school

now need an education system that can meet the diverse needs of individual students in 21st-century Britain. Examples of this include the promotion of specialist schools which are allowed to build on their strengths (for example, in technology or languages) and thus raise standards of achievement. Also the promotion of faith schools has been related to higher standards of achievement.

Since 2002 academies have also been promoted. These may be former comprehensives that were failing, taken out of LA control and funded by government and private sponsors in order to raise achievement levels. These schools are allowed to select part of their intake, raising concerns that they will exclude the less able or those with special educational needs.

The introduction of academies has increased diversity in the choice of schools.

Changes in academies
WRITTEN ACTIVITY

Read the information below, then answer the questions that follow.

> Academies are often former failing comprehensive schools that have been taken out of LA control. The aim was to reinvest in them to regenerate education in their local area. Their social profile is now changing, with a reduction in the numbers of students eligible for free school meals. However, the proportion of students receiving free school meals in academies is still three times the average for secondary schools.

1 What were academies set up to do?
2 Why is the number of students entitled to free school meals an indicator of social background?
3 Identify one piece of evidence to suggest that academies have provided diversity in education to meet the needs of individuals. Identify one piece of evidence to suggest that this may increasingly not be the case.

A post-comprehensive era?
DISCUSSION ACTIVITY

In a small group, discuss whether you think promoting a range of different school types such as specialist schools, faith schools and academies is a useful idea. Would it be better to have no diversity or choice, with all schools being of one type?

CHECK YOUR UNDERSTANDING

1 Identify and briefly explain three educational reforms that have taken place since 1997.
2 State one important change in the education system since 1997 and explain how this change may have increased or decreased educational opportunities.

KEY POINTS

A wide range of policies since 1997 have focused on raising standards, reducing inequalities and promoting diversity and choice in education.

TOPIC 13 How can social class affect achievement?

OBJECTIVES

Explain the nature–nurture debate

Examine patterns of achievement based on social class

Certain groups (for example, working-class children, boys, some ethnic minorities) appear to perform relatively badly within the educational system, for instance when measured in terms of examination results and entry to higher education. Such groups are said to underachieve educationally.

The nature–nurture debate: is it our genes or is it our social environment?

Nature

This theory suggests that the explanation for educational success and failure lies with natural intelligence. The more extreme view sees intelligence as largely inherited, that is, as genetic. Educational success and failure are seen as reflecting the different ability levels we are born with.

Nurture

This theory suggests that the explanation for educational success and failure lies with the social environment. Educational achievement is related to social factors such as class, gender, ethnicity, peer groups, family and school organization.

Explaining different levels of attainment

Research into educational attainment has gone through various stages.

- During the 1960s and 1970s social class was seen as an important influence on people's lives, so much of the research examined social class and how it could affect achievement levels. Although many of the studies carried out now seem dated, their findings still have relevance for today.

- Later research, in the 1980s and 1990s, focused on a growing interest in the importance of gender and ethnicity as influences on people's lives. Consequently, research into educational achievement has reflected this.

- Many of the areas of importance identified during research on social class, such as parental encouragement and teachers' attitudes, have been re-examined from the point of view of gender and ethnicity. For example, differences in the treatment of male and female students by teachers has been examined.

- More recently, researchers have noted the ways in which class, gender and ethnicity combine to influence a person's educational achievement.

What do the statistics tell us about social class and achievement?

The term 'social class' is one way of describing a person's position in society (see Chapter 8). An individual's social class is usually determined by looking at their occupation or at their parents' occupations. In addition, whether or not a

Glossary terms: nature   nurture

child has access to free school meals can be seen as linked to lower income and thus to social class background. Statistics tend to show that the higher a student's social class background is, the greater the chance of that student achieving high educational qualifications.

Sociologists have put forward a number of explanations for the relative underachievement of working-class students. Such explanations can be divided into:

- the influence of home environment/background
- the influence of the school environment.

Social class and achievement
WRITTEN ACTIVITY

Examine the following statistics, then answer the questions that follow.

Attainment of 5 or more GCSE grades A*–C in year 11 (2003–2006), percentages

Parental occupation	2003	2006
Higher professional	76	81
Lower professional	65	73
Intermediate	53	59
Lower supervisory	41	46
Routine	33	42
Other/not classified (e.g. no occupation)	34	34

Academic achievement in year 11 GCSE (2006), percentages

Free school meals	5+ A*–C	8+ A*–C	5–7 A*–C	1–4 A*–C	5+ D–G	1–4 D–G	none
No	61	45	15	22	11	4	3
Yes	31	18	13	27	20	14	8

Source: Youth Cohort Study, 2008

1 Identify the patterns in each table.
2 Make a list of factors or ideas that might explain these patterns in achievement.

CHECK YOUR UNDERSTANDING

1 Explain what is meant by 'nature'.
2 Identify and briefly explain one way in which an individual's social environment could influence their achievement.

KEY POINTS

Sociological explanations for differences in achievement mainly focus on the social environment. Social class is a key factor here, with students from higher social class backgrounds having a greater chance of achieving higher qualifications.

TOPIC 14 # How can material factors affect achievement?

OBJECTIVE
Examine the influence of material deprivation on achievement

One question that is asked is, "How can the home environment affect educational achievement?" A range of explanations has been put forward in answer to this question, based on individuals' home background or environment.

The material environment and material deprivation

In spite of 'free schooling', there is still an obvious connection between the material conditions of the home and educational achievement.

The Child Poverty Action Group has stressed the costs of things like school uniforms, sports kits and special materials, which may result in poorer children being kept away from school or being sent home. There is a stigma attached to children who are treated in this way.

Living conditions also have an effect. Poor housing, overcrowding, lack of privacy or quiet places to do homework adversely affect performance at school (Douglas, 1967). These conditions are more likely to apply to working-class children. In addition, research has revealed that absenteeism is higher among such children.

Material deprivation?

Many working-class areas, especially in the inner cities, may lack pre-school facilities, such as nursery schools and playgroups, although the introduction of the Sure Start programme may have had some impact here.

Halsey, Heath and Ridge (1980) showed that a higher percentage of working-class children than middle-class children left school at the first possible opportunity. Again, many of the policies introduced by New Labour to combat social exclusion, such as EMAs and Aim Higher, were designed to change this situation.

What causes underachievement?

DISCUSSION ACTIVITY

For each of the factors listed, explain how they could lead to educational underachievement:

- lack of new school uniform or sports kit
- lack of privacy or quiet place in the home
- poor diet, e.g. no breakfast before arriving in school
- poor attendance through illness
- not having attended a nursery school.

Glossary terms: material deprivation

On the other hand, middle-class children may have a head start as their higher social class position and income may lead to better-quality housing and a greater availability of books and study facilities at home, for example their own room, access to the internet, or the ability to afford private tuition.

Social class and pre-school children

Read the extract, then answer the questions that follow.

> Research for the Department for Education and Skills conducted in 2002 by Leon Feinstein of University College London claimed that, even by 2 years of age, pre-school children showed different aptitudes for completing simple 'educational' tasks and that the differences depended on income and class background. He estimated that a rise in home income of £100 a week was equal to a 3% improvement in the tests. Poorer parents, Feinstein noted, tended to be more passive and less engaged with the world around them – and to use a narrower vocabulary with their pre-school children. Children who do badly at pre-school level are least likely to have school success.

Source: Williams (2003)

1 Identify the factors that affected pre-school children's achievement levels.

2 Explain how the use of a 'narrower vocabulary' might influence a pre-school child's achievement.

3 Explain how doing badly at pre-school level might influence future school success.

Assessing material deprivation

Try to put forward some criticisms of material deprivation as an explanation for different achievement levels.

CHECK YOUR UNDERSTANDING

Identify and briefly explain two possible ways in which material deprivation could influence educational achievement.

KEY POINT

The concept of material deprivation suggests that children from more privileged backgrounds in general have better material facilities in the home.

TOPIC 15   How can parental attitudes affect achievement?

OBJECTIVE
Examine the influence of parental values and cultural deprivation on educational achievement

Parental attitudes and expectations

While material conditions seem to be of great importance in working-class areas, parental attitudes seem to be a more important factor in more prosperous areas.

The government's Plowden Report (1967), and sociological research by Douglas in the same year, both stressed the importance of parental attitudes in determining educational success. The general conceptions of middle-class and working-class values, as perceived by sociologists, are summarized in the table below.

Middle-class values	Working-class values
Desire for control over their lives.	A more passive attitude with a fatalistic acceptance of other people being in control.
Emphasis on future planning.	Emphasis upon present or past.
'Deferred gratification' – being prepared to make sacrifices now in order to fulfil future ambitions; investing for the future. Sacrificing money and time now to ensure a better future (e.g. staying on at school or going to college/university).	'Present gratification' – living for the moment with little attempt to plan for the future or get a job.
Individual achievement stressed – by their own efforts, individuals will improve their position.	Collective action stressed – working people will achieve improvements by sticking together (e.g. trade union activities).

Some researchers have suggested that middle-class and working-class parents socialize their children into different sets of values. It has been suggested that middle-class values contribute to the development of ambition, disciplined study and striving for success among middle-class children. Working-class values are less likely to lead to such success, as there is an emphasis on present gratification and a tendency to accept one's position fatalistically (in other words, to believe that you cannot change your circumstances).

Middle-class parents' knowledge of how to 'work the system' may also be an important factor in their children's success – how to hold their own in disagreements with teachers about the teaching of their children; how to fight sexual discrimination; knowing what books and periodicals to buy and having the money to buy them.

It is argued that middle-class parents expect more from their children and are more interested in their progress, shown, for example, in more frequent visits to school.

Glossary terms: cultural deprivation

Cultural deprivation

Working-class children and those from some minority ethnic groups may suffer as a result of cultural deprivation. It is suggested that schools are based on white middle-class values and assumptions, so children from this background have a better opportunity for academic success. For example, family visits to a library or museum will encourage an interest in learning and general knowledge, and middle-class families are more likely to make such visits. The middle-class home is seen as a place where books, educational toys and electronic media are the norm. The working-class child, it is argued, is less likely to receive this kind of upbringing.

DISCUSSION ACTIVITY

What is 'white, middle-class culture'?

Explain what is meant by the idea that, in school, 'white, middle-class culture dominates'.

Describe how this idea could explain working-class underachievement.

STRETCH AND CHALLENGE ACTIVITY

The involvement of parents

1 Are school visits and parents' evenings a useful way to measure parents' interest in their children's education? List reasons why this might be a good method and also any possible problems with this approach.

2 What method(s) would you use to measure whether or not parents were encouraging their children? Make a note of these and list any possible problems with your approach.

WRITTEN ACTIVITY

Social capital

Read the following comments from a middle-class student:

> Well, I know some GPs who sort of teach there [at university]. I know one who teaches at Imperial and one who teaches at UCL [University College London] and they both recommended it. And then we went to the open days and I really liked them both. I really liked UCL – and I went to a 'women in maths' day at UCL and that was really good as well… Then there's the teacher whose daughter went to Cambridge [university] and so I spoke to her about it, her course… And then on my work experience I got to speak to about four or five different GPs, because I was spending time with lots of them, so they all told me which one they would recommend.

Source: Ball (2003)

1 What type of social background were the people who helped this student likely to be from?
2 Explain what advantage middle-class students might have as a result of their social background.

CHECK YOUR UNDERSTANDING

Identify and explain two possible ways in which parents' values and attitudes could influence educational achievement.

KEY POINTS

Middle-class and working-class parents are argued to have different values and expectations regarding education. Middle-class values may lead children to fit in better with the school environment, while working-class children may be culturally deprived.

How might the school affect achievement?

OBJECTIVE

Examine the influence of labelling and the self-fulfilling prophecy on educational achievement

We will now look at explanations that stress the influence of the school environment and the way the school is organized.

Teachers are unavoidably involved in making judgements about pupils. These judgements often affect a child's chances of educational achievement.

Several studies have noted the effect of teachers' expectations on their students' performance and their assessments of the students' performance. Some teachers may judge children who are well behaved as 'bright', but be more questioning about the good performance of less well behaved children. This is known as the 'halo effect': students may be typecast on the basis of early impressions based on their appearance, manners, speech and homes. Teachers, in effect, label students.

Many sociologists suggest that some teachers' assessments of students tend to reflect the teachers' views of what middle-class and working-class students should be capable of, rather than their *actual* performance. Gillborn and Youdell (2000) take this a step further by linking the labelling process to the pressure on schools to appear successful in league tables. This may influence teachers' ideas about which students have the ability to do well. The result is that 'able' students are seen as middle class. The 'less able' are placed in lower sets and entered for lower-tier exams. In this way, pressure from the education system and marketisation may lead some teachers to act on these labels.

The 'halo' effect.

Labelling students

1 Describe four ways in which teachers label students.

2 For each of the four ways chosen, explain why working-class students may be more likely to receive negative labels.

3 Some students may try to 'reject' the label they are given. Identify and explain one way in which this might happen.

If teachers have low expectations of working-class children, they may see the student as only being capable of reaching a certain level of academic achievement, and he or she may see no point in trying to develop the student's performance any further. This is known as a 'self-fulfilling prophecy'.

The idea of a self-fulfilling prophecy may put students under pressure to bring their own 'self-image' into line with the teacher's judgement of them. What is the

Glossary terms: labelling self-fulfilling prophecy

Testing the self-fulfilling prophecy

Read the following details of a study by Rosenthal and Jacobson, called *Pygmalion in the Classroom* (1968). The study was designed to test the theory of the self-fulfilling prophecy.

> Teachers in an elementary school in California were told by the researchers that they had identified a number of students – the 'spurters' – who were likely to make rapid academic progress. The teachers were led to believe that the spurters had been identified as a result of high scores in IQ tests.
>
> In reality, the spurters had simply been selected randomly by the researchers and did not display any greater ability than their classmates. However, a year later it became clear that the spurters had, indeed, made significantly greater progress than the other students.
>
> Rosenthal and Jacobson concluded that the progress of the spurters was a result of the teachers' expectations of them. These higher expectations had been communicated to the students and they had come to believe in the teachers' 'prophecy' about them.

1 In what ways could the teachers have communicated their high expectations to the spurters?

2 What do you think happened to the other students who were not labelled as spurters?

3 If you were a parent of a child at that school, how would you have felt about the research?

4 Can you think of any factors other than the teachers' 'prophecy' that could have influenced the spurters' achievements?

point in trying to improve your maths if the teacher has told you that you are hopeless in the subject? Even if the student resists the teacher's assessment of them, they might still find it difficult to improve their performance because the teacher may deem it a waste of resources to spend time working with them. In effect, the student is forced to accept the teacher's 'prophecy' about them.

Again, it is thought that working-class students are more likely to receive a negative 'prophecy' from teachers, whereas middle-class students will receive a more positive one.

STRETCH AND CHALLENGE ACTIVITY

Ethics in Rosenthal and Jacobson's research

Note down some reasons why this study may be considered unethical. Was this the only way to research the self-fulfilling prophecy?

CHECK YOUR UNDERSTANDING

1 Explain what is meant by 'labelling'.

2 Identify and explain one possible effect of the self-fulfilling prophecy on students.

KEY POINTS

Processes within the school may be influential on students' achievements. Teachers may label students and this may lead to a self-fulfilling prophecy. These labels can be positive or negative and students can accept them or attempt to reject them.

TOPIC 17 What is the influence of streaming, subcultures and school organization?

OBJECTIVES

Examine the influence of streaming and the counter-school subculture on educational achievement

Examine the influence of school organization on achievement

Effects of streaming

Streaming into different ability groups, based upon an assessment of general ability, can be seen as an ideal way to meet the educational needs of individual students. For example, students will receive a level of work that is appropriate to their needs and abilities and will be working alongside students of similar ability. Equally, teachers will be able to produce materials and lessons that meet the needs of the students more effectively, as they know what ability range they are to teach.

However, streaming may have undesirable effects, similar to the self-fulfilling prophecy mentioned in Topic 16. For example:

- Students in the lower streams tend to be disheartened and this may result in them not trying to improve.

- Even when students are not disheartened, teachers may pay less attention to the students in the lower stream than to those in the higher stream.

- Streaming is often linked to social class, with a disproportionately higher number of lower-stream students being drawn from the working class.

- Transfers between streams are rare in practice.

Some schools have tried to overcome these problems by having mixed-ability groups, or have tried a compromise by having subject setting. With the introduction of the National Curriculum, some research suggests that streaming has been on the increase as schools 'set' students according to their ability to achieve different levels of the curriculum.

❖ DISCUSSION ACTIVITY

Streaming

In a small group, discuss the following points:

1 Explain how streaming could affect a student's exam performance.

2 How would you explain why a higher number of lower-stream students come from working-class backgrounds?

The school 'counter-culture' and peer-group pressure

Studies by Hargreaves (1967) of an English boys' secondary modern school and by Lacey (1970) of a grammar school, suggest that one of the effects of streaming is to lead to the development of a school subculture which is opposed to the learning objectives of the school.

Hargreaves argued that the lower-stream secondary modern schoolboys tended to reject the academic values and standards of behaviour expected by the school, which had labelled them as 'failures'. The boys had evolved a 'counter-culture' which stressed defiance of teachers and carrying out daring exploits. Lacey found a similar counter-culture in the

School 'counter-culture'.

lower streams of the grammar school he studied. The evidence seemed to point to the fact that streaming led to students being put off any form of learning from the school.

School organization

A well-organized school (for example, with clear rules and good leadership) tends to have better results than a poorly organized school. For example, a study by a research team led by Michael Rutter in 1979, based on a sample of inner London secondary schools, found that schools taking children from similar backgrounds achieved very different results.

The schools with the best results had certain things in common:

- They were well organized, with strong leadership.
- Teachers were dedicated and well prepared.
- There was a strong emphasis on academic achievement.
- Praise and encouragement of students was emphasized, rather than criticism and punishment.

Many of these findings are supported by MacBeath and Mortimore in the Improving School Effectiveness Project's (2001) findings.

In this way, the quality of the school is thought to play a role in improving student achievement in general and in attempting to overcome social class differences.

STRETCH AND CHALLENGE ACTIVITY

Is a well-organized school the answer?

Note down arguments for and against the idea that a well-organized school can compensate for other unsatisfactory school or home background factors in affecting the educational achievements of different social classes.

WRITTEN ACTIVITY

Home v school

Create two lists of relevant factors, one headed 'home factors', the other headed 'school factors'.

1 For each set of factors, rank them in order of 'most important' or 'most useful' idea to 'least important' or 'least useful' idea. Be prepared to explain your choices.

2 Do you consider home factors or school factors to be the most important influence on achievement levels between social classes? Make a note of the reasons for your choice.

CHECK YOUR UNDERSTANDING

1 Identify and explain two possible effects of streaming in schools – one positive and one negative.

2 Identify and explain two possible effects of the counter-school subculture in schools.

KEY POINTS

Streaming in schools can have both a positive and a negative influence on students' achievements. Some students may become part of a counter-school subculture which may affect their achievement. The way in which a school is organized may have some effect in reducing the influence of social class differences in achievement.

TOPIC 18   Why has achievement for females improved?

OBJECTIVES
Describe different patterns of achievement for students by gender
Explain reasons for improvements in the educational performance of girls

Differences in male and female achievement

Official statistics reveal some differences in educational achievement based on gender.

Looking at gender and achievement

WRITTEN ACTIVITY

Examine the following statistics, then answer the questions that follow.

Percentage achieving 5+ A*–C grades at GCSE

	2004/5	2005/6	2006/7	2007/8
Males	52	54	57	60
Females	62	64	66	69

Source: adapted from DCSF 2008

Percentage achieving A–C grades at A level by subject 2005/6

	Males	Females
Chemistry	73	77
Physics	68	76
Maths	78	83
History	72	77
Sociology	67	75
Art and design	71	80
English	73	75

Source: adapted from DCSF 2008

1 Outline the differences in achievement levels between female and male students at GCSE and A level.

2 Make a list of factors or ideas that might explain these differences in achievement.

Girls are more academically successful, for example:

- In England for Key Stage 1 (5–7-year-olds) to key Stage 3 (11–14-year-olds), girls scored consistently higher than boys in the summer of 2007.
- More women than men entered full-time undergraduate courses at university – 54 per cent were women in 2006.

Source: DCSF (2008)

How can we explain these differences?

The feminist movement

The feminist movement has led to changes in attitudes towards women's roles and expectations. In the past, boys were usually expected to go on to work and support a family. Girls were expected to make marriage and motherhood their primary concerns. Feminism has helped to challenge these ideas and to give girls greater confidence in their abilities.

Wilkinson (1994) states that: "women's aspirations and their image of themselves have profoundly altered in the past quarter of a century". Wilkinson describes a generation of confident, assertive, ambitious women with goals and expectations far beyond those of earlier generations, partly as a result of earlier gains made by the women's movement.

Changing job opportunities

In the future, it is predicted that more women than men will be working. It is also predicted that there will be further decreases in traditionally 'male' jobs in manufacturing and engineering, but a continued increase in 'female' jobs in service industries.

Some researchers also argue that the skills seen as most desirable by employers are those traditionally associated with women, for example flexibility, teamwork and good communication skills.

Legal changes and equal opportunities policies

The Sex Discrimination Act (1975) makes sex discrimination in education illegal. It has raised awareness of equal opportunities in schools and colleges. For example, Kelly's research (1981) demonstrated that science was a 'male' subject as a result of textbook images, male role models and the dominance in the classroom of male teachers and male students. As a result, national projects such as GIST (Girls into Science and Technology) and GATE (Girls and Technology Education) were set up to try to encourage girls' participation and success in science and technical subjects. In addition, training packs for teachers were developed to look at aspects of the hidden curriculum and teachers were encouraged to make their resources more 'girl friendly'.

The introduction of the National Curriculum

The National Curriculum has meant that girls and boys in both primary and secondary schools have equal access to the same subjects, and some subjects are compulsory for all students, such as science.

While some researchers have argued that this has led to improvements in girls' performances in science and technology, others have argued that it has not helped to encourage girls to choose these subjects at A-level or degree level.

> **❖ DISCUSSION ACTIVITY**
>
> **Female achievement**
>
> Outline and explain how the ideas described help us to explain improvements in female achievement in exam results and university attendance.

Women are aiming for the top jobs.

> **CHECK YOUR UNDERSTANDING**
>
> Identify and explain three factors that might be leading females to achieve better grades than males at GCSE level.

> **KEY POINTS**
>
> Although achievement levels for both males and females have improved, female achievement levels are higher overall. A range of factors in both the education system and the wider society can be identified to help explain this pattern.

TOPIC 19   How can we explain differences in subject choice between males and females?

OBJECTIVE

Identify factors which might influence subject choices for females and males

Murphy and Elwood (1999), argue that children learn their gender roles within the home. This relates to how parents treat their children and the expectations they have of them. These early experiences may lead to children associating themselves with certain broad subject areas later on. For example, boys may have more experience of science-related equipment outside of school and this familiarity helps them to see science as a 'male' subject.

For other researchers, such as Mitsos and Browne (1998), factors within the school are also important. These might include: gender stereotyping in textbooks or the continued 'absence' of female role models in science and maths textbooks; continued stereotyping by teachers; male domination of equipment in the science classroom.

Patterns in subject choice at A-level   ✏ WRITTEN ACTIVITY

Examine the statistics on gender and subject choice, then answer the questions below.

1 Identify which subjects seem to be most strongly dominated by males and which by females.

2 Note down some ways in which you might explain these patterns, bearing in mind that female students outperform males in each of these areas at GCSE level (A–C grades).

3 What effects might these patterns have on future career choices?

Entries by subject at A-level 2005/6

	Males	Females
Chemistry	17 720	16 814
Physics	18 687	4 970
Mathematics	30 637	19 168
History	20 546	20 127
Sociology	5 674	18 566
Art and Design	11 558	25 778
English	24 223	53 924

Source: DCSF (2008)

Making a choice of subjects   🔍 RESEARCH ACTIVITY

Carry out some research on student subject choices.

1 Select a sample of students who either have made, or will be making, choices about subjects for GCSE, A-level or university degree.

2 Use questionnaires or unstructured interviews to find out what factors may influence their choices.

3 Try to use your results to explain differences in subject choice between male and female students at both A-level and degree level.

Some researchers have seen single-sex schools as benefiting female students' achievement levels. In particular, they are thought to help to improve girls' performance in traditionally 'male' subject areas, such as maths. This may also then have an influence on subject choices made at GCSE level and post-16.

Another theory which has been tried out in a small number of mixed-sex schools is that of single-sex classrooms. The idea here is that female and male students are taught separately for certain subjects in an attempt to remove the disruptive influence of the opposite sex.

> **STRETCH AND CHALLENGE ACTIVITY**
>
> **Influences on subject choice**
>
> How might the wider society influence subject choices? You might consider the media, advertising, role models and so on.

ARE SINGLE-SEX SCHOOLS AND CLASSROOMS BEST?

DISCUSSION ACTIVITY

Read the extract and consider the questions that follow.

> Teaching girls in single-sex schools, long an obsession of many parents worried about their daughters being distracted by boys, makes no difference to their attainment according to a comprehensive study by Alan Smithers, Professor of Education at Buckingham University and one of Britain's most respected school experts.
>
> "[…] the reason people think single-sex schools are better is because they do well in league tables," said Smithers. "But they are generally independent, grammar or former grammar schools and they do well because of the ability and the social background of the pupils."
>
> […] a growing movement in the US suggests that boys' and girls' brains develop differently, so they benefit from separate teaching styles. In Britain, more and more mixed schools are using single-sex classes because of concerns over boys' results.
>
> […] this study comes after research published last month in Scotland showed that even in a co-educational school, separating pupils into single-sex classes failed to improve boys performance. Rather… the move led to greater indiscipline.

Source: Anushka Asthana, *The Observer*, 25 June 2006

Using the extract and your own ideas, discuss the possible benefits and problems of both single-sex schools and classrooms in the following areas:

- for raising achievement levels
- for students making subject choices
- for students' social development.

CHECK YOUR UNDERSTANDING

Identify and explain three reasons why male and female students often choose different subjects in higher education.

KEY POINTS

Differences exist in subject choices between males and females – particularly in post-16 education. These differences may be related to influences from home, the wider society or from within the education system. Single-sex schools and classrooms have been identified as a possible way of addressing these differences as well as to raise achievement generally.

TOPIC 20 Why is the performance of female students improving faster than that of male students?

OBJECTIVE

Explain reasons for the underachievement of males compared with females in education

Statistics suggest that the achievement levels of males, although improving, are not doing so at the same rate as that of females. A number of explanations have been suggested for this trend.

Harris's (Harris et al, 1993) research into the attitudes of 16-year-olds from mainly working-class backgrounds has shown that:

- Boys are thought to be suffering increasingly from low self-esteem and poor motivation.

- Boys seem to be less willing to struggle to overcome difficulties in understanding their work.

- Boys are less likely to work consistently hard than girls and are more easily distracted. In areas such as coursework, boys found it more difficult to organize their time effectively.

- Girls are more willing to do homework and to spend more time on it.

- Girls give more thought to their futures and to the importance of qualifications in achievement of this, whereas boys do not seem as concerned.

Do girls try harder than boys?

Although things may have changed since Harris's study was carried out, more recent research has identified some further explanations:

- Moir and Moir (1998) suggest that schools have become too 'girl friendly' and boys are now forced to learn in ways that do not suit them. This may include an emphasis on verbal skills and a non-competitive environment.

- Katz (2000) argues that peer pressure, the fear of ridicule and the need to fit in, all contribute to boys not being seen to 'try'.

- Katz also argues that low self-esteem in boys may be linked to images of incompetent men found in advertising, sitcoms, soaps and so on. This low self-esteem may also be linked to the decline in traditional male jobs, leaving boys uncertain about their futures and lacking motivation.

- Others have suggested that women have reassessed their role in society and recognize that work and a

Do media images damage boys' self-esteem?

career (and thus education) is very much a part of their role. Boys, however, are now going through this process of reassessment of what is 'masculine' in society. At present being a 'geek' is not part of masculinity and this may be a barrier to some boys taking education seriously.

Why do some male students underachieve?

In a small group, discuss the explanations given for male underachievement in relation to females.

1 Which ones do you agree or disagree with? Make a note of these.
2 Discuss and make a note of at least two other possible explanations.
3 Take each explanation in turn and try to suggest why it is happening.

STRETCH AND CHALLENGE ACTIVITY

Changing patterns according to gender

We have examined the changes in patterns of achievement according to gender. While female students still seem to choose 'female' subjects at A-level and degree level, it is clear that they are now outperforming males in all areas and that this may lead to some important changes.

Using the information in this section, describe three possible consequences of the changing patterns in attainment according to gender.

RESEARCH ACTIVITY

Arrange to carry out unstructured interviews with a small number of male and female students. Try to find out their views on the factors that might be leading to different levels of performance.

CHECK YOUR UNDERSTANDING

1 Identify and explain two factors that may be leading males to achieve at a lower rate than females.
2 Explain one way in which social class background could lead to differences in achievement rates for males.

KEY POINTS

Although achievement levels for males are increasing overall, they appear to be under-performing compared with female students. A number of factors have been linked to this pattern. These relate to the influence of males' own attitudes to studying, changes within schools and the education system, and changes in the wider society in terms of traditional male roles.

TOPIC 21 — What are the patterns for ethnicity and achievement?

OBJECTIVE
Identify differences in achievement levels for different ethnic groups

What do the statistics tell us?

Statistics show that educational achievement is, to some extent, related to ethnicity. Students from some ethnic backgrounds tend to underachieve educationally (that is, they do not achieve their full potential and tend to perform relatively poorly in exams), while others overachieve.

◉ Eye on the exam

As well as developing your sociological knowledge and your ability to assess and criticise this material, it is also important to be able to interpret tables, graphs and charts correctly.

Educational attainment among the ethnic groups — WRITTEN ACTIVITY

Examine the following statistics on ethnicity and achievement, then answer the questions that follow.

Academic attainment in Year 11, 2006 (percentages)

Ethnic origin	5+ A*–C grades
White	58
Mixed	55
Indian	72
Pakistani	52
Bangladeshi	57
Other Asian	77
Black African	55
Black Caribbean	44
Other	56

Source: Youth Cohort Study (2008)

1 Identify the patterns in educational attainment for different ethnic groups.
2 Give some examples to show how gender influences the patterns of attainment for different ethnic groups.
3 What differences do you notice in the ways in which people's ethnic backgrounds have been categorized in the two tables?

Achievement at GCSE 2007 5+ A*–C grades (percentages)

Ethnicity	males	females
White	55	64
White British	55	64
Irish	61	66
Gypsy/Romany	13	15
Mixed	**52**	**63**
White and black Caribbean	42	55
White and black African	57	58
White and Asian	66	73
Asian	**57**	**69**
Indian	70	79
Pakistani	47	60
Bangladeshi	52	64
Other Asian	57	72
Black	**46**	**59**
Black Caribbean	41	56
Black African	50	61
Other black background	43	57
Chinese	**82**	**85**

Source: adapted from DCSF (2008)

Are there any problems with using such statistics?

Note that many studies use categories to classify ethnic groups that are too general, for example, studies that use the term 'Asian' would not allow us to see differences in achievement levels between Indian, Pakistani and Bangladeshi students.

Also, most of the statistics produced do not allow us to examine the possible influence of social class background in relation to ethnicity.

Explaining the relationship between ethnicity and educational achievement

As with social classes and female and male students, it is clear that factors other than nature or genetically inherited abilities may be more important in explaining the relative success or failure of different ethnic groups. Indeed, the Swann Committee, which was appointed by the government in 1985 to examine the position of ethnic minorities in the education system, ruled out IQ as a cause of differences in attainment.

Researching ethnicity and achievement

STRETCH AND CHALLENGE ACTIVITY

What sorts of issues might a researcher need to consider when looking at reasons for differences in achievement levels for different ethnic groups? These might include ethical issues and decisions about appropriate methods to use.

Eye on the exam

An important skill in sociology is to be able to see links between the different topics studied. For ethnicity and educational achievement, links can be made to gender and social class factors.

Differences in ethnic background may be highlighted in some school situations.

CHECK YOUR UNDERSTANDING

1 Identify and briefly explain one problem in using statistics to examine the educational achievement of different ethnic groups.
2 Identify two factors other than nature or genetically inherited ability that might explain differences in achievement for different ethnic groups.

KEY POINTS

Statistics show different levels of achievement for different ethnic groups. Research suggests that IQ is not a major factor and that other factors relating to social background may be most influential on achievement levels.

TOPIC 22 Are social class and cultural factors influential?

OBJECTIVE

Explain how social class and cultural factors may influence the achievement of some ethnic groups

The home and social class background

These explanations stress the importance of social class and culture to educational success.

Reid (1996) pointed out that differences in achievement may be due to class factors or class in combination with ethnicity. Class position may also be influenced by the types of work offered to groups coming to Britain as well as the class background and resources that people had prior to arriving in Britain. In this way, many of the factors affecting the attainment of working-class and middle-class students may also affect some ethnic minority students. In other words, there is a kind of 'doubling up' of factors. Thus, some of the differences in achievement between ethnic groups may simply reflect social class differences.

Ethnicity, class and achievement

✿ **DISCUSSION ACTIVITY**

Read the extract, then answer the question that follows.

> Minority ethnic pupils are more likely to experience deprivation than white British pupils, especially Pakistani, Bangladeshi, black African and black Caribbean pupils. For example, 70% of Bangladeshi pupils and almost 60% of Pakistani and black African pupils live in the 20% most deprived post code areas (as defined by the Index of Multiple Deprivation) compared to less than 20% of white British pupils.

Source: DFES research paper (2006)

Discuss how the information in the extract supports the idea that social class may be a key influence in explaining differences in achievement between different ethnic groups.

Cultural differences

This view suggests that the cultural norms and values of some ethnic minority groups may be different from 'mainstream' cultural norms and values. This may affect students' achievement because schools are seen to be institutions where white, 'mainstream' norms and values dominate.

It has been argued that the language spoken at home may also be an important factor affecting achievement. Some children who have only recently arrived in the UK may speak English as a second language and, as a result, they may be disadvantaged at school. However, as Clarke (1997) points out, the issue of language may be more complex than it at first appears. Some students from various parts of India, Pakistan or Bangladesh may speak up to eight languages. This may lead to some confusion when English is introduced as an additional language or, alternatively, may demonstrate an ability to quickly absorb and use a new language. The fact that students from an Indian background are such high achievers at present, perhaps demonstrates that language may not be an important factor.

Parental expectations

Some sociologists have argued that educational success and failure can be explained by the level of encouragement received from parents or guardians. From this point of view it has been argued that parents from some ethnic minority groups are less interested in their children's education than parents from other groups. However, there is plenty of evidence to suggest that this view is inaccurate.

A study by Inner London Education Authority in 1987 reported that Indian families put pressure on their children to succeed and that this affected their performance in a positive way. In a number of areas African-Caribbean parents established Saturday schools because they were worried about their children's underachievement. Indeed, Ken Pryce's study of the African-Caribbean community in Bristol in 1979 showed that parents had very high academic aspirations for their children.

More recently, Bhatti (1999) found that for some Asian parents, who were often poorly educated themselves, there was a strong desire to help their children's education more. However, the parents in her sample felt a sense of frustration at their lack of knowledge of school and the education system, the school's lack of interest in them and the gap between their own experiences and their children's, which led to a difficulty in understanding their children's daily lives.

🍀 DISCUSSION ACTIVITY

Is school dominated by a white, mainstream culture?

Discuss how the following aspects of school life may affect the achievements of some ethnic minority students.

- Expectations about clothing may not take into account some minority cultures' norms and values.
- Teaching staff may not be from minority groups.
- The holidays celebrated may not be those of some minority groups.
- The types of food available may not meet the needs of all minority cultures.

CHECK YOUR UNDERSTANDING

Identify and explain two home factors that may affect attainment levels for some ethnic groups.

Identify and explain two ways in which gender may be influential in the attainment levels of different ethnic groups.

KEY POINTS

Various explanations have been given relating to cultural differences. However, social class background and gender also seem influential, suggesting that explanations relating to these two factors are also relevant.

TOPIC 23 What is the role of the school in ethnicity and achievement?

OBJECTIVE
Explain how the school and processes such as labelling may affect achievement

The type of school attended

Research suggests that the main factor in explaining differences in educational attainment is the school attended.

Smith and Tomlinson (1989), in a study of 18 comprehensive schools, identified a range of important influences within the school, including the quality of teaching and the resources available and the attitudes and policies relating to providing equal opportunities within the school. They concluded that ethnic minority students who went to good schools would do as well as white students in these schools.

Labelling and teacher expectation

Some sociologists argue that some teachers have stereotyped views and expectations of students due to the child's ethnic origin. These stereotypes may also reflect social class background and gender differences. For example, some teachers may have higher expectations of Asian students – they are considered to be capable and hardworking – with Asian girls seen as quiet and passive.

Research also shows that some teachers believe that children from an African-Caribbean background are less academic than those from other ethnic backgrounds, with African-Caribbean boys being seen as more disruptive. Teachers expect less, so these students do not receive as much encouragement as other students. However, as Mirza (1997) notes, there is evidence that African-Caribbean girls have a strong desire and motivation to succeed which may allow them to reject the negative labels given to them. In this way, the teachers' labels may lead to a self-fulfilling prophecy through which the students' educational achievement is affected, but this may depend on a variety of factors such as gender.

The hidden curriculum

Some sociologists explain ethnic underachievement in terms of the hidden curriculum. For example, it is argued that subjects that students study (for instance history) are biased towards a white European culture. Some books may present stereotypical images of some minority groups, or they may ignore ethnic minorities altogether. This may lead to, for example, some students feeling a sense of not being valued which may, in turn, lead to underachievement.

These explanations stress the importance of the school environment to educational success for ethnic minorities.

Teachers' labels and stereotypes

Mac an Ghaill (1992) found in interviews with Asian and African-Caribbean students that teachers might label students in terms of subject ability, with African-Caribbean girls encouraged to do music and sport. For some Asian students, whether they were seen as 'bad' depended on whether they were the main minority ethnic group in a school. Stereotypes included assumptions about arranged marriage and that Asian female students would be neat and know little about football.

1 What do the comments of the students tell us about the usefulness of the general term 'ethnic minority' when looking at teachers' labels and stereotypes?

2 One African-Caribbean girl states that she was encouraged to do music and sports. Why do you think teachers selected these particular subjects?

3 One girl stated that teachers stereotyped Asians as 'bad' in her school if they were the main minority ethnic group. What might this tell us about the attitudes of some teachers?

4 What points do the students make about the different stereotypical labels given to female students?

Were Smith and Tomlinson correct?

Smith and Tomlinson's research has been criticized because:

- of the size of the sample
- of the failure to include a mix of schools with both large and small numbers of students
- the sample was not nationally representative
- some schools had large numbers of African-Caribbean students and some had small numbers.

1 Explain how the points listed may affect the value of Smith and Tomlinson's research.

2 Note down some other possible problems associated with research into this area.

CHECK YOUR UNDERSTANDING

1 Identify and explain two ways in which teachers might influence the educational attainment of ethnic minority students.

2 Explain two ways in which the hidden curriculum might influence the school lives of ethnic minority students.

KEY POINTS

The concept of labelling can be used to explain some teachers' attitudes to different ethnic groups. This is made more complex by differences in labels relating to gender. Also, labels may vary between ethnic groups. The hidden curriculum may also present stereotypical images of some groups.

How might discrimination and a lack of black teachers be important?

OBJECTIVES

Explain some possible sources of discrimination within education
Examine the possible effects of a lack of black teachers

Racism

Racism may take different forms within the school environment (for example, some teachers and students may hold racist attitudes), and may be both intentional and unintentional. More recently, the notion of institutional racism has been highlighted by the Macpherson Report (1999), which followed the racially motivated murder of Stephen Lawrence (see page 45). This refers to the idea that some schools, or perhaps the educational system as a whole, may be unknowingly or unintentionally discriminating against some groups as part of the institution's day-to-day working.

Another area of concern for some researchers has been the role of discrimination in the process of setting, streaming and exam entries (Gillborn and Youdell 2000). Here, as a result of some teachers' attitudes, some ethnic minority students may be more likely to be placed in lower sets or streams and to be entered for lower-level papers in exams.

It is argued that many students may feel rejected by the school. As a result, they may reject the school and, consequently, not achieve their full academic potential. Research by Modood (1997) and Mason (2000) has linked the formation of strong African-Caribbean student subcultures to this process. If these subcultures challenge racism in the school they are likely to reinforce teachers' labels of them as 'troublemakers'.

Other examples of research in this area include:

- Wright (1992) found that Asian children may face discrimination based on exclusion from discussion work as a result of teachers' assumptions about their language abilities.

- Wright also found, during research into primary classrooms, that African-Caribbean males may be more likely to receive negative attention and criticism from teachers, even in situations where peers of other ethnic origins shared in an offence.

Racism in schools

WRITTEN ACTIVITY

One student in Mac an Ghaill's study (Mac an Ghaill, 1992) felt that the education system was racist. He mentioned a lack of black people in textbooks, a narrow English and European perspective in history, and the exclusion of his language and culture.

1 Identify the range of different ways in which racism may be taking place.

2 For each area you have identified, explain the types of response students may make and how this might affect attainment levels in school.

3 For each area, explain how you might seek to combat this form of racism.

- Scott Fleming, in a case study on sport and ethnicity (1993), found that some aspects of South Asian culture – such as observing prayer times during the day – were seen as 'problems' by PE teachers, leading to students being regarded as unable to play in team matches.

A lack of black teachers

Research has shown that teachers from ethnic minority backgrounds are significantly under-represented in schools in Britain overall, although there may be variations between areas. A DCFS survey of teachers' ethnic backgrounds in the Local Authority sector in 2008 showed that 94 per cent of teachers described themselves as white; 1.7 per cent as black/black British; 2.6 per cent as Asian/Asian British and 0.8% per cent described themselves as Mixed. As well as this, they may be less likely to be in positions of authority.

DISCUSSION ACTIVITY

Do we need more teachers from ethnic minority groups?

Wright (1992) noted in his study that teachers treated African-Caribbean students unfairly. One student wanted just black people and teachers in his school as he thought that this would stop him being picked on.

1 Why might it be useful to have more teachers from ethnic minority backgrounds in schools?

2 Why do you think teachers from ethnic minority backgrounds are under-represented in schools in Britain?

Some sociologists feel that this situation can influence the school experiences of ethnic minority students.

STRETCH AND CHALLENGE ACTIVITY

Home v school

1 Read through the various factors that sociologists feel may affect the attainment of ethnic minority groups and rank these in order of importance.

2 Decide which is of greater influence – home or school factors. Note down an explanation for your choice.

CHECK YOUR UNDERSTANDING

Identify and briefly explain two ways in which discrimination may be taking place within the education system.

KEY POINTS

There are variations in achievement levels for different ethnic groups. Discrimination and racism in education may affect student achievement. A lack of teachers from ethnic minority groups may also be influential. There are also variations in achievement within ethnic groups related to social class, background and gender.

It is important not to assume that the members of a particular classified group all share the same attitudes, values and experiences.

5 Crime and Deviance

What is is meant by crime and deviance?

OBJECTIVE
Explain the difference between crime and deviance

Many of us are likely to have experienced crime personally at some point in our lives. Some of us, for example, may have committed a crime or been the victim of one. Others may have experienced crimes as both offenders and victims. Even if we have not had direct experience of crime, we will definitely have come across it second-hand in the mass media, for instance in the press, TV news broadcasts and reality-based crime programmes such as *Crimewatch*.

Issues related to crime and deviance are controversial and cause a lot of debate within the media and among politicians. Crime is also a major focus of public concern and debate. These debates focus on wide-ranging issues such as detecting, reducing and preventing crime, policing and police powers, overcrowding in prisons, the growth of internet crime and identity theft, terrorism, human trafficking, antisocial behaviour and teenage crime.

Sociologists are interested in studying criminal activity but they also explore the role of deviance in society. The distinction between crime and deviance is an important one in sociology. A crime is an illegal act which is punishable by law. Crime involves actions such as robbery, fraud or shoplifting that break the criminal law and, if detected, can result in criminal proceedings. Deviance refers to behaviour which does not conform to a society's rules and norms. It is disapproved of by most people in that particular society and, if detected, is likely to lead to negative sanctions (see page 9).

Deviant behaviour

DISCUSSION ACTIVITY

To help you to understand more about what deviance is, consider the following actions:

- keeping a parcel left on a neighbour's doorstep
- buying DVDs at bargain prices, knowing they are illegal copies
- smoking cannabis on the bus
- assisting a relative to commit suicide
- getting too much change at a charity shop and keeping the extra money.

1 In a small group, discuss the examples and decide whether you think any of this behaviour can be classed as deviant.

2 Of those acts that you have classed as deviant, identify the most serious and the most trivial. Discuss why you have picked these out and note down your reasons.

Glossary terms: antisocial behaviour   crime   deviance   negative sanctions

Goode (2008) defines deviance as behaviour, beliefs and physical characteristics that break social norms and produce negative reactions. In his view, deviance may be mild or it may be more extreme. In the case of mild deviance, such as telling a little lie or parking illegally, the penalties imposed might involve harsh words or a small fine. However, we would not think of the person who tells a lie or parks on double yellow lines as a deviant. Extreme deviance includes behaviour or beliefs that are so far outside the norms that they generate very strong negative reactions from others. Examples include people who have been extremely heavily tattooed or pierced and people who claim they have been abducted by aliens (Goode, 2008).

Body modification as extreme deviance?

STRETCH AND CHALLENGE ACTIVITY

How far do you agree with Goode (2008) that body modification is an example of extreme deviance?

Is deviance necessarily illegal?

We have seen that a crime is an illegal act, while deviance involves behaviour that does not conform to a society's norms or social rules. Some, but not all, deviant acts are also against the law. This means that deviant behaviour includes both legal and illegal activities. Legal deviance is behaviour that is considered 'abnormal' in some way by most people in a society but is not against the law. Illegal deviance is criminal behaviour which is punishable by the state.

Is crime necessarily seen as deviant?

Some acts are illegal but they are not necessarily always considered deviant. It is a criminal offence to use a hand-held mobile phone while driving or supervising a learner driver (except to call 999 in an emergency when it is unsafe to stop). In practice, however, it is not unusual to see people using a mobile phone while driving.

WRITTEN ACTIVITY

Deviance and the law

Consider the following examples:

1 murder
2 alcohol dependency
3 smoking at the office
4 parking on double yellow lines
5 shoplifting.

List those acts which:

a) are both deviant and illegal
b) are deviant but legal
c) are illegal but would not usually be considered as deviant.

CHECK YOUR UNDERSTANDING

1 Explain what sociologists mean by the term 'deviance'.
2 Explain the difference between crime and deviance.

KEY POINTS

A crime is an illegal act that is punishable by law. Deviance is behaviour which the majority of people disagree with, or which goes against the rules and norms of a society.

Deviant acts can be – but are not always – illegal. Illegal acts are not necessarily considered deviant.

TOPIC 2 When is an act seen as deviant?

OBJECTIVES

Explain the view that deviance is socially defined

Explain the idea that what is classified as criminal or deviant can change over time and vary between cultures

Many sociologists argue that while crime involves legally defined behaviour, deviance is socially defined. According to this view, whether an act is seen as deviant or not depends on the particular social setting in which it takes place. To understand this idea better, consider the example of nudity. There is nothing deviant about nudity in itself. In the shower, bedroom or sauna, for example, nudity is generally seen as perfectly acceptable. By contrast, in a supermarket, at a pop concert or on a football pitch, nudity would be seen as deviant. In certain social contexts and settings, therefore, nudity is seen as appropriate and fitting. In other situations, however, it would be seen as deviant and might also be illegal.

Sociologists argue that what is considered 'deviant' does not depend on the act itself but on how other people react to it; how they see, define and label the act. Selling drugs, for example, is likely to be seen as a deviant act if done by a drug dealer on a street corner but not if done by a pharmacist at the local chemists. Deviance, therefore, is defined according to the social setting in which the act takes place – it is socially defined.

Sociologists support the claim that deviance is socially defined by highlighting historical and cultural variations in what is considered deviant behaviour.

What does the historical evidence tell us about deviance?

Historical evidence suggests that what is classified as deviant can change over time. The following examples illustrate this idea.

*   In the past, a number of cultures carried out human sacrifice. During the 15th century, the Aztec civilization in Mexico, for instance, offered captive warriors as sacrifices in order to keep the sun alive.

Is the same act always deviant?   ❖ DISCUSSION ACTIVITY

1   In a small group, look at the following examples and discuss whether there are any circumstances in which they might be considered acceptable:
    *   spraying CS gas in someone's face
    *   setting fire to someone's pudding
    *   breaking someone's nose
    *   claiming to be Elvis Presley
    *   carrying a gun
    *   executing a person.

2   Make a note of three important points arising from your discussion about whether these acts might be seen as acceptable.

3   Write a short paragraph to explain the idea that what is considered as deviant can depend on who does it and the setting in which the act takes place.

- Victorian England had some very different standards for what was considered appropriate behaviour compared with those of today. For example, capital punishment (having the death sentence for certain crimes) was practised.

- Attitudes towards suicide have varied over time and between cultures. During the Second World War, Japanese Kamikaze pilots dive-bombed and deliberately crashed their planes into enemy ships, resulting in their own deaths. This was considered by the Japanese to be a heroic act.

- Since the Second World War, attitudes to issues such as sex outside marriage, divorce, abortion, homosexuality and smoking have changed in Britain. The social stigma or disgrace that was attached to extra-marital births during the 1950s, for example, has now almost disappeared.

What does the cross-cultural evidence tell us about deviance?

Evidence suggests that behaviour classified as deviant can vary from one culture to another. The following examples illustrate the idea that norms and social rules vary cross-culturally.

In the USA the police carry guns.

- Cultures differ in their expectations regarding what is appropriate dress for men, women and children.

- In the USA, it is acceptable for police officers and members of the public (within limits) to carry guns.

- Some countries have the death penalty. According to Amnesty International, at least 5186 people were sentenced to death across 53 countries in 2005.

- In Switzerland, assisting someone to die is not a criminal offence if it is done for honourable motives. There are clinics, used by Swiss people and increasingly by people from abroad, which help people to end their lives.

What does the evidence tell us about crime?

What is classified as criminal behaviour can also change over time and vary between cultures. For example:

- In the 1920s it was illegal to produce and drink alcohol in the USA.

- In Saudi Arabia, there are laws against the public interaction of women with men other than their husbands.

CHECK YOUR UNDERSTANDING

1 Give two examples of acts which are against the law but which are not usually considered to be deviant.

2 Give two examples of deviant acts which are not against the law.

KEY POINTS

Deviance is defined according to the social setting in which it takes place. Behaviour classed as 'deviant' can vary according to who performs the act and where they do so.

What is classified as deviant also varies between cultures and over time.

TOPIC 3 What is the difference between formal and informal rules?

OBJECTIVE
Explain the difference between formal and informal rules

Formal rules

The idea of rules is central to the study of crime and deviance. Sociologists distinguish between formal and informal rules. Formal rules are written down, for example, in the form of laws or codes of conduct. These formal, written rules have official status and punishment, penalties or negative sanctions are usually imposed on those caught breaking them.

Formal rules guide people's behaviour in many social settings such as schools, workplaces, police stations, motorways and on public transport. Pedestrians, cyclists and car drivers, for example, all have different rules that they must follow and these are listed in the Highway Code. At work people are expected to follow the rules about health and safety.

Formal rules at school | WRITTEN ACTIVITY

1 Why might it be necessary to have formal, written rules concerning teacher and student behaviour in the school or college setting?

2 List four of the formal rules in your school or college and, for each, give one reason why you think the rule is either necessary or unnecessary.

Informal rules

Generally, we do not give much thought to the informal or unwritten rules which govern many aspects of social life. They are 'taken-for-granted' rules or guidelines on how we are expected to behave in particular social settings. We would probably not be expected, for example, to ask permission before getting ourselves a drink or taking a shower at home. At a distant relative's house, however, we would be much more likely to ask permission first. Even though we may not always consciously think about the informal or unwritten rules which govern social life, they can still have a powerful influence over how we behave in particular situations.

Life without rules | DISCUSSION ACTIVITY

1 In a small group, discuss what our lives would be like if there were no rules, or if most people ignored the rules. Does society need rules? Which rules? Why? Who benefits from the rules? Does anyone lose out?

2 Note down the three most important points that were made during your discussion.

Glossary terms: formal and informal rules   negative sanctions

Breaking the informal rules

Look at the following cartoons which illustrate examples of informal or taken-for-granted rules being ignored or broken.

1 Note down two informal rules that govern how we are expected to behave at a supermarket checkout queue and two informal rules which govern how we are expected to dress for a job interview.

2 What is likely to happen if we break these rules?

3 Make a list of at least three informal rules which you have obeyed today. Explain briefly why you obeyed each of these rules.

Why do you think the idea of rules is central to the study of crime and deviance?

Eye on the exam

As part of your revision, you could test yourself to see whether you understand the key terms and ideas. Jot down what you think a term (such as 'formal rules') means and then check it against the definition given in the glossary. You don't need to come up with an identical definition, as long as you've got the main idea. Check anything you don't understand with your teacher.

CHECK YOUR UNDERSTANDING

Identify and explain two differences between formal and informal rules.

KEY POINTS

Rules may be formal, that is written down as laws or codes of conduct. Alternatively, they may be informal, that is unwritten and taken for granted.

TOPIC 4 What are social order and social control?

OBJECTIVES

Explain the term social order
Explain the term social control

What is social order?

For people to live and work together, a certain amount of order and predictability is needed. It could be argued that social order and predictability are necessary if society is to run smoothly without chaos or continual disruption. In studying social order, sociologists focus on the many aspects of social life which are stable and ordered. Sociologists are interested in exploring how and why social order is achieved and maintained over time. There are two main approaches to explaining how social order works in society – the consensus approach and the conflict approach.

The consensus approach to social order

According to the consensus approach, social order and stability depend on co-operation between individuals and groups who work together for the same thing. Generally, this co-operation happens in situations where people believe that they share common interests and goals. For example, sociologists who follow the functionalist approach believe that society is based on consensus, which means that broadly speaking people agree about norms and values. This consensus arises from the process of socialization (see page 10), during which we learn and come to share the norms and values of our society. Functionalists argue that social order is maintained over time because most people support and agree to abide by the rules.

The conflict approach to social order

A second approach believes that there is a conflict of interests between different groups in society. Clashes occur because groups do not share common interests and goals. Marxists, for example, believe that there is conflict between powerful and less powerful groups of people in capitalist society (see page 56). According to Marxists, the main groups, or social classes, are the bourgeoisie and the proletariat. The bourgeoisie are the ruling class who own the big businesses which employ the proletariat or working class.

Eye on the exam

Remember to refer to the relevant sociological approaches (e.g. the consensus and conflict approaches or the functionalist and Marxist approaches) in your answers.

Consensus v conflict approaches

WRITTEN ACTIVITY

1 Have a look at a recent copy of a daily newspaper. Read through it and choose two articles that cover issues which have generated conflict between individuals or groups.

2 For each article, state briefly what has caused the conflict.

3 Do you think that society, in general, seems to be held together by consensus or disrupted by conflict? Write a paragraph explaining your views.

Glossary terms: social control methods   social order

Class conflict occurs between these two groups because they have opposing interests. The bourgeoisie want to make more profits while the proletariat want higher wages. However, social order and stability are generally maintained partly because the bourgeoisie have the power to enforce order. They are able, for example, to influence the type of laws that are passed.

What is social control?

We have seen that much of everyday life is subject to rules, either formal or informal. The question we must now ask is: why do most people conform to, or go along with, most of these rules most of the time? In addressing this question, sociologists point out that people's actions and behaviour are controlled or constrained by the social groups they mix with and by the wider society in which they live. In other words, much of our behaviour is socially controlled.

The phrase 'methods of social control' refers to the processes by which people are encouraged or persuaded to conform to (follow) the formal and informal rules. It also applies to the ways in which social groups or societies deal with behaviour that violates or breaks these rules. Social control methods may involve sanctions or other social reactions to deviance that aim to limit or reduce the frequency of deviant acts. A positive social control sanction might be a promotion at work and a negative one might be a prison sentence.

Social control in action.

The processes of social control

WRITTEN ACTIVITY

In order to explore the processes of social control, choose one setting with which you are familiar, for example a football match, a shopping precinct or your home.

1   State three rules that you follow in your chosen setting.

2   Explain briefly why you stick to each of these rules.

3   If the rules were broken, what would happen to you (the individual) and to society?

CHECK YOUR UNDERSTANDING

1 Identify and explain one difference between the consensus and conflict approaches to social order.

2 Explain what sociologists mean by 'methods of social control'.

KEY POINTS

Social order is necessary for society to run smoothly. The functionalist approach argues that social order is based on consensus (agreement). The Marxist approach argues that social order is based on the power of the ruling class over the working class.

Much of our behaviour is socially controlled by groups and society.

TOPIC 5 What is the difference between formal and informal social control?

OBJECTIVE

Explain the difference between formal social control and informal social control

In exploring how social control operates, sociologists highlight the important role of the 'agencies of social control'. These are the groups and organizations in society which ensure that most people comply with, or stick to, the rules most of the time. Sociologists have identified two distinct types of social control: formal and informal social control.

Formal social control

Formal social control is based on written rules and laws. It is usually associated with the ways the state regulates and controls people's actions and behaviour. The 'agencies of formal social control' are those bodies in society which make the laws, enforce them or punish people who break the law:

- The Houses of Parliament consist of the House of Commons and the House of Lords. Their role is to legislate, that is to make the laws which regulate our behaviour.

- The role of the police force as an agency of formal social control is to maintain order, enforce the law, investigate crime and apprehend offenders.

- The role of the judiciary (the courts) is to deal with alleged offenders and to convict and sentence those found guilty of a criminal offence. Sentences include a fine or a term of imprisonment. Such sanctions are official and are backed by the state.

Agencies of formal social control

WRITTEN ACTIVITY

Study these four photographs and, for each one, identify which agency of formal social control is being represented.

Middlesex Guildhall Crown Court

Santa Fu Prison, Germany

Stoke Newington Police Station, London

The Houses of Parliament

Glossary terms: agencies of social control   formal social control

- The role of the prison service, as part of the penal system, is to confine prisoners. Prison, as an agency of social control, punishes convicted law breakers and deters them and other people from committing crime.

Informal social control

Informal social control is based on unwritten rules and processes such as the approval or disapproval of other people. Informal social control is enforced by social pressure – by the reactions of group members such as families, friends, peers or colleagues. These reactions to behaviour may be in the form of positive or negative sanctions. Positive sanctions reward individuals who comply with or behave according to the group's expectations by, for example, praising them or giving them a gift. Negative sanctions punish those who do not conform by, for instance, ridiculing them, ignoring them, playing practical jokes on them, gossiping about them, hitting them or arguing to try to persuade them to change their behaviour.

Informal processes of social control — DISCUSSION ACTIVITY

Informal social control operates through positive and negative sanctions. In a small group, identify two ways in which such sanctions (positive and/or negative) may work in each of the following examples:
- a school student who is seen as hard working and dedicated
- a neighbour who works as a prostitute
- a married MP who is caught committing adultery
- a teenager who rescues a drowning child.

Make a note of the outcome of your discussion.

STRETCH AND CHALLENGE ACTIVITY

Families, peer groups, schools, workplaces and religions are all examples of agencies of social control. Which other important social process are these groups and institutions linked to?

CHECK YOUR UNDERSTANDING

1 What do sociologists mean by 'formal social control' and 'informal social control'?
2 Identify two agencies of formal social control and explain, in each case, how they control a person's behaviour.
3 Identify two of the ways in which peer groups encourage members to conform to their rules.

KEY POINTS

Formal social control is based on written rules and laws. Informal social control is based on informal social processes and is enforced through social pressure.

TOPIC 6 — What non-sociological explanations are there for criminal and deviant behaviour?

OBJECTIVES

Discuss biological and psychological factors that may influence criminal and deviant behaviour

Explanations for why people break the rules and engage in criminal or deviant behaviour include psychological, biological and social factors. We have seen that psychologists are concerned with individual behaviour and focus on individual differences in aggression or personality (see page 7) in their explanations. Now we will look at some of the psychological factors that may influence criminal and deviant behaviour before turning to biological explanations.

Psychological explanations for criminal and deviant behaviour

Psychologists have explained criminal behaviour in several different ways. Some explanations focus on the personality traits (or features) of individual offenders.

Being impulsive is an example of a personality trait that some psychologists have linked to criminal tendencies. Impulsive people act without thinking. They rarely stop to consider or weigh up the consequences of their actions or behaviour. So the idea here is that some people commit crime because they are impulsive and act on the spur of the moment. They do not stop to think about the chances of getting caught and ending up in prison, or about how their behaviour might affect other people.

Criminal personality · ✎ WRITTEN ACTIVITY

> It is common for us to attach labels to criminals and try to explain their behaviour through describing them as having a certain character trait. For example, it is common to refer to some criminals as 'psychos' – particularly in films and the newspapers. This type of person is actually called a psychopath. Labels such as these have been developed by psychologists to help us understand the different types of personality category that people fit into. Not all of these are criminal, but it is assumed that many criminals have similar personality characteristics.

Source: adapted from Marsh, 2006

1 Why have psychologists developed terms like psychopath?
2 What sort of personality traits or features might many criminals have in common?

💡 STRETCH AND CHALLENGE ACTIVITY

Can you think of any examples of crimes that are likely to require a lot of thought and careful planning, rather than being committed on the spur of the moment?

Biological explanations for criminal and deviant behaviour

Biological explanations look for biological causes for criminal activity. These causes are particular biological characteristics within the individual. In focusing on individuals, biological explanations are similar to psychological explanations.

The work of Lombroso is often discussed to illustrate the biological approach. Lombroso was a 19th-century Italian doctor and criminologist who believed that crime could be explained in terms of genetically determined physical characteristics. In his view, some people were born criminals. They could be identified by various physical features such as their large jaw, high cheekbones, big ears and extra fingers, toes and nipples!

More recent biological explanations focus on the genetic basis of criminal and antisocial behaviour. For example, it is argued that some people are more likely to commit violent crimes because of the genes they have inherited.

Do your genes make you a criminal? ❖ DISCUSSION ACTIVITY

Though we may feel today that Lombroso's biological explanation of crime is outdated, the following extract from a newspaper article describes the case of a young man in the USA who, his lawyer argued, was born to kill. Biological explanations of crime such as this suggest that some people are more likely to break the law because of their genes. Read the extract, then answer the questions that follow.

> In 1991, Tony Mobley, aged 25, walked into a pizza store and casually shot the manager in the neck after robbing the till and joking that he would apply for the job vacancy when the man was dead. Now Mobley is waiting on Death Row and his last chance of a reprieve rests with a plea from his lawyer that the murder was the tragic consequence of a genetic predisposition. The genes of Tony Mobley, his lawyers argue, meant he was born to kill.

Source: adapted from Steve Connor, *The Independent on Sunday*, 12 February 1995

1 In a small group, discuss whether you agree that a person could be born a criminal. Explain your views.

2 Can you think of any other factors that might explain why a person turns to crime?

3 Make a note of three important points made during your discussion.

CHECK YOUR UNDERSTANDING

1 Sociologists and psychologists study people but differ in their approach. Describe one main difference between these two approaches.

2 Describe one similarity between biological and psychological approaches to explaining criminal behaviour.

KEY POINTS

The causes of criminal and deviant behaviour have been explained in terms of psychological, biological and social factors. Psychological explanations focus on the psychological traits of individual offenders, such as being impulsive. Biological explanations focus on the genetic basis of criminal and antisocial behaviour.

TOPIC 7 # How do sociologists explain criminal and deviant behaviour?

OBJECTIVE

Discuss sociological explanations of crime and deviance based on inadequate socialization, the opportunity structure and relative deprivation

Sociologists reject psychological and biological explanations of human behaviour. They explain involvement in crime and deviance in terms of social rather than genetic or personality factors. Beyond this, however, sociologists disagree on how to explain crime and deviance. Some sociological approaches see crime and deviance as based on learned behaviour, which develops through the socialization process. In this view, deviance is a result of learning deviant behaviour from interaction within families (inadequate socialization). Other explanations focus more on the availability of legal and illegal opportunities in a person's life or relative deprivation.

Inadequate socialization

Young people's involvement in criminal and deviant behaviour has been explained in terms of the negative influence of family background and home environment. New Right approaches, for example, suggest that children from parentally deprived homes – in which parents do not take responsibility for the social upbringing of their children (see page 55) – tend to be more prone to crime.

The proud parents?

Such explanations generally focus on what they see as ineffective socialization practices, such as inadequate parenting and lack of parental supervision of children, which lead to delinquency. For example, delinquent teenagers are seen as inadequately socialized into society's norms and values.

However, it is not just families that are seen as failing to socialize children effectively into society's values. Other agencies of socialization, such as schools, religions and the mass media, are also highlighted. For example, lack of discipline in schools and the decline in the influence of religious values are also seen as reasons for inadequate socialization. Furthermore, these approaches suggest that the mass media (including the film and music industry) glamorize gun crime and violence.

The opportunity structure

Some sociologists have explained juvenile (relating to young people) and adult crime in terms of the levels of legal and illegal opportunities available to the individual. In areas where the levels of employment and educational opportunities are low, people may turn to illegal ways of achieving success. The following extract from William's study of the "Cocaine Kids", teenage members of a cocaine ring in New York City, illustrates the idea of the availability of legal and illegal opportunity structures.

Glossary terms: relative deprivation

Legal and illegal opportunities

Read through the extract, then answer the question that follows.

> These studies took me to the Bronx, Harlem and Washington Heights – areas of high unemployment and diminishing resources, especially for young people. But while quality entry-level jobs were disappearing, illegal opportunities were emerging with considerable force because of the growth of a powerful and profitable multi-national drug industry.
>
> The Cocaine Kids, and many of the kids coming behind them, are drawn to the underground economy because of the opportunities that exist there. The underground offers status and prestige – rewards they are unlikely to attain in the regular economy – and is the only real economy for many.

Source: Williams (1989) p. ix

Identify the legal and illegal opportunities available to the "Cocaine Kids".

💡 STRETCH AND CHALLENGE ACTIVITY

What do you think the author means by the terms "underground economy" and "regular economy"?

👁 Eye on the exam

Remember to use the relevant key concepts and terms (such as relative deprivation) in your answers.

Relative deprivation

Some approaches link particular crimes to relative deprivation. Relative deprivation occurs where groups or individuals feel that they are unfairly disadvantaged compared with other similar people. For example, an individual may feel that they do not earn enough at work compared with colleagues with similar levels of qualifications.

A young male, for instance, might want a lifestyle based on having lots of money to spend on designer clothes, expensive jewellery and fast cars. He went to school with people just like himself who now have such a lifestyle. For him, however, the reality is unemployment or a training programme. In this case, the gap between his expectations and reality may make him feel relatively deprived.

The experiences of relative deprivation leave the individuals or groups feeling discontent. This discontentment may then lead to involvement in crime and deviance.

♣ DISCUSSION ACTIVITY

Agree or disagree?

In a small group, discuss how far you agree with each of the three explanations of criminal and deviant behaviour discussed here (inadequate socialization, the opportunity structure and relative deprivation).

CHECK YOUR UNDERSTANDING

Identify and explain fully two social factors which might lead people to become criminals.

KEY POINTS

Sociologists focus on social factors. Their explanations of crime and deviance include socialization patterns, opportunity structures and relative deprivation.

TOPIC 8 | **What other sociological explanations of criminal and deviant behaviour are there?**

OBJECTIVE

Explain sub-cultural and Marxist theories of criminal and deviant behaviour

We have examined some of the ways sociologists explain crime and deviance. Other theories, including sub-cultural and Marxist approaches, have also been put forward by sociologists.

Sub-cultural theories

Some sociologists explain both juvenile delinquency and adult crime in terms of the values of a particular subculture and the influence of the peer group. Albert Cohen (1955) studied juvenile delinquency among working-class boys in North America. He argued that individuals did not carry out delinquent acts such as vandalism or violence on their own. Cohen saw juvenile delinquency as a group phenomenon. Young males learn to become delinquents by becoming members of groups or gangs in which delinquent behaviour already exists as 'the done thing'. Delinquency is to do with being part of a delinquent subculture or a way of life among boys' gangs in urban neighbourhoods of large cities.

Cohen linked juvenile delinquency to the education system in America. He argued that schools have middle-class values and expectations. As a result, working-class boys cannot compete on the same terms as middle-class boys to acquire status and qualifications through education. Working-class boys experience status frustration in trying and failing to meet middle-class expectations at school. Being part of a delinquent subculture enables these boys to gain status within their group and also to flout the school rules and hit back at the school system that has branded them as failures.

Delinquency is seen as part of a group subculture or way of life within urban neighbourhoods.

Deviance among young people has also been linked to school subcultures and peer group influences in the education system in Britain. Paul Willis (1977) explores the cultural practices of the 'lads', a group of 12 non-academic, working-class boys in a Midlands' secondary school. These lads were strongly anti-school and were influenced by values that stressed masculinity and toughness. Through the anti-school culture, the lads openly resisted the values of the school and the authority of their teachers. They also rejected the boys who did conform, who they called "ear'oles".

For the lads, time at school was spent "skiving", "dossing" and "having a laff" rather than studying. They expected their future jobs to involve manual labour (for example, working in a factory or on a building site) rather than in "pen pushing" (for instance, working in an office) and therefore viewed academic qualifications as pointless.

❀ DISCUSSION ACTIVITY

Delinquency as a group phenomenon

In a small group, discuss how far you agree with the view that delinquency among young people is a group rather than an individual activity.

Note down three points arising from your discussion.

Marxist explanations

Marxists explain crime by looking at the type of society we live in and who has power within it. They are critical of capitalist societies in which a small group of very wealthy and powerful people – the bourgeoisie – own the means of production, such as the land, factories and big businesses. Marxists argue that the bourgeoisie exploit poorer working-class people – the proletariat – in order to make as much profit as possible.

Capitalist society is based on values such as materialism (valuing material possessions), consumerism (wanting more and better consumer goods such as mobile phones, designer clothes and cars) and competition between individuals to have these possessions and consumer goods (keeping up with the neighbours).

Marxists argue that the media continually reinforce these values through advertising in magazines, in television game shows and even Hollywood films based on the lives of the super-rich. In such a society, it is likely that some people will try to get the things they want through any means possible, including illegal means. In this view, crime can be seen as a by-product of the way capitalist society is organized.

Marxists are critical of the laws enforced in a capitalist society. Criminal law, they argue, is made by, and works in the interests of, those who own property. Consequently, it is not surprising that many laws relate to the protection of private property. Marxists argue that, given such a legal system, it is likely that working-class people will be caught breaking the law while crimes committed by the powerful bourgeoisie go undetected. For example, benefit fraud is generally seen as being more serious and costly than tax evasion, even though far more revenue is lost through tax evasion than through benefit fraud.

STRETCH AND CHALLENGE ACTIVITY

How far do you agree that the media reinforce values such as materialism and consumerism?

WRITTEN ACTIVITY

In your view, is the photograph opposite showing an artist or a delinquent at work? Explain your view.

CHECK YOUR UNDERSTANDING

1 Identify and explain fully one way in which sociologists have explained crime and deviance among teenage boys.

2 Some sociologists who follow the Marxist approach argue that crime can be seen as a by-product of the way capitalist society is organized. Explain what they mean by this.

KEY POINTS

Sub-cultural theories explain crime and delinquency in terms of the values of a particular subculture and the influence of the peer group.

Marxist theories explain crime as resulting from the way capitalist society is structured.

TOPIC 9 · How does labelling theory explain criminal and deviant behaviour?

OBJECTIVE
Discuss labelling theory as an explanation of criminal and deviant behaviour

According to official statistics, there is a relationship between people's involvement in crime and social factors that affect them, such as social class, age, gender, ethnicity and locality. Labelling theory explores how and why certain people (for instance, working-class boys) become labelled as deviant or criminal. A deviant label (such as prostitute, delinquent or drug addict) is like a sticky tag that can be attached to an individual or group.

Cicourel (1976) undertook participant observation (see page 30) with police and probation officers in two cities in California (USA) to study day-to-day police, probation and court activities. He focused on juveniles (young people) and found that the way a particular juvenile was viewed by officials had a significant impact on how that individual was dealt with. The decision on whether or not to bring an individual to court was largely influenced by the probation officer's view of 'the typical delinquent'.

A delinquent type, in the officials' view, is from a low-income, broken home, has a bad attitude towards authority, poor school performance and is a member of a minority ethnic group. If an individual's background fits that of 'the typical delinquent' then they are more likely to be charged and, if found guilty, to be labelled a delinquent. According to Cicourel, a middle-class white boy is less likely to be seen as a typical delinquent, even when behaving in the same way or committing the same act. Consequently, he is more likely to receive a warning rather than be charged with a criminal offence.

So, according to Cicourel, a delinquent is someone who has been labelled as such. To be labelled a delinquent is more the result of the reaction of other people, such as probation and police officers, than it is of an individual's actual behaviour.

Stereotyping

Labelling is often linked to stereotyping. Members of some groups, for example, people with mental health problems, are sometimes labelled and treated according to stereotypes.

Labelling someone as deviant may help to create a self-fulfilling prophecy (see page 126) by pushing people further towards deviance. For example:

- A young woman starts taking illegal drugs. Over time, her use increases.
- She is publicly identified, labelled and marked out as a 'drug addict'.
- This label influences how people behave towards her and how they respond to her. She is rejected by her family, loses her job and her home and comes to see herself as deviant.

DISCUSSION ACTIVITY

Labelling theory in action

In a small group, discuss the following scenario:

Ben, a middle-class boy, and Bill, a working-class boy, are apprehended in a large department store on suspicion of shoplifting. They are not together and do not know each other. According to labelling theory, what is likely to happen to each boy and why?

Make a note of the outcome of your discussion.

Glossary terms: stereotypes

- She turns to shoplifting as a way to finance her drug dependency, thus becoming involved in further crime and deviance.
- She now meets others in the same situation as herself and becomes involved in a deviant subculture and lifestyle.

The cause of deviance is not, according to this view, in the action itself but in the reaction of others to it.

DISCUSSION ACTIVITY

Shopping centre outlaws 'hoodies'

The following newspaper article focuses on the social reaction to 'hoodies'. It makes a link between antisocial behaviour (defined in the Crime and Disorder Act (1998) as acting in a manner that actually causes or is likely to cause harassment, alarm or distress) and youths wearing hooded tops. Read the extract, then answer the question that follows.

The country's biggest shopping centre has banned youths wearing hooded tops to stop antisocial behaviour. The Bluewater shopping centre in Kent yesterday introduced a "zero tolerance approach to intimidating conduct" after shoppers complained about groups of loitering teenagers. Baseball caps and other clothing that obscures the face were also banned, to make sure those misbehaving could be identified on CCTV. Bans on 'hoodies' are becoming increasingly common, having been introduced in Folkestone, Merseyside, Corby and Kettering. In January 2005, two 15-year-olds in Leamington Spa received antisocial behaviour orders specifically banning them from wearing hoodies. Those wearing hooded tops at Bluewater will be denied entry or told to leave if they pull their hoods up after they get in.

Source: adapted from David Sapsted, *The Telegraph*, 12 May 2005

In a small group, discuss the possible reasons why youths wearing hooded tops are more likely than other young people to be seen as a problem or threat. Make a list of the possible reasons.

STRETCH AND CHALLENGE ACTIVITY

To what extent do you think 'hoodies' are being labelled as deviant and treated according to stereotypes?

CHECK YOUR UNDERSTANDING

What do sociologists mean by the following terms?

a) deviant label   b) stereotype

KEY POINT

Labelling theory explores how and why certain people (such as working-class boys) come to be labelled as deviant or criminal.

TOPIC 10 — What are the main sources of statistical data on the extent of crime?

OBJECTIVE
Discuss the main sources of statistical data on the level of crime

There are two main sources of statistical data on the extent or the level of crime:

- surveys of the public, such as victim surveys and self-report surveys
- official statistics on crimes recorded by the police, such as those shown in the table.

Victim surveys

Victim surveys question people about their experiences of crime. The British Crime Survey (BCS), for example, was first carried out in 1982 and is now done every year. The results are published by the Home Office, along with police recorded crime rates.

The BCS measures crime through surveys with a sample of over 40 000 households (see page 37). It interviews people aged 16 and over who live in private households in England and Wales. It asks them whether they have been victims of particular offences within the last 12 months and, if so, whether they reported these crimes to the police.

The BCS covers crimes against the person (such as assault) and property crime (such as car theft or burglary). However, it does not cover all crime recorded by the police. Crimes such as murder, fraud or so-called 'victimless' crimes (where there is no direct victim) such as drug use, are not covered.

Self-report studies

Self-report studies question people about their offending. The Offending, Crime and Justice Survey (OCJS), for example, is commissioned by the Home Office. This study was first carried out in 2003. It measures the extent of self-reported offending, drug use and antisocial behaviour in England and Wales, particularly among those aged 10–25. By asking people about their offending, it provides information on offenders and offences that are not necessarily dealt with by the police or courts.

Problems with survey data   ✎ WRITTEN ACTIVITY

The BCS and the OCJS are household surveys and so do not cover homeless people or those living in institutions such as prisons. Nor do they cover all crimes.

1 Identify and explain two possible limitations of each of these surveys as sources of data. You could, for example, consider any limitations associated with interviewing people generally or you could think about likely problems in asking people to report on their own involvement in crime or their experiences of crime. Alternatively, you could consider how representative the samples are.

2 In pairs, compare your answers and note down any points you have missed.

Glossary terms: self-report studies   victim surveys

Official statistics of crimes recorded by the police

Official statistics of crimes recorded by the police are published by the Home Office each year in a publication entitled *Crime in England and Wales*. Sociologists use these statistics as a secondary source of data (see page 16). They are helpful in enabling researchers to identify trends in recorded crime over time. For example, by comparing statistics collected in the late 1800s with recent figures it is possible to examine long-term trends in recorded crime. These statistics are also helpful in identifying trends in the rate of particular crimes over time. In addition, they allow comparisons of crime rates in different parts of the UK.

The different sources of statistical data on the level of crime tend to provide different pictures. BCS estimates of crime are higher than the figures on crimes recorded by the police. According to BCS figures covering 2006/07, approximately 11.3 million crimes were committed against adults living in private households in England and Wales. By comparison, approximately 5.4 million crimes were recorded by the police in England and Wales in 2006/07.

Recorded crime
WRITTEN ACTIVITY

The table below shows crimes recorded by the police in 2006/07 in England and Wales according to the type of offence. We can see, for example, that violence against the person accounted for 19 per cent of all recorded crime. Study this information, then answer the questions.

1 Which type of offence accounted for:

a) the highest percentage of recorded crimes in England and Wales in 2006/07

b) the second-lowest percentage?

2 Were more drugs offences or burglary recorded in 2006/07?

Crimes recorded by the police in England and Wales, 2006/07

Type of offence	Percentages
Theft and handling stolen goods	36
Criminal damage	22
Violence against the person	19
Burglary (e.g. housebreaking)	11
Fraud and forgery	4
Drugs offences	4
Robbery	2
Other offences	1

Source: adapted from *Social Trends* (2008)

CHECK YOUR UNDERSTANDING

1 What is a victim survey?

2 Describe briefly how a victim survey is carried out.

3 What is a self-report survey?

KEY POINTS

Official statistics on police recorded crime are published in the UK by the Home Office.

Victim surveys and self-report studies also provide statistical data on the extent of crime. British Crime Survey estimates of crime are higher than the figures on crimes recorded by the police.

How far do official statistics on recorded crime measure the extent of crime?

OBJECTIVE

Discuss how far official statistics on recorded crime measure the extent of crime

Although official statistics on crime recorded by the police appear to be a straightforward measure of the extent of crime in any one year, they have limitations. Recorded crime represents only a partial picture of the total amount of crime committed. Issues to consider when examining whether official statistics on recorded crime provide an accurate picture of how much crime there is include the discovery, reporting and recording of crime.

Discovery and witnessing crime

Are all crimes known about? If a crime has not been witnessed or discovered in the first place, it cannot be reported to the police. It cannot, therefore, be counted in official statistics on recorded crime. For example, a victim may be unaware that a crime has actually taken place. If a thief takes a £5 note from a wallet containing around £45, for instance, this may go unnoticed by the owner. Similarly, a victim must recognize and define an incident such as a smashed window as criminal rather than accidental damage if there is any chance of it being reported.

Criminal or accidental damage?

Reporting crime

Are all of the crimes that are witnessed or discovered actually reported to the police? Many less serious offences are not reported and so cannot be recorded by the police. Victim surveys such as the BCS suggest that many people who have been victims of crime do not report it to the police. According to the 2007/08 BCS, for example, 58 per cent of victims of crime said the offence was not reported to, or known about by, the police. This under-reporting helps to explain why the actual recorded crime figure is lower than BCS estimates of crime.

The likelihood of reporting crime to the police varies according to the type of offence. The 2007/08 BCS, for example, suggests that 93 per cent of motor vehicle theft is reported to the police. This proportion is relatively high, probably because people must report car theft to the police before they can claim from their insurance company. Burglaries where something is stolen are also more likely than some other crimes to be reported. Offences such as vandalism, assault without injury and theft from the person are least likely to be reported.

Reasons for not reporting a crime to the police include:

- The crime is considered too trivial, for example theft of a cheap ring, or it is thought that the police could do nothing about it.
- The victim suffered no loss.
- The victim may believe that the police will handle it insensitively; this is possibile with crimes such as rape.

The British Crime Survey

Study the following information taken from the BCS, then answer the questions.

1 According to these figures, what percentage of burglaries in which something was stolen was reported to the police?

2 Why do you think this proportion was relatively high?

3 What percentage of vandalism was reported to the police?

4 Why do you think this proportion was relatively low?

Reporting rates based on 2007/08 BCS

Type of offence	Percentages
Theft of vehicle	93
Burglary with loss	76
Burglary no loss (including attempts)	54
Theft from vehicle	44
Robbery	43
Vandalism	35
Assault with no injury	34
Theft from the person	32

Source: adapted from Jansson et al (2008) p. 39.

- Victims of violent crime may consider the issue to be private, do not want to involve the police and deal with it themselves.
- When a crime is committed in the workplace, employers may prefer to dismiss the employee rather than involve the police. The term 'white-collar crime' refers to crime committed by white-collar employees (broadly, those in relatively high-status positions, such as accountants or lawyers) in the course of their employment. It includes theft from an employer or 'fiddling' travel expenses. It is under-represented in crime statistics.

Recording crime

Are all reported crimes actually recorded by the police? The police may not necessarily record a crime that is reported to them. They may, for example, consider the crime to be too trivial or they may doubt the honesty or accuracy of the complainant's report. The police may decide that there is not enough evidence of an offence having been committed to justify recording it.

Sociologists argue that official statistics ignore the hidden or 'grey' figure of crime, which includes unreported and unrecorded crime. As a result, they tend to treat official statistics on recorded crime with caution.

CHECK YOUR UNDERSTANDING

Identify and explain two reasons why the recorded rate of crime may not include all crimes committed.

KEY POINT

Not all crime is discovered, witnessed, reported or recorded, so official statistics on police recorded crime do not tell the whole story.

TOPIC 12 **What is meant by the 'social construction' of official crime statistics?**

OBJECTIVE

Outline the view that official crime statistics are socially constructed

Official statistics on police recorded crime may appear to provide a straightforward and factual account of how much crime takes place each year. However, when sociologists examine how these statistics are actually collected or compiled, they question whether they provide a valid or true picture. This is because official crime statistics are 'socially constructed' (see page 39). In other words, they are the outcome of a series of choices and decisions made by the various people involved, such as victims, witnesses and police.

The social construction of crime statistics

WRITTEN ACTIVITY

The following diagram illustrates the series of decisions that are made by witnesses, victims and police officers in the process of constructing statistics on crime recorded by the police. Examine the diagram and explain the stages involved in this process.

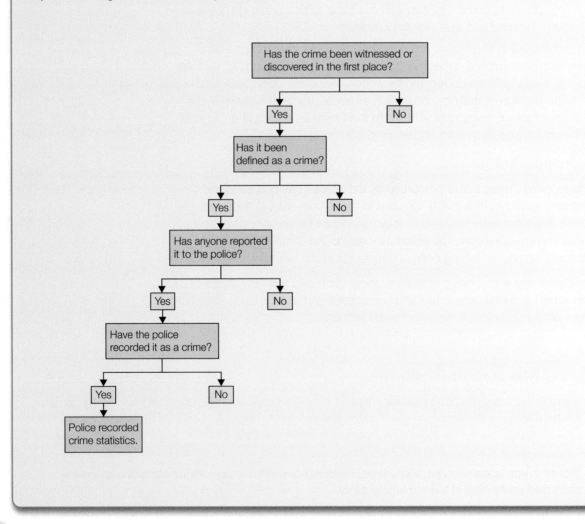

Pros and cons of official statistics on crime

WRITTEN ACTIVITY

Drawing on information from this and the previous topic, make a list of:

• the advantages of official statistics on recorded crime

• the limitations of official statistics on recorded crime.

STRETCH AND CHALLENGE ACTIVITY

What is meant by the view that official statistics on crime recorded by the police are 'socially constructed'?

Eye on the exam

Some of the more challenging exam questions ask you to "discuss how far sociologists would agree" with a particular view or statement. For example, a question might ask you to: "Discuss how far sociologists would agree with the view that deviant and criminal behaviour results from inadequate socialization."

Such questions are worded to encourage you to assess and evaluate information and evidence. In other words, to gain high marks, you will need to provide evidence and arguments for and against the view given in the question.

In tackling the above question, you need to discuss the view that deviant and criminal behaviour results from inadequate socialization. To achieve top marks, however, you also need to tackle "how far". You could do this by discussing other sociological explanations of crime and deviance such as opportunity structures, relative deprivation, sub-cultural explanations, Marxist explanations and labelling theory.

You also need to reach a clear conclusion on the issue of "how far" or to what extent. Your conclusions about how far should be based on the arguments and evidence you have provided in your response.

CHECK YOUR UNDERSTANDING

1 Explain why a victim survey might show the number of crimes actually committed more accurately than police statistics.

2 Discuss how far sociologists would agree that statistics on recorded crime measure how much crime there is.

KEY POINTS

Official statistics on police recorded crime are based on a series of decisions made by, for example, victims and police officers. As such, they do not provide a true picture of crime levels.

TOPIC 13 What is the relationship between involvement in crime and age?

OBJECTIVES

Describe the patterns in the relationship between age and involvement in crime as shown in statistical data

Explain these patterns

If we take official statistics at face value, there is a relationship between involvement in criminal activity and social characteristics such as social class, age, gender, ethnicity and locality (area). Maguire (2007) notes that there are many more males, young people, black people, poor people and poorly educated people in the prison population relative to the general population.

Findings from sociological research reveal a less clear-cut picture than official statistics about who commits crime. Self-report studies have found that between 40 and almost 100 per cent of respondents admit to having committed at least one criminal offence during their lifetime.

Official statistics suggest a link between age and offending behaviour, with younger people, particularly males, being more likely to engage in criminal activity than older people. In 2006, for example, around 6 per cent of all 17-year-old males in England and Wales were found guilty of, or cautioned for, serious (indictable) offences. By contrast, less than 1 per cent of men in age groups over the age of 45 were found guilty of, or cautioned for, indictable offences.

Findings from self-report studies suggest that the majority of young people do not engage in crime. Additionally, young people who do engage in crime tend to commit relatively minor offences. Data from the 2004 Offending, Crime and Justice Survey, for example, indicate that 74 per cent of younger interviewees (that is, around three-quarters of the 5000 young people aged 10 to 25) said that they had not committed any of the offences they were asked about during the previous year. Of those who said they had committed one of these offences, many had committed relatively minor offences or had only offended occasionally.

How do we explain these patterns?

- Peer group pressure may encourage some young people to engage in criminal activity. We have seen, for example, that delinquency has been linked to group subcultures.
- Young people may seek excitement, which could lead them into trouble with the police. Some sociologists argue that the experience of rule breaking in itself has attractions in terms of generating feelings of excitement and an adrenaline rush.
- There may have been a breakdown in the social control of some young people, both at home and at school.

DISCUSSION ACTIVITY

Age and offending

In a small group, discuss other possible reasons why:

a) some young people are more likely to offend than others

b) young people are generally more likely to offend than people in their parents' or grandparents' age groups.

Make a note of four points arising from your discussion.

Offenders' age and gender

This table provides information on the proportion of males and females aged 10, 15, 17 and 20 and the proportion in older age groups who were found guilty of, or cautioned for, indictable (serious) offences in England and Wales in 2006. For example, 0.28 per cent of boys and 0.07 per cent of girls aged 10 were found guilty of, or cautioned for, indictable offences. Study this information, then answer the questions below.

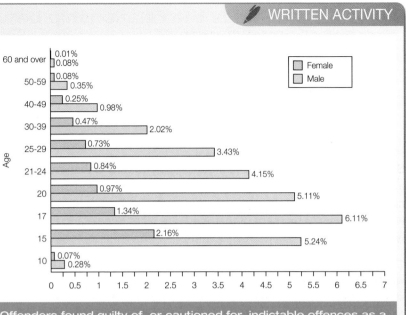

Offenders found guilty of, or cautioned for, indictable offences as a percentage of the population in England and Wales, by age and sex, 2006.

Source: adapted from *Criminal Statistics 2006, England and Wales* (Ministry of Justice, 2007) p. 79

1 According to these figures, what was the peak offending age for males in England and Wales in 2006?

2 What was the peak offending age for females?

3 Do these statistics tend to suggest that young people are more likely or less likely to offend as they enter their 20s and 30s?

4 Was the proportion of 20-year-old females found guilty of, or cautioned for, indictable offences in 2006 greater or smaller than that of males aged between 40 and 49?

These statistics tell us about the age and gender of convicted or known offenders. Identify one group which these statistics do not tell us about.

Identify and explain two possible reasons why people aged 20 and under are more likely to be found guilty of, or cautioned for, serious offences than those aged over 45.

Official statistics on police recorded crime suggest that criminal activity is more commonly found in particular social groups such as young males. Possible explanations for this include peer group pressure.

What is the relationship between crime and gender?

OBJECTIVES

Describe the patterns in the relationship between gender and involvement in crime as shown in statistical data

Explain these patterns

Statistics suggest that females are less likely to offend than males. In 2006, for example, 99 900 women and 407 100 men were found guilty of, or cautioned for, indictable (serious) offences in England and Wales. In other words, around 20 per cent of the offenders were female and 80 per cent were male.

In 2006, the most common indictable offence which both men and women were found guilty of, or cautioned for, was theft or handling stolen goods. This accounted for around 50 per cent of all female offences and 30 per cent of all male offences. Additionally, the 2004 OCJS found that males were more likely than females to say that they had committed an offence during the previous year. Males were also more likely than females to say they had offended frequently and had committed serious offences.

One view is that females tend to be less involved in crime than males because of gender socialization. From early childhood, we have different expectations of children's behaviour according to their gender. In general, girls are expected to be more passive and boys more active. If boys and men conform to society's views of masculinity, they may be under pressure to be macho and 'tough'. These sorts of expectations based on gender may lead males into conflict with the police and into criminal activity such as alcohol-related crime.

Another view is that females have fewer opportunities than males to commit criminal offences because their behaviour is more closely monitored. Young girls, for example, tend to be supervised more carefully by their parents than young boys. Similarly, more restrictions are usually placed on adolescent girls than on adolescent boys. As adults, women often have more domestic responsibilities than men and so have less opportunity to become involved in criminal behaviour.

It may be that those in authority within law enforcement hold stereotyped beliefs about women and men. One example is that female offenders are seen as 'sad' rather than 'bad' and, therefore, they need help rather than punishment. Consequently, female offenders, particularly those who conform to gender stereotypes, may be treated more leniently than males within the criminal justice system. This could apply at every stage, that is during reporting, police response, trial and sentencing. This is sometimes referred to as the 'chivalry' effect

Girls and boys are often socialized differently.

Offenders by sex and type of offence

The following pie charts show the types of offence that male and female offenders were found guilty of, or cautioned for, in 2006. For example, 0.3 per cent of female offenders and 1.37 per cent of male offenders were found guilty of, or cautioned for, motoring offences in 2006. Study the information in the pie charts, then answer the questions that follow.

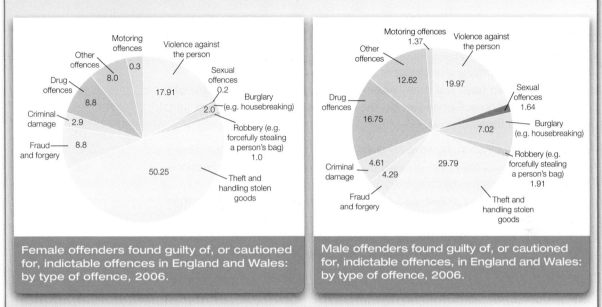

Female offenders found guilty of, or cautioned for, indictable offences in England and Wales: by type of offence, 2006.

Male offenders found guilty of, or cautioned for, indictable offences, in England and Wales: by type of offence, 2006.

Source: adapted from *Criminal Statistics 2006, England and Wales* (Ministry of Justice, 2007) p. 66

1 Which offence was the second most common for both males and females in 2006?

2 Which offence was least common for women in 2006?

3 Which offence was least common for men in 2006?

4 Drug offences accounted for 8.8 per cent of female offenders in 2006. What percentage of male offenders did drug offences account for?

What do the cards opposite tell us about expectations surrounding masculinity and femininity?

How would you explain the fact that there are far fewer women than men in prisons in England and Wales?

Official statistics on police recorded crime suggest that more men commit crime than women. Possible explanations for this include gender socialization and the chivalry effect.

TOPIC 15 **How do we explain women's increasing involvement in crime?**

OBJECTIVE

Explain the increasing involvement of women in crime

Although females are less likely to offend than males, recent statistics suggest that the number of female offenders in the UK is increasing. Some explanations for this increase focus on the changing position of women in society. While becoming more independent and gaining equality in the workplace, women have lost many of the constraints or controls that kept them away from crime. Consequently, they now have similar legal and illegal opportunities to those of men.

An alternative explanation, however, argues that the majority of women have not benefited substantially from equality in the workplace or in the professions. On the contrary, women are more likely than men to be unemployed or employed in low-paid, unskilled, part-time jobs. As a result, more women than men live in relative poverty. According to this view, women's increased involvement in crime is related to their economic situation and their experiences of poverty. This helps to explain why female offenders tend to be poor and why they often engage in crimes such as shoplifting.

It is also argued that the female crime rate has increased because more women are now being arrested, charged and convicted rather than because more women are actually committing crimes. According to this view, changing attitudes towards gender and crime mean that the more lenient treatment of women within the criminal justice system (the 'chivalry' effect) is now less common. Joan Garrod (2007), for example, notes that the increase in the

---

Girl gangs muscling in on street violence   ✏ WRITTEN ACTIVITY

The following extract about girls' involvement in gangs is taken from a newspaper. Read the extract, then answer the question that follows.

> Hundreds of girls are joining criminal gangs involved in violence and drugs, experts warned yesterday. Alarmingly, at least three all-girl gangs are roaming the streets in London. A report by the Metropolitan Police Authority found that 10 per cent of gang participants are women and evidence suggests girls as young as seven are joining up.
>
> The deputy chairman of the Metropolitan Police Authority said yesterday: "The Met has long been aware of the involvement of females in criminal activity. It has always been there. What I am worried about now is exclusively girl gangs."
>
> Campaigners have warned more must be done to find out exactly how many girls are in gangs, with some estimates suggesting they make up around a third of membership.

Source: adapted from James Slack, *Daily Mail*, 22 August 2007

According to this article, what aspect of females' involvement in crime has changed recently?

Glossary terms: social problems

number of women in prisons over the last 10 years is almost entirely due to harsher sentencing rather than because women have started to commit more serious crimes.

Researching girl gangs
WRITTEN ACTIVITY

Young people's involvement in gangs is considered a serious social problem, generating a lot of media coverage and public debate in recent years. Imagine that you are putting together a research proposal in order to try to get funding for a project on young females and gangs. In your proposal, you must identify your research aims and outline the research methods you plan to use. You must also show that you have thought about the ethical issues that may arise during your research.

In a small group, put together a research proposal for a study of young females' involvement in gangs. Ensure that you include the following information:

1 The title of your proposed research study.

2 Your research questions, aims or hypotheses.

3 At least one primary research method that you plan to use in your investigation and an explanation of how and why you would use it.

4 At least one secondary source of data, explaining how you would use it.

5 A discussion of at least two ethical issues that may arise during the process of doing your research and how you plan to deal with them.

STRETCH AND CHALLENGE ACTIVITY

1 What is meant by the 'chivalry' effect?

2 What evidence is there to suggest that the chivalry effect is becoming less significant?

DISCUSSION ACTIVITY

The newspaper article opposite identifies the emergence of "exclusively girl gangs". In a small group, discuss the possible reasons why the emergence of exclusively girl gangs might cause public concern. How far are they likely to cause more concern than mixed or exclusively boy gangs?

Make a note of three main points raised during your discussion.

CHECK YOUR UNDERSTANDING

Identify and explain two reasons why the number of female offenders in the UK is increasing.

KEY POINTS

Recent statistics suggest that the number of female offenders in the UK is increasing.

Possible explanations for this include the changing social position of women and changing attitudes to gender and crime.

TOPIC 16 **What is the relationship between involvement in crime and ethnicity?**

OBJECTIVE

Describe the patterns in the relationship between ethnicity and involvement in crime as shown in statistical data

Statistics from the Ministry of Justice (2008) show that members of some ethnic groups are over-represented in the prison population relative to their proportion in the general population. Black people, for example, are around five times more likely than white people to be in prison.

The general population

WRITTEN ACTIVITY

The first line of the following statistics shows the ethnic composition of the population of England and Wales, according to the 2001 census. The next line shows the prison population according to ethnicity.

We can see, for example, that people of Asian heritage make up 4.7 per cent of the general population but 6 per cent of the prison population. Examine this information, then answer the questions that follow.

Proportion of ethnic groups in the prison population in England and Wales, 2006/07

	Ethnicity (%)					
	White	Black	Asian	Other	Unknown/not recorded	Total
General population (aged 10 and over) at 2001 Census	91.3	2.8	4.7	1.2	0.0	100
Prison population	81.5	11.0	6.0	1.1	0.4	100

Source: adapted from Ministry of Justice (2008)

1 What percentage of the general population comprises 'black' ethnic groups?

2 What percentage of the prison population comprises 'white' ethnic groups?

3 Members of which ethnic groups are under-represented among those in prison and which are over-represented among those in prison, relative to their proportion in the general population?

In 2006, 80.8 per cent (around four-fifths) of all male British nationals and 82.7 per cent of all female British nationals in prisons in England and Wales were white.

Statistics from the Ministry of Justice (2008) show that black people are around seven times more likely than white people to be stopped and searched by the police. They are three-and-a-half times more likely to be arrested.

Glossary terms: ethnic group

The prison population

The following statistics examine British nationals in prison according to their ethnicity and gender. They show, for example, that 0.2 per cent of male British nationals and 0.4 per cent of female British nationals in prison were members of Chinese or other ethnic groups. Examine this information, then answer the questions that follow.

Prison population of British nationals in England and Wales: by sex and ethnic group, 2006

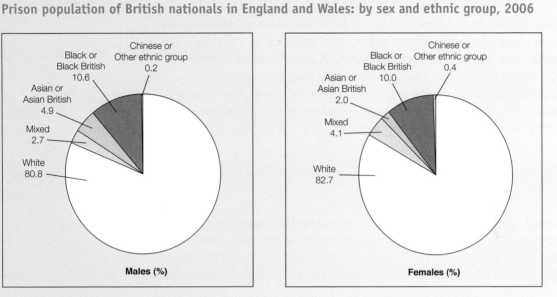

Males (%)

Females (%)

Source: adapted from *Social Trends* (2008)

1 Among which ethnic groups is the proportion of female prisoners greater than that of males?

2 Which ethnic group made up:

   a) the largest proportion of both male and female prisoners?

   b) the second-largest proportion of both male and female prisoners?

   c) the smallest proportion of both male and female prisoners?

Drawing on this information, write a paragraph to summarize the relationship between ethnicity and the prison population as shown in official statistics.

Identify two ethnic groups whose members are over-represented in prison relative to their proportion in the general population.

Members of some ethnic groups are over-represented while others are under-represented in the prison population relative to their proportion in the general population.

How do we explain the patterns in statistics on crime and ethnicity?

OBJECTIVE

Explain the patterns in the relationship between ethnicity and involvement in crime as shown in statistical data

We could take the statistics at face value and see them as reflecting the level of crime within each ethnic group. This would involve arguing, for example, that there are more black people in prison relative to their proportion in the general population because they commit more crime than members of other ethnic groups. If we assume for the moment that this is actually the case, then one possible explanation is that higher proportions of black people experience unemployment so the level of crime may be linked to poverty and relative deprivation.

An alternative approach, however, rejects the idea that the statistics reflect the actual levels of crime in society and argues instead that the statistics exaggerate crime among particular ethnic groups. Crime statistics can be seen as reflecting the way that policing is carried out and bias within the criminal justice system. A number of sociologists have argued that black people are more likely to be targeted, prosecuted, convicted and sentenced for longer periods of time than people from other ethnic groups. The Macpherson Report also identified institutional racism (see page 45) within the Metropolitan Police.

Ethnicity and the criminal justice process

✎ WRITTEN ACTIVITY

We can see from the following table that people of Asian heritage comprise 4.7 per cent of the general population but 8.1 per cent of those stopped and searched by the police. From this it can be argued, for instance, that people of Asian heritage are over-represented among those stopped and searched, relative to the general population. Examine this information, then answer the questions below.

Proportion of ethnic groups at different stages of the criminal justice process in England and Wales, 2006/07

	Ethnicity (%)					
	White	Black	Asian	Other	Unknown/not recorded	Total
General population (aged 10 and over) at 2001 census	91.3	2.8	4.7	1.2	0.0	100
Stops and searches	72.3	15.9	8.1	1.5	2.1	100
Arrests	83.1	9.6	5.3	1.3	0.7	100
Cautions	81.3	6.4	4.4	1.2	6.6	100

Source: adapted from Ministry of Justice (2008)

Relative to their proportion in the general population, members of which ethnic group are:

a) most likely to be stopped and searched?

b) over-represented among those arrested?

c) under-represented among those cautioned?

Is policing fair?

The following extract is from an article that explores whether policing focuses more on some groups (such as young black men) than others. Read through the article, then answer the questions that follow.

A view often expressed by sociologists and criminologists is that some people are 'criminalized' while other (often more serious) offenders avoid police attention.

Since catching offenders 'in the act' is actually rare, police officers tend to focus their attention on individuals they think are 'likely' to be offenders. They do this by developing a profile of a 'typical' offender. These informal profiles are largely based on two sources of information.

- First, officers' own views and previous encounters with offenders. However, these encounters are problematic because they are rarely systematic. Most offenders are never caught and those who are caught are either unlucky or slow (thus not necessarily representative of offenders in general).

- Second, information from the public. However, accounts of offenders given by victims or witnesses usually involve no more than descriptions of sex, age and ethnicity – presumably because these are often the characteristics most obvious to onlookers.

The central problem, therefore, is that police have to operate with profiles that rely on such characteristics (young, black males etc.) rather than on anything that is clearly linked with potential or undetected offending. If the criteria usually used to select individuals for police attention are characteristics that someone can have little or no control over (e.g. age, gender, ethnicity and social class) rather than particular behaviours which they can influence, then only a narrow group of people becomes subject to police attention, on grounds that are often not justifiable.

Source: adapted from Townsley and Marshall (2006)

1 In the first sentence, the authors refer to the view that some offenders avoid police attention. Identify two examples of crimes that appear to avoid police attention.

2 According to the authors of this article, what two sources of information are profiles of 'typical' offenders based on?

Drawing on this article, write a paragraph to explain why the policing of young black men can be seen as unfair.

CHECK YOUR UNDERSTANDING

Discuss how far sociologists would agree that crime statistics exaggerate crime levels among particular ethnic groups.

KEY POINT

Crime statistics are seen as reflecting policing methods and bias within the criminal justice system.

TOPIC 18 · What is the relationship between involvement in crime, social class and locality?

OBJECTIVES
Describe the patterns in the relationship between social class, locality and crime
Explain these patterns

Social class

There is evidence that working-class people are over-represented in the prison population in proportion to their numbers in the general population. Marsh (2006), for example, notes that the vast majority of women within the prison system are working class or underclass (the most disadvantaged social group at the bottom of the class structure).

Over-representation of working-class people in the prison population

If we take the statistics at face value then it could be argued that:

- Most people want to be successful and affluent (well off). Working-class people have relatively fewer opportunities to succeed through legal channels such as education and employment. Consequently, they are more tempted to turn to crime for financial gain.

- Working-class subcultures may stress deviant or criminal behaviour, which can bring status within particular peer groups.

Alternatively, the statistics may reflect bias within the criminal justice system, which includes the police and courts. According to this view, the law is strictly enforced against working-class people who engage in robbery or burglary. By contrast, crimes such as business fraud committed by members of powerful groups are under-recorded in the official statistics.

White-collar and corporate crime

The term 'white-collar crime' refers broadly to crimes committed by people in relatively high-status positions (such as managers in business, accountants or lawyers) during the course of their work. Examples include tax evasion, fraud and misuse of expense accounts. Such crimes are conducted within the context of everyday business and workplace activity rather than, for instance, on the streets. This helps to prevent white-collar crime from being discovered. Nelken (2007) argues that with white-collar crimes, the problem is to discover whether there has actually been an offence rather than to identify the culprit. Fraud, for example, is frequently undetected. Furthermore, the police are often not called when an offence has been committed. Consequently, much white-collar crime is likely to be undiscovered, unreported and unrecorded.

DISCUSSION ACTIVITY

Discovering white-collar crime

In a small group, discuss how far you agree with Nelken's view that the problem with white-collar crimes is to discover whether there has actually been an offence rather than to identify the culprit.

Why might it be difficult to discover whether there has actually been an offence?

Make a note of three points arising from your discussion.

Glossary terms: corporate crime

Corporate crime refers to crimes committed by employees on behalf of the organization or company they work for. Corporate crime includes offences against consumers, such as the manufacture and sale of unsafe products or unfit foods. It also includes environmental offences involving, for instance, pollution of water and air. Tombs (2005) notes that there is little effort by the government to keep statistics on corporate crime. For example, the main forms of crime statistics kept by the Home Office do not include identifiable types of corporate crime.

Corporate crime includes environmental offences involving pollution of water and air.

Locality

There is a link between crime rates and locality (area). In general terms, the crime rate in urban areas is higher than in rural areas. Data from the 2007/08 British Crime Survey show that the risk of being a victim of any household crime (burglary, vehicle-related theft or vandalism) is lower in rural than in urban areas. Additionally, the risk is higher in the most deprived areas than in the least deprived areas.

How do we explain these patterns?

- Inner-city crime can be seen as a response to social inequality and economic deprivation. According to this view, higher levels of unemployment and relative poverty are found in urban areas than in the suburbs. Such factors are seen either as the causes of crime or as the context within which crime is committed.

- There could be more opportunities to commit crime in urban settings. In city centres, for example, there are more targets and temptations, such as department stores and parked cars, than in rural areas.

- Cities may have lower levels of social control than rural areas.

- Statistics may, however, reflect different policing methods. In rural areas, the police may be more likely to deal informally with offenders who commit less serious offences than to charge them.

CHECK YOUR UNDERSTANDING

1 a) What do sociologists mean by the terms 'white-collar crime' and 'corporate crime'?

   b) Explain two reasons why white-collar and corporate crime may be under-represented in crime statistics.

2 Explain briefly why there appears to be more crime in urban areas than in rural areas of the UK.

KEY POINTS

Official statistics suggest that criminal activity is more common in particular social groups or localities. However, studies of white-collar and corporate crime paint a more complex picture.

TOPIC 19 # What is the significance of criminal behaviour for victims of crime?

OBJECTIVES

Identify the different types of research into the victims of crime

Discuss these different types of research

Since the 1980s, sociologists, policy makers and politicians have focused increasingly on the experiences of the victims or survivors of crime. Young (2007) identifies three types of research on crime victims: measurement research; studies of the impact of crime; studies of the role of victims in the criminal justice system.

Measurement research

Measurement research examines the types and numbers of people who are victims of crime. Victim surveys such as the British Crime Survey (see page 37) provide statistical information on the victims of crime, such as their social characteristics. These surveys also provide statistics on the 'grey figure' of unreported crime. Contrary to popular opinion, such data indicate that young men aged 16 to 24 are most at risk of experiencing criminal violence.

Walklate (2007) has undertaken extensive research on the victims of crime. She notes that some people are more likely than others to become crime victims. She identifies four key factors: class, gender, age and ethnicity.

For example, people who live in the most deprived areas are most likely to be victims of crimes such as burglary and vehicle-related criminal damage.

	High risk from crime
Class	The poor, living in private rented housing
Gender	Males
Age	The young
Ethnicity	Minority ethnic groups

In the following extract, Walklate outlines some of the patterns between factors such as deprivation and age, and the likelihood of becoming a victim of crime.

As Dixon et al. report, in England and Wales, people on an income of less than £10,000 are: 1.6 times more likely to be mugged; 1.3 times more likely to be burgled; and 4.2 times more likely to feel insecure walking alone after dark in their neighbourhood than people on incomes of £30,000 and more.

In addition, age features as a factor. Younger people rather than older people seem to be most at risk from crime of all kinds, but at risk from personal crime (violence) in particular.

Source: adapted from Walklate (2007) p. 68

Studies of the impact of crime

Sociologists are interested in understanding how crime impacts on people's lives. Research has focused on the impact on victims of particular types of crime such as domestic violence, burglary and stalking. The findings indicate

Glossary terms: repeat victimization

that crime impacts on victims in different ways. The impact may be physical (e.g. injury during an assault); financial (e.g. having to replace uninsured stolen items); psychological (e.g. feeling stressed or insecure after an assault or burglary); or social (e.g. affecting victims' family relationships).

Walklate (2007) notes that crime does not impact on all members of society in the same way. The impact of crime may be particularly problematic where someone is a victim regularly over time – known as 'repeat victimization' – or where victims experience crime routinely, that is as part of their daily lives. Racial harassment or domestic violence, for example, may occur not only repeatedly but also routinely in people's everyday lives.

Since the 1970s, organizations supporting crime victims have become more widespread. Victim Support, for example, is a national charity which helps people to cope with crime. Trained volunteers provide information, for instance, on police and court procedures, compensation and insurance.

> ### ✿ DISCUSSION ACTIVITY
>
> ## Victims of crime
>
> In a small group, discuss the possible reasons why members of some groups, for example young males or the poor, are more likely than others to become victims of crime.
>
> Make a note of three possible reasons.

Studies of the role of victims in the criminal justice process

Victims are increasingly involved in the criminal justice process because people now understand that without their co-operation in reporting crime, providing evidence and acting as witnesses in court, most crime would go unpunished (Hoyle and Zedner, 2007). For example, restorative justice programmes aim to repair the harm and damage caused by criminal behaviour. Such programmes may, for instance, require offenders to meet the victims of their crimes in order to make amends.

> ## Crime behind closed doors
> ### 💡 STRETCH AND CHALLENGE ACTIVITY
>
> Walklate (2007) argues that victim surveys focus on 'crime of the streets' or conventional crimes such as robbery and burglary. Consequently, they tend to overlook crime occurring 'behind closed doors' such as white-collar crime or abuse of the elderly, women and children.
>
> Drawing on Walklate's ideas, explain one limitation of victim surveys as a source of information about crime victims.

> ### CHECK YOUR UNDERSTANDING
>
> 1 Identify two key factors that influence the likelihood of becoming a victim of crime.
> 2 Identify two crimes that people on lower incomes are more likely to be victims of than those on higher incomes.
> 3 Describe and explain two ways in which crime may impact on individual victims.

> ### KEY POINT
>
> Research into the victims of crime includes measurement research, studies of the impact of crime and studies of the role of victims in the criminal justice system.

TOPIC 20 — What is the significance of criminal behaviour for communities and society?

OBJECTIVE

Explain the ways that crime impacts on communities and society

Fear of crime

Sociologists explore the impact crime has on communities and societies. One way that crime may impact on communities is by generating fear of crime. BCS figures highlight the fact that the public worry about and fear particular crimes such as violent crime, burglary and car crime.

Worry about crime
WRITTEN ACTIVITY

BCS respondents are questioned on their worry about crime. The following information shows changes in the proportion of people who answered that they were 'very worried' about burglary, violent crime and car crime. Examine this information, then answer the questions that follow.

Percentages of respondents who answered 'very worried' when asked how worried they were about particular crimes (England and Wales)

	2000	2006/07
Burglary	19	13
Violent crime	24	17
Car crime	21	13

Source: adapted from *Social Trends* (2008)

1 Which crime caused most worry in 2000 and also in 2006/07?

2 Have the percentages of respondents who answered 'very worried' increased or decreased over the period of time shown?

Fear of crime is one way that crime impacts on everyone, to some degree, regardless of whether they have actually been victims of crime. Sometimes, the level of anxiety may not be in proportion to the actual risk. The BCS of 2005/06, for example, found that 38 per cent of respondents were 'fairly worried' about credit card crime and another 19 per cent were 'very worried' about it. Although such anxiety is quite widespread, the BCS of 2006/07 found that only 4 per cent of plastic card users in England and Wales were actually victims of fraud.

Williams (2008) notes that people are now expected to take on more responsibility for protecting themselves from crime. The idea is that, rather than relying on the police to prevent crime, citizens should try to reduce their chances of becoming the victims of crime. They could do this by, for instance, installing domestic burglar alarms.

DISCUSSION ACTIVITY

Fear of crime and risk of becoming a crime victim

In a small group, discuss the possible reasons why the fear of crime (for example, credit card crime) may not necessarily be in proportion to the actual risk. Which social groups do you think experience most anxiety about crime? Why do you think this is?

Make a note of three points arising from your discussion.

Crime is seen as causing tensions in communities and societies that could potentially be destructive. For example, crime can lead people to believe that neighbourhood and community ties are breaking down. Over recent years in Britain, there has been more emphasis on engaging communities to fight crime in their locality. Crimestoppers encourages people to fight crime by providing a phone line so that people can call anonymously with information about crime and to report illegal activities. Similarly, the National Benefit Fraud Hotline was set up so that people can report anyone they suspect of fraudulently claiming benefits.

Several schemes try to involve people in improving safety within their local community. Neighbourhood Watch, for instance, advises its members about home security and how to make communities safer.

We're closing in
with over 3000 fraud investigators

DWP

Benefit fraud is a crime and you could face a prison sentence
TARGETING ⊙ BENEFIT THIEVES

An advertisement for the government campaign against benefit fraud.

The costs of white-collar and corporate crime

Clinard and Meier (2001) identify three kinds of costs (or harm) that are linked to white-collar and corporate crime. These are financial, physical and social.

- **Financial harm** covers the economic impact associated with white-collar and corporate crime, such as loss of taxation revenue.

- **Physical harm** may be suffered by employees, consumers and the community. It includes sickness, injury and death resulting from environmental pollution, the sale of defective car tyres and unfit foods, or work-related exposure to substances linked to lung disease.

- **Social costs** include mistrust that may develop between professionals and clients or employers and employees.

Along similar lines, Tombs (2005) suggests that corporate crime reduces social trust not only in the corporations that supply us with food, clothes and services but also in governments for failing to regulate the corporations' activities. Tombs also argues that the economic and physical costs of corporate crime generally fall on those in society who are already relatively disadvantaged. For example, people on tighter budgets are more vulnerable to buying items (such as cheaper meat contaminated with E. coli) that may result in them becoming victims of corporate crime.

> **◉ Eye on the exam**
>
> Don't worry if you can't remember the names of all of the sociologists you have studied. It is possible to show that you know the relevant sociological ideas and arguments without always referring to sociologists by name.

CHECK YOUR UNDERSTANDING

1 Explain one way in which crime may impact on communities.

2 Describe two costs associated with white-collar or corporate crime.

KEY POINT

Crime impacts on neighbourhoods, communities and on society generally.

TOPIC 21 · **Why is youth crime seen as a social problem?**

OBJECTIVES

Recognize that crime and deviance generate public debate

Explain why teenage crime is seen as a social problem

Debates on crime and deviance

Issues related to crime and deviance are controversial and can generate heated debate among politicians and within the media. These debates focus on issues such as the growth of internet crime and identity fraud, terrorism and the treatment of terrorist suspects, human trafficking, antisocial behaviour, fear of young people and crime committed by teenagers.

Crime is a major focus of public concern and debate. The media play a role in setting the agenda (deciding on the focus) of public debates and discussions about crime and deviance. TV news broadcasts do this, for example, by focusing on some items, stories and views and excluding others. In this way, the public see particular issues as social problems. It is argued that the media increase the public's worries about law and order. Reiner (2007) notes that various studies of news reports have found that violent crimes are over-represented compared with their incidence in official statistics on crime. He also argues that news stories exaggerate the risks of crime faced by groups such as white people of higher status, and they over-represent women, children or older people as victims of crime.

Youth crime as a social problem

Youth crime and antisocial behaviour among teenagers are issues of particular concern to British politicians, policy makers and the public. Pitts (2005) notes that youth crime is often front-page news in the UK and, as a result, it is also a source of anxiety among members of the public. Juvenile crime and deviance, in other words, are considered social problems that concern people in today's society. Behaviour seen as problematic includes antisocial behaviour, drug taking, binge drinking, gangs and violent crime including gun and knife crimes in British cities.

Members of the public consider antisocial behaviour among teenagers as a problem partly because they think that it has negative consequences. People think that the fear it generates is damaging to community life and to community ties. Incidents of vandalism and graffiti are seen as costly in economic terms. More serious incidents of violence and teenage knife crime are seen as costly in terms of the young lives lost and the devastation caused within victims' families.

Newburn (2007) points out that, according to official statistics, a significant proportion of crime is committed by young people. This, together with adult fears about youth crime, leads to young offenders being society's number one 'folk devil'. The term folk devils refers to social groups that are seen as deviant and as troublemakers. Such groups are represented by the media as a threat to society.

Glossary terms: folk devil · moral panic · scapegoating

Antisocial behaviour

The BCS asks respondents about antisocial behaviour in their area. The following table shows the percentage of respondents who said that teenagers hanging around on the streets was a very big problem or a fairly big problem in their area. Examine this information, then answer the questions that follow.

1 Did a higher or lower proportion of respondents say that teenagers hanging around on the streets was a very big or fairly big problem in their area in 2006/07 than in 1992?

2 How far would you agree that 'teenagers hanging around on the streets' provides a satisfactory measure of antisocial behaviour?

1992	20
2000	32
2003/04	27
2006/07	33

Source: *Social Trends* (2008)

The media portrayal of young people as folk devils can result in a 'moral panic' or a public outcry about their behaviour. A moral panic is when the media reports in such a way that relatively trivial acts are sensationalized and exaggerated. Minor acts of vandalism committed by young people, for example, are regarded as typical of all young people and as a threat to social order. A moral panic also involves a process of scapegoating young people or blaming them for society's problems (see page 224).

Governments in Britain have tried to control youth crime and reduce antisocial behaviour among young people by policies such as fining parents for their children's misbehaviour. Other policies include curfews, exclusion zones and Antisocial Behaviour Orders (though ASBOs are not only imposed on young people). Several commentators have pointed out, however, that such measures can be counterproductive. ASBOs, for example, can be a status symbol or a badge of honour among the young.

DISCUSSION ACTIVITY

'Hoodies' revisited

Look back at the information on the social reaction to young people who wear 'hoodies' (see page 161).

In a small group, discuss:

1 To what extent are young people who wear 'hoodies' being treated as folk devils?

2 How far can the 'hoodies' ban be seen as reflecting a moral panic, public outcry or overreaction to young people and their behaviour?

3 How might the ban on 'hoodies' impact on young people?

Make a note of three points arising from your discussion.

STRETCH AND CHALLENGE ACTIVITY

Why do you think having an ASBO can be a source of status? (For ideas on this, you could refer to the sub-cultural explanations of crime and deviance earlier in this chapter.)

CHECK YOUR UNDERSTANDING

1 Describe one kind of problem behaviour believed to be associated with teenagers in recent years.

2 Explain why it is considered by members of the public to be a problem.

KEY POINTS

Crime is a major focus of concern and debate among politicians, the media and the public. Teenage crime in particular is seen as a social problem.

TOPIC 22 — What are the links between racism and crime?

OBJECTIVE

Discuss the social problem of racism

Describe government attempts to tackle racially motivated crime

We have seen that the chances of being a victim of crime are linked to ethnicity and that members of some minority ethnic groups are among those at high risk of crime. Racially motivated crime and racism more generally are examples of social problems. This is because they are damaging or harmful to individuals and society.

Phillips and Bowling (2007) indicate that there have been more than 150 racist murders over the last 35 years in Britain. They argue, however, that most crime (around 85 per cent) committed against minority ethnic communities is not racially motivated.

Social problems require solutions. One way in which British governments have tried to tackle racially motivated crime is by introducing legislation. The Crime and Disorder Act 1998, for example, created new offences including:

- racially aggravated assault
- racially aggravated criminal damage
- racially aggravated harassment.

A racially aggravated offence is one in which:

- the offender demonstrates hostility to the victim based on the victim's membership of a 'racial' group, or
- the offence is motivated by hostility towards members of a 'racial' group because they are members of that group.

Racially aggravated offences have a higher maximum penalty than offences that are not racially aggravated. The maximum penalty for racially aggravated criminal damage, for example, is higher than that for criminal damage.

The figures in the box below give an indication of the extent of racially motivated crime victimization among different ethnic groups.

Respondents interviewed in the 2002/03 British Crime Survey who had been victims of racially motivated crime in the previous year:

- 4 per cent of 'mixed-race' respondents
- 3 per cent of Asian respondents
- 2 per cent of black respondents
- 2 per cent of Chinese/other origin respondents
- less than 1 per cent of white respondents.

Source: Salisbury and Upson (2004)

Glossary term: racist victimization

According to data from the British Crime Survey (Jansson, 2006), 20 per cent of vandalism victims from black and minority ethnic groups thought the vandalism had been racially motivated. By contrast, less than 1 per cent of white victims of vandalism thought the incident had been racially motivated.

The term 'racist victimization' is used in cases where individuals are targeted and victimized because of their race, ethnicity or religion (Phillips and Bowling, 2007).

Recorded crime rates ✏️ WRITTEN ACTIVITY

Recorded crime rates now include incidents of racially or religiously aggravated offences. In 1999/2000, for example, 10 758 incidents of racially or religiously aggravated harassment were recorded. This figure rose to 28 485 in 2006/07 and dropped by 7 per cent to 26 495 in 2007/08. Racially or religiously aggravated harassment accounted for 11 per cent of all police recorded harassment in 2007/08.

Several researchers, including Walklate (2007), argue that such figures are likely to underestimate the extent to which routine harassment is part of the everyday lives of people from minority ethnic groups.

1 In which year did the number of racially or religiously aggravated offences peak, according to recorded crime rates?

2 What do you think researchers mean by 'routine harassment'?

💡 STRETCH AND CHALLENGE ACTIVITY

Why do you think recorded crime rates may underestimate the extent of routine harassment in the everyday lives of people from minority ethnic groups?

Tackling racism and racially motivated crime 🍀 DISCUSSION ACTIVITY

How effective do you think legislation is in reducing racism and racially motivated crime? Can you think of other ways of addressing these social problems?

Make a note of the main points made during your discussion.

CHECK YOUR UNDERSTANDING

Explain one way in which governments have tried to tackle racially aggravated crime in recent years.

KEY POINT

Racism and racially aggravated crime are examples of social problems that governments have tried to tackle in recent years.

6 The Mass Media

TOPIC 1 **What are the mass media?**

OBJECTIVES

Explain what the term 'mass media' means

Consider the press as an example of the mass media

The term 'mass media' refers to forms of communication (media) that reach large (mass) audiences. The mass media are a central part of life in modern societies. Many of us wake up to the radio in the morning, listen to music on our iPod on the bus, surf the internet at lunch time or watch television in the evening. In this way, most people come across the mass media on a daily basis. In fact, it would probably be almost impossible to avoid the media completely.

As well as being significant to individuals, the mass media are important in economic life. For example, online shopping has become increasingly popular over the last decade. Many businesses now rely on the internet, e-mail or mobile phones to communicate with their customers. The mass media's central role in society and their widespread presence in our daily lives help to explain why sociologists are interested in studying them.

Online shopping has taken off.

The media can be divided into traditional and new media.

Traditional media include:

- newspapers
- magazines
- books
- television
- radio
- cinema.

New media include:

- the internet
- mobile phones
- digital radio
- cable and satellite TV
- DVDs
- video games.

One way of making sense of the range of mass media available to us is to explore the distinction between the press, broadcast and electronic media. In this topic, we will examine the press in more detail.

The press in Britain

The 'press' includes newspapers and magazines. In Britain, the press are privately owned and are run as profit-making businesses. Newspapers and magazines are financed through income from advertisements and sales. This means that they are in competition with each other.

The traditional media include newspapers.

Some newspapers are published daily while others are published weekly. Some, such as *The Guardian* and the *Daily Express*, are produced for a national market while others, such as the *Manchester Evening News* and London's *Evening Standard*, are produced and distributed regionally.

Traditionally, newspapers used to be divided into three groups. These were:

- quality broadsheets such as *The Guardian*, the *Daily Telegraph* and the *Times*
- middle-market tabloids such as the *Daily Mail* and *Daily Express*
- mass-market tabloids or 'red tops' such as the *Sun* and the *Mirror*.

All quality newspapers used to be published as broadsheets, which means they have pages around twice the size of the pages of the middle-market and mass-market tabloids.

However, over the last few years some of the quality newspapers have moved from broadsheet to compact editions. The Independent was the first quality national newspaper to launch a compact tabloid edition in 2003 and the *Times* is now published as a compact tabloid.

The quality press and the tabloids

🔍 RESEARCH ACTIVITY

For this activity, your group will need one copy of a mass-market tabloid newspaper and one copy of a national quality newspaper published on the same day.

1 Compare the content of the two newspapers and discuss the similarities and differences between them. For example, do they both have horoscopes, cartoons and crosswords? Are there sections on famous celebrities, scandal and gossip? How much emphasis is there on topics such as international news, politics, fashion and sports? How much space is taken up by photographs and headlines?

2 Note down three similarities and three differences between the quality and the mass-market newspapers.

💡 STRETCH AND CHALLENGE ACTIVITY

How far is the distinction between the quality press and the tabloids a useful one today?

CHECK YOUR UNDERSTANDING

1 Explain, with examples, what sociologists mean by the term 'mass media'.

2 Explain briefly, with examples, what is meant by 'traditional media' and 'new media'.

KEY POINTS

The mass media are forms of communication that reach a mass audience. They can be divided into three categories: press, broadcasting and electronic media.

What are the broadcast and electronic media?

OBJECTIVE

Explain what broadcast and electronic media are

Broadcasting in Britain

Broadcasting refers to television and radio. In Britain, some broadcasting is publicly funded, but most is financed privately. Public service broadcasting (PSB) operates through the BBC (British Broadcasting Corporation), which is funded by income from the television licence fee. Because it offers a public service, the BBC is expected to provide high standard programmes that deal with a range of subjects and satisfy the interests of different audiences.

Commercial broadcasting is funded mainly through advertising. Advertisers pay for commercials to promote their products. Additionally, companies may sponsor particular television programmes by paying for their company's logo to appear at the beginning and end of the programmes, as well as either side of a commercial break.

Satellite and cable television are funded partly by advertisers. They are also funded by income from subscription fees, Pay Per View and income from audience members who phone or text programmes.

Television broadcasting

The table below shows some of the main television networks in Britain, examples of the channels they provide and their means of distribution (the way they are broadcast). With terrestrial channels, broadcasts are delivered by ground transmitters rather than by satellite or cable signals.

The digital television switchover taking place in the UK is the process of turning off the analogue television signal and replacing it with a digital signal, which is clearer and gives a better picture. It started in 2008 and is due to be completed in 2012. Freeview is a digital terrestrial service that provides many digital channels for free.

Networks	Examples of TV channels	Distribution
BBC	BBC 1, 2, 3, 4 CBBC, BBC News 24, BBC Parliament	terrestrial analogue*, Freeview, cable, satellite
ITV	ITV 1, 2, 3, 4	terrestrial analogue*, Freeview, cable, satellite
Channel 4	C4, E4, More4, Film4	terrestrial analogue*, Freeview, cable, satellite
Five	Five, Five Life, Five US	terrestrial analogue*, Freeview, cable, satellite
Sky	Sky Movies, Sky1, Sky Sports 1, Sky Sports 2, Sky News	Freeview (News and Travel only), cable, satellite

* Until the switchover from analogue to digital TV.
Source: adapted from Branston and Stafford (2006)

Sponsorship

Some commercial television programmes are sponsored by companies such as Specsavers, Sainsbury's and Carphone Warehouse.

1 Note down three television programmes that receive sponsorship and, for each, identify their sponsor.

2 Give two possible reasons why such companies pay to sponsor television programmes.

Radio broadcasting

The following table shows some of the main BBC and commercial radio stations in Britain.

BBC Radio	National (e.g. Radio 1, 2, 3, 4, Radio Five Live)
	Local (e.g. BBC Radio Merseyside, BBC Radio Suffolk)
Commercial Radio	National (e.g. Classic FM, talkSport)
	Local (e.g. Piccadilly Key 103, Capital Radio)

Electronic media

The internet is an electronic medium (singular of media) which became available in the 1990s. The internet is a huge, interconnected set of computer networks spanning the globe. The World Wide Web is a collection of documents, video, sound, images and other resources. These are often linked by hyperlinks and accessed via their internet address (Oates, 2008). The internet hosts:

- the World Wide Web
- services such as e-mail.

Anyone can put things on the internet – you do not have to be a media professional to generate content for the internet. We can create (rather than just consume) media output such as websites and blogs, and we can upload music. We can also contribute articles to online projects such as Wikipedia, the online encyclopaedia. Additionally, individuals can join social network sites, such as MySpace, YouTube and Facebook.

Through the internet we can now produce content as well as consuming media content. Why is this seen as a significant change in our relationship with the media?

Social network sites are among the most-visited sites in the UK.

1 What does the term 'broadcasting' refer to?

2 Describe one way in which people can create content on the internet.

Broadcasting (TV and radio) may be funded publicly or privately. The internet became available in the 1990s and hosts the World Wide Web and e-mail.

TOPIC 3 — What technological developments have affected the mass media over the last 30 years?

OBJECTIVE
Explain developments in mass media technology over the last 30 years

Over the last 30 years, there have been important developments in the technology of the mass media. Some of these are outlined below.

Television has changed dramatically due to new technologies. In 1980, there were just three television channels in Britain: BBC 1, BBC 2 and ITV. They were all terrestrial channels. Since then, the number of channels available has increased significantly. In addition to receiving Channel 4 and Channel 5, we can now subscribe to a range of satellite and cable television channels.

Digital broadcasting provides multi-channel television with high-quality pictures and sound. It can be received by subscribing to a digital satellite service such as Sky, or to a digital cable service such as NTL. It can also be received through a digital terrestrial service called Freeview. New television sets may have a built-in Freeview tuner. You can also receive digital TV via a set-top box decoder and normal TV aerial. You make a single payment to Freeview for the set-top box but you do not have to pay a subscription.

Press the red button!

Digital TV services offer interactivity. Viewers can interact with the TV by pressing the red button on their digital television handsets to enter competitions or vote for someone on a reality show. Increasingly, the content of television programmes has a cross-media dimension. This means that you can interact with the programme through other forms of media such as mobile phones and the internet. For example, popular programmes such as *The X Factor* and *Strictly Come Dancing* have an interactive element to them where viewers send texts from their mobile phones.

Digital technology allows images, sounds and information to be delivered across the internet, mobile phones and television. When different types of media, telecommunications and computing come together in this way, it is known as convergence. Some mobile phones, for example, can send and receive texts and e-mails and connect to the internet.

Digital technology in action.

Digital radio services allow more stations to be broadcast with better sound quality than through analogue services. We can now listen to digital radio stations on digital televisions.

Services such as Teletext on ITV and Ceefax on BBC give us access to regularly updated news and information on a variety of subjects via our television screens. Through dedicated television channels and the internet, we can now access 24-hour rolling news. As a result, we can access breaking news stories and follow events as they unfold.

Glossary terms: convergence   interactivity

Newspaper production now involves the use of the latest technology such as computerized layout and digitized printing. Electronic versions of newspapers can be accessed via the internet.

Multi-channel television
✣ DISCUSSION ACTIVITY

1 In a small group, discuss what the benefits of multi-channel television might be to the viewer. Can you think of any disadvantages?
2 Note down at least two benefits and two disadvantages of multi-channel television.

Technological developments
✒ WRITTEN ACTIVITY

Copy and complete the following table. Under 'What the term means', write down your definition of the term. In the next column, note down the advantages and disadvantages of this for the consumer.

Development in technology	What the term means	What the development means for the consumer
Digitalization		
Interactivity		
Convergence		
The internet		

💡 STRETCH AND CHALLENGE ACTIVITY

How far do you agree that some groups might benefit more than others from these developments? Which groups might be left behind?

CHECK YOUR UNDERSTANDING

Describe and explain two ways in which the technology of the mass media has developed over the last 30 years.

KEY POINT

Important developments in mass media technology over the last 30 years include cable and satellite TV, digitalization, interactivity, convergence and the internet.

How widespread is newspaper readership?

OBJECTIVES
Outline national daily newspaper circulation figures
Identify changes in newspaper readership

We encounter the mass media almost everywhere and most of us have regular access to at least one medium of mass communication. Sociologists are interested in studying the media audience or consumers. One area of interest is how much media we actually consume: how many newspapers are sold each day, which television programmes have the largest audiences and how often we use the internet.

People engage in a wide range of activities in their leisure time, such as socializing with friends, going shopping and playing sport. Some of the activities that people do in their free time, such as watching TV, playing computer games or reading newspapers are related to the mass media.

Newspaper circulation

Newspaper circulation figures

DISCUSSION ACTIVITY

The table provides circulation figures for 10 national daily newspapers in September 2007. There is a mixture of quality, middle-market and mass-market newspapers.

Examine these figures then answer the following questions.

1 Write down the heading 'National daily newspaper circulation figures, September 2007'.

2 List the 10 newspapers in order of circulation, starting with the one with the highest circulation and finishing with the lowest.

3 In a small group, decide whether each of the 10 newspapers is a quality, middle market or mass-market publication. Note down your answers.

4 In your group, decide whether the quality, middle-market or mass-market publications have the highest circulation figures. Note down your answer.

Newspaper	Circulation
Daily Express	794 252
Daily Mail	2 365 499
Daily Mirror	1 584 742
Daily Star	811 988
Daily Telegraph	890 973
Financial Times	441 219
Guardian	367 546
Independent	251 470
Sun	3 128 829
Times	635 653

Source: Audit Bureau of Circulations (ABC) & Brad UK Media Ownership Guide 2007

Trends in newspaper readership

Drawing on data from British Social Attitudes surveys, Curtice and Mair (2008) examine the changes in newspaper readership between 1983 and 2006. In 1983, 77 per cent of adults in Britain said they regularly read a daily morning newspaper. By 2006, however, only 50 per cent did so.

Curtice and Mair found that not all newspapers have suffered a decline in readership. The readership of quality newspapers such as the *Daily Telegraph* and *The Independent* has remained fairly stable. The decline is among the readership of the popular newspapers such as the *Daily Mail* and *Daily Mirror*. The changes are shown in the table below.

Curtice and Mair (2008) found little evidence to suggest that this decline in readership is linked to the development of electronic versions of newspapers available online. For example, only 3 per cent of those who did not read a newspaper regularly in 2006 consulted a newspaper website at least three times per week.

Changes in newspaper readership 1983–2006

Percentage of adults who say they regularly read a daily morning newspaper (at least three times a week) in Britain

	1983 (%)	2006 (%)
Popular newspapers	57	33
Quality newspapers	10	12

Source: adapted from Curtice and Mair (2008)

WRITTEN ACTIVITY

According to this information:

1 What percentage of respondents regularly read a daily morning popular newspaper in 1983?

2 What percentage of respondents regularly read a daily morning quality newspaper in 2006?

3 By what percentage did the proportion of adults who regularly read a daily morning popular newspaper decline between 1983 and 2006?

4 By what percentage did the proportion of adults who regularly read a daily morning quality newspaper increase between 1983 and 2006?

STRETCH AND CHALLENGE ACTIVITY

Some commentators are concerned about the decline in newspaper readership. Why do you think the decline is seen as a cause for concern?

CHECK YOUR UNDERSTANDING

Describe one change in newspaper readership over the last 25 years.

KEY POINTS

Sociologists study how much media we consume. There has been a decline in the readership of popular newspapers in the last 25 years.

TOPIC 5 How much television do audiences watch?

OBJECTIVES

Outline the growth in ownership of digital TV services
Describe TV viewing habits

Sociologists are interested in studying television audiences. One area of interest includes how much television we watch each day and which programmes attract the biggest audiences.

Television viewing habits

WRITTEN ACTIVITY

The Taking Part survey asked adults in England about their television viewing habits. The table shows some of the findings from this survey.

According to this information:

1 What percentage of respondents watch television for around 3 hours per day?

2 What percentage of respondents watch comedy programmes?

3 Which type of programme is most popular?

Adults in England...	Percentages
watch TV for an average of 2 hours per day	27
watch TV for an average of 3 hours per day	23
watch the news (national or local)	65
watch films	61
watch comedy	54
watch live sport coverage	51

Source: *Social Trends* (2008)

Audiences and broadcasters

WRITTEN ACTIVITY

The pie chart shows the proportion of the television audience that different broadcasters attracted in 2007. Study this information and answer the questions below.

1 What percentage of audience share does Virgin attract?

2 What percentage of audience share does Five attract?

3 Which broadcaster attracts the biggest share of the audience?

4 Which two broadcasters together attract over 55 per cent of the audience?

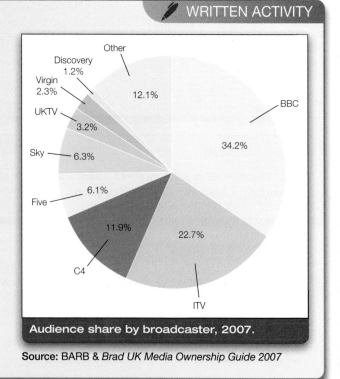

Audience share by broadcaster, 2007.

Source: BARB & *Brad UK Media Ownership Guide 2007*

Ownership of a digital television service (including digital, satellite and cable receivers) has grown steadily since the 1990s. In 1996/97, 19 per cent of UK households owned a digital television service and by 2005/06, 65 per cent of households owned one. By March 2007, 81 per cent of homes in the UK had a digital television service.

People often subscribe to a digital television service to access more channels or particular channels. Supporters of multi-channel television emphasize the wide choice of channels it offers to consumers. We can now subscribe to and watch channels that are dedicated to particular interests, for example, music, news, sport or films. Other reasons include the higher quality of the picture. Critics, however, argue that having more channels does not necessarily guarantee that viewers have more choice. They just have more of the same.

Most popular TV programmes

✎ WRITTEN ACTIVITY

The table provides information on the top 10 most popular programmes broadcast in the UK between January and November 2007. Study this information and answer the questions that follow.

1 Television programmes can be divided into 'types' of programme, such as current affairs, soaps, documentaries and films. Although 10 different programmes are shown in the table, we can divide these into types. Identify four different types of programme that appear in the table.

2 Which television channels broadcast the programmes with the biggest audiences?

Top 10 performing programmes in the UK, January–November 2007

	Programme	Millions	Channel
1	Rugby World Cup Final 2007 Sat 20th Oct 19:29	13.13	ITV1
2	Coronation Street Mon 15th Jan 20:30	13.08	ITV1
3	The Vicar of Dibley Mon 1st Jan 21:33	13.08	BBC1
4	Concert for Diana Sun 1st July 20:10	12.22	BBC1
5	Britain's Got Talent Sun 17th June 20:00	11.58	ITV1
6	EastEnders Mon 9th Apr 21:03	11.56	BBC1
7	Dancing On Ice Sat 17th Mar 18:29	10.04	ITV1
8	Doc Martin Mon 29th Oct 21:01	9.92	ITV1
9	The X Factor Sat 18th Aug 19:39	9.79	ITV1
10	Comic Relief – The Big One Fri 16th Mar 18:59	9.73	BBC1

Source: BARB & *Brad UK Media Ownership Guide 2007*

CHECK YOUR UNDERSTANDING

Identify two reasons why people get a digital television service.

KEY POINTS

Ownership of a digital television service has grown steadily since the 1990s. Watching television is a popular activity in leisure time.

TOPIC 6 What use do people make of the internet?

OBJECTIVES

Describe how widespread internet access is
Identify reasons for accessing the internet

Internet access

Currently, people can access the internet via a desktop or laptop computer, a hand-held computer, a mobile phone or a digital television.

In the UK, the internet can be accessed relatively easily.

- Household internet access has grown rapidly in the UK from 10 per cent of households in 1998/99 to 55 per cent in 2005/06. By 2007, 61 per cent of UK households had internet access.

- Household access to the internet is linked to income. High-income households are more likely than low-income households to have internet access. In 2005/06, for example, 93 per cent of households in the highest income group (out of 10 income groups) and 17 per cent in the lowest income group had an internet connection.

Access to and use of the internet ✎ WRITTEN ACTIVITY

Adults in the UK...	Percentage	
	2001/02	2006
used the internet in last 3 months and lived in households with internet access	37	52
used the internet in last 3 months, but lived in households without internet access	11	7
do not use internet but have household access	9	9
do not use internet and do not have household access	43	31

Source: adapted from *Focus on the Digital Age* (ONS, 2007) pp. 3–4

According to this information:

1 What percentage used the internet in the last 3 months but did not have internet access in their household
a) in 2001/02?   b) in 2006?
2 What percentage neither used the internet nor had access in their household in 2006?
3 What was the increase between 2001/02 and 2006 in the proportion of people that used the internet in the last 3 months and had internet access in their household?

👁 Eye on the exam

When you are doing your revision, have a look at the CHECK YOUR UNDERSTANDING questions for the topic you have revised. Can you answer these questions without re-reading the material in the topic? Remember to ask your teacher if there is anything you are not sure about.

Reasons for accessing the internet

People access the internet for many reasons. They use it to:

- look for information
- send and receive e-mails
- browse generally
- buy and sell
- bank online
- play games
- make travel arrangements
- visit chat rooms
- download music
- read online news
- listen to radio
- watch television.

The most common reasons people use the internet are to find information about goods and services and to send and receive e-mails. In 2007, 86 per cent of UK adult internet users had used the internet during the three months before the interview to find information about goods and services. In addition, 85 per cent used the internet to send and receive e-mails.

People's use of the internet varies depending on their age. In 2007, young people aged between 16 and 24 were more likely than people in other age groups to play or download games, films, music or images and to look for information about education on the internet.

Researching media consumption — RESEARCH ACTIVITY

1 Design a short questionnaire to find out about the participation of people from different age groups in activities related to the media. You could begin by producing a list of eight media-related activities, such as watching television and going online. You could then design questions about whether people participate in each of these activities and, if so, how regularly, for example, daily, weekly or monthly.
2 Pilot your questionnaire on a sample size of 10.
3 Make a note of the three most significant results from your pilot questionnaire.

STRETCH AND CHALLENGE ACTIVITY

How far do you think having access to the internet at home is a necessity? How far is it a luxury? Are people who do not have the internet at home disadvantaged when, for example, it comes to doing homework or applying for jobs?

CHECK YOUR UNDERSTANDING

1 Identify two reasons why people use the internet.
2 Which households are more likely to have internet access at home?

KEY POINTS

Household access to the internet has grown rapidly since the late 1990s. People access the internet, for example, to send e-mails and find information about goods and services.

What are the effects of the mass media on their audiences?

OBJECTIVE

Discuss the 'hypodermic syringe' and 'uses and gratifications' approaches to studying the impact of the mass media on audiences

Members of the public, politicians and policymakers have, for a long time, been concerned about the power of the media and its possible harmful effects on audiences. For example, debates have focused on how far the media can influence people's political attitudes and behaviour and how far violent content on the screen can lead to real-life violence. Researchers disagree on the issue of how the mass media impact on their audiences.

The 'hypodermic syringe' approach

During the early 20th century, it was believed that the mass media of the time (which did not include television) could have a lot of power over the audience. The press, for example, was regarded as a potentially powerful means of controlling and persuading people.

The hypodermic syringe model is one of the earliest approaches to studying the effects of the media on audiences. The idea behind this approach is that the audience receives daily injections of messages from television and newspapers. These messages work like a drug. They are seen as having a direct and powerful effect on the audience's attitudes and behaviour.

The hypodermic syringe model saw the media as having a powerful effect on behaviour.

The uses and gratifications approach

While the hypodermic syringe approach emphasizes what the media do to their audiences, the uses and gratifications model focuses on what audiences do with the media. The uses and gratifications approach focuses on how we, as members of the audience, use the media. It examines the individual needs that are gratified, or met, by the media. Some of us, for example, watch television quiz programmes because they offer excitement, education and a chance for us to try to beat the experts.

McQuail (1987; 2003) found that the needs which television most satisfied were for the following:

- Information – we might watch daily news broadcasts or documentaries to find out what is happening in the world.
- Personal identity – we might watch programmes such as *Trisha* because they enable us to gain insight into ourselves.
- Personal relationships – we could watch a soap opera, for instance, as a substitute for real-life companionship or as a source of conversation.
- Entertainment and diversion – we watch comedy shows, for example, to escape from our problems, to relax or to fill time.

Glossary terms: power

The hypodermic syringe

Read through the extract below, then answer the question that follows.

> In the early twentieth century, there was a widespread belief that the mass media could exert powerful effects on people. It was believed that the media could be used for propaganda purposes (such as spreading a set of political beliefs).
>
> Theorists discussed such concepts as the 'hypodermic needle' effects, which maintained that the media only needed to present a persuasive message and the audience would accept it and act upon it in exactly the way the message-sender desired.
>
> However, this view was challenged in the years following the Second World War. Scholars observed firstly that such direct effects were not always measurable, and secondly that consumers would not routinely accept, without question, everything the media told them.
>
> The belief in the powerful effects of the media was therefore replaced by the idea that the media had only limited effects on audiences.

Source: adapted from Gunter (2008)

Describe briefly how the hypodermic syringe approach appears to view the audience.
For example, are people seen as critical or uncritical?

1 The extract identifies two criticisms of the hypodermic syringe approach. Briefly explain these in your own words.

2 In your opinion, how might the hypodermic syringe approach view the power of advertisements over the audience?

The popularity of reality TV

The table on page 197 shows that some reality TV programmes are very popular and can attract millions of viewers.

In a small group, discuss why people watch reality TV programmes such as *The X Factor*, *I'm a Celebrity... Get Me Out of Here*, *The Apprentice* or *Big Brother*.

Make a note of three possible needs that such programmes might satisfy for viewers.

Describe three ways in which audiences use the mass media.

The impact of the mass media on audiences has been disputed. Supporters of the hypodermic syringe model argue that the media could have powerful effects on people's behaviour or beliefs. The uses and gratifications approach examines what people do with the media and what needs the media satisfy.

What are the effects of the media according to the decoding approach?

OBJECTIVE

Discuss the decoding approach to studying the impact of the mass media on audiences

Some researchers are interested in the idea of audience members as 'decoders'. Abercrombie (1996) explains this approach as follows:

> We are all familiar with the idea of a spy decoding a message from his or her controller. In the same way, the television audience decodes or interprets a message from a TV programme. The difference is that, with a spy message, there is only one possible correct meaning which the spy carefully decodes. In the television message, however, there are several possible meanings and so there are several different ways of decoding the message.

Source: adapted from Abercrombie (1996)

This approach suggests that the content of a particular television programme, such as a news bulletin, has several possible meanings. It may, therefore, be decoded or interpreted in a number of ways.

Different sections of the audience may decode or interpret the contents of a television programme in very different ways. The way a particular programme is decoded may depend on, for example, the social and cultural backgrounds of different sections of the audience. For example, a worker involved in strike action is likely to interpret news bulletins about the strike differently from the senior managers.

The contents of news bulletins may be interpreted in different ways.

How we decode a particular programme is shaped by our cultural and social backgrounds, our age, gender and ethnicity. How we actually respond to the programme's messages depends on our own reading of it.

Decoding TV programmes   ❖ DISCUSSION ACTIVITY

1 In pairs, choose two of the following television programmes:

- *Neighbours*
- *Question Time*
- *Blue Peter*
- *The Bill*
- *Friends*
- *News at Ten and Weather*
- *Doctor Who*
- *Little Britain*
- *The Simpsons*
- *Top Gear.*

2 For each, suggest how the programme might possibly be decoded or interpreted by the four people listed below. In your discussion, you could focus on how watchable, relevant and interesting each of the four might find the two programmes.

- a school girl aged 10
- a male university student aged 21
- a female GP aged 36
- a retired bus driver in his 70s.

3 Make a note of four points arising from your discussion.

The decoding approach sees the audience very differently from the way the hypodermic approach sees it. While the hypodermic syringe approach views the audience as passively receiving media messages, the decoding approach sees audience members as actively interpreting these messages.

Eye on the exam

The CHECK YOUR UNDERSTANDING question below is an example of the more challenging exam questions which ask you to "discuss how far sociologists would agree" with a particular view or statement.

To gain high marks in such questions, you will need to assess and evaluate information and evidence. In other words, you should provide evidence and arguments for and against the view expressed.

In tackling the question below, you could discuss the hypodermic syringe approach to illustrate the view that the mass media have a direct and immediate effect on audiences. To achieve top marks, however, you also need to tackle 'how far'. You could do this by discussing alternative sociological explanations of the effects of the mass media on audiences, such as the decoding approach.

You also need to reach a clear conclusion on the issue of 'how far' or to what extent. Your conclusions about 'how far' should be based on the arguments and evidence you have provided in your response.

Comparing approaches

WRITTEN ACTIVITY

Copy and complete the following table comparing different views of the media.

	Decoding approach	Hypodermic syringe approach
View of the audience		
View on how powerful the media are		
View of media messages – one message or many messages?		

STRETCH AND CHALLENGE ACTIVITY

Which of these two approaches do you think provides a more satisfactory account of the relationship between the media and the audience?

CHECK YOUR UNDERSTANDING

Discuss how far sociologists would agree that the mass media have a direct and immediate effect on audiences.

KEY POINT

The decoding approach views audience members as active interpreters of media messages.

TOPIC 9 **What is the role of the mass media in the socialization process?**

OBJECTIVES

Describe the mass media's role in the socialization process

Describe the links between socialization, identity development and the mass media

Socialization is an important concept in sociology (see page 10). It describes the process through which we learn the culture of the society or group we are born into. The agencies of socialization are central to the process of socialization. They are the groups and institutions which contribute to the socialization process (see page 10). Agencies of socialization include families, schools, peer groups, religions, workplaces and the mass media.

Mass media as an agency of socialization

The mass media play an important role in the socialization process. They are powerful sources of information and knowledge about the world. Magazines, for example, often have advice on life and relationships.

Sometimes, the media put forward messages about gender. Gauntlett (2008), for example, points out that in 2007, the UK supermarket chain Iceland was still using the slogan "That's why mums go to Iceland" in its TV advertisements. By providing messages about the role of women, the media can be seen as contributing to gender socialization.

Gunter (2008) points out that the media's influences may be subtle. However, these influences build up over time. Take, for example, exposure to advertisements with women promoting washing-up liquid and men promoting cars. Repeated over time, such stereotyped portrayals could encourage the idea that decisions about washing-up liquid are best taken by women and decisions about cars are best taken by men. (See Chapter 5 Crime and Deviance for a discussion about stereotypes.)

Socialization, identity and the mass media

The agencies of socialization play an important part in the development of our identities. Identity refers to how we see ourselves (our self-identity) and how other people see us. Sources of identity include our gender, age, ethnicity, social class, religion and sexuality.

Even though we may not consciously think about identity, we make choices throughout our lives related to our own identity, how we see ourselves and how we want others to see us. Such choices relate to clothing, jewellery, hairstyle, tattoos, piercings and leisure activities. Decisions about our relationships, friendship groups, careers and political beliefs are also related to issues of identity.

Traditionally, sociologists saw people's social class or gender as key parts of their social and political identities. Identity was generally linked to occupation and status. Ball et al (2000) express this in terms of "we are what we do". For example, when people say, "I'm a house-husband" or, "I'm a musician" they are expressing this aspect of their identity.

Glossary terms: identity sexuality

Expressing aspects of identities through dress

Examine the photographs below and, for each, discuss and note down what possible aspects of the individual's identity are being expressed through dress.

However, Ball and colleagues (2000) argue that the identities of young people today cannot be understood in terms of traditional categories of class and gender. In fact, very few of the young people interviewed by Ball et al referred directly to their social class or gender. Some young people from minority ethnic groups, however, saw their 'race' as a key aspect of their identity.

The mass media, identity and lifestyles

In developing our identities, we make choices about our lifestyles or way of living. We could choose, for example, a lifestyle focused on success at work or one centred on clubbing. Gauntlett (2008) argues that the mass media are important in spreading ideas about many modern lifestyles, such as dance music and clubbing.

> A young person interested in dance music and clubbing might 'learn' about this scene first of all from the glossy dance music magazines. Real-life experience might lead this view to be adapted or replaced. But the magazines would still exert an influence by associating the lifestyle with glamour, or drugs, or whatever.

Source: adapted from Gauntlett (2008)

Explain briefly one way in which the mass media can spread ideas about modern lifestyles.

CHECK YOUR UNDERSTANDING

1 Identify and explain one way in which the media play a role in the socialization process

2 What do sociologists mean by the term 'identity'?

3 Describe one way in which the mass media might play a part in the development of people's identities.

KEY POINT

The mass media are an important agency of socialization and play a key part in developing people's social identities.

TOPIC 10 What is the mass media's role in political socialization?

OBJECTIVES

Explain the term political socialization
Discuss the influence of the mass media on voting behaviour

The mass media and political socialization

During the process of political socialization, we acquire political values, beliefs and preferences. The political views we develop, in turn, affect whether we participate in political activities and the way we vote. The media are significant in the political socialization process because they are often our main source of information about politicians and current affairs. In democracies, the media are seen as having an important role during election campaigns.

The mass media and voting behaviour

Traditionally, most newspapers in Britain have tended to side with one political party or another. Over the years, for example, the *Daily Telegraph* has supported the Conservative Party and the *Daily Mirror* has supported the Labour Party. A newspaper's political outlook or leaning can affect which stories are covered in detail and how they are reported. Curtice and Mair (2008) argue that someone who reads one particular newspaper regularly is likely to be exposed to a slant on current affairs that could encourage them to vote for one party over another.

In general terms, we can say that since 1945, the press has been more supportive of the Conservatives than of Labour. Consequently, many Labour Party members have felt that the Conservative Party has had an unfair advantage during elections.

During the 1992 general election campaign, for example, five out of six national tabloid newspapers supported the Conservative Party. *The Sun,* for instance, made it clear that it was not in favour of a Labour victory. Such coverage could influence our views of particular politicians and their party. When the Conservative Party's unexpected victory was announced, *The Sun* claimed, rightly or wrongly, to have influenced the outcome of the general election.

During the 1997 general election, however, newspaper coverage was more balanced. For example, *The Sun* announced its support for Tony Blair and New Labour. A total of six national dailies backed the Labour Party. Curtice and Mair (2008) note that it is not clear whether the newspapers' switch to Labour helped to bring Labour many votes. It may be that newspapers feared losing readers unless they switched to the party that many of their readers were already backing. If this is the case, the press may not be so powerful in influencing voting behaviour.

DISCUSSION ACTIVITY

The media and elections

If the mass media have the power or ability to influence the outcome of elections, and are slanted towards one political party or another, then this could be seen as a major problem in a democracy.

In a small group, discuss the possible reasons why this could be seen as a cause for concern in democracies. Make a note of three reasons.

Glossary terms: political socialization   democracy

WRITTEN ACTIVITY

The press and the 2005 general election

The table shows the national daily newspapers' party support in the 2005 general election campaign.

1 Which party did the mass-market tabloids tend to support?

2 What outcomes did the middle-market tabloids want?

3 Which party did the 'quality' press tend to support?

Mirror	Labour victory
Express	Conservative victory
Sun	Labour victory
Daily Mail	Not a Labour victory
Daily Star	No preference declared
Daily Telegraph	Conservative victory
Guardian	Labour victory
Times	Labour victory
Independent	More Liberal Democrats
Financial Times	Labour victory

Source: adapted from Scammell and Harrop (2005)

Curtice and Mair (2008) outline two concerns that are often raised in relation to the press's influence on voting behaviour:

- The press has too much influence on how people vote.
- The press's negative coverage of politics and criticism of all politicians has discouraged voters from voting at all.

Curtice and Mair point out that these concerns assume that newspapers influence relatively large numbers of readers and voters. However, as we have seen, their analysis of data from British Social Attitudes surveys (see page 195) suggests that readership of popular newspapers has fallen sharply. Curtice and Mair note that the decline in readership could actually be seen as healthy for British democracy. If readership is declining, then:

- newspapers' ability to influence the outcomes of general elections (as *The Sun* claimed to have done in 1992) will also have declined
- fewer people will be exposed to the press's supposedly negative coverage of politics and politicians that discourages people from voting at all.

However, the decline in readership of popular newspapers can also be seen as unhealthy for democracy. This is because popular newspapers will be less likely to play a role in providing information to people who are not particularly interested in politics.

STRETCH AND CHALLENGE ACTIVITY

How has *The Sun*'s support for Labour changed since the 1992 general election?

CHECK YOUR UNDERSTANDING

1 Identify one way in which the media may influence the results of a general election.

2 Explain why this could cause concern in a democratic society.

KEY POINT

The mass media, along with other agencies of socialization, play an important part in developing people's political beliefs and voting behaviour.

TOPIC 11 · What are the patterns of ownership within the press?

OBJECTIVE
Describe patterns of newspaper ownership

The concentration of newspaper ownership has been a long-standing source of concern in Britain. At the turn of the 20th century, for example, the rise of press barons such as Lord Northcliffe (who founded the *Daily Mail* in 1896) in England and Pulitzer in the USA fuelled fears about the press's influence in democracies.

Critics feared that these press barons would use their ownership of newspapers to restrict the flow of information and debates. For example, it was believed that they could potentially abuse their power as newspaper owners to:

* promote their own political beliefs
* criticize politicians, political parties and other individuals and views they disagreed with.

Press ownership today

Newspapers in Britain are all privately owned and a small number of large corporations own the majority of them. This means that, potentially, some individuals in a particular corporation have a lot of power because the

Ownership of the press

WRITTEN ACTIVITY

The information in the table shows national media publishers in 2007. Study this information, then answer the following questions.

According to this information:

1 Which company publishes *The Guardian*?
2 Which company publishes *The Sun*?
3 How many organizations in total publish the bulk of national newspapers?

Publisher	Newspapers
News International	*The Sun, News of the World* *Times, Sunday Times* *The Times Literary Supplement*
Trinity Mirror	*Daily Mirror, Sunday Mirror* *The People* *Scotland's Daily Record* *Sunday Mail*
Daily Mail and General Trust	*Daily Mail* *The Mail on Sunday*
Northern and Shell	*Daily Express, Sunday Express* *Daily Star, Daily Star – Sunday*
Guardian Media Group	*The Guardian* *The Observer*
Independent News and Media	*The Independent* *Independent on Sunday*
Pearson	*The Financial Times*
Telegraph Media Group	*Daily Telegraph* *Sunday Telegraph*
Newsquest	*The Herald*

Source: adapted from Audit Bureau of Circulations (ABC) & *Brad UK Media Ownership Guide 2007*

company is family-owned or because they have controlling shareholdings. By contrast, *The Independent* was set up to avoid the situation in which powerful individuals are able to dominate.

WRITTEN ACTIVITY

Newspaper publishers' market share

Critics of concentrated press ownership argue that, in order to safeguard democracy:

- the power to communicate should be distributed more widely
- ownership of the press should be spread out as widely as possible.

The pie chart shows the market share of national daily papers according to publisher.

1 What percentage of the market share of national daily newspapers did
  a) Trinity Mirror have?
  b) the Telegraph Media Group have?

2 Which two groups together account for over 50 per cent of sales of national daily newspapers?

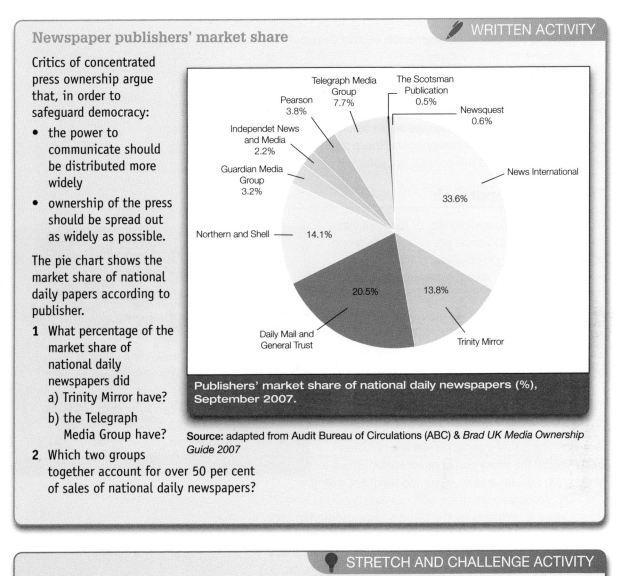

Telegraph Media Group 7.7%
The Scotsman Publication 0.5%
Pearson 3.8%
Newsquest 0.6%
Independet News and Media 2.2%
Guardian Media Group 3.2%
News International 33.6%
Northern and Shell — 14.1%
20.5%
13.8%
Daily Mail and General Trust
Trinity Mirror

Publishers' market share of national daily newspapers (%), September 2007.

Source: adapted from Audit Bureau of Circulations (ABC) & *Brad UK Media Ownership Guide 2007*

STRETCH AND CHALLENGE ACTIVITY

1 Does this information suggest that ownership of the press is spread out widely or concentrated? Write a short paragraph to explain your answer.

2 Explain why concentration of press ownership might be a problem in a democracy.

CHECK YOUR UNDERSTANDING

Describe and explain one characteristic of press ownership in Britain.

KEY POINTS

In the UK, newspapers are privately owned and ownership is concentrated. Potentially, some individuals in media corporations have a lot of power.

TOPIC 12 # What is the pluralist approach to press ownership and content?

OBJECTIVE

Discuss the pluralist approach to the debate on ownership, control and content of newspapers

A key concern among sociologists today is whether, through their ownership or control of the media, particular individuals and organizations have the power to impose their views on audiences. In the debates on ownership and control of newspapers, there are two broad approaches: the pluralist approach and the conflict approach.

The pluralist approach

According to this view, a plurality or range of views and interests exists in society and no single group dominates. This range of opinions and views is reflected in the wide variety of newspapers and magazines available to us.

Diverse publications such as the *Morning Star, the Telegraph, The Sun, Gay Times, Woman's Weekly, Country Life, Hi-Fi World, Mojo, The Voice* and *Viz* give scope for everyone's views to be catered for. Those who support the pluralist approach argue that all points of view, voices and interests are represented within this wide range of content.

Pluralists argue that there is no real link between ownership of the press and content. Newspapers simply give people what they want to read. For example, *The Sun* carries very little international news because its readers do not want it, not because the owners have decided to exclude it. Owners cannot influence the content of newspapers because if they tried to give us what we do not want, we would simply stop buying their product. In this case, firms who fail to provide what we want are unlikely to succeed in the market and could face bankruptcy.

Diversity in publishing.

Pluralism and freedom of the press

The pluralist view supports the idea of freedom of the press. In the view of pluralists, the press is and should be free from the control and interference of owners. Pluralists argue that freedom of the press exists because:

*   We, as members of the public, exercise control through our market power. We can easily switch newspapers if we are unhappy with the content of a particular newspaper. Hence, the market controls content and the consumer is sovereign.
*   Owners cannot simply dictate content but have to give us what we want to buy.

Glossary terms: pluralism

- There is freedom to set up new newspapers if existing ones do not meet market demands.
- We can put forward our views on an issue and have them published by writing letters to the editor of a newspaper.
- On a day-to-day basis, the media professionals, such as newspaper editors and journalists, rather than the owners exercise control over content.

Eye on the exam

Remember to refer to the relevant sociological approaches (e.g. the pluralist approach) in your answers.

WRITTEN ACTIVITY

The diminishing power of media owners

Read through the information below, then answer the question that follows.

With developments in digital technology, some commentators suggest that the power and influence of media owners will diminish. They also suggest that concentration of ownership will become less of a concern. This is because:

- In theory, digital technology enables anyone to produce media. Through internet blogs, for example, consumers can create content and engage in public debate.
- Digital technology has led to an increase in the variety of media products available to us.
- The internet is becoming more accessible and affordable to everyone.

Explain one reason why developments in digital technology may mean that concentration of ownership will become less of a concern in the future.

STRETCH AND CHALLENGE ACTIVITY

Not everyone agrees with these views regarding the likely effects of developments in digital technology on the power and influence of owners. Can you identify one possible criticism of these views?

Eye on the exam

The stretch and challenge activity above asks you to critically examine ideas and information. As such, it provides a good opportunity for you to practise your evaluation skills.

CHECK YOUR UNDERSTANDING

1 According to the pluralist approach, how does the market control the content of newspapers?

2 Identify two reasons why, according to the pluralist view, freedom of the press exists.

KEY POINTS

Sociologists disagree on how much power and control owners exercise over content.

According to pluralists, no single group dominates, all viewpoints are represented within the printed media and consumer demand determines the news content.

TOPIC 13 · What is the conflict approach to press ownership and content?

OBJECTIVE

Discuss the conflict approach to the debate on ownership, control and content of newspapers

The conflict approach

The conflict approach views society as based on conflicting interests between different groups. The owners of newspapers are seen as part of a powerful and wealthy minority group. They are in a strong position to put their own personal views and interests across to the rest of us because, as owners, they are able to control the content of newspapers. They do so in their own interests.

If, for example, a large business concern owns a chain of newspapers, it is likely to encourage the production of news stories and advertisements which support the views of the business world. It is likely to discourage the production of material which is critical of big business. Articles written from the viewpoint of trade unions and environmental groups, for example, are less likely to appear.

On occasions, press owners have intervened directly to influence content. Harry Evans was hired as editor of the *Sunday Times* from 1967 to 1981 and editor of the *Times* from 1981 to 1982. He was allegedly fired from his post as editor of the *Times* by Rupert Murdoch, the owner, as a result of his (Evans') political policy.

Supporters of the conflict approach point to the following developments within the media as evidence to back up their views:

* There has been an increasing concentration of press ownership in the hands of a few companies and individuals. As part of this process, smaller companies have been swallowed up by media giants.

* Since the early days of the press barons, multimedia conglomerates such as News Corporation have emerged. Conglomerates are formed by different firms merging. They have stakes across a range of different media, for example in newspapers, books, films and digital TV services. Trinity Mirror, for instance, owns five national newspapers, more than 150 regional newspapers and more than 200 websites.

* These multimedia (or cross-media) conglomerates operate on a global rather than a national scale. This means that a small number of multinational companies now have interests in media across the globe.

* As a result of these developments, a large proportion of what we see, hear and read now comes from a few huge multinational media empires.

👁 Eye on the exam

Remember to use the relevant key terms (such as conglomerates and multimedia ownership) in your answers.

Glossary terms: conglomerate

CASE STUDY: RUPERT MURDOCH

- Rupert Murdoch is Chairperson and Chief Executive Officer of News Corporation, of which News International in the UK is a part. News Corporation owns newspapers in the UK including *The Sun,* the *News of the World*, the *Times*, the *Sunday Times, The Times Literary Supplement* and several evening and weekend newspapers. News International has a 33 per cent share of the national daily newspaper market (see page 209).

- News Corporation is one of the largest and most influential media groups in the world. It has interests in newspapers not only in the UK but also in Australia and the USA.

- In addition to its newspaper interests, it also has shares in magazines, HarperCollins book publishers, television films, Twentieth Century Fox Film, and cable and satellite broadcasting including a share in BSkyB.

- News Corporation's assets include MySpace, the social networking site.

Multimedia ownership

DISCUSSION ACTIVITY

Some individuals and groups express concern about developments in multimedia (or cross-media) ownership. They believe that the government should restrict the growth of such media empires.

1 In a small group, discuss the possible grounds for concern associated with cross-media ownership.

2 Make a note of two possible problems.

Comparing approaches

WRITTEN ACTIVITY

Copy and complete the following table comparing different views on press ownership and content.

	Pluralist approach	Conflict approach
Whose interests dominate in society?		
Who or what influences press content?		

STRETCH AND CHALLENGE ACTIVITY

Which of these two approaches do you think provides a more satisfactory account of the relationship between press ownership and content?

CHECK YOUR UNDERSTANDING

Identify and explain one factor which may influence the content of news.

KEY POINTS

The conflict approach argues that a small group of powerful press owners control the content of news. Recent developments (e.g. cross-media conglomeration) mean that much of what we read comes from a few multinational media empires.

TOPIC 14 How are news stories selected and presented?

OBJECTIVE

Outline the power of the media in agenda setting and norm referencing

We have discussed the view that those who own or work within media organizations such as newspapers have power over content. We will now examine the ways in which this power may be exercised in the selection and presentation of news.

Selection of news

✤ DISCUSSION ACTIVITY

In a small group, identify three issues that are hot topics in the news at the moment. Discuss the possible reasons why these particular issues have hit the news. How far does media coverage of these issues influence what topics we think and talk about?

Make a note of three points arising from your discussion.

It is easy for us to take the content of news on television and in newspapers at face value rather than question what is covered. Sociologists, however, focus on the issue of how news is selected and presented.

Potentially, there are an infinite number of issues and viewpoints in society, as well as countless events happening each day across the world. Sociologists are interested in exploring what is selected and covered as 'news' and what is ignored. They question why particular issues, events and viewpoints are included on television and in the press while others appear to be excluded. In considering this question, sociologists see the news as being manufactured or made.

Sociologists are also interested in examining how material is presented. Is it presented in a fair and neutral way or in a biased and one-sided way? Is it presented positively or negatively? Agenda setting and norm referencing are two processes that the media employ in selecting and presenting news content.

Agenda setting

The mass media have the power to 'set the agenda'. This refers to the way the news media focus public attention on particular issues and topics. In doing so, they tell us what the relevant and important issues are at any moment in time. Television news programmes, for example, may not tell us what to think but they do influence what we think about. They do this by discussing some issues and leaving out other topics.

In this sense, they set the agenda of public discussion and debate by including some views, stories and information and excluding others. Potentially this gives them a lot of influence over people's political views and the way they vote in elections.

Glossary terms: agenda setting   folk devil   gatekeepers   norm referencing

The role of media 'gatekeepers'

Media gatekeepers are the programme controllers, editors, journalists and owners who decide what to cover and how to present it. They can 'open the gate' to certain issues, events or points of view and 'close the gate' to others. This means that media gatekeepers are in a strong position to set the agenda of public debate and to influence what topics we think about.

Norm referencing

The mass media also have power in relation to norm referencing. The term 'norm referencing' describes the way in which the news media outline the acceptable boundaries of behaviour. The behaviour and views of some groups or organizations are presented positively and those of others are presented negatively. In this way, positive images of some groups (such as nurses and fire fighters) and negative images of others (such as asylum seekers and teenage parents) are created. Through this norm referencing, the media have the power to shape public opinion.

Some groups are presented positively and others are presented negatively in the media.

WRITTEN ACTIVITY

The media and folk devils

Groups such as lone mothers, environmentalists and animal rights activists are often presented negatively in the media. The consequences may be that we do not take their views seriously, we condemn their behaviour or we demand that action should be taken against them. In Cohen's (2002) view, unmarried mothers have the status of folk devils (see pages 184 and 224).

He argues that in the early 1990s, 'girls' were presented in the media as getting pregnant in order to become entitled to state benefits, 'extra handouts' or to jump the queue for public housing.

Identify one group that is presented negatively in the media and describe the consequences of this negative portrayal.

CHECK YOUR UNDERSTANDING

Explain one way in which those who own or work within media organizations may use their power to select and present news.

KEY POINTS

Sociologists study how news is selected and presented. They identify the media's role in agenda setting and norm referencing.

What other factors affect how news is selected and presented?

OBJECTIVE

Describe how factors such as news values, the profit motive, advertisers, the state and legal constraints affect the content of news

We have identified several factors that affect what we see, hear and read in the news and how it is presented. One view, as we have seen, is that content is heavily influenced by the views of owners. Owners, for example, have the power to hire and fire editors and other media professionals who produce the news.

The BBC, however, is technically without owners; it is 'owned' by the state. Consequently, the debate regarding the owners' influence on news content is not strictly applicable to the BBC.

Another view, from the pluralist approach, suggests that one of the most important influences on content is simply consumer demand within a competitive market.

In addition to the possible influences of owners and consumers, a number of other factors have been identified by researchers. These include: news values, the profit motive, advertisers, the state and legal constraints.

News values

The media operate by a set of values about what is considered 'newsworthy', that is, what events, issues and personalities they think their audience will find interesting or topical. Editors allocate staff, space and time to different topics according to the 'news values' of these topics. Some issues and personalities are considered by editors to be particularly newsworthy.

Before her death, Diana, Princess of Wales, for example, was considered newsworthy by the popular press and today, her sons are. Other personalities considered newsworthy include the Beckhams. Even trivial stories about their lives are likely to make news.

On a television news broadcast, items that can be filmed are more newsworthy than ones that are mainly based on interviews and 'talking heads'. As a result, items that can be illustrated with film are more likely to be included. This also explains why economic and financial news is often shown using animated graphics.

Newsworthy personalities.

The profit motive

Newspapers exist as businesses and operate to make a profit. This means that the profit motive will have an influence on content. Press gatekeepers will consider possible stories in terms of whether they are likely to achieve big circulations. Similarly, commercial broadcasting has to make a profit and so needs to attract and keep an audience.

Glossary terms: news values

Advertisers

Advertisers are an important source of revenue for newspapers. Advertisers in the press may have an influence on content in so far as they could withdraw their business if they disagree with a paper's stand on a particular issue.

The state and legal constraints on content

- Complaints about media content are handled by the British Office of Communication (Ofcom). The Press Complaints Commission deals with complaints about the editorial content of newspapers and magazines.

- The media are subject to laws of libel, which prevent the publication of false statements that damage a person's reputation. A number of celebrities, including Kerry Katona, Kate Hudson, Jimmy Nail and Kate Garraway, have been involved in libel court cases with newspapers.

- During national emergencies and wars, governments have attempted to influence media coverage. During the Iraq war (2003), for example, a row broke out between the British government and the BBC about television coverage of the war. The government complained about the BBC reporting the lack of popular and political support in Britain for the war. The director of BBC news claimed that the government tried to intimidate the BBC in its reporting of events leading up to the war and also during the war itself (Williams, 2004).

Eye on the exam

The CHECK YOUR UNDERSTANDING question below is another example of a question that is asking you to debate an issue and to argue for and against a viewpoint.

Internal and external influences on content

WRITTEN ACTIVITY

One way of summarizing the various influences on mass media content and the way news is selected and presented is by dividing the influences into internal and external factors. Internal factors are influences, practices or pressures that exist within media organizations. External factors are influences or pressures that come from outside the media.

Copy and complete the table. Add at least another three points under each heading.

Influences on the content of the mass media and the way news is selected and presented	
Internal influences	**External influences**
• The role of gatekeepers. •	• Consumer demand. •

CHECK YOUR UNDERSTANDING

Discuss how far sociologists would agree that press owners are a major influence on the content of newspapers.

KEY POINT

Influences on content include news values, advertisers, the government and laws.

TOPIC 16 How are black people represented in the media?

OBJECTIVE
Discuss media representations of black people

One important area of the study of media content concerns representations. Sociologists are interested in studying the media's portrayal or representation of different social groups, such as black people and women, and the images presented of them. One area of interest is how far the media present realistic images and how far they encourage stereotyping (distorted or exaggerated images of social groups – see page 160).

Research shows that in television drama productions during the 1950s, 1960s and 1970s, black people were either absent or under-represented. When black people were represented, the media often employed negative stereotypes.

Television programmes during this time often presented black people in stereotypical roles such as criminals. Black people were also presented in a narrow range of roles such as singers, dancers, musicians or sports people.

Further research suggests that during the 1960s and 1970s, news reporting tended to simplify race issues and reported on them in a negative and unbalanced way. Issues that emphasized the problems associated with countries in Africa and Asia, such as famine, poverty and war, were over-reported. In Britain, reports often associated black people with crime, conflict and riots.

Cottle (1994) sees such news reporting in the 1960s and 1970s as effectively hiding the very real problem of racism in Britain. He points out that studies in the 1970s and 1980s identified how Britain's black population were criminalized. By this, he means that media reporting gave the impression that black people were prone to crime.

There have been reports in the media linking black people to mugging, violent street protests and inner-city riots. An important element of such distorted coverage was that black people came to be defined as a threat to society's values (see page 224 on moral panics). The media, however, chose to ignore continuing social inequalities and the growing anger at police harassment.

Abercrombie (1996) believes that there were considerable changes in the representation of race and ethnicity on television in the 1990s. For example there were now more black actors and presenters. More importantly, he argues, black actors were now playing ordinary characters rather than being presented as stereotypes. *The Cosby Show* in America was particularly significant in this respect because:

- all the main characters were black
- they were presented in realistic, non-stereotypical ways
- they were presented as successful members of upper-middle-class society.

✿ DISCUSSION ACTIVITY

Black actors on TV

Abercrombie (1996) gives examples of programmes such as *EastEnders* and *The Bill* in which black actors play ordinary characters rather than stereotypes.

1 In a small group, discuss how far you agree that such programmes do present black actors in ordinary roles. Have you noticed any stereotypes?

2 Discuss specific examples from recent episodes of these programmes.

3 Now make a note of three significant points raised during your discussion.

Other researchers, however, suggest that the mass media still represent black people in distorted ways. Bagguley and Hussain (2008), for example, discuss media representations of people of South Asian heritage in Britain. They argue that there is a constant drip of media stories on forced marriage, crime and a refusal to integrate or fit in.

In their research on the riots in Bradford in 2001, Bagguley and Hussain (2008) investigated the communities' views on how the media reported the riots.

The interviewees believed that the mainstream media were:

- highly selective in what they reported on, for example, journalists "were more interested in gangs of Asian youths bricking the police" than the causes of events
- biased, for example, interviewees felt that the role of the far right (the National Front) in provoking the riots was ignored. Interviewees also felt that disturbances that involved white people were not given enough attention.

Additionally, interviewees saw the media as never providing positive news about the British Asian community and as not attempting to present their views.

Negative portrayal of British Asian communities ✎ WRITTEN ACTIVITY

Claire Alexander (2004) comments on the negative portrayal of British Asian communities in the mass media.

> This can be seen in the obsession with arranged marriage, runaway girls and cultural breakdown. It can also be seen in the demonization of young Asian men, symbolized in the rise of a series of new 'folk devils' – the underclass, the Fundamentalist and the 'gang'.

Source: adapted from Alexander (2004) p. 135

Identify two themes that the media focus on when reporting on British Asian communities.

💡 STRETCH AND CHALLENGE ACTIVITY

Explain, in your own words, Alexander's view on the representation of British Asians in the media.

CHECK YOUR UNDERSTANDING

Discuss how far sociologists would agree that mass media images of people from minority ethnic groups are stereotypical rather than realistic.

KEY POINT

Sociologists examine the ways in which members of minority ethnic groups are represented in the media and whether these groups are stereotyped.

TOPIC 17 How is gender represented in the media?

OBJECTIVE
Discuss how women and men are represented in the media

Sociologists have undertaken research on images of gender in children's books, advertising, television, films, newspapers and magazines. During the 1970s, research indicated that mass-media representations of women tended to be stereotypical rather than realistic. Images of women did not reflect the range of roles which they actually played in society.

Sue Sharpe (1994) focused on images of women and men in children's books. She argued that there are still lots of traditional images of men and women around. However, there has been some progress since the 1970s. For example, books that present men and women in less stereotyped ways are increasingly common.

Research highlights the stereotyping of women in a number of media products, including television advertisements, pop videos and magazines. In 1990, Cumberbatch carried out research for the Broadcasting Standards Council (1990) on the way in which women and men are represented in television advertisements. His findings are summarized here:

- Nearly two-thirds of people in advertisements were men.
- The vast majority of voice-overs in advertisements were male.
- Women in advertisements were more likely than men to be young and blond.
- Men were more likely than women to be shown in a professional work setting.
- Women were frequently shown with a male partner.

We have seen that, more recently, the shop Iceland has advertised using a slogan which suggests that a mother's role includes doing the grocery shopping (see page 204).

Women in the sports news

Women are often invisible in much press and television coverage of sport. When women's sport is reported, it is often trivialized. Women's football, for example, is covered only patchily. Williams (1997) examined coverage of women's football on television and in newspapers in the 1990s. He found little coverage of women's football compared with that of men and schoolboys' football.

Newspapers and television do cover women's tennis but arguably in ways that trivialize the achievements of women players.

Men's magazines

Gauntlett (2008) undertook research on men's magazines such as *FHM, Loaded, Maxim, Nuts, GQ* and *Zoo*. He highlights several key themes of masculinity that are presented in these magazines. These themes include the following: men like (to look at) women; men like cars, gadgets and sport; men need help, for example with fashion and grooming; men are fascinated by bravery and danger.

RESEARCH ACTIVITY

Studying voice-overs

Over a period of one week, watch a total of 15 television advertisements which have voice-overs.

1 For each of these advertisements, make a note of the product being advertised and the gender of the voice-over.

2 What proportion of the voice-overs were male and what proportion were female?

3 Was there any link between the type of product being advertised and the gender of the voice-over?

4 Write a brief report on your findings and conclusions.

Women's tennis

Read through this article from *The Sun* newspaper, then answer the question that follows.

Phwoar-ty Love

Sexy smashers are sending pulses racing as the tennis world heads for a sizzling summer.

With the French Open in full swing and Wimbledon on the horizon, a bevy of court stunners are showing off their red-hot form.

A new survey has put Anna Kournikova back at No 1 in the list of top tennis totty – but a whole host of skirted beauties are lining up to claim her throne.

And there was plenty on show at Roland Garros yesterday.

Daniela Hantuchova and American teenager Ashley Harkleroad sent the temperature soaring on the day when they both featured in the poll by British tennis magazine *Ace*.

Leggy pin-up Hantuchova surrendered her crown as top babe and had to settle for second place behind Kournikova while busty Harkleroad, only 18, was a newcomer at No 10.

Source: Charlie Wyett, *The Sun*, 29 May 2003

Identify three examples of ways in which this article could be seen as treating women as sex objects.

One view of this type of portrayal is that it sees women's tennis as less important than men's. How far would you agree with this view?

Gauntlett argues that these magazines all project the same images of women, men, and men's interests and concerns. These include semi-naked women, sport and drinking. Critics of such magazines argue that they present narrow and stereotypical images of gender. Other commentators suggest that articles in these magazines are meant to be read as humorous.

Discuss how far sociologists would agree with the view that the mass media often present stereotypical rather than realistic images of women.

Sociologists examine the ways in which women and men are represented in the media and whether they are stereotyped.

TOPIC 18 Does the internet influence the distribution of power in society?

OBJECTIVES

Discuss the internet's role in a democracy

Explain what is meant by the digital divide

The internet is a global communications network. By the 1990s, internet access in Britain was available via computers in public libraries and internet cafes. It was also found in many homes, schools and workplaces. We can now also access the internet via mobile phones and digital televisions.

One view is that the internet could help democracy by spreading power more widely between different individuals and groups. Via the internet, for example, people can get information, express political opinions and exert influence. In this way, the internet could empower people, that is, give them more power.

The internet and democracy

In a democracy, the internet is seen as increasing citizens' access to political information. We can now go online to access e-government resources including information on local government web pages and on Directgov. Twenty years ago, it would have been almost impossible to access this sort of political information.

The internet is also seen as aiding citizens to communicate with politicians by, for instance, e-mailing local councillors or MPs.

Individuals who are concerned about global warming can use the internet to find people who share their concerns. Pressure groups such as Greenpeace can go online to publicize their organizations and attract new members.

Some researchers suggest that the internet gives opportunities to citizens in democracies to become more involved in politics. It:

- provides information about political topics quickly and cheaply
- enables people to respond to news reports
- provides an interactive environment so people can create content, produce news and publish their views via their own websites or blogs (web logs)
- allows people to be organized to take part in political actions on behalf of a cause. E-mail can be used, for example, to mobilize members of anti-war or pro-hunting groups to take part in a protest.

E-mail played an important role in mobilizing members of the Countryside Alliance to take part in the 'Liberty and Livelihood' march in London in 2002. This march was organized to protest against the government ban on hunting with dogs (Oates, 2008).

RESEARCH ACTIVITY

Directgov

Directgov is the official UK government website for citizens. Information about all public services can be found here.

Log onto the Directgov website (http://www.direct.gov.uk/en/index.htm).

1 Identify three topics or subjects that are covered on this website.

2 Identify three audience groups for whom information is available.

Glossary terms: digital divide   pressure group   stratification

The internet can be seen as an important democratic tool (Baker, 2007) because it increases people's capacity to participate, communicate, and circulate lots of different information. The internet can also provide an open space for discussion between people around the world.

Other approaches, however, are less optimistic about the internet's role in increasing participation. One view accepts that much political activity, including publicity and mobilizing, is now conducted online. Nonetheless, there is little evidence that political activity has increased as a result. According to this view the use of the internet for political purposes:

1   is not widespread compared with its other uses, such as for shopping or entertainment

2   only involves individuals and groups who have the resources to use it regularly. This is because 'e-democracy' requires technology and funding to start up and keep going.

The Countryside Alliance 'Liberty and Livelihood' march in London in 2002.

What is the digital divide?

Boyle (2005) identifies an important new form of stratification in the UK. He uses the term 'digital divide' to describe this new division between those who have access to new media technology such as the internet and digital TV, and those who do not have access to these.

The digital divide

WRITTEN ACTIVITY

Oates (2008) identifies several digital divisions. These include divisions based on:

• **Wealth:** richer people are more likely to have the equipment and means to access the internet.
• **Education:** the more education a person has had, the more likely he or she is to use the internet.
• **Age:** younger people tend to use the internet more often and in more varied ways than older people.
• **Geography:** just 3.5 per cent of the population of Africa is online.

Source: adapted from Oates (2008)

1   Explain what sociologists mean by the digital divide.
2   Identify two digital divisions and explain briefly what they are based on.

CHECK YOUR UNDERSTANDING

Identify two arguments for and two arguments against the view that the internet empowers people and groups in a democracy.

KEY POINTS

The internet is seen as potentially increasing people's capacity to participate in a democracy. The digital divide, however, excludes some people from participating online.

What is the role of the mass media in the process of deviancy amplification?

OBJECTIVE
Explain the terms moral panics and deviancy amplification

Stan Cohen (2002) argues that the media are involved in the creation of moral panics. Moral panics involve exaggerating the extent and significance of a social problem. An important aspect of a moral panic is that a particular group is cast as a folk devil. In other words, it becomes defined as a threat to society's values. The group is portrayed in stereotypical terms by the mass media.

Folk devils of the 1960s

Cohen undertook a case study of the moral panic surrounding mods and rockers during the 1960s. Events in 1964 in Clacton, a small holiday resort on the East coast of England, were the starting point. Easter Sunday in 1964 was the coldest for 80 years. A few groups of bored young people started scuffling on pavements and throwing stones at each other. The mods and rockers factions started separating out. Cohen describes what happened next:

> Those on bikes and scooters roared up and down, windows were broken, some beach huts were wrecked and one boy fired a starting pistol in the air. The vast number of people crowding into the streets, the noise, everyone's general irritation and the actions of an unprepared and undermanned police force had the effect of making the two days unpleasant, oppressive and sometimes frightening.

Source: Cohen (2002)

The incidents described by Cohen were reported in most national newspapers the next day. Reports included sensationalist headlines about what happened. In this way, the mods and rockers were cast as folk devils.

Cohen argues that the media exaggerated the seriousness of the events in terms of:
- the numbers of young people taking part
- the numbers involved in violence
- the amount and effects of any damage or violence.

In Cohen's view, the media distorted what was actually going on and created a false image of young people and their activities. Cohen describes this process as amplification, which involves exaggerating and distorting something that has actually happened. Such amplification, Cohen suggests, encouraged other young people to behave in the way portrayed by the media. This resulted in further disturbances and led to the public outcry which Cohen calls a moral panic.

People reading newspapers and watching scenes on television began to see the mods and rockers as a threat to law and order. The police, responding to the public outcry, acted harshly and this led to further arrests. Cohen's point is that the media can actually amplify deviance or provoke more deviant behaviour.

Cohen is aware that, today, many readers may not have heard of mods and rockers. He points out, however, that the processes which bring about moral

Glossary terms: amplification of deviance   moral panic

panics remain important. He highlights the more recent moral panics that have surrounded school shootouts, welfare cheats and refugees.

Sensationalist headlines

Mass-market and middle-market tabloids are sometimes criticized for exaggerating and sensationalizing their headlines and stories.

1 In pairs, examine a recent copy of one of these newspapers. Identify any articles in which the headlines appear to sensationalize, exaggerate or distort the seriousness of the events, incident or social problem being described.
2 Note down which articles you have identified and your reasons for doing so.
3 Team up with another pair and explain why you have identified these particular articles.

The internet and moral panics

More recently, there has been public concern about the ill-effects of the internet. McQuail (2003) views the anxieties over the internet as an example of a moral panic. Read through this extract, then answer the questions that follow.

The internet has become the latest medium to provoke a 'moral panic' at the ease with which explicit sexual (and other undesirable) content can enter the home and be accessed even by children. Other worries include:

- the unreliability of sources
- invasion of privacy
- defamation (attacking a person's character)
- fraud and other cybercrime
- facilitating crime and terrorism.

Source: adapted from McQuail (2003) p. 6

1 Identify one area of concern about the internet that focuses specifically on children.
2 Identify two other worries associated with the internet.

STRETCH AND CHALLENGE ACTIVITY

McQuail also suggests that the unregulated character of the internet, its attraction and widespread presence are at the heart of the new anxieties about it.

Explain, in your own words, what he means by this statement.

CHECK YOUR UNDERSTANDING

1 Explain what sociologists mean by a moral panic.
2 Identify and explain one way in which the mass media might influence our views on how much crime there is in society.

KEY POINTS

The media can exaggerate and distort deviance and crime. In doing so, they can amplify or provoke more of it. Such amplification can lead to a public outcry or moral panic.

TOPIC 20 **What contemporary social issues are related to the mass media?**

OBJECTIVE
Discuss areas of public concern about the mass media

We have seen that there has been public concern about the possible ill-effects of the internet. Another area of public concern about the media is the potential harm they can do, particularly to children. There is long-standing public anxiety about the media's ability to produce violent and aggressive behaviour among children.

Media exposure and violence

Much of the early research on the links between exposure to the media and real-life violence was carried out in laboratories using experiments. In 1963, Bandura conducted research with nursery school children. The children were put into four groups, some of which watched a short film showing an adult punching a large inflated plastic doll and hitting it with a mallet. The children were then placed in a room with several different toys, including a doll and mallet. Many of the children who had seen the film copied the violent behaviour shown in it.

Such research findings seemed to support the hypodermic syringe view of the effects of the media on audiences (see page 200). They fuelled debates on whether violence on the screen influenced the audience's behaviour. In the 1990s, for example, concern was raised about the effects of films such as *Child's Play 3* and *Natural Born Killers*. It was alleged, for instance, that *Natural Born Killers* led to a spate of copycat murders in the USA.

In 2008, the Advertising Standards Agency (ASA) ruled that two posters advertising the film *Wanted* could be seen to condone violence by glamorizing or glorifying the use of guns.

Sociologists have informed the debates on the media and violence. Their research has shown, for example, that children are able to distinguish between fictional and factual material on television and that children do not passively accept television messages. Instead, they actively interpret or make sense of these messages.

Gauntlett (2001) identifies problems with much research on media violence. He argues that to understand violent people and the causes of their behaviour, researchers should actually study violent people. Studies which question teenage offenders with histories of violence and compare them with non-offending young people have found that young offenders:

• watched less television and video than other teenagers

• had less access to technology

DISCUSSION ACTIVITY

Violent films

1 In a small group, discuss whether:
   a) violent films may lead to copycat behaviour
   b) the likelihood is so great as to justify censorship of films.

2 Make a note of three important points that were made during your discussions.

Artificial studies

Read through this extract about studies of violence, then answer the question that follows.

> Careful sociological studies of media influences require a lot of time and money. Consequently, they are heavily outnumbered by simpler studies which often put their subjects into artificial situations (but then pretend they are studying the everyday world).
>
> Experiments involve forcing participants to watch a particular programme which they would not have chosen if left to their own devices and – just as artificially – observing them in a particular setting afterwards.
>
> Here, behaviour of children towards an object is often taken (artificially) to represent how they would behave towards a real person. Furthermore, this all rests on the mistaken belief that children's behaviour will not be affected by the fact that they know they are being tested and/or observed.

Source: adapted from Gauntlett (2001) p. 56

Why are there relatively few careful sociological studies of media influences?

- had no particular interest in violent programmes
- either enjoyed the same material as non-offending teenagers or were not interested in watching television.

Gauntlett points out that studies which actually interview those involved in violence fail to show a strong connection between screen violence and real-life violence.

Peak and Fisher (1996) argue that television is not to blame for violence and crime. Television has been used as a scapegoat for deep-rooted social problems. They suggest that the causes of violence and crime are more likely to be found in poverty, unemployment, homelessness, abuse and personality traits.

💡 STRETCH AND CHALLENGE ACTIVITY

1 Identify two problems with studies of media influences based on experiments.
2 What term do sociologists use to describe people's behaviour being affected because they know they are being observed as part of a study?

CHECK YOUR UNDERSTANDING

Identify and explain two areas of public concern about the mass media.

KEY POINTS

Areas of public concern and debate focus on the harmful effects of the media, particularly in relation to children, and anxieties over the internet. Sociological research has informed these debates.

7 Power

What is power?

OBJECTIVE
Explain what is meant by 'power'

Power is a key concept in sociology. Sociologists study the way that power relationships work in society. They are particularly interested in exploring inequalities in power between different individuals and social groups.

There are several ways of defining power. Max Weber (1864–1920) was one of the most influential early sociologists to study power. He argued that an individual or group has power when they are able to get what they want despite opposition from other people. In Weber's view, we exercise power over someone when we influence them, even against their will.

What are the sources of power?

According to Weber, power may be based on either coercion or authority. **Coercion** involves the use of force. We obey an individual or group because we feel that we have no choice; we are forced into obeying against our will. Coercive power includes the threat or use of physical violence or torture. Kidnappers, for example, exercise coercive power when they demand a ransom and receive the payment in exchange for the release of hostages.

Authority is exercised over us when we willingly obey someone because we think it is the right thing to do. In this case, force is unnecessary because we agree to obey. A teacher, for example, exercises authority over students in the classroom when they willingly complete homework and hand it in on time.

Other sociologists are inspired by the work of Karl Marx (1818–83), another highly influential early sociologist. These sociologists see power as closely linked to social class relationships. Power is held by members of the bourgeoisie – the economically dominant property-owning class. Marxist approaches argue that the bourgeoisie use their power to exploit the proletariat – the working class.

What are the sources of authority?

Max Weber identified three types of authority. These are traditional authority, legal rational authority and charismatic authority. In each of these cases, the people who are being subjected to the authority (such as the student in the classroom) accept the exercise of power (in this case, by the teacher). They give their consent and see the power as legitimate or proper.

Traditional authority

Traditional authority is based on custom and tradition. We accept the authority of an individual or group because it is customary for us to do so. In Britain, for example, the monarch exercises authority based on tradition.

Glossary terms: apartheid   authority   charismatic authority   coercion

Legal rational authority

In the case of legal rational authority, we obey an individual or group because of the position they hold within an organization. For example, the democratically elected president of a nation exercises legal rational authority over its people. In the workplace, employees accept the office manager's authority to supervise their work because this is set out in their job descriptions.

Legal rational authority in action.

Charismatic authority

In the case of charismatic authority, we obey an individual because we believe that he or she has extraordinary personal qualities which inspire us. Charismatic leaders are seen as exceptional people. The authority of some religious leaders, for instance, is based on their charisma. Mahatma Gandhi (1869–1948) is an example of a charismatic religious leader. He used his charismatic authority to lead the struggle for India's independence from Britain.

Before the move to democracy in South Africa, Nelson Mandela, a charismatic political leader, led a large popular movement against apartheid. Such examples show that charismatic leaders can act to bring about social change.

Charismatic leaders can be a force for social change.

Weber recognized that, in practice, an individual's authority may be based on a mix of two types of authority. For example, as South Africa's democratically elected president (1994–99), Nelson Mandela exercised both legal rational and charismatic authority.

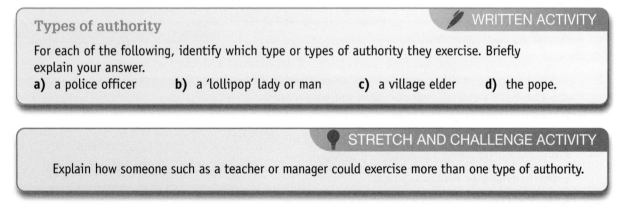

Types of authority   ✎ WRITTEN ACTIVITY

For each of the following, identify which type or types of authority they exercise. Briefly explain your answer.
a) a police officer   **b)** a 'lollipop' lady or man   **c)** a village elder   **d)** the pope.

💡 STRETCH AND CHALLENGE ACTIVITY

Explain how someone such as a teacher or manager could exercise more than one type of authority.

CHECK YOUR UNDERSTANDING

1   Explain what sociologists mean by the terms 'power', 'coercion' and 'authority'.

2   What do sociologists mean by the following terms?
traditional authority   legal rational authority   charismatic authority

KEY POINTS

People exercise power when they get what they want in spite of opposition. Power can be based on coercion (the use of force) or authority (consent or agreement). Weber identified three types of authority: traditional, legal rational and charismatic.

TOPIC 2 What is a democracy?

OBJECTIVE

Explain what is meant by the terms 'democracy' and 'citizenship'

Different societies have different political systems. In some systems, power is concentrated in the hands of just a few people, and in others it is distributed more widely. In many nations, including the UK, the political system is based on democracy.

What is democracy?

The term 'democracy' literally means 'government by the people'. In a democracy, power is distributed widely and the government's power is based on consent and legal rational authority rather than on coercion. There is a distinction between direct democracy and indirect or representative democracy.

Democracy in action.

In a **direct democracy**, the citizens of the country take part directly in the decision-making process. They can, for example, vote on proposals for particular policies, and the results of the vote will determine whether or not the proposals become law.

In an **indirect democracy**, citizens elect representatives who make political decisions for them. In Britain, we have representative or parliamentary democracy. We elect Members of Parliament (MPs) who govern on our behalf.

Features of democracies

DISCUSSION ACTIVITY

In the following list, you will find four features of democracies and four features of undemocratic political systems. In pairs, discuss which are features of democracies and why. Make a note of your decisions and your reasons.

1 Elections are held during which people can vote freely for whichever candidate they choose.
2 There is tight government control of the press and television.
3 Freedom of speech and expression is allowed.
4 One individual or elite group rules.
5 Organizations such as trade unions are free to meet.
6 Pressure groups are banned.
7 The legal system and police force are independent of the government.
8 Fair trials are denied.

What is citizenship?

The term 'citizenship' is used in several different ways. It can refer to being a member of a particular state, such as the UK. In this sense, citizenship is a political and legal status. All UK citizens have full legal rights, for example to

Glossary terms: citizens   citizenship   democracy   direct democracy   pressure group

Opinions on UK democracy

Opinion polls are a type of survey that use fixed-choice questions to find out things like:

- people's views on topical issues, for example whether they agree with a proposed airport expansion
- how people intend to vote, for instance: 'How would you vote if there were a general election tomorrow?'

Some commentators argue that aspects of the political process in the UK are not democratic. For example, the head of state (the monarch) and MPs in the House of Lords are not elected.

1 Devise a poll to find out people's opinions on whether:
- Britain should have an elected head of state
- MPs in the House of Lords should be elected.

Remember to ask fixed-choice questions and include all possible answers that respondents might give (for example 'don't know').

2 Pilot your opinion poll on a sample of ten people. Try to ask equal numbers of men and women, younger and older people.

3 Write a paragraph outlining the results of your pilot opinion poll.

vote in elections and to be treated equally. Citizenship also involves responsibilities, for instance to respect the law and pay tax.

Citizenship can also be about active involvement in public life and participation in the political process. The term 'active citizenship' is sometimes used to describe activities such as voting, joining a pressure group or being interested in current affairs. Active citizenship is seen as key to democracy. For example, citizens' active participation in the political process can help to make governments respond to public opinion.

Citizenship education involves learning how to become an informed and active citizen. At school, for example, students may study topics such as rights and responsibilities, equality and what it means to be British.

STRETCH AND CHALLENGE ACTIVITY

In your view, what does being a good citizen involve?

CHECK YOUR UNDERSTANDING

1 What do sociologists mean by the term 'democracy'?
2 Explain one difference between direct and representative democracy.
3 Identify and explain two ways in which the term 'citizenship' is used.

KEY POINTS

Representative democracy is a system of government in which citizens choose their representatives through elections. Commentators disagree about how democratic Britain is. The hereditary monarchy is seen as an example of an undemocratic institution.

Citizenship can refer to political and legal status or to active involvement in public life.

TOPIC 3 # What is the state?

OBJECTIVES

Explain what is meant by 'the state'

Explain contrasting views of the state

The state and its institutions

The state is a central part of the political process. It refers to the various institutions that organize and regulate society by making, implementing and enforcing laws. In the UK, the state exercises authority over England, Northern Ireland, Scotland and Wales. Some state powers, however, have been passed to the Welsh Assembly, the Scottish Parliament and the Northern Ireland Assembly.

The main institutions of the UK state

Parliament: the Houses of Commons and Lords	The civil service: the bureaucracy	The judiciary: the courts
Legislative power	*Executive power*	*Judicial power*
Parliament has a key role in the legislative (law-making) process. The government sets out its proposals in the form of Bills, which must be passed in Parliament before becoming law. MPs in the Commons are elected. Part of MPs' role is to represent their constituents' interests.	The role of the civil service is to advise government ministers on policy and to implement (carry out) government policy. The civil service is politically neutral (apolitical), so it does not take sides with one political party over another and does not involve itself in political debate.	The judiciary consists of judges who operate within the court service. They, along with the police force, are concerned with law enforcement.

The 'government' of the UK consists of those Members of Parliament (MPs) who are ministers, selected by the Prime Minister, who is the leader of the governing party. The Cabinet is made up of senior ministers (such as the Chancellor of the Exchequer) who meet regularly to discuss government policy. Although the legal system, the military and the police force are all part of the state, they are independent of the government.

The Cabinet meets regularly to decide on government policy.

Contrasting views of the role of the state

We can identify two broad approaches to the study of power and the state: the pluralist approach and the conflict approach. These approaches differ in their views on who holds power in society, how it is used and whose interests are represented by the state.

According to the pluralist approach, a range of competing groups and interests exists in society (see page 210). Political power is shared between these groups. No single group or individual dominates decision making or always gets its own way. Rather than siding with one group over another, the state's role is to act as an umpire or neutral referee. In doing so, it regulates and manages the different interests and serves the needs of all citizens.

Glossary terms: constituents   state

Sociologists from the conflict or Marxist approach argue that those in positions of power within the state (such as top judges and senior civil servants) tend to come from a narrow social and educational background. Many are from privileged backgrounds, having been educated in private schools and Oxford or Cambridge University. By contrast, people from state schools and newer universities hold relatively few positions of power.

The Marxist approach sees power in capitalist societies as concentrated in the hands of the few. Power is used to benefit the minority. The state's role is to protect the interests of the bourgeoisie. Those in powerful positions within the state are either drawn from or serve the interests of the bourgeoisie. This group's economic dominance gives it political power, so state policies generally benefit its members.

Top judges and the 'old school tie'

WRITTEN ACTIVITY

Seven per cent of the school-aged population in England and Wales attends private schools.

1 What percentage of current UK-educated top judges attended fee-paying schools?

2 What percentage of current top judges who went to a UK university studied at Oxford or Cambridge?

Type of education received by UK-educated leading judges*

% who attended:	1989	2004
fee-paying schools	76	75
maintained schools	24	25
Oxford or Cambridge	88	81
other university	12	19

(*The Law Lords and Judges in the Appeal and High Courts)

Source: adapted from a report by The Sutton Trust (2005)

STRETCH AND CHALLENGE ACTIVITY

Write a paragraph discussing whether the educational background of leading judges reflects that of the wider population and how far this has changed between 1989 and 2004.

CHECK YOUR UNDERSTANDING

Identify and explain two differences between the pluralist and conflict approaches to the role of the state.

KEY POINTS

The state consists of institutions that make, implement and enforce laws. The pluralist approach sees power as distributed widely among different groups, with the state refereeing between them. The conflict approach sees power as concentrated in a few hands, with the state serving the interests of the privileged minority.

TOPIC 4 # What is the role of general elections in the political process?

OBJECTIVES

Explain the role of general elections in the political process

Outline the role of political parties in general elections

The role of general elections

General elections are held every five years (or less). People elect MPs to represent them in the House of Commons. The party with the most MPs forms the government and puts its policy programme into effect.

In UK general elections, the vast majority of people aged over 18 have the right to vote. This enables them to vote for one candidate and is known as a 'one person, one vote' system. We cast our vote in a secret ballot in the constituency in which we live.

General elections are based on the system of 'first past the post' or 'winner takes all'. This means that a candidate in a particular constituency needs only one more vote than their nearest rival to win a seat in the House of Commons. An advantage of the first-past-the-post system is that each constituency elects its own MP, whose job it is to represent constituents' interests. It also ensures that one political party usually gains sufficient seats to form the government. One problem, however, is that many MPs will be elected even though more than half of their voting constituents did not vote for them.

The first-past-the-post system works against smaller parties whose support is spread out geographically rather than concentrated in a few constituencies. Critics argue that the first-past-the-post system is unfair and undemocratic. Smaller parties would get more seats with a system of proportional representation (PR). With PR, a party would win seats according to the total number of votes it received throughout the UK rather than in one constituency.

The role of political parties

In a representative democracy such as the UK, citizens have the right to form, join and become active in the political party of their choice. A political party is

---

Results from the 2005 UK general election

WRITTEN ACTIVITY

The Conservative candidate for Croydon Central won by 75 votes.

The Conservative candidate for Kensington and Chelsea won by 12 418 votes.

The Labour candidate for Crawley won by 37 votes.

The Labour candidate for Bootle won by 16 357 votes.

A safe seat is one that a particular party wins election after election. A marginal seat is one that a party holds with only a small majority, so it could easily change hands at the next election.

1 Which seat could be considered a safe seat for the Conservative Party?

2 Which seat could be considered a marginal seat for Labour?

Glossary terms: constituency electorate mandate manifesto

an organization that wants to form a government. In most cases, political parties have policies on a range of issues, such as education, welfare and crime control.

Before a general election, each political party publishes its policy proposals in its election manifesto. The party that wins the general election forms the government. It can then claim a mandate for its policies. In other words, it can claim that support for its policies derives from the electorate (those people entitled to vote).

Votes cast and seats won in the 2005 general election
WRITTEN ACTIVITY

Critics argue that with the first-past-the-post system, there is an imbalance between the votes cast for the various political parties and the outcome in terms of the number of seats won in the House of Commons. In the 2005 general election, for example, the Liberal Democrats got 22 per cent of the votes but only 9.6 per cent of seats.

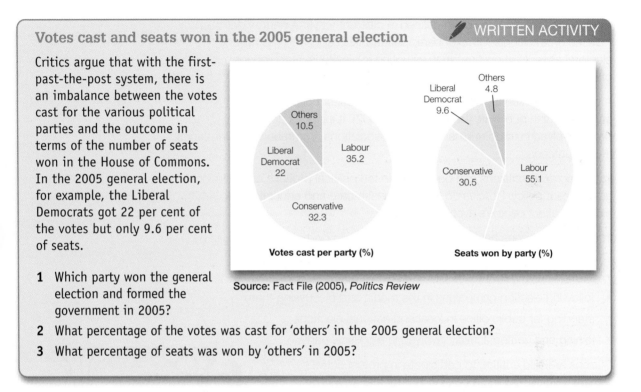

Votes cast per party (%) — Others 10.5, Liberal Democrat 22, Labour 35.2, Conservative 32.3

Seats won by party (%) — Others 4.8, Liberal Democrat 9.6, Conservative 30.5, Labour 55.1

Source: Fact File (2005), *Politics Review*

1 Which party won the general election and formed the government in 2005?

2 What percentage of the votes was cast for 'others' in the 2005 general election?

3 What percentage of seats was won by 'others' in 2005?

STRETCH AND CHALLENGE ACTIVITY

Write a paragraph to show that some parties lose out from the first-past-the-post system while other parties can benefit from it.

CHECK YOUR UNDERSTANDING

Identify and explain one advantage and one disadvantage of the first-past-the-post system of voting.

KEY POINTS

In general elections, the electorate votes for MPs who represent them in the House of Commons. A political party has beliefs and policies on issues such as education and defence. The party that wins a general election can claim that it has the authority (mandate) to carry out its policies.

What opportunities do people have to participate in the political process?

OBJECTIVES

Describe the different ways in which people can take part in politics
Identify changes in political participation over time

Political participation

Political participation has been defined in different ways. A narrow definition focuses on traditional forms of participation linked to governmental and electoral aspects of politics, such as voting in elections, standing for public office and being involved with a political party.

A broader definition of political participation focuses more widely on engagement in public life (Beetham et al, 2002). It includes activities such as being involved in trade unions, tenants' associations, community organizations and volunteering.

In democracies, citizens can participate in the political process and influence government policy. Policies on housing, health care and education, for example, affect people's everyday lives.

In Britain, all citizens have the right to participate in politics and public life by, for example:

- voting in referendums and elections
- following election campaigns in the media and discussing them
- standing for public office in local and national elections
- joining and getting actively involved in a political party.

Citizens are also entitled to participate in protest activities by, for example, signing a petition, contacting an MP or the media, or joining a pressure group.

Beetham and his colleagues (2002) argue that citizen participation can help to make government more democratic during the long gaps between elections. Active participation ensures that:

- the government is made aware of the views of citizens
- informed citizens act as a check on, and form of control over, the government and elected representatives.

Participation in non-electoral political activities at Speakers' Corner.

How has political participation changed?

Participation in the political process in Britain appears to have changed significantly over the last 50 years. In general, traditional forms of participation are declining. For example, there has been a decline in:

- voter turnout in UK general elections, particularly since the 1992 election
- membership of political parties over the last decade
- the strength of voters' identification with a political party over the long term.

Glossary terms: apathy   turnout

The Power Commission

The Power Commission investigated reasons for the decline in participation in formal democratic politics (for example, voting and standing for office) in Britain. In 2006, it reported that voting in elections seems irrelevant to growing numbers of people. It found evidence that people feel:

- they no longer want to get involved in formal politics or join political parties
- politicians and political institutions are untrustworthy, failing and disconnected from them
- their views and interests are not influential enough in political decision making.

However, the report also rejected the idea that people are politically apathetic (uninterested in all forms of politics). Political apathy is a myth because people, for example, undertake voluntary work, sign petitions, join protest marches and support consumer boycotts.

WRITTEN ACTIVITY

Changes in inclination to participate in protest activity, 1983–2002

The table shows how likely people were to participate in various protest activities. It shows the proportion of respondents who said they would do each thing if a harmful or unjust law were being considered by parliament.

1 What percentage of respondents said they would go on a protest or demonstration in 1983?

2 What percentage said they would contact an MP in 2002?

3 Which activity were respondents most likely to say they would do in 2002?

% saying they would:	1983	2002
Contact MP	46	51
Contact media	14	27
Go on a protest or demonstration	8	18
Sign a petition	55	63
Speak to an influential person	10	19
Form a group of like-minded people	6	8

Source: adapted from Curtice and Seyd (2003)

STRETCH AND CHALLENGE ACTIVITY

Describe the overall change in people's likelihood to participate in protest activity between 1983 and 2002. How far does this change suggest that there is a crisis in political participation?

CHECK YOUR UNDERSTANDING

1 Describe two ways in which citizens can participate in protest activity.

2 Explain two reasons for the decline in participation in formal politics.

KEY POINTS

In democracies, citizens have the right to participate in politics, for example, by joining a political party or protesting. Participation in formal party politics has declined over the last 50 years. Other forms of participation and protest, however, are on the increase.

TOPIC 6 **What are the social influences on general election turnout?**

OBJECTIVES

Describe the links between social characteristics and turnout in general elections

Explain why some people do not vote in general elections

Links between social characteristics and turnout in general elections

The term 'turnout' refers to the proportion of eligible voters (people who are allowed to vote) who actually vote in an election. Between 1945 and 2005, 17 general elections were held in the UK. Turnout between 1945 and 1997 was relatively stable and did not fall below 70 per cent of the electorate. More recently, however, turnout has fallen sharply. In the 2001 general election, for example, turnout fell to a low of 59.4 per cent and in 2005, it increased only slightly to 61.3 per cent.

UK general election turnout

WRITTEN ACTIVITY

According to this information:

1 In which year was turnout the highest?

2 In which year was turnout the lowest?

3 What percentage of registered voters did not vote in 2005?

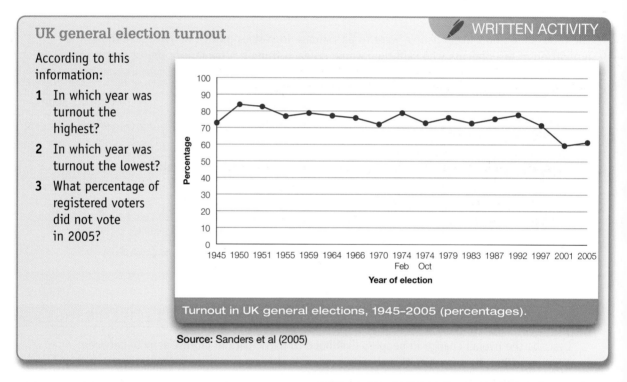

Turnout in UK general elections, 1945–2005 (percentages).

Source: Sanders et al (2005)

STRETCH AND CHALLENGE ACTIVITY

1 Write a paragraph describing the pattern of turnout between 1945 and 2005.

2 Explain why a low turnout at a general election can be seen as a cause for concern in a democracy.

Social factors such as age, gender, ethnicity and social class influence the patterns of voting. In the 2005 general election, there were links between turnout and social characteristics such as age and social class.

Why do some people not vote in general elections?

- People do not see much difference between the two main parties (Labour and the Conservatives). These parties' policies and politicians have become increasingly similar. This leads people to believe there is no real choice between the main parties, their policies and politicians.

- People feel that they already know what the election's outcome will be. If people consider that the election result is a foregone conclusion, they may think it is pointless to vote.

- Turnout was low in 'safe' Labour seats in 2005. People in these seats may have abstained (not voted) because they were disillusioned with Labour, or because they were disillusioned with all politicians and politics.

- However, some commentators see low turnout as reflecting public satisfaction with the current government and contentment with the way the economy is performing, rather than reflecting disillusionment.

- Another possible explanation for the gradual fall in turnout is that voters are less motivated to get involved in politics when there are so many other ways of filling their time.

However, Curtice (2005) notes that there is little evidence that voters are less motivated to participate. During the 2005 campaign, for example, a MORI opinion poll reported that 61 per cent of respondents were 'very' or 'fairly' interested in politics. This figure has not fallen over the last 30 years.

Age and turnout

DISCUSSION ACTIVITY

1 Fewer than four in ten people aged 18–24 voted in the 2005 general election. In a small group, discuss the possible reasons why young people are less likely to vote than older people. How far is this a cause for concern in a democracy?

2 Make a note of three points arising from your discussion.

Eye on the exam

If an exam question asks you to provide more than one reason (for example, 'Explain two reasons ...') then you must ensure not only that you give the correct number of reasons but also that you give completely different reasons.

CHECK YOUR UNDERSTANDING

Explain two reasons why a person who is entitled to vote in a general election might not use their vote.

KEY POINTS

Turnout in general elections has declined since 1945. The likelihood of a person voting in a general election is linked to social factors such as age and social class. Reasons for abstaining include lack of choice or disillusionment.

TOPIC 7 — How do social class, gender and age influence voting behaviour?

OBJECTIVE
Explain how social class, age and gender influence voting behaviour

Sociologists are interested in understanding why the electorate votes the way that it does. Several social factors influence voting behaviour. These include social class, gender and age.

Social class and voting behaviour since 1945

Up until the 1970s, social class was seen as the most important influence on voting behaviour in Britain. Most voters voted for one of the two main parties – Labour and the Conservatives – and support for these parties was based broadly on social class. A person's social class was determined by their occupation. Working-class people (in manual jobs) tended to vote Labour while middle-class people (in non-manual occupations) tended to vote Conservative.

Over the last 35 years, however, the social class structure has changed. Rallings and Thrasher (1997) pointed out that, between 1979 and 1992, the proportion of manual workers in the electorate declined from 41 per cent to 34 per cent. A smaller and smaller proportion of the electorate could now be seen as typically working class. This meant that Labour's traditional electoral base was being eroded.

Despite this, in 1997 the Labour Party (or 'new Labour' as it became known under Tony Blair's leadership) won a landslide election victory. It gained support both from manual workers (part of the working class) and clerical workers (part of the middle class). New Labour was successful partly because it managed to appeal to people from different social classes.

Social class and party preference   ✎ WRITTEN ACTIVITY

The following table shows the link between social class and voting in the 2005 general election. AB and C1 are middle class while C2, D and E are working class.

2005 General Election (percentages)

Social class	Conservative	Labour	Liberal Democrat	Other
AB (professional middle class)	37	28	29	6
C1 (lower middle class)	37	32	23	8
C2 (skilled workers)	33	40	19	8
DE (manual workers)	25	48	18	9

Source: adapted from Kavanagh and Butler (2005) p. 198

1 What percentage of skilled workers voted Labour?
2 Which party was most popular among the professional middle class?
3 Which party was most popular among manual workers?

Glossary terms: class dealignment

One view is that social class is no longer as strong a predictor of voting behaviour as it was in the past. The term 'class dealignment' refers to the weakening of the links between social class and voting behaviour. Kavanagh and Butler (2005) note that the social class divide in voting was possibly weaker than ever in the 2005 general election. In 1992, for instance, the Conservatives had a lead of 32 per cent over Labour among professional middle-class voters. In 2005, however, this lead fell to 9 per cent. Labour had managed to attract a large part of what used to be the Conservative core vote.

A second view, however, suggests that social class remains an important influence on voting behaviour. From the 2005 general election results, we can see that the professional and lower middle classes were more likely to vote Conservative. The working classes were more likely to vote Labour, as were people living in rented accommodation. In the view of Rowe (2005), the link between social class and party support continued along traditional lines in 2005.

> **STRETCH AND CHALLENGE ACTIVITY**
>
> To what extent was support for Labour and the Conservatives based on social class in the 2005 general election?

Age, gender and voting behaviour

Traditionally, young people have been more likely to vote Labour and older people have been more inclined to vote Conservative. In the 1997 general election, Labour led the Conservatives in all age groups except those over 65. In 2005, Labour led the Conservatives in all age groups except those over 55.

Since the 1940s, women have been more likely than men to vote Conservative. This pattern, however, appears to be changing. In the 1997 general election, younger women were more likely to vote Labour than younger men. Norris and Wlezien (2005) suggest that the traditional gender gap in voting has reversed and that, overall, women were more likely to vote Labour than men in 2005. For example, 38 per cent of women and 34 per cent of men voted Labour while 32 per cent of women and 34 per cent of men voted Conservative.

CHECK YOUR UNDERSTANDING

1 Why do Kavanagh and Butler suggest that the social class divide in voting was possibly weaker than ever in the 2005 general election?

2 Why does Rowe argue that the link between social class and party support continued along traditional lines in 2005?

3 Identify one change that has taken place in the relationship between gender and voting behaviour over the last 50 years.

KEY POINTS

One view is that social class is no longer the most important influence on voting behaviour. Another view suggests that the traditional links between class and voting remain significant. Traditional patterns of voting behaviour based on gender have changed but the link between age and voting persists.

TOPIC 8 # What are the patterns between ethnicity, religion, region and voting behaviour?

OBJECTIVE
Describe the patterns between ethnicity, religion, region and voting behaviour

While factors such as social class and age are important, they are not the only social influences on voting behaviour. Other significant influences include ethnicity, religion and region.

Ethnicity and voting behaviour

Sociologists highlight the link between ethnicity and voting behaviour. Traditionally, the Labour Party has received strongest support from British Asian and black communities. In the 1992 general election, for example, 81 per cent of minority ethnic voters voted Labour and 10 per cent voted Conservative. In 2001, 73 per cent voted Labour and 12 per cent voted Conservative (Rowe, 2002).

This link can be explained partly in terms of social class as many minority ethnic voters are in low-paid jobs. Another factor that plays a part is Labour's image as the party taking an interest in the problems and issues facing black Britons.

> ### ◉ Eye on the exam
>
> In an exam question on voting behaviour, remember to use the relevant sociological concepts such as social class and ethnicity. It is also important to draw on evidence to back up any points you make.

Religion and voting behaviour

In some countries, religion is an important factor in political life and in voting behaviour. In Northern Ireland, for example, links between religion and politics are important.

Religion can influence voting behaviour in Britain and, for instance, a party's policies may put off voters from a particular religion. Curtice (2005) suggests that Muslim voters might no longer be prepared to support Labour because of the Labour government's decision to join the USA in invading Iraq in 2003. For example, in the 2005 general election, Labour's vote fell on average by over 5 per cent more in constituencies with a relatively large Muslim population than it did in those with no or a small Muslim population.

Region and voting behaviour

Traditionally, the Conservative Party has been more popular in the South of England outside London, while the Labour Party has been more popular in the North of England and Scotland. In the May 1997 general election, this divide became more marked as the Conservative Party lost all of its 10 seats in Scotland. It also lost its single seat in Wales.

People living in inner-city areas are more likely to support Labour while those in rural areas and the suburbs are more likely to vote Conservative. After the 1997 general election, the Conservative Party was left with almost no representation in urban areas. Its support was based mainly in the countryside and some suburbs.

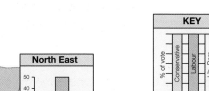

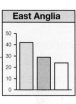

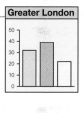

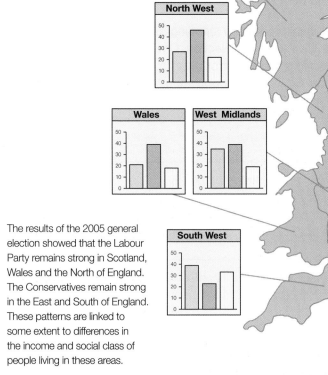

The results of the 2005 general election showed that the Labour Party remains strong in Scotland, Wales and the North of England. The Conservatives remain strong in the East and South of England. These patterns are linked to some extent to differences in the income and social class of people living in these areas.

Regional voting patterns in the 2005 general election.

Factors affecting voting behaviour

WRITTEN ACTIVITY

Copy out and complete the table, adding the other factors (age, ethnicity, religion, region) that influence voting behaviour

Factor	How it affects voting behaviour
Social class	
Gender	

CHECK YOUR UNDERSTANDING

To what extent would sociologists agree that social class is still the most important influence on the voting behaviour of British citizens?

KEY POINT

Social factors that affect voting behaviour include ethnicity, religion and geography.

How far are MPs' social backgrounds typical of those of the UK population?

OBJECTIVES

Describe the social characteristics of MPs

Explain reasons for the low number of female MPs

Citizens have the right to participate in the political process by standing for public office, for example in a local council or UK Parliament election. One view is that politicians such as MPs and councillors should mirror the population in terms of their social backgrounds. So, if a city's population contains around 30 per cent of black people, then 30 per cent of the city's councillors should also be black.

The social characteristics of MPs

The social backgrounds of MPs, however, are not representative of the UK population's backgrounds. Members of some social groups (for example, men and university educated people) are more likely than others to participate in politics by becoming MPs. Other social groups (such as working-class people)

WRITTEN ACTIVITY

Social composition of the House of Commons, May 2005

The first column in the table lists different social groups and the second column shows the number of MPs belonging to these groups, following the 2005 general election. The third column shows the number of MPs needed if they were elected in proportion to their numbers in the overall UK population. For example, 128 females MPs were elected. However, we would need 336 female MPs in order for the number of female MPs to reflect the proportion of females in society.

	Actual number of MPs	Number of MPs needed
Women	128	336
Ethnic minorities	15	51
University education	440	206
Oxbridge education*	164	4
Private school	206	45
Aged under 30	3	106
Aged over 65	43	135
Professional	242	72
Manual worker	38	239

Source: Cole (2006)

* Oxford or Cambridge university education

1 Which groups are under-represented among MPs in the House of Commons?

2 Which groups are over-represented among MPs in the House of Commons?

STRETCH AND CHALLENGE ACTIVITY

1 Write a paragraph describing the social background of MPs in the Commons.

2 Why might the under-representation of some groups be considered a cause for concern in a representative democracy?

Glossary terms: all-women short list   discrimination

Who participates in voluntary activities?

Social factors such as gender and age influence the pattern of participation in voluntary activities. Higher proportions of people aged 16-24 participate in informal volunteering than those aged 65 and over. However, similar proportions of those aged 16-19 and 65-74 engage in formal volunteering. Women are more likely than men to engage in both formal and informal volunteering.

Volunteering and socio-economic status

WRITTEN ACTIVITY

The chart shows participation in voluntary activities (percentages in England, 2005) at least once a month in the previous year by socioeconomic classification

1 Among which occupational group was there little difference in the proportions of respondents who engaged in formal and informal volunteering?

2 What percentage of respondents in intermediate occupations volunteered informally at least monthly?

3 What percentage of respondents in semi-routine occupations volunteered formally at least monthly?

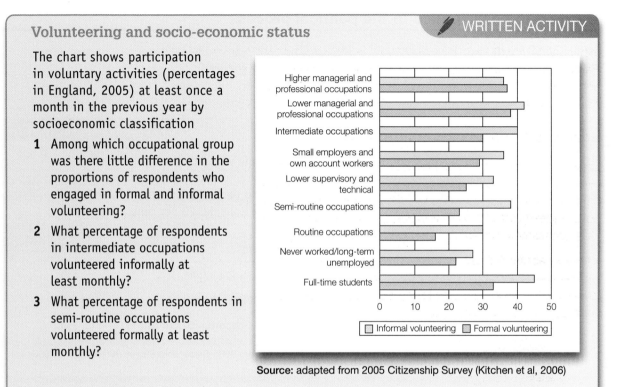

Source: adapted from 2005 Citizenship Survey (Kitchen et al, 2006)

STRETCH AND CHALLENGE ACTIVITY

To what extent would you agree that the likelihood of volunteering formally is linked to people's socioeconomic status?

CHECK YOUR UNDERSTANDING

Identify one difference between formal and informal volunteering.

KEY POINTS

Individuals can contribute to their local communities by volunteering, either formally or informally. Women are more likely to volunteer than men. Relatively high proportions of younger people participate in informal volunteering. Over one-third of people in managerial and professional occupations participate in formal volunteering.

TOPIC 15 | What barriers are there to participation in the political process?

OBJECTIVES

Identify barriers to participation in the political process
Explain variations in participation between individuals and groups

Barriers to participation in the political process

Even though all UK citizens have the right to participate in the political process, not everyone exercises this right (see page 236). Research has identified several barriers to participation.

Barriers to involvement in volunteering

WRITTEN ACTIVITY

The 2005 Citizenship Survey found that 39 per cent of people who did not participate in formal voluntary activities or participated infrequently said they would like to take part or participate more often. Barriers to participation were mainly related to the likely time commitment involved. For example, 29 per cent of respondents said that looking after children or home prevented them from participating in formal volunteering.

1 What percentage had not heard of opportunities to help?

2 Which barrier to participation was mentioned by the biggest proportion of respondents?

Work commitments	59%
Do other things in spare time	31%
Looking after children/home	29%
Had not heard of opportunities to help	15%

Source: adapted from 2005 Citizenship Survey (Kitchen et al, 2006)

The 2005 Citizenship Survey (Kitchen et al, 2006) also identified barriers to participation in civic activities such as being a school governor or involvement in a decision-making group. Barriers include: lack of time; lack of money; lack of access to transport; lack of information; personal circumstances such as having caring responsibilities; fear of crime.

Some individuals are more likely than others to participate in a social organization such as a political party, trade union, environmental group, parents' association, tenants' group or women's group. The British Household Panel Survey (quoted in ONS, 2004) highlights several factors that influence participation in social organizations in Britain. These include:

- **Household composition:** those containing childless couples and non-related people are most likely to be members of a social organization; those containing lone-parent families are least likely to be members.

- **Educational qualifications:** people with higher educational qualifications are more likely to be members of, or active in, social organizations than those with no qualifications.

- **Employment status:** employed people are more likely to be members of, or active in, social organizations than unemployed people.

- **Income:** people in higher-income households are more likely to be members of, or active in, social organizations than those in lower-income households.

Explanations of the variations in participation

Denver (2002) identifies four broad theories that explain variations in the levels of political participation between individuals and groups.

Social location

Individuals and social groups have different amounts of resources, such as information and skills. These resources are linked to people's social location or their social characteristics, including their gender, age, educational qualifications, occupation and income. The likelihood of participating in politics is linked to these social characteristics. So, for example, people who go to university are more likely than other people to acquire relevant skills and information which will enable them to participate more fully in politics.

Rational choice

People make a rational or conscious choice about whether or not to participate in politics. They will participate if the incentives or benefits of doing so outweigh the costs. Costs may include the time, effort and money involved; benefits may include believing that voting can actually change things.

Socialization

Political behaviour and attitudes develop through the socialization process (see page 206). People become inclined towards various forms of behaviour through interacting with, for example, families and communities. While some people are socialized into patterns of active involvement in politics, others are not.

Psychology or personality

Research into political participation has focused on individuals' psychological traits and personalities. Findings indicate that professional politicians and full-time workers for political parties tend to have extrovert (outgoing) personalities and lots of self-confidence.

STRETCH AND CHALLENGE ACTIVITY

Identify one difference between the explanation for variations in political participation based on socialization and that based on psychology or personality.

CHECK YOUR UNDERSTANDING

1 Identify two possible barriers to political participation.
2 Identify and explain two reasons why levels of political participation may vary between different individuals and social groups.

KEY POINTS

The likelihood of participating in the political process varies according to an individual's social location, views on the costs and benefits involved, socialization and personality.

TOPIC 16 How do we measure participation in the political process?

OBJECTIVE
Identify problems in measuring political participation

Researchers have highlighted problems in measuring the extent of civic and political participation. Much research on levels of participation is based on social surveys (see page 18). One problem concerns what the term 'political' means to respondents and what they class as political. For example, in one survey, 60 per cent of respondents claimed not to have discussed politics or political issues in the past two or three years. However, when presented with a list of 17 local, national and international political issues, only 6 per cent of respondents said that they had not discussed any of these in the last year (Electoral Commission and Hansard Society, 2007).

The use of surveys has been criticized as a means of investigating young people's participation. Questionnaires may underestimate their involvement because they often do not include the sorts of activities that young people may participate in. Surveys (such as the British Household Panel Survey) tend to question respondents about involvement in organizations such as trade unions, parents' associations, tenants' groups, professional and pensioner organizations. These organizations are likely to be less relevant to young people's lives. Critics argue that more appropriate questions are necessary to measure the extent of young people's participation (ONS, 2004).

Young people's political participation

DISCUSSION ACTIVITY

A key feature of recent debates about British youth concerns their low levels of engagement in formal politics. There is evidence of:

- low levels of interest in national politics among young people
- high levels of mistrust of politicians
- a sense of distance from the political process.

There is also evidence that while many young people feel strongly about many local and national issues, they have little knowledge about how they can influence policies in these areas, or little confidence as to whether this can be effective.

Source: adapted from Eden and Roker (2002)

1 In a small group, discuss how far you would agree that the image of British youth which has emerged from recent debates reflects the reality.

2 Note down three points made during your discussion.

How do we measure young people's political participation?

WRITTEN ACTIVITY

It is important to clarify what is meant by 'politics'. Large-scale surveys sometimes underestimate the extent of young people's political engagement by focusing on a relatively narrow range of indicators.

Young people's involvement in community-based organizations and pressure groups is often understated. This is partly because young people themselves often understate their level of political engagement by thinking of 'politics' as 'official' party politics.

As a number of studies have shown, young people are often enthusiastic and committed activists within a range of campaigning organizations with broadly 'political' goals, such as environmentalism, human rights and animal rights.

Source: adapted from Fahmy (2004)

1 Why do some surveys underestimate the extent of young people's political participation?
2 Why do young people themselves sometimes understate how politically engaged they are?
3 What sort of political activities are young people often involved in?

STRETCH AND CHALLENGE ACTIVITY

According to Fahmy, why is it important to make it clear what we mean by 'politics' when researching young people's political participation?

RESEARCH ACTIVITY

Researching people's political participation

1 Design a pilot survey to investigate the extent of people's political participation. Remember to include a wide range of measures covering formal (official party) politics and involvement in activities such as protest marches, volunteering and signing petitions.
2 Pilot your questionnaire on a sample of ten people.
3 Make a note of the three most significant results from your pilot questionnaire.

Young people are active within a range of campaigning organizations.

CHECK YOUR UNDERSTANDING

Explain two problems with using surveys to examine levels of political participation.

KEY POINTS

There are problems in measuring political participation. Surveys may underestimate people's involvement in politics.

TOPIC 17 · What is the welfare state?

OBJECTIVE
Explain the term 'welfare state'

The term 'welfare state' describes a system in which the state takes responsibility for protecting the health and welfare of its citizens, and for meeting their social needs. The state does this by providing services and benefits. In Britain, the welfare state was established as a safety net to protect the most vulnerable members of society and to guarantee them an adequate level of income, health care, education and housing.

Origins of the British welfare state

The origins of the British welfare state go back to the reforms of the Liberal government between 1906 and 1919. Free school meals were introduced in 1906 and old-age pensions were introduced in 1909.

However, it was not until the 1940s that the welfare state was firmly established. Its foundations were laid by the Beveridge Report (1942), which identified the five giant evils that the state was to combat. These were Want, Disease, Ignorance, Squalor and Idleness. The Beveridge plan envisaged a cradle-to-grave provision of benefits, including unemployment and sickness benefits. Particular groups, such as the elderly, widows and orphans were provided for. The idea was that everyone would pay insurance contributions while they were in work and, in return, they would be entitled to benefits when they were unable to work.

The welfare state works as a safety net.

In 1945, after a landslide general election victory, the Labour Party formed the post-war government (1945–50, 1950–01). Its aims were:

- To remove poverty and redistribute income more equally. In July 1948, a social security system came into operation. This was designed to help people should they need financial support, for example because of unemployment, ill health or retirement.
- To tackle disease by providing free health care to all. The NHS came into operation in July 1948.
- To tackle ignorance by providing free secondary education to all children. Butler's Education Act 1944 had introduced a system of free secondary state education and, in 1947, the school leaving age was raised to 15.
- To remove squalor by replacing poor housing with adequate state and private provision.
- To tackle idleness and unemployment through job creation.

DISCUSSION ACTIVITY

From the cradle to the grave

1 In a small group, discuss what the phrases 'cradle-to-grave provision' and 'the welfare state as a safety net' mean.

2 Note down your group's definition of these phrases.

What services are provided by the welfare state today?

Today, the welfare state provides services related to, for example, health, education, housing and welfare benefits. It also provides social services such as meals-on-wheels and child protection.

Glossary terms: contributory benefits local benefits national benefits

The National Health Service

The NHS provides various healthcare-related services such as general practitioners (GPs), hospitals, opticians, dentists and the ambulance service. These are funded by central government from national taxation.

National insurance benefits

National benefits, including national insurance (NI) benefits, are the responsibility of central government. NI benefits are contributory benefits. This means that, in order to qualify for them, the claimant must have paid sufficient contributions into the NI scheme. For example, people in paid employment pay part of their weekly or monthly earnings into the NI scheme. If they become unemployed, they are entitled to claim NI benefits provided that they have paid sufficient NI contributions.

The range of welfare benefits changes over time as governments introduce new ones and phase out old ones. Current examples of NI benefits include contribution-based Jobseeker's Allowance and the state retirement pension.

Non-contributory benefits

Non-contributory benefits are designed for people in financial need who have not paid enough NI contributions to qualify for NI benefits. Current examples include Income Support. Additionally, Working Tax Credits top up wages, and Child Tax Credits are payments for children.

Local benefits

Local benefits are the responsibility of local councils, for example Lambeth or Teesside Councils.

NHS provision.

RESEARCH ACTIVITY

Benefits and services

Log on to the Department for Work and Pensions' website at www.dwp.gov.uk. Identify two benefits or services provided by the welfare state today and briefly explain who they are for.

RESEARCH ACTIVITY

Local benefits

Log on to your local council's website. Identify two benefits provided by your local council and briefly explain what they are.

Examples of local benefits and services

Housing benefit	For people on low incomes who pay rent.
Education benefits	School clothing grants and free school meals.
Social services	Community support (home help) and meals-on-wheels.

CHECK YOUR UNDERSTANDING

1 Explain what sociologists mean by 'the welfare state'.

2 Explain one difference between contributory and non-contributory benefits.

KEY POINTS

The welfare state takes responsibility for its citizens' health, welfare and social needs.
The state provides services related to education, training, health, housing and benefits.

on-contributory benefits   welfare state

TOPIC 18 **What are the different political positions in debates about the welfare state?**

OBJECTIVE

Identify different political positions in debates about the welfare state

Welfare issues provoke heated debates among politicians, the public and the media because they involve important questions about how society tackles poverty and inequality. Welfare issues are controversial because welfare provision is funded by income from taxation.

One major area of debate concerns the role of the state in supplying social welfare and how far the state should be responsible for welfare provision. There are different political positions in these debates.

The Labour Party believes that the welfare state has an important role to play in society. It argues that the Labour government has done a lot since it came into power in 1997 to help the welfare state work better. Within the NHS, for example, the Labour Party identifies key achievements such as shorter waiting lists, increased numbers of doctors and nurses, financial investment in the NHS and provision of new NHS walk-in centres.

In tackling poverty, Labour sees its successes in terms of lifting children out of poverty, helping people into work and cutting the number of long-term unemployment claims among young people.

DISCUSSION ACTIVITY

The state's responsibility for welfare provision

1 Discuss how far the state should take responsibility for citizens' health, welfare and social needs.

2 How far should citizens, families, charitable organizations (such as Age Concern or Barnardo's), or profit-making businesses (such as private nursing homes) be involved in supplying welfare?

3 Note down three points arising from your discussion.

Labour and welfare reform

WRITTEN ACTIVITY

In this extract, Gordon Brown, the Prime Minister, outlines his views on welfare reform.

> It is very important for the government to give help to people who need it, when they need it. This may be because people might lose their job, or people might need help and advice to get them back to work.
>
> We want people to help us, by taking the help and support we offer them and getting ready to find a job. We want a system that gives more help and support to people but expects more from people in return. I think that this is the right thing to do, helping people get better skills so they can make the most of what they can do and build a better life for themselves, their families and their local area.

Source: adapted from Brown, G. (2008)

1 What does Gordon Brown see as the government's role in relation to welfare provision?

2 What does Labour expect from the people who receive benefits?

Glossary terms: dependency culture

The Conservative Party believes that Britain's welfare state, while helping to tackle some serious social and economic problems, has created others. For example, the welfare system enables people to choose a life on benefits and fails to encourage everyone who can work to find work. The welfare state is linked to the development of a dependency culture involving long-term dependency on welfare benefits and deliberate avoidance of work.

The Conservatives and welfare reform

✎ WRITTEN ACTIVITY

In this extract, David Cameron, the Conservative Party leader, outlines his views on welfare dependency and reform.

It is not acceptable that nearly five million of our fellow citizens are on out-of-work benefits. Mass welfare dependency is a waste of the country's human resources and a huge drain on the taxpayer – benefits cost the country over £100 billion a year, by far the biggest item in public spending. But worse than this, benefit dependency is a tragedy for the people involved, one of the primary causes of low aspirations and social breakdown.

Our plans for welfare reform will help those who want to work into sustained employment, and cut benefits for those who refuse to work. They will give some of our most deprived citizens the opportunity to live independent and fulfilling lives.

Source: adapted from Cameron, D. (2008)

1 Why does Cameron object to what he describes as welfare (or benefit) dependency?

2 How does his party plan to reform welfare provision to tackle this?

Support for the welfare state

❖ DISCUSSION ACTIVITY

Many people continue to support the NHS. Discuss the possible reasons for this continued support. Should NHS provision be extended or slimmed down?

Make a note of three points raised during your discussion.

💡 STRETCH AND CHALLENGE ACTIVITY

Identify one difference between Labour and the Conservatives in their positions on the welfare state.

CHECK YOUR UNDERSTANDING

Identify two reasons why welfare issues provoke debate.

KEY POINTS

Welfare issues are controversial. Political parties have different positions on the welfare state.

TOPIC 19 — How have governments attempted to tackle social problems such as poverty?

OBJECTIVES

Explain the terms 'social problems' and 'social policies'
Describe government attempts to tackle poverty

Social problems and policies

Social problems involve social conditions, situations or behaviour that are viewed as undesirable and so require action to try to 'solve' them (Davies, 2002). We have seen that the Beveridge Report (1942) identified five giant evils that the welfare state was to combat. Today, poverty remains a social problem alongside issues such as discrimination and unemployment. They are undesirable features of society that need tackling through social policy.

The term 'social policy' refers to the actions taken by policy makers and governments to tackle social problems and promote people's wellbeing. There is little agreement, however, on the aims and goals of social policy or the ways in which governments should act to finance welfare services. An important question concerns how resources should be allocated to promote welfare.

One approach sees the main goal of welfare services as reducing poverty by redistributing income from rich to poor. In this view, state benefits should be 'targeted' on people with the lowest incomes.

Tackling poverty

Despite the development of the welfare state, poverty continues to be a major concern for policy makers. Alcock (2008) views poverty as a core social policy issue. Policy makers and politicians, however, disagree on what to do about poverty.

Political party views on poverty — WRITTEN ACTIVITY

In the 1980s, the Conservative government did not believe that specific policies were needed to combat poverty beyond the provision of social security benefits. The Conservatives' argument was that, by the standards of poverty at the end of the 19th century, few people in Britain were now poor. As a result, there was no need for further policy action.

The Labour government under Tony Blair took a different view. It identified child poverty in particular as a serious social problem and pledged to end it by 2020.

Source: adapted from Alcock (2008)

Identify one difference between the Conservative governments of the 1980s and the Labour government under Tony Blair in their views on how much poverty there was.

STRETCH AND CHALLENGE ACTIVITY

Explain briefly how government views on how much poverty exists are linked to their policies on poverty.

Glossary terms: means test   poverty

One way of trying to reduce the number of people in poverty in Britain today is by state provision of financial support through means-tested benefits. A means (or income) test establishes whether a person is in need of financial help before they receive it. Whether or not a claimant qualifies for means-tested benefits, and how much they receive, depends on factors such as their income and savings. To receive means-tested benefits, an individual's or family's income and savings must fall below a certain level.

One advantage of means-tested benefits is that resources and help can be targeted at those in most need. However, critics identify several problems with means testing. For example:

- Those in need may not actually claim the benefits to which they are entitled because the claims process is too complex and intrusive.
- Means-tested benefits may label and stigmatize claimants.
- Means tests may trap people in poverty. This is because an increase in income may reduce the benefits to which people are entitled. For example, an employed person who is receiving means-tested benefits could get a wage rise but be no better off, or even worse off, if they now earn too much to qualify for benefits. This is sometimes called 'the poverty trap'.
- Means tests may discourage people from saving.

Most benefits are selective or targeted at those in greatest need on the basis of a means test. Child benefit, however, is a universal rather than a selective benefit. In other words, it is available to anyone with responsibility for a child, regardless of their income or savings. Universal benefits are less likely than means-tested benefits to stigmatize (or label) recipients. There is no stigma attached to child benefit, for example, and take-up rates are high.

The Labour government introduced a national minimum wage in 1999. Deacon (2008) argues that the minimum wage has not had a significant impact on wage inequalities. For example, in 2006, half of all children experiencing poverty lived in households in which at least one adult was working. In these cases, paid employment does not necessarily provide a route out of poverty.

Critics of government attempts to reduce poverty argue that:

- benefit levels are inadequate to meet people's basic requirements and should be increased to ensure that people can afford basic necessities
- successive governments have failed to significantly reduce the high levels of poverty in Britain.

DISCUSSION ACTIVITY

The debate on child benefit

Some people are critical of universal benefits such as child benefit.

1 In a small group, discuss possible reasons for and against paying child benefit universally rather than selectively. Try to consider possible reasons related to individual children, families and society as a whole.

2 Note down two reasons for:
a) maintaining child benefit for all
b) paying it only to families on low incomes.

CHECK YOUR UNDERSTANDING

1 Identify and explain one reason why governments might decide to use means-tested benefits to tackle poverty in Britain.

2 Outline one disadvantage of using means-tested benefits to tackle poverty.

KEY POINT

Governments attempt to address social problems such as poverty through social policies such as means-tested benefits or the minimum wage.

TOPIC 20 How have governments attempted to tackle unemployment?

OBJECTIVES

Understand why unemployment is seen as a social problem

Describe government attempts to tackle unemployment

Official measurements of unemployment count all those people aged 16 and over who do not have a job, who want to work, are available to start work in the next two weeks and who have been seeking a job in the last four weeks. The unemployment rate refers to the percentage of economically active people (those aged 16 and over who are either in work or looking for work) who are unemployed. The UK unemployment rate changes over time. It was low in the early 1970s at around 4 per cent. It peaked at 11.9 per cent in 1984 and again at 10.4 per cent in 1993. Since then, unemployment rates have generally fallen. However, the unemployment rate rose by 1.1 per cent in 2008, reaching 6.3 per cent for October to December.

Unemployment is viewed as a social problem for the people experiencing it, their communities and children living with unemployed parents or guardians.

Unemployment as a social problem

WRITTEN ACTIVITY

In the following extract, the author explains why unemployment is seen as a social problem.

> For millions of people, paid employment is not only their major source of income, it is also the basis of their social standing and self-esteem. People without such work are at greater risk of poverty and are more likely to experience ill health. Their children are less likely to do well at school and to obtain secure, well-paid jobs. Unemployment is also linked to a range of other social problems. Communities in which unemployment is high are also disproportionately affected by crime, family breakdown and antisocial behaviour.

Source: adapted from Deacon (2008)

Make a list of the reasons why unemployment can be seen as a serious social problem for those experiencing it, their children and communities.

While high rates of unemployment are associated with social problems, high rates of employment are good for governments. For example, they:

- boost government revenue from income tax and reduce spending on state benefits
- make it easier to fund other social policies and to meet the likely costs of an ageing population (Deacon, 2008).

In recent years, the attention of policy makers has focused on the numbers of people who are 'economically inactive'. This term refers to people who are neither in work nor actively seeking it. The main causes of inactivity are

Glossary terms: economically inactive   unemployment rate

long-term sickness, disability or unpaid caring responsibilities. As Deacon points out, inactivity, like unemployment, is associated with poverty and disadvantage. The terms 'the jobless' or 'the workless' are increasingly used by policy makers to cover both unemployed and inactive people.

One way governments have tried to address unemployment and inactivity is through welfare-to-work policies. Deacon (2008) sees welfare-to-work programmes as designed to:

- increase job opportunities for people who are claiming benefits, for example, through job creation schemes and work experience schemes
- improve claimants' skills and motivation through, for example, provision of education and training initiatives and counselling services
- give claimants a greater financial incentive to take advantage of the opportunities available by, for example, increasing the benefits paid to those in work through tax credits.

Unemployment and government programmes — RESEARCH ACTIVITY

Governments have attempted to tackle unemployment by introducing programmes such as the New Deal. This programme helps unemployed people on benefits to look for employment and includes training and preparation for work. Specific New Deal programmes are now available for groups such as people with disabilities, lone parents, young people and those aged 25 and over.

Using the internet as a source of information, find one current government programme that is designed to tackle unemployment and explain briefly what the programme involves. You could begin by looking at the DWP's Jobcentre Plus website at www.jobcentreplus.gov.uk.

Compulsory programmes — DISCUSSION ACTIVITY

1 In a small group, discuss how far you agree that involvement in government programmes should be compulsory for people (such as lone parents, unemployed people and those with disabilities) who receive benefits from the state.

2 Make a note of three points arising from your discussion.

Protests have taken place in Britain linked to social policy and welfare issues.

CHECK YOUR UNDERSTANDING

1 Identify two social problems associated with unemployment.

2 Identify and explain one way in which governments have tried to tackle unemployment and economic inactivity.

KEY POINTS

Unemployment is problematic for individuals and communities. Social policies are increasingly targeted at economically inactive people such as lone parents.

How have governments attempted to tackle discrimination, including issues arising from an ageing population?

OBJECTIVE

Describe government attempts to tackle discrimination and address the ageing population

Discrimination occurs when people are treated differently and less favourably, for example because of their gender, ethnicity or age. One way in which governments have tried to tackle discrimination is through legislation (laws). It is unlawful to discriminate on the grounds of gender, race, age, religion, belief, disability or sexual orientation.

Examples of equality and anti-discrimination laws include:

- Equal Pay Act 1970 and Sex Discrimination Act 1975
- Race Relations Act 1976
- Civil Partnership Act 2004
- Disability Discrimination Act 2005.

The 1976 Race Relations Act outlawed direct discrimination, indirect discrimination and victimization. Indirect discrimination occurs where a member of one group is at more of a disadvantage than another because of a requirement or a restriction, such as having to wear a particular uniform at work. Victimization occurs when a person who complains about discrimination is treated less favourably. The Act covered education, employment and the provision of services. It made it unlawful to discriminate against anyone on the grounds of 'race', colour, nationality or ethnic or national origin.

It is unlawful to discriminate on the basis of gender when recruiting staff.

Tackling discrimination

DISCUSSION ACTIVITY

According to a survey carried out for the Equality and Human Rights Commission in 2007, discrimination and disadvantage are still common across Britain. Some forms of discrimination are complex and deep-rooted. Sometimes people choose to ignore the rights of others even when this is against the law.

We have laws in this country to protect us from discrimination, unequal treatment and to preserve our rights. The Equality and Human Rights Commission is a public body that has powers to enforce the equality laws and shape public policy.

Source: adapted from Equality and Human Rights Commission (2008)

1 In a small group, discuss why discrimination is a social problem that needs to be tackled. Why do you think discrimination is still common across Britain? Apart from legislation, how might governments tackle discrimination?

2 Make a note of the main points arising from your discussion.

Researching discrimination at work

It is unlawful to treat someone at work less favourably than another person would be treated in similar circumstances because of their sex, race, religion, belief or sexual orientation. Discrimination can occur in relation to pay, recruitment, promotion, dismissal, pregnancy, maternity or requests to change working hours. Harassment or bullying at work on grounds of someone's sex or race is also unlawful.

Source: adapted from Equal Opportunities Commission (2004)

Imagine that you are investigating race discrimination in a large financial company.

1 Explain one ethical issue that could arise during the research process.

2 Identify one primary method of research that you would use, and explain why this method would be better than another primary method for getting the information you require.

3 Identify one secondary source you would use, and explain why you would use this source.

Policy issues arising from an ageing population

Older people have been a major focus of social policy since the early 20th century (Walker and Maltby, 2008). Britain's ageing population (see page 82) means that older people continue to be an important policy focus. Walker and Maltby (2008) identify key social policy issues affecting older people today, including age discrimination in the labour market and pensions.

People aged 50–60 face discrimination in the labour market from employers who believe that older workers cannot adapt to new technology (Walker and Maltby). While no research evidence supports such beliefs, they still limit the opportunities open to older workers.

The Employment Equality (Age) Regulations 2006 introduced regulations against age discrimination in employment and training. While the legislation covers the whole age range, it is more likely to benefit older people. However, employers are still permitted to implement a retirement age of 65.

Many older people's main source of income is from the state, for example from pensions and disability benefits. Some estimates suggest that poverty affects at least 20 per cent of people on pensions. Some commentators argue that state pensions are inadequate and should be improved.

CHECK YOUR UNDERSTANDING

Explain fully one way in which governments have attempted to tackle discrimination.

KEY POINTS

Governments have tackled discrimination through legislation. There is evidence, however, that discrimination persists. Older people are a major focus of social policy.

TOPIC 22 How do power relationships operate in everyday situations, such as between parents and children?

OBJECTIVES

Explain how power relationships can operate in everyday life

Describe how power relationships may operate between parents and children

Power, as we have seen, may be based on authority or coercion (see page 228). In a democracy, the government exercises legal rational authority when it makes decisions on policies to tackle social problems such as discrimination and poverty (see page 229). As an elected body, the government has the authority to devise social policies and have them implemented.

Power relationships in everyday life

Power is also present in day-to-day relationships between people and in everyday settings such as classrooms and workplaces. We enter into power relationships when we try to control or influence the behaviour and decisions of other people. We also enter into power relationships when other people try to control or influence our behaviour. In this sense, all areas of social life involve elements of power when influence, authority, control, constraint or coercion is exercised.

In everyday life, holding and exercising power is about being able to make your own interests count, achieve your aims and influence the behaviour of others. Power relationships operate in everyday situations where there are inequalities in power between individuals and groups. They may operate, for example, between:

- children, parents and guardians
- students and teachers
- children and their peers
- employers and employees
- members of the public and the police.

Power relationships between children, parents and guardians

Families operate as agencies of social control (see page 153) and parents or guardians are authority figures within families. They are expected to exercise authority over their children and to discipline them when necessary. Parents exercise power when they try to influence their children's behaviour or actions

---

People with power?

DISCUSSION ACTIVITY

It is possible to distinguish between holding power and using it. In a small group, discuss the extent to which the following people have the power to influence your behaviour and decisions. In what ways do they exercise power over you in practice?

- parents or guardians
- the police
- teachers
- employers
- peers

Make a note of the main points raised during your discussion.

STRETCH AND CHALLENGE ACTIVITY

What do sociologists mean when they suggest that power relationships operate in everyday life?

against their will. They might, for example, forbid their teenage children to camp out at a music festival, go on holiday with friends or play loud music indoors.

Traditionally, parents (particularly fathers) were powerful figures and children had few rights. However, we have seen that relationships between parents and children have changed over the last 50 years (see page 66). Since the 1950s, for instance, sociologists have identified a shift of power and attention towards children in working-class families (Cunningham, 2007). Parents, for example, became less strict and started having more democratic or equal relationships with their children than they had with their own parents.

It is now recognized that children have rights within families. They have the right to have their opinions taken into account in decisions that concern them, such as where to live in the event of parental divorce.

Eye on the exam

It is important to get as much practice at examination questions and papers as possible. Try answering some questions under timed conditions.

Should smacking be banned?

DISCUSSION ACTIVITY

The idea of parental responsibility includes parents' responsibility for disciplining their children. There is concern among politicians, children's organizations and the public about whether parents should smack their children to control their behaviour. In other words, should parents be able to exercise power over their children based on coercion?

In 2004, legal changes were introduced and any punishment that left physical marks or caused mental harm was outlawed. Many campaigners, however, believe that children should be protected from all forms of physical punishment and violence, including a mild slap.

1 In a small group, discuss whether:
- smacking is based on authority or coercion
- parents should have the power to smack their children to enforce discipline
- smacking should be a criminal offence.

2 Note down three points that were raised during your discussion.

CHECK YOUR UNDERSTANDING

Identify two ways in which parents exercise power over their children.

KEY POINTS

Power relationships operate in everyday life. Parents exercise power over their children when they influence, control or constrain their behaviour against their will.

How might power relationships operate in classrooms and schools?

OBJECTIVE

Describe how power relationships may operate between teachers and students

In everyday relationships, individuals in positions of authority within organizations may exercise power over others. In a school setting, for instance, teachers exercise legal rational authority based on their position within the authority structure. It is this position, together with their professional training and knowledge, which gives teachers the authority to make decisions concerning teaching and learning. They are able to decide, for example, what topics students will study during particular lessons, whether to spend time on class discussion or silent reading and what to set for homework.

Teachers also have the power to enforce school rules. For example, they are authorized to tell students to stop running in the corridor for health and safety reasons. Teachers' authority, however, is limited to particular school contexts. While they could tell their students to form an orderly queue in the canteen, for instance, their status as a teacher does not authorize them to tell adults to form queues at bus stops or airport check-in desks.

Teachers may also exercise a form of authority based on their charisma (see page 229). Such teachers can be seen as exceptional individuals who inspire their students. We should bear in mind, however, that some students do not necessarily conform to the school rules or authority structure. They may be part of a deviant subculture that resists the authority of teachers (see page 128).

Relationships between teachers and their students have changed over time. In general, they have become more informal and democratic. During the 1960s, for example, many schools routinely used physical punishment (or exercised coercive

---

Discipline in schools   ❖ DISCUSSION ACTIVITY

The extract below sets out government policy on school discipline and punishment.

> The school's discipline policy and any school rules must be based on the governors' statement on how children should behave (which all schools must have). Under the Human Rights Act 1998, any punishment or treatment must not be 'inhuman or degrading'. It must be suitable taking into account what the child has done.
>
> Physical punishment such as smacking, caning or shaking a child is illegal in all schools. School staff may use 'reasonable force' to stop a child: committing a crime, hurting someone or damaging something.

Source: www.direct.gov.uk/en/Parents/ParentsRights/DG_4002948

1 In a small group, discuss the possible reasons why the use of physical punishment is now illegal in schools. To what extent does this reflect changing attitudes to children's rights?

2 Make a note of three points arising from your discussion.

power) as a last resort to discipline students. Today, while schools still operate as an agency of social control and enforce adult authority, changes in the law mean that they no longer have the power to use corporal (physical) punishment.

Recent educational policies can be seen as reflecting a shift in thinking about the balance of power between teachers and students. For example, by law, schools must now take students' views into account when deciding on policies that affect them.

Involving pupils in decision making
WRITTEN ACTIVITY

> The Education and Skills Act 2008 has now become law. This Act will have a massive impact for school councils across the country. It states that schools' governing bodies must 'invite and consider' the views of their pupils on major policy issues that will affect them.
>
> So the people who make the biggest decisions in your school (the governing body) will have to ask you what you think about these decisions, and listen to your views.
>
> Schools that are doing this well already often use class councils. This ensures that all pupils have a chance to have their say.

Source: adapted from Schools Councils UK, www.schoolcouncils.org/front-page/News/pupils-get-a-real-voice-what-to-do-now

1 How might this legislation affect the balance of power and influence between pupils and teachers?

2 Why do you think relationships between pupils and teachers have changed over the last 50 years?

STRETCH AND CHALLENGE ACTIVITY

How might these changes help prepare pupils to be active citizens?

Decision making in action?
DISCUSSION ACTIVITY

1 In a small group, discuss how far you think students should be actively involved in making decisions on each of the following issues:
   - the canteen menu
   - facilities at school
   - the appointment of teachers.

2 Make a note of the main points raised during your discussion.

CHECK YOUR UNDERSTANDING

Identify one way in which the relationship between students and teachers has changed over the last 40 years and explain why the relationship has become more democratic.

KEY POINTS

Teachers exercise legal rational authority based on their position within the school's authority structure. Some also exercise charismatic authority. Relationships between teachers and students have become more democratic and students are now being involved in decision-making processes.

TOPIC 24 — How do power relationships operate between the public and the police and between employees and employers?

OBJECTIVES

Describe how power relationships may operate between members of the public and the police

Describe how they may operate between employers and employees

Members of the public and the police

The police force operates as an agency of social control and its role involves enforcing the law (see page 152). Like teachers and parents, the police play a part in enforcing adult authority over young people.

Police officers exercise power over members of the public in the form of legal rational authority based on the position they hold within the police force. They have powers to stop and search, arrest and detain members of the public. They may also exercise coercive power or reasonable force as a last resort.

Police officers' authority is based on written rules, and their interaction with the public is governed by codes of practice. These codes seek to strike the right balance between police officers' power and the public's rights and freedom. However, interaction with police officers may sometimes provoke resistance among members of the public.

The use of dispersal powers

WRITTEN ACTIVITY

The following extract is from a study exploring young people's interaction with the police and the use of dispersal (separating and moving on) powers.

Under the 2003 Anti-Social Behaviour Act, dispersal orders give the police new powers in authorized areas to disperse groups of two or more people where their presence or behaviour has resulted, or is likely to result, in a person being harassed, intimidated, alarmed or distressed. The powers are controversial due to the discretion (freedom to decide and act) they give to police and because they may involve stepping on individuals' rights.

Where targeted at groups of youths, dispersal orders can antagonize young people who frequently feel unfairly labelled for being in public places with their friends.

In one case study area, 61 per cent of young people thought that dispersal orders were unfairly targeted at young people, and in the other area 43 per cent thought so. Two-fifths of young people in both areas thought that dispersal orders had increased conflict between the generations. Where enforced without clear explanation, dispersal orders can damage police relations with youths and provoke defiance in some.

Source: adapted from Crawford and Lister (2007)

1 Identify two ways in which young people view dispersal orders.
2 Under what circumstances might dispersal orders damage relations between the police and young people and provoke defiance in some?

1   Some commentators are concerned that groups can be dispersed simply because of their presence rather than because of their behaviour. Why do you think some critics object to the police's power to disperse groups because of their presence?

2   The authors suggest that "increased levels of police contact may foster negative feelings towards the police. This, in turn, may amplify deviance." What do they mean by this?

Employers and employees

One view of employer and employee relationships argues that these are based on legitimate authority and operate through formal rules. For example, employees sign employment contracts and are free to resign if their employer behaves unreasonably. Workers' rights regarding the minimum wage, equality, working conditions, health and safety and redundancy are all protected in law.

Other views, however, suggest that in reality, unequal power relationships operate in the workplace. For example, it is argued that:

● the employment contract is based on an unequal balance of power between employer and employee

● employers have the power to hire and fire workers

● many employees are not involved in decision making at work

● some employers do not fulfil their responsibilities, for example in relation to the minimum wage.

Traditionally, workers' resistance to management decisions on pay and conditions took the form of negotiation through official trade unions or strikes. Today, employees can exercise power at work through industrial action such as strikes, go-slows or overtime bans. However, legislation has reduced unions' power to undertake industrial action. Unions are now required to follow the correct procedure in organizing industrial action. For example, before taking strike action, a secret postal ballot of union members must be held and the majority must support the action.

Some commentators suggest that trade union power is limited. For example, unions have only veto power or the ability to block employers' policies. They lack power to help formulate policies in the first place (Giddens, 2006).

DISCUSSION ACTIVITY

Influence at work

Research suggests that manual workers have less influence in decision making at work than professional or managerial workers. In a small group, discuss the possible reasons for this and note down two reasons.

CHECK YOUR UNDERSTANDING

1   Identify one way in which interaction between the public and police may be problematic.

2   To what extent is there an equal balance of power between employees and employers?

KEY POINT

Some interactions (e.g. between the police and public or employees and employers) may generate conflict and resistance.

8 Social Inequality

What is social inequality?

OBJECTIVE

Explain the terms 'social inequality' and 'social stratification'

Social inequality

Social inequality exists in all known societies. One of the main concerns of sociology is to understand these inequalities and how they impact on people's lives. Social inequality refers to the uneven distribution of:

- resources such as money and power
- opportunities related to, for example, education, employment and health.

Focusing on social inequality highlights important differences between individuals and groups in their access to, and share of, these resources and opportunities. Studies of inequality explore:

- the nature of inequality
- how much inequality there is and who gets what
- why some people get more than others.

Inequality in Britain today.

Social class, gender, ethnicity and age are all sources of inequality in the UK. In other words, resources and opportunities are distributed unequally between individuals and groups based on their class, gender, ethnicity and age. Piachaud (2009) argues that the causes of inequality within the UK include large differences between people in terms of inherited wealth, education and access to the labour market.

Social inequality	🍀 DISCUSSION ACTIVITY

In a small group, discuss the possible reasons why social inequality has existed in all known societies. How far do you think that social inequality is bound to exist in all societies? How far do you think it is possible to reduce social inequality?

Make a note of three points raised during your discussion.

Social stratification

Social stratification is a key concept in sociology. It describes the way society is structured in a hierarchy of strata or layers that are unequally ranked one above another. A social hierarchy is shaped like a pyramid and each layer is smaller but more powerful than the one below it. The most privileged group in society forms the top layer and the least favoured group forms the bottom layer.

Stratification involves inequality between social groups in the distribution of economic and social resources such as wealth, income, status and power.

Glossary terms: income   social inequalities   social stratification   wealth

These inequalities persist or carry on over time.

- Wealth refers to ownership of assets such as property, land and works of art. It also includes money held in savings accounts and shares in companies.

- Income may be received in cash (for example wages) or in kind (for instance the use of a company car).

- Status refers to social standing or the prestige that an individual in a particular social position is given by other members of the community or society.

- Power relates to the ability of an individual or group to get what they want, despite any opposition from other people (see Chapter 7).

The group in the top rank of the social hierarchy is likely to have much more wealth, income, status or power than the one at the bottom. Sociologists argue that an individual's position within a stratification order is the outcome of social factors such as their gender, age, ethnicity and class. In contemporary Britain, these are the main criteria by which people tend to be stratified.

Sociologists examine structured inequality between the different layers. They focus on inequalities (for example, in educational opportunities, income and health) between groups such as men and women or middle-class and working-class people. They also explore how these inequalities persist or carry on over time.

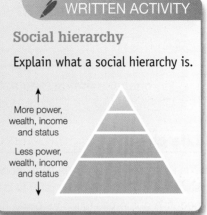

WRITTEN ACTIVITY

Social hierarchy

Explain what a social hierarchy is.

More power, wealth, income and status

Less power, wealth, income and status

WRITTEN ACTIVITY

Inequalities in Britain

In Britain there are vast inequalities in wealth, income and virtually everything else. Compared with children of top professionals and managers, the children of unskilled workers are 50 per cent more likely to die in infancy. As adults, the unskilled group are roughly twice as likely to die before reaching retirement age, and ten times more likely to have no natural teeth. Children from the top group are six times more likely to go to university. They are also six times more likely to stay in the top group than are those born at the bottom to rise to the top.

Source: adapted from Roberts (2001)

1 Which two social groups is Roberts comparing?
2 Identify two areas of life in which there are inequalities between these groups.

STRETCH AND CHALLENGE ACTIVITY

How might sociologists explain these class-based differences in life expectancy and infant mortality?

CHECK YOUR UNDERSTANDING

What do sociologists mean by the terms 'social inequality' and 'social stratification'?

KEY POINTS

Social inequality and stratification are key concerns in sociology. Social inequality refers to the unequal distribution of resources and opportunities. Stratification describes the way society is structured in a hierarchy of unequal layers.

TOPIC 2   What are life chances?

OBJECTIVES

Explain the term 'life chances' and describe the relationship between life chances and social factors such as class, gender and ethnicity

Describe inequalities in health

Life chances

The idea of life chances is a key concept in studying social inequality and stratification. Life chances refer to people's chances of achieving positive or negative outcomes (such as being healthy or ill, wealthy or poor) as they progress through life. These outcomes relate to many aspects of life including health, education, housing, wealth and income.

Life chances or opportunities are not distributed equally between different individuals or groups. This is because social factors such as class, gender and ethnicity affect life chances. Those in higher social classes, for example, have access to more of the things considered desirable in life (such as good healthcare and decent housing) than those in other social classes. Life chances are also shaped by inequalities in wealth, income, power and status.

Researchers have identified marked inequalities between different social classes in relation to:

- life expectancy at birth (see page 80)
- morbidity (having an illness or a disease)
- income and wealth
- housing

- infant mortality
- educational outcomes (see Chapter 4)
- poverty
- employment prospects.

The picture becomes more complicated when we examine the links between life chances, gender, ethnicity and age. For example, the chances of experiencing poverty are linked to gender, ethnicity and age as well as class.

Inequalities in health

Inequalities in health refer to differences in health outcomes between social groups or geographical areas (Shaw et al, 2006). Based on data from the 2001 census, Shaw and her colleagues argue that inequalities in healthcare and health outcomes still exist in contemporary Britain. They found fewer doctors in areas where a higher proportion of people needed medical care. In practice, this means that people in most need of medical services receive the least.

In the UK, factors such as where you live and your gender are related to life expectancy. For example, life expectancy in England is longer than in the other UK countries. It is also longer among women than men.

Life expectancy has improved and people now live longer (see page 80). Despite this, however, relative differences in health and life expectancy between groups of people and between areas persist (Shaw, 2002). In fact, Shaw argues that the life expectancy gap between different social classes has widened.

Glossary terms: life chances

The life expectancy gap

In the mid-1990s, the life expectancy gap between those in professional occupations and those in unskilled manual jobs was 6.4 years for women and 9.5 years for men.

There is overwhelming evidence that poverty and inequalities in material wellbeing underlie inequalities in health. Poverty and poor health are closely linked. Over the past 20 years, the number of people living in poverty grew significantly. There were also growing income inequalities in Britain, driven by factors such as the increase in 'work rich' families (with two adults in paid work) and 'work poor' families (with no adults in paid work).

Source: adapted from Shaw (2002)

1 What does Shaw mean by 'the life expectancy gap'?
2 Was the life expectancy gap between social classes bigger for men or for women in the mid-1990s?
3 Identify one factor that is behind these inequalities in health.

STRETCH AND CHALLENGE ACTIVITY

Explain one factor that is driving the growing income inequalities in Britain.

Reducing health inequalities

RESEARCH ACTIVITY

One view is that inequalities in health could be reduced by spending more money on healthcare. For example, if people paid more tax, and this extra government income was spent on healthcare, this could fund a reduction in health inequalities.

1 Devise an opinion poll to find out whether people would be prepared to pay higher taxes to reduce inequalities in health. Remember to ask fixed-choice questions and include all possible answers (for example, 'don't know').
2 Pilot your opinion poll on a sample size of ten. Try to ask equal numbers of men and women, younger and older people.
3 Write a short paragraph outlining the results of your pilot opinion poll.

CHECK YOUR UNDERSTANDING

1 What do sociologists mean by 'life chances'?
2 Identify two social factors that affect life chances and opportunities.

KEY POINTS

Life chances refer to people's chances of having positive or negative outcomes (such as being healthy or ill) over their life. They are distributed unequally and are influenced by class position, gender and ethnicity. For example, the life expectancy gap between different social classes has widened.

What different forms of stratification are there?

OBJECTIVE

Describe forms of stratification based on religion, ethnicity and class

Forms of stratification can vary between different societies at one point in time. They can also change within one society over time. Slavery, for example, existed as a form of stratification in ancient Greece and Rome and in the southern states of the USA in the 19th century. Under slavery, one group claims the right to own another group and treat them as property.

Stratification systems differ according to whether status is ascribed or achieved. With ascribed status, social positions are fixed at birth and unchanging over time. With achieved status, they are earned on the basis of personal talents or merit. Promotion at work, for example, can be earned through experience, ability or effort.

Stratification systems also differ according to how open or closed they are, that is, how easily an individual can move up or down between the strata. In an open society, movement up or down between the different strata is possible. In a closed society, such movement is much less likely to occur. The term social mobility is used to refer to movement between the layers or strata. In societies where status is ascribed, there is little social mobility. However, in achievement-based societies there is movement between the layers.

Social position may be ascribed at birth.

The caste system in traditional India

The caste system in India is an example of a stratification system. Here, people are born into a particular caste and their social position is ascribed at birth. The system is closed so there is little movement between the different layers. Each caste was traditionally associated with particular occupations, as shown in the table.

The caste system is linked to the Hindu religion. Hindus believe that they are born into

Main castes	Types of occupation	Status
Brahmin	Priests, teachers	Higher status
Kshatriyas	Soldiers, land owners	↑
Vaishyas	Merchants, traders	Lower status
Shudras	Servants, manual workers	↓
Dalits ('Untouchables')	Do the worst jobs in society	Social outcasts

a particular caste and deserve to be there as a result of their behaviour in their previous life. By living according to the rules now, Hindus can ensure that they will be reborn into a higher caste in the next life. In this way, they can progress through the ranks of the caste system. Inequality between different groups was justified as stemming from religious belief.

Apartheid

Apartheid in South Africa (1948–94) was based on a government policy of racial segregation, and ethnicity was used as the basis for stratification.

Glossary terms: achieved status   apartheid   ascribed status   caste   social mobility

Apartheid applied to all aspects of society and so access to health, education, housing and employment was segregated according to whether a person was black, white or coloured.

Under apartheid, a person's social position was ascribed at birth. Black people were denied the citizenship rights and opportunities available to white people. So, their life chances were much worse, with little scope for mobility.

Apartheid in South Africa.

Social class

In modern industrial societies such as Britain, social class is seen as the main form of stratification. Social class is based on economic factors such as occupation and income (how people earn a living) rather than on religious teachings or racist ideas. This form of stratification is said to be an open one in that class position can be achieved and social mobility is possible.

Sociologists also emphasize the significance of sources of inequality based on gender, ethnicity and age in class-based societies. For example, men and women in the same class may have very different life chances in relation to promotion and pay at work. Feminist approaches in particular would see gender as a more important source of inequality than social class.

More power, wealth, income and status

Less power, wealth, income and status

Upper class

Middle class

Working class

Social class-based strata.

Comparing different forms of stratification

WRITTEN ACTIVITY

Copy out and complete this table comparing caste, apartheid and class.

	Caste	Apartheid	Social class
What is stratification based on?			
Is social position ascribed or achieved?			
Is the system open or closed?			
Is social mobility possible?			

STRETCH AND CHALLENGE ACTIVITY

Why might basing status on ascription rather than achievement be seen as unfair?

CHECK YOUR UNDERSTANDING

Explain two different forms of stratification.

KEY POINTS

Different forms of stratification have existed between societies and over time. They include caste, Apartheid and class.

TOPIC 4 **How have sociologists explained social class?**

OBJECTIVE

Explain Marx's and Weber's views on class

What is social class?

Social class is a key concept in sociology and the term is used frequently. Nonetheless, there is no agreed definition of social class and sociologists view it in different ways (Roberts, 2001). The ideas of both Karl Marx and Max Weber have been central in developing sociological views on social class. In fact, they continue to shape debates on class in the early 21st century (Crompton, 2008).

Marx on class

Karl Marx (1818–83) saw capitalist society as a highly stratified system. He identified two main classes: the bourgeoisie (the ruling class) and the proletariat (the working class). Membership of these classes was determined by economic factors – that is, ownership and non-ownership. The wealthy bourgeoisie owned the means of production through their ownership of property, big businesses, land and factories. The proletariat did not own any property and had to sell their labour to the bourgeoisie in order to survive.

These two classes had very different interests. For example, while the bourgeoisie aimed for ever-increasing profits, the proletariat sought higher wages. Marx saw the bourgeoisie as exploiting the proletariat and this situation led to conflict between these classes.

Marx on class

WRITTEN ACTIVITY

Copy out and complete this table to summarize Marx's views on the differences between the bourgeoisie and proletariat.

	Bourgeoisie	Proletariat
Ownership	•	•
Interests	•	•

Marx believed that the bourgeoisie would decline in size and get much richer, while the proletariat would grow in size and become increasingly poor. Eventually, the proletariat would rebel, leading to a revolution or radical change in society. As a result, the social class system would disappear and people would live in a more equal society.

A revolution has not occurred in Britain, partly as a result of increased standards of living and the development of the welfare state. However, sociologists drawing on the Marxist (or neo-Marxist) approach today highlight the enormous differences in the distribution of wealth and power between property owners and workers in society. Neo-Marxists see this as the key division in society.

Weber on class

Max Weber (1864–1920) argued that classes were formed in marketplaces such as the labour market. In the labour market, one class of people hired labour and another class sold their labour. Weber saw the processes of hiring labour and the rewards (or life chances) that arose from this as crucial in explaining class.

Weber argued that a class is a group of people who have similar access to life chances, that is, chances of being successful (or otherwise) and opportunities in education, health and so on. Weber identified four main classes:

- property owners
- the petty bourgeoisie (e.g. shopkeepers)
- professionals
- the working class.

These different class situations reflected different life chances in the labour market. Members of the working class, for example, shared similar life chances in the labour market. However, they had different life chances from property owners.

Like Marx, Weber saw class as based on the distribution of economic resources such as wealth. However, Weber also stressed the importance of non-economic factors such as status (prestige) and power (political influence) in determining life chances and in shaping patterns of stratification.

Weber distinguished between class and status. While classes were formed in marketplaces, status groups could be identified by the prestige or honour attached to their styles of life. Weber argued that each of the four classes had a different amount of status, wealth and power.

In Marx's view, ownership was the most significant division in society. Other inequalities (such as status) arose from class divisions. Weber, however, saw class and status as two separate aspects of stratification. In Weber's view, a person's status may differ from their class (or economic) position. For instance:

- members of the aristocracy (such as a Lord or Lady) may have no savings but their title gives them status
- nurses may lack wealth but have high status
- National Lottery millionaires may be very wealthy but lack status.

Economic position and status do not necessarily go hand in hand.

Weber on class

Copy out and complete this table to summarize what Weber meant by class, status and power.

WRITTEN ACTIVITY

Class	
Status	
Power	

CHECK YOUR UNDERSTANDING

Identify one similarity and one difference between Marx's and Weber's views on social class.

KEY POINTS

Marx identified two main classes. Class membership was determined by economic factors (ownership and non-ownership). Weber identified four main classes, reflecting different life chances. Weber saw class, status and power as important in determining life chances.

TOPIC 5 — How does the functionalist approach view stratification?

OBJECTIVE
Explain the functionalist approach to stratification

The functionalist approach was popular and influential, particularly among North American sociologists in the mid-20th century. This approach explains social practices (such as stratification) in terms of the functions they perform for the wider society.

The functionalist approach argues that some positions in an advanced industrial society are more important than others because they are vital to the continuation of society. The holders of these top positions require specific high-level skills and qualifications in order to perform their roles effectively. Not everyone in society has the talent or ability to fill these positions. The few who have the raw talent and potential need to undergo lengthy periods of education and training in order to develop the necessary skills. This means sacrifices of one kind or another.

The functionalist approach argues that talented people will only be persuaded to undertake the lengthy training required to qualify for important positions if they can see rewards at the end of it. In order to motivate talented people to make the necessary sacrifices while in education and training, top positions have to look desirable. So these positions must provide access to rewards that are both scarce and valued in society. Such rewards could include, for example, high status, generous salaries, bonuses and pension schemes, and perks such as a company car and private health cover.

According to this approach, a system of inequality or unequal rewards and prestige is necessary in all societies to attract the most talented people to the most important occupations. Such a system is functional for society because, although scarce rewards are distributed unequally, this is done in a way that everyone considers fair.

The functionalist approach to stratification

WRITTEN ACTIVITY

The following table covers six points related to the functionalist approach to stratification. However, there is still work to be done on it. For each of the six issues, you need to decide which option is correct. For example, does the functionalist approach see status as ascribed or achieved (see page 280)? Once you have made your decisions, copy out the table with the correct answers.

1	Status	Ascribed or achieved?
2	Talent is distributed equally.	Yes / no?
3	Positions are earned on the basis of talent.	Yes / no?
4	Society is closed.	Yes / no?
5	Social mobility is not possible.	Yes / no?
6	Social mobility is desirable.	Yes / no?

Jobs, talent and pay

In a small group, look at this list of jobs:

- City banker
- English teacher
- Heart surgeon
- High court judge

- Member of a successful boy band
- Midwife
- Politician
- Professional footballer

- Reality TV star
- Refuse collector
- Vicar
- TV chat show host.

1 In your group, discuss and note down which three jobs fit each of the following criteria:

a) require the highest levels of talent or education

b) the most important in terms of the contribution they make to society

c) deserve the highest earnings

d) are usually very highly paid.

Did the same three jobs come up each time?

2 Write down the two most significant points that were made during your discussion.

STRETCH AND CHALLENGE ACTIVITY

Identify two possible criticisms of the functionalist approach to stratification.

Eye on the exam

Try to refer to the relevant sociological terms (such as ascribed status and social mobility) and approaches (such as the functionalist approach) in your answers.

CHECK YOUR UNDERSTANDING

Identify one difference between the functionalist and Marxist (see Topic 4) approaches to social inequality.

KEY POINTS

The functionalist approach argues that some positions are vital to society but not everyone has the talent to fill these posts. To attract the best-qualified people, top positions must provide access to desirable rewards such as high pay and status. Stratification is functional for society because it ensures that the most important jobs are filled by the most talented and qualified people.

TOPIC 6 How is social class measured?

OBJECTIVE
Describe and assess the different social class scales

Occupation is often used as a way of measuring social class. Occupation is used because it is related to factors such as levels of pay, working conditions, social status and life chances.

The Registrar General's classification

The Registrar General's social class scale was the UK's official government class scale from 1911, when it first appeared, until 1998. This classification distinguishes between manual and non-manual occupations. Manual occupations are jobs that involve some physical effort. They can be skilled, semi-skilled or unskilled. These are seen as working class. Non-manual occupations require no physical effort. Skilled non-manual, intermediate and professional occupations are seen as middle class.

The Registrar General's social class scale

This scale identifies five social classes. Classes I, II and III (Non-manual) were seen as middle class and III (Manual), IV and V were seen as working class.

I   Professional occupations such as solicitors, surgeons and architects.

II   Managerial and technical occupations such as teachers, nurses and aircraft pilots.

III (N) Skilled non-manual occupations such as clerical workers, secretaries and receptionists.

III (M) Skilled manual occupations such as bus drivers, electricians and hairdressers.

IV   Partly skilled occupations such as postal delivery workers, bartenders and caretakers.

V   Unskilled occupations such as labourers, refuse collectors and cleaners.

Problems with the Registrar General's scale

- Classifications based on occupation cannot accommodate people without jobs (such as students, retired and unemployed people). In practice, retired and unemployed people were allocated to a class based on their most recent occupation. However, those who had never worked, such as young unemployed people, were difficult to place.

- Other people without occupations were allocated to a class according to the class of the head of the household in which they lived. In practice, the class of a married woman who was a homemaker was based on her husband's occupation.

- Men and unmarried women were allocated to a class on the basis of their own occupations. When more married women went into paid employment in the 1970s, the practice of assessing the class position of a family or couple on the basis of the male's occupation was challenged.

- Occupational class scales and job titles do not tell us about an individual's wealth and property. It was not clear where the wealthy upper class or National Lottery millionaires should be placed.

WRITTEN ACTIVITY

Different social classes in a hospital setting

Examine the people who are shown at work in this photograph. For each of the jobs shown, identify which social class the person doing the job belongs to according to the Registrar General's scale.

- The same job title, such as doctor, lecturer or farmer, may hide significant differences. The title 'farmer', for example, could hide huge differences in wealth, income, status and qualifications depending on the size and type of farm involved.

The NS-SEC

The NS-SEC (National Statistics Socio-economic Classification) has replaced the Registrar General's scale as the UK's official classification. The NS-SEC is also based on occupation, but one advantage is that it covers the whole adult population including, for example, people who are unemployed. Another advantage is that it is seen as able to measure and predict health and educational outcomes. The NS-SEC scale groups together occupations that have similar:

- rewards from work such as pay and fringe benefits (including, for example, health insurance and a company car), career prospects and job security

- employment status (whether an employer, self-employed or an employee)

- levels of authority and control (for example, how far people are responsible for other workers and how far they are supervised by others).

To cover the population completely, three other categories ('Students', 'Occupations not stated or inadequately described' and 'Not classifiable for other reasons') are added.

> **STRETCH AND CHALLENGE ACTIVITY**
>
> **Assessing class position on men's occupations**
>
> Why do you think the practice of assessing the class position of a family or couple on the basis of the male's occupation was challenged?

The NS-SEC class scale

1 Higher managerial and professional occupations:

　1.1 Employers [in large organizations] and higher managerial occupations, e.g. senior sales manager.

　1.2 Higher professional occupations, e.g. solicitors.

2 Lower managerial and professional occupations, e.g. social workers, teachers.

3 Intermediate occupations, e.g. clerks, secretaries, computer operators.

4 Employers [in small businesses] and own account workers [the self employed], e.g. farmers.

5 Lower supervisory and technical occupations e.g. maintenance engineer, car mechanic.

6 Semi-routine occupations, e.g. cooks, bus drivers, sales assistants, teaching assistants

7 Routine occupations, e.g. waiters, cleaners, labourers

8 Never worked and long-term unemployed

CHECK YOUR UNDERSTANDING

Identify one similarity and one difference between the Registrar General's and the NS-SEC scales.

KEY POINTS

Occupation is often used to measure social class because it is related to factors such as status and life chances. The NS-SEC is seen as overcoming many of the problems with the Registrar General's scale.

TOPIC 7 What is gender?

OBJECTIVE
Explain what sociologists mean by 'gender'

Gender is one of a number of social divisions alongside age, ethnicity and class. Feminist approaches in sociology have highlighted the importance of exploring gender and gender inequalities in contemporary society.

What is the difference between sex and gender?

Sociologists distinguish between sex and gender. The term 'sex' refers to whether a person is considered male or female. It concerns biological differences between men and women, for example in relation to their bodies and role in reproduction. These physical characteristics are ascribed at birth and are usually fixed throughout life.

Sex
Male   Female

Gender
Masculine   Feminine

Gender describes the different social practices, expectations and ideas that are associated with masculinity and femininity.

Families often socialize their sons and daughters differently and so children develop a gender identity – that is, they come to see themselves as masculine or feminine. Virtually from birth, for instance, we differentiate between girls and boys in the names we give them and the style and colour of the clothes we dress them in. Male babies, for example, are more likely to be dressed in blue clothes while female babies are more likely to be dressed in pink.

His or hers? What do you think?

As babies get older, we continue to differentiate between them, for example in the toys we give them. Young children are often given different books and toys (such as Iron Man or Spider Man for boys and Barbie or My Little Pony for girls) according to their gender.

Many sociologists have concluded that the process of socialization is highly gendered. By this, they mean that socialization prepares us for social roles related to our gender, such as breadwinner or housewife.

Sociologists explore the ways that gender is constructed or shaped by social processes such as socialization. Agencies of socialization such as families, schools and the mass media are central in how we learn masculinity and femininity. For example, they may teach us that girls and boys should behave in different ways. While girls should be kind and caring, boys should be independent and strong.

❖ DISCUSSION ACTIVITY

Pink and blue worlds

Some commentators argue that everyday life, particularly for younger children, is divided into a pink world for girls and a blue world for boys.

1 In a small group, discuss how far you would agree with this view of everyday life.

2 Make a note of three points arising from your discussion.

Glossary terms: gender

Gender in everyday life

Holmes (2009) argues that, as part of the socialization process, girls and boys are channelled into doing different kinds of things.

> Girls and boys are dressed in different kinds of clothes, do different school subjects, usually end up in different jobs and are portrayed differently in everything from magazines to movies to television shows. From birth, girl children and boy children are treated differently, and every day of our lives involves interacting with other people according to their gender. We talk to girls/women differently about different things, assuming they are more delicate and will be interested in, say, clothes or children or cooking. Meanwhile, boys/men are treated as though they are tough and likely to be interested in sport or cars.

Source: adapted from Holmes (2009)

1 Drawing on this information, identify two ways in which girls and boys are channelled into doing different kinds of things.
2 Describe one way in which we might interact with other people according to their gender.

Sociologists argue that many of the differences between men and women are created by society rather then being based on biology. They argue this because what is seen as masculine and feminine behaviour has varied historically and between different cultures. It depends on how a particular society understands gender at a particular time. Gender, in other words, is socially constructed.

Cross-cultural differences in gender

> H&M, the Swedish retailer, will open the first women-only department store in Saudi Arabia as part of moves to bring more women into the country's workforce. Saudi Arabia has strict laws that prohibit the public interaction of women with men other than their husbands. These extend to restrictions on working and driving. As the store will be staffed by women, the Saudi Government has insisted that only females will be able to shop there.

Source: adapted from D. Robertson, *The Times*, 19 May 2008

Identify and note down two points from this information to support the view that the role of women varies cross-culturally.

CHECK YOUR UNDERSTANDING

1 Explain one difference between sex and gender.
2 Explain one way (other than pink and blue clothes and toys) in which girls and boys are socialized differently.

KEY POINTS

The term gender describes the different social practices and ideas that are associated with masculinity and femininity. Sociologists argue that gender is based on social rather than biological differences. The socialization process, for example, is gendered.

TOPIC 8 # What inequalities are based on gender?

OBJECTIVES
Identify inequalities linked to gender
Explain gender inequalities in employment

Inequalities linked to gender

Many changes have taken place over the last 40 years to address gender inequality in areas like education and employment. These changes are partly linked to the introduction of anti-discrimination laws (see pages 268–9). Following the Equal Pay Act (1970), employers must pay men and women the same salary when they are doing the same work or work of equal value. The Sex Discrimination Act (1975) has made it unlawful to discriminate or treat someone less favourably (for example, at work or school) because of their sex.

As a result of such legislation, many practices that treated people differently on the basis of their gender (such as listing girls and boys separately on school registers) were changed. The term 'sexism' refers to discrimination on the basis of sex. Historically, most sexism was directed at women, but the term also applies to discrimination against men.

Li et al (2008) note that women today are increasingly likely to achieve good educational qualifications, jobs and salaries. Feminist approaches, however, suggest that gender inequality is still the most important source of division in society today. Holmes (2009), for example, argues that society is still organized in ways that tend to benefit men more than women. This is because we live in a patriarchal society. In other words:

- society is controlled mainly by men who have considerable power within politics and the workplace
- men generally have a bigger share of rewards such as wealth and status.

Feminist approaches focus on inequalities resulting from gender, for example in terms of power, and how they impact on everyday life. Gender inequalities are seen as 'man made', so it is possible to create a more equal society.

Gender inequalities at work

Despite legislation passed nearly 40 years ago, gender inequalities in the labour market persist. Often, men and women do not work

Men and women's employment rates: 1971 and 2007   WRITTEN ACTIVITY

Work is a source of status and power as well as income, so it is important to examine whether inequality in paid work persists. Men's and women's employment rates are becoming increasingly similar, as the UK statistics in the table show.

	Working-age men	Working-age women
1971	92%	56%
2007	79%	70%

Source: *Social Trends* (2008)

By how many percentage points did:
a) men's employment rate fall over this period?   b) women's employment rate rise?

Glossary terms: glass ceiling

together in the same occupations. For example, fire fighting is male dominated and nursery nursing is female dominated. In 2007, 19 per cent of employed men were working in skilled trades compared with around 2 per cent of women. In contrast, 20 per cent of employed women were in administrative or secretarial occupations compared with less than 5 per cent of men. The image of invisible walls is used to illustrate this divide between female and male occupations.

When women and men work in the same occupation, women are more likely to be in lower- or middle-level jobs while men tend to hold the higher-grade and senior management posts. In 2007, for example, 19 per cent of men and 11 per cent of women were employed as managers or senior officials. It is argued that women are held back by a 'glass ceiling', an invisible barrier to promotion.

Many women are employed in low-status, part-time jobs. Women, on average, still earn significantly less than men. Li et al (2008) found that women had worse pay levels than men of similar ages and educational levels. Women also had worse chances than men in terms of accessing employment and accessing professional and managerial jobs.

Explanations for the persistence of inequality at work include:

- **Sex discrimination within the workplace.** This means that women continue to be treated less favourably than men simply because they are women. However, Li et al (2008) found that women report lower levels of being denied a promotion than men.

- **Women's triple shift.** Dunscombe and Marsden (1995) argued that many women bear the burden of working a triple shift. This involves paid employment, domestic labour (housework and childcare) and 'emotion work' (making children and partners feel good). So, it could be argued that some women are held back when applying for promotion at work or developing a career.

- **Childcare provision.** Some critics argue that Britain has inadequate or expensive childcare provision for the under-5s. If this is the case, it may act as a barrier, preventing women with young children from participating in full-time, paid employment or in staying in employment long enough to progress in their career.

STRETCH AND CHALLENGE ACTIVITY

Identify one possible reason why the male rate of employment declined between 1971 and 2007.

DISCUSSION ACTIVITY

Jobs for the girls!

1 In a small group, discuss possible reasons why women today might be more likely to enter jobs which were traditionally thought of as men's jobs.

2 Note down three reasons.

CHECK YOUR UNDERSTANDING

1 Describe two ways in which British governments have tried to reduce inequalities between women and men over the last 40 years.

2 State two reasons why women tend to earn less, on average, than men in the UK.

KEY POINTS

Despite legislation, women still experience inequality in employment in relation to, for example, pay. Possible reasons include women's triple shift and discrimination.

TOPIC 9 What is ethnicity?

OBJECTIVE
Explain what sociologists mean by ethnicity

What is ethnicity?

We have seen that Apartheid in South Africa (1948–94) was based on a government policy of racial segregation in which ethnicity was the main basis for stratification. Some sociologists argue that in contemporary societies such as the UK and USA, there are inequalities between different ethnic groups arising from discrimination. As a result, ethnicity, like social divisions based on class and gender, affects the life chances of individuals and groups.

An ethnic group is a social group whose members share an identity based on their cultural traditions, religion or language. The term 'ethnic minority' describes a group of people who are from a different ethnic group from the general population who, in turn, may be described as the 'ethnic majority'. Britain is a culturally diverse society and is home to a rich mix of minority ethnic groups including those of Irish, Polish, Greek Cypriot, Indian and African-Caribbean heritage.

The term 'race' has been used in different ways. It has been used to refer to the idea that humankind could be divided up into different 'racial groups' on the basis of natural, physical characteristics. Some 'races' were thought to be

Ethnicity and the population

WRITTEN ACTIVITY

1 Which ethnic group does the majority of the population in Britain belong to?

2 What percentage of the population was made up of the Indian ethnic group?

3 How many people belonged to the black Caribbean ethnic group?

4 Identify two groups that are seen as minority ethnic groups.

Population by ethnic group, GB, 2001

	Numbers	Percentages
White British	50 366 497	88.2
White Irish	691 232	1.2
Other white	1 423 471	2.5
Mixed	673 798	1.2
Indian	1 051 844	1.8
Pakistani	746 619	1.3
Bangladeshi	282 811	0.5
Other Asian	247 470	0.4
Black Caribbean	565 621	1.0
Black African	484 783	0.8
Other black	97 198	0.2
Chinese	243 258	0.4
Any other ethnic group	229 325	0.4
All ethnic groups	57 103 927	100.0

Source: *Focus on Ethnicity and Religion* (ONS, 2006)

superior to others and this belief was used to justify the oppression of one group by another. The colonization of parts of Africa and Asia in the 19th century by Europeans, for example, was justified in this way. More recent scientific evidence, however, has led scientists to reject the idea of different biological 'races'.

Sociologists reject the idea that humankind can be divided into different 'racial groups'. Instead, they argue that 'racial differences', like gender differences, are created by society rather than rooted in biology. However, sociologists (as well as many politicians and policy makers) recognize that racism or racial discrimination exists. Racism occurs when people are treated differently and less favourably on the basis of their ethnicity.

What changes have taken place to address inequality based on ethnicity?

Changes have taken place over the last 40 years to address inequality based on ethnicity in areas such as education, employment and criminal justice. These changes are partly linked to:

- The introduction of equality and anti-discrimination legislation – the 1976 Race Relations Act, for example, outlawed direct discrimination, indirect discrimination and victimization (see page 268).

- The establishment of the Commission for Racial Equality, which later merged with the Equal Opportunities Commission to become the Equality and Human Rights Commission (see page 268). These organizations have helped to tackle racism and discrimination.

- The recognition that institutional racism existed within organizations such as the Metropolitan Police and must be addressed (see page 45).

- Equal opportunities policies or statements supporting diversity in the workplace and in education (see page 131).

Some commentators argue that inequalities based on ethnicity are much less significant today than they were 40 or 50 years ago. For example, black people are making inroads into the world of politics, the media, the arts, literature and sport. As a result, ethnicity is no longer seen as such a major social division compared with the situation in the past.

STRETCH AND CHALLENGE ACTIVITY

Explain the difference between the terms 'ethnic group' and 'minority ethnic group'.

People from minority ethnic backgrounds are making inroads into politics, the arts and sport.

Eye on the exam

The question in CHECK YOUR UNDERSTANDING specifies a particular time frame. It asks you to focus on 'the last 40 years' so you must ensure that your answer addresses this time frame.

CHECK YOUR UNDERSTANDING

Describe one way in which British governments have tried to reduce inequalities based on ethnicity over the last 40 years.

KEY POINTS

One view is that changes in attitudes and practices (such as the recognition that institutional racism must be addressed) have taken place to address inequalities based on ethnicity. As a result, ethnicity has become a less significant social division than in the past.

TOPIC 10 What inequalities are based on ethnicity?

OBJECTIVE
Identify links between ethnicity, inequality and life chances

While some commentators argue that inequalities based on ethnicity are now much less significant, others argue that in some of the most crucial areas, such as employment, education and the criminal justice system, little has actually changed for the better.

Ethnicity and unemployment

Unemployment is an important indicator of inequality. It can be linked to social problems such as poverty and homelessness as well as ill health.

Unemployment and ethnicity　　　WRITTEN ACTIVITY

The table provides figures on the unemployment rates among different ethnic groups. Study this information and answer the questions.

Unemployment rates 2001 England and Wales Percentages

	Men of working age	Women of working age		Men of working age	Women of working age
White British	6	4	Bangladeshi	19	22
White Irish	7	4	Black Caribbean	17	10
Indian	7	7	Black African	18	16
Pakistani	16	18	Chinese	8	8

Source: *Focus on Ethnicity and Religion* (ONS, 2006)

Unemployment rates in each ethnic group were higher among young people aged 16–24 than in older age groups.

1 Among which ethnic group was male unemployment the highest?
2 Among which ethnic groups was female unemployment the lowest?

STRETCH AND CHALLENGE ACTIVITY

Drawing on this information, write a paragraph to summarize the links between ethnicity and unemployment.

Having educational qualifications improves the life chances and quality of life of all ethnic groups (Li et al, 2008). However, prejudice and discrimination in the labour market exist and so the life chances and quality of life of some ethnic groups are negatively affected.

Is there fair employment based on ethnicity?

Li and colleagues (2008) examined the position of different ethnic groups in relation to paid employment in 2004/05. They focused on whether minority ethnic groups have the same employment chances as their white British peers of the same age and educational level.

The researchers found that all minority ethnic groups had much worse chances of accessing employment than their white peers. The researchers compared the chances of getting professional and managerial jobs, levels of pay and whether different groups reported having similar levels of being refused a job or denied a promotion. Their findings are presented below.

We can see, for example, that weekly earnings are much worse for men and somewhat worse for women of Pakistani/Bangladesh ethnicity than their white British peers.

	Chances of getting professional and managerial jobs	Weekly earnings	Job and promotion refusals
Black Caribbean	Much worse for men	Much worse for men	Much worse
Indian	Yes	Yes, similar	Somewhat worse
Pakistani/Bangladeshi	Much worse	Much worse for men, somewhat worse for women	Somewhat worse for men, not for women
Chinese	Yes	A little worse for men, not for women	Yes, similar

Source: adapted from Li et al (2008), p. 98

1 Which minority ethnic groups had the same access to professional and managerial jobs as their white British peers?

2 Overall, do men or women from minority ethnic groups seem to fare better in relation to their earnings?

Drawing on the information above, write a paragraph to show that:

a) Different minority ethnic groups are positioned differently in relation to employment.

b) It is important to examine gender alongside ethnicity when investigating inequality in employment.

Identify two differences in the life chances of some minority ethnic groups compared to those of their white British peers.

There is evidence to suggest that, despite changes, discrimination based on ethnicity (for example in the labour market) persists. However, members of some ethnic groups (such as those of Indian heritage) are much better placed than others (such as those of Pakistani/Bangladeshi heritage) in terms of employment so it is difficult to generalize.

How do sociologists approach the study of age?

OBJECTIVE

Explain what is meant by age

Chronological age

One way of looking at an individual's age is simply in terms of how long they have been alive. Someone born in 1990, for example, would be 19 years old in 2009. This is known as a person's chronological age. Your chronological age is used to determine whether you are allowed to participate in a range of activities. For example, it would be unlawful for someone with a chronological age of 12 to buy an alcoholic drink in a pub in England. However, the chronological age for purchasing alcohol varies between societies.

Biological age

A second way of looking at age is in biological terms. In this case, a person's age may be related to the physical changes taking place in their bodies. For example, puberty begins at a relatively early point in life, while the appearance of greying hair and wrinkles generally indicate that a person has reached a later point in life. Biological changes are usually linked to a person's chronological age.

Age as a social category

Vincent (2001) notes that age is one of the few social categories used in all societies. In some societies, age is not particularly important, but in others it is a key category.

Sociologists are interested in exploring the ways that age is seen in social terms. We may, for instance, have different social expectations of people and treat them differently according to how old we think they are. For example, we would probably not expect a 78-year-old to tell us that their hobbies included skateboarding and listening to thrash metal music. Similarly, we might be surprised to learn that a 6-year-old was a classical music fan and that their favourite television programme was the *Antiques Roadshow*.

Social expectations about age may influence how we view behaviour.

Sociologists argue that age (like gender and ethnicity) is socially constructed. Expectations surrounding age vary from society to society and over time. We can examine this variation by looking at childhood.

Attitudes to age   ❖ DISCUSSION ACTIVITY

Discuss and note down what the following expressions tell us about society's attitudes to age.

Act your age!   Toy boy.

Mutton dressed as lamb.   Pester power.

You're as old as you feel.   You can't teach an old dog new tricks.

Childhood

Research suggests that, in the past, childhood was very different from that experienced by children in Britain today. For example, Ariès (1962) indicates that in medieval times, children over five were seen as small adults who participated in the adult world of work and leisure.

In the 19th century, child labour was the norm among working-class families (see page 66). Poverty forced children to work long hours, for example in cotton mills or factories, to help support their families. Children were seen as particularly suited to sweeping chimneys or pulling sleds of coal through narrow passages in mines. In contrast, child labour is not only considered unacceptable but is also illegal in contemporary Britain.

Since Victorian times, many changes have taken place in laws relating to children in Britain. For example, restrictions have been imposed on employing children, and full-time compulsory education has been introduced (see page 66). In this way, the position and status of British children can be seen as having changed historically, with children today clearly having a different status from adults. Some commentators, however, suggest that childhood may now be changing in important respects. Many children, for example, resemble adults in being active consumers of fashionable clothes, accessories and brands.

In many contemporary societies, childhood is seen as a separate stage to youth and adulthood. Children are regarded as dependent and vulnerable. They are protected by law against exploitation, for example in the workplace. However, in other cultures, the separation of childhood and adulthood is less marked. Some children are expected to fend for themselves or to play an adult role at work. In this way, expectations surrounding childhood can be seen to vary cross-culturally.

RESEARCH ACTIVITY

Researching child labour

Estimates suggest that, globally, one in six children is engaged in child labour. You can find information about child labour from organizations such as UNICEF. Log on to the UNICEF website at:

http://www.unicef.org/protection/index_childlabour.html.

How does UNICEF define child labour?

Child labour.

CHECK YOUR UNDERSTANDING

1 What does it mean to describe age as a social category?

2 Identify one example to show that expectations surrounding childhood have varied over time.

KEY POINTS

We can look at age as a biological and social category. Sociologists explore the ways in which expectations surrounding age vary cross-culturally and historically.

How do sociologists view youth?

OBJECTIVE
Explain youth as a stage in the transition from childhood to adulthood

Youth is seen as a period of transition between childhood and adulthood. In contemporary Britain, youth is regarded as an important stage of development during which individuals 'grow up' and move from the status of child to adult. As part of this process, they move from a state of dependence on their parents to one of independence. The transition between childhood and adulthood may involve:

- increasing independence from families, parents and guardians
- moving from the family home to another household
- finishing full-time education
- moving into full-time paid employment
- gaining more status in society.

Age and youth in England and Wales   DISCUSSION ACTIVITY

Age (years)	Rights and responsibilities
10	Criminally responsible
12	Buy a pet
13	Minimum age for paid employment, under licence (age 11 on farms)
14	Ride a horse on the road wearing protective head gear
15	Kept under remand, subject to conditions
16	Age of sexual consent
17	Licence to drive a car
18	Vote in elections
21	Become an MP
26	Full rate of housing benefit

Source: adapted from Mizen (2002)

1 In a small group, discuss how far these different age-based restrictions seem sensible and logical. In your view, should any of them be changed?

2 Make a note of three points arising from your discussion.

DISCUSSION ACTIVITY

Mizen (2002) notes that among politicians, policy makers and even youth researchers, there is no obvious agreement about the age at which youth can be said to begin or end. As far as the law stands, youth could begin at 10 (the age of criminal responsibility in England and Wales) and end at 26 (when the full range of welfare benefit entitlements is available) or at any age in between.

1 In a small group, discuss the age at which you think 'youth' begins and ends.
2 Make a note of your decision and the reasons for it.

In practice, young people may continue to be financially dependent on their parents or other family members into their twenties and beyond (see pages 68–9). Full-time students or unemployed young people may live at home because they cannot afford to live independently. This means that the transition from childhood to adulthood in contemporary Britain is not necessarily clear-cut or precise. Additionally, we need to bear in mind that young people are not a uniform group. For example, they are divided according to gender, ethnicity, social class and location. These factors will influence their transitions into adulthood.

In contemporary Britain, we take the idea of youth, youth culture and the existence of teenagers for granted. However, the category of youth is seen by researchers as a relatively recent development. In Britain, youth is a 20th-century product. One view is that 'teenagers' emerged as a social category in the 1950s. They could be identified by the style of clothes they wore, their haircuts and the music they listened to.

Other societies would not necessarily recognize the notion of 'youth' as a separate stage of life that can last several years. In societies where the worlds of adulthood and childhood are less separate, the transition from childhood to adulthood may be easier and quicker to complete. In some cultures, this transition may be marked by initiation ceremonies (Pilcher, 1995).

Youth is a 20th-century product.

STRETCH AND CHALLENGE ACTIVITY

Is the passage from childhood to adulthood in Britain marked in any way? Do 18th- or 21st-birthday celebrations count as marking the transition to adult status?

The 'Chisunga' initiation ceremony of the Bemba people of Zambia

WRITTEN ACTIVITY

According to Richards (1982), the 'Chisunga' initiation ceremony marks the transition from girlhood to womanhood. It takes place after a girl has had her first period.

The Chisunga ceremony comprises many individual rituals, including the physical testing of the girl through various ordeals, her social isolation as a form of ritual separation and the singing of ritual songs.

The ceremony lasts over a month and ends with the girl's change of status being marked by the end of her social isolation.

She is bathed, dressed in new clothes, brought out of the hut and placed on a new mat outside its door. The girl sits silently in front of the villagers, who throw small presents onto the mat. After the ceremony, girls are considered ready for marriage, and often a marriage ceremony immediately follows.

Source: adapted from Pilcher (1995)

What does the Chisunga initiation ceremony mark?

CHECK YOUR UNDERSTANDING

Identify two features of the move from childhood to adulthood.

KEY POINTS

In some cultures, the transition from childhood to adulthood is clearly marked by initiation ceremonies. In others, the transition is more extended and less clear cut.

TOPIC 13 How do sociologists study older age?

OBJECTIVE
Describe sociological approaches to the study of older age

Many of the aspects of older age that we take for granted in contemporary Britain, such as retirement or pensions, are relatively recent developments. Before the introduction of state retirement pensions in 1908, older people worked until they were physically unable to continue. Retirement has only been the norm in Britain since the mid-20th century.

The status of older people can vary between different cultures. In contemporary Britain, getting old is often seen as something to be avoided. Some people try to combat the ageing process by resorting to hair dye, plastic surgery or Botox injections. In some reality TV programmes, members of the public undergo surgery and dental work in order to look younger. In other cultures, however, older age is viewed as something to look forward to, with older people being valued and enjoying high status in society.

The ageing process is sometimes viewed as something to combat or defy.

Defying age or growing old gracefully?   ❖ DISCUSSION ACTIVITY

1 In a small group, discuss the possible reasons why people might want to look younger than they are. What does this tell us about the status of older people in society?

2 Note down three points arising from your discussion.

Old age as a pleasure   ✒ WRITTEN ACTIVITY

For the Venda-speaking people of Southern Africa, old age is regarded as a 'pleasure'. Signs of old age, such as greying hair or the birth of a grandchild, are welcomed as indications of a person's approaching contact with the 'real' world of the spirits. In cultures where the afterlife is given great significance, old people's closeness to death increases rather than reduces their status.

Source: adapted from Pilcher (1995)

Identify two differences between people in Britain and the Venda-speaking people in how old age is viewed.

💡 STRETCH AND CHALLENGE ACTIVITY

Drawing on examples such as the Venda-speaking people of Southern Africa, or from your own experience, explain how ideas about 'age' can vary from culture to culture.

The term ageism (or age discrimination) is used to describe a situation in which a person is treated differently and less favourably on the basis of their age. Young people and older people tend to be more vulnerable to ageism than other groups.

Age discrimination claims triple in a year

The number of age discrimination claims being lodged at employment tribunals has more than tripled. Figures released by the Tribunal Service show that claims rose from 962 in 2006 to 2940 in 2007. Solicitors expect the number of age discrimination claims to soar over the next few years.

In 2007, the average payout for successful age discrimination cases was £8695, compared with £10 044 for sex discrimination and £17 308 for race discrimination.

Selina Scott, the television presenter, was awarded a six-figure settlement from Channel Five. The 57-year-old accused the broadcaster of ageism after it offered her a high-profile role but then gave the job to two younger broadcasters.

Source: adapted from Ben Leach, *The Telegraph*, 7 December 2008

Explain one way in which people can now challenge age discrimination.

For example, they may experience negative stereotyping on the basis of their age (see page 269). People in their 50s and 60s, for instance, may find it difficult to get a job because some employers hold stereotyped ideas about their inability to learn new skills.

As a result of the Employment Equality (Age) Regulations, which came into force in 2006, there are now regulations against age discrimination in employment and training (see page 269).

It is important to appreciate that, like youth, older people cannot be seen (or lumped together) as a uniform group. Older people's position and experiences differ according to whether they are 'young old' (65–75) or 'old old' (in their mid 80s, 90s or older) (see page 84).

The social position of older people varies between individuals and groups. Many may face poverty while others enjoy an affluent lifestyle and have a high-status position in society. For example, many judges, MPs, world statesmen and women and wealthy company directors are in their 60s, 70s and 80s. It is also important to recognize that age may be linked to other social divisions based on gender, ethnicity and class. The life chances of an elderly, working-class, widowed black woman, for example, may be much worse than those of a newly retired, middle-class, married white man.

STRETCH AND CHALLENGE ACTIVITY

How far do you agree that ageism is as much a social problem as sexism and racism?

DISCUSSION ACTIVITY

Gender and TV newsreaders

1 In a small group, discuss the possible reasons why male news presenters on TV include some aged 60 or more, while women presenters are usually aged under 50.

2 Note down two possible reasons.

CHECK YOUR UNDERSTANDING

1 What is meant by age discrimination?

2 Identify one way in which governments have tried to reduce age discrimination in Britain over the last ten years.

KEY POINTS

Age discrimination is increasingly recognized as a social problem in Britain and legislation has been introduced to tackle this. However, the status of older people varies between societies. Within Britain, the position of older people varies according to their social class, gender and ethnicity.

TOPIC 14   How are wealth and income distributed in Britain?

OBJECTIVE
Describe how wealth and income are distributed

It is important to examine how wealth and income are distributed because they influence life chances. For example, many people with high incomes can choose between NHS and private healthcare, or between private and state education. However, most people in low-income households will not have these choices.

Wealth refers to the ownership of assets (things that people own) that are valued at a particular point in time. Marketable assets are things that can be sold to make money, such as houses, land, works of art and jewellery. Wealth also includes money in savings accounts and shares in companies. Wealth is often passed down the generations through inheritance in families. It may also be built up by saving or by the value of assets such as houses or land going up.

Income refers to the flow of resources which individuals and households receive over a specific period of time. Income may be received in cash (for example wages) or in kind (for instance, a discount scheme or petrol allowance). Sources of income include wages, welfare benefits and pensions (see the pie chart).

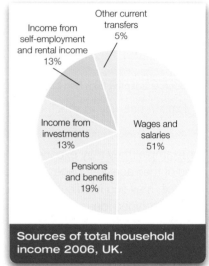

Income from self-employment and rental income 13%

Other current transfers 5%

Wages and salaries 51%

Income from investments 13%

Pensions and benefits 19%

Sources of total household income 2006, UK.

Source: *Social Trends* (2008)

The distribution of wealth   ✎ WRITTEN ACTIVITY

1 What percentage of wealth did the most wealthy 1% own in 1991?

2 What percentage of wealth did the least wealthy 50% own in 2001?

3 By how many percentage points did the wealth held by the most wealthy 5% increase between 1991 and 2001?

Distribution of marketable wealth less value of dwellings, UK

Percentage of wealth owned by:	1991 (%)	2001 (%)
Most wealthy 1%	29	33
Most wealthy 5%	51	58
Most wealthy 10%	64	72
Most wealthy 25%	80	86
Most wealthy 50%	93	97

Source: adapted from *Social Trends* (2004)

The distribution of wealth

In Britain, there are vast inequalities in the distribution of both wealth and income (Roberts, 2001). However, wealth is distributed even more unevenly than income. The most important element of household wealth in the UK is residential buildings (such as houses and flats). Of total assets in 2006, 45 per cent were held in the form of residential buildings.

💡 STRETCH AND CHALLENGE ACTIVITY

Write a paragraph to summarize changes in the distribution of wealth in the UK between 1991 and 2001.

In Britain, we can identify a number of people, sometimes referred to as the super-rich, who are multimillionaires. The super-rich comprise:

- those who own wealth in the form of shares in industry, finance and commerce
- upper-class landowners such as the Duke of Westminster (see below) who have inherited their wealth.

Britain's super-rich

RESEARCH ACTIVITY

Sunday Times Rich List 2008

Lakshmi Mittal and family	Roman Abramovich	The Duke of Westminster
Ranking: 1	Ranking: 2	Ranking: 3
Age: 57	Age: 41	Age: 56
Worth: £27,700,000,000	Worth: £11,700,000,000	Worth: £7,000,000,000
Source of wealth: Steel	Source of wealth: Oil; industry	Source of wealth: Property

Source: http://business.timesonline.co.uk/tol/business/specials/rich_list/rich_list_search/

The *Sunday Times Rich List* is updated every year. Access the latest version of the Rich List by logging on to:
http://business.timesonline.co.uk/tol/business/specials/rich_list/rich_list_search/

Who holds the top three positions in the current Rich List?

The distribution of income

Income is distributed unevenly between households in the UK. Income inequality has widened over the last 30 years. For example, in 1979, the top 10 per cent of people in the UK received 21 per cent of income and the poorest 10 per cent received 4 per cent of income. In 2007, the top 10 per cent received 40 per cent of income and the poorest 10 per cent received 3 per cent of income.

The increase in income inequality can be explained partly by the huge salaries and bonuses paid to the highest earners. In 2005/06, for example, a chief executive of a top 100 company in Britain could expect to earn around £2.9 million. However, following the credit crunch, which began in 2008, huge bonuses are less likely to be paid.

CHECK YOUR UNDERSTANDING

1 What is the difference between wealth and income?

2 Identify two ways in which having a high income may improve life chances.

KEY POINTS

Life chances are influenced by wealth and income. There are huge inequalities in the distribution of wealth and income in Britain which appear to be growing.

TOPIC 15   What is social mobility?

OBJECTIVES
Explain what the term 'social mobility' means
Identify routes and barriers to social mobility

The term 'social mobility' refers to people's movement up or down between a society's strata. In Britain, it refers to movement between social classes. Upward social mobility, for example, would include movement from a routine occupation to a higher professional occupation on the NS-SEC scale (see page 287).

Social mobility is currently a hot topic and is of interest not only to sociologists but also to politicians and policy makers. This is partly because it is seen as an important measure of how open society is (see Topic 3). High rates of upward and downward mobility can be used to argue that:

* status is based on achievement rather than ascription. This means that society provides equality of opportunity and operates as a meritocracy. A meritocratic society is one in which individuals' achievements are based on their own talents and efforts rather than their social origins and backgrounds.

* individuals are rewarded on the basis of personal qualities rather than inherited wealth or personal connections (Crompton, 2008).

There are two types of social mobility:

1 Intra-generational social mobility refers to the movement of an individual over the course of their life from one occupational classification to another. Intra-generational mobility might occur, for example, as a result of being promoted or changing career.

2 Intergenerational social mobility refers to movement between the generations of a family. If a child enters a different occupational classification from his or her parents, then we can say that intergenerational mobility has occurred.

The extent of social mobility can be described in three ways:

1 **long range:** from the bottom strata to the top or from the top to the bottom

2 **short range:** for example, from an unskilled to a skilled manual job

3 **self-recruitment:** where children remain in the same class as their parents.

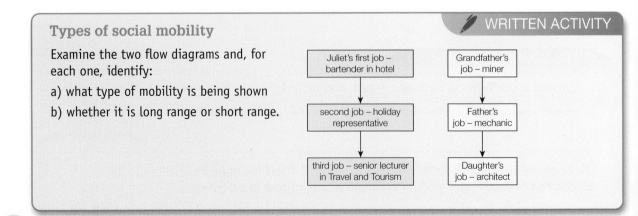

WRITTEN ACTIVITY

Types of social mobility

Examine the two flow diagrams and, for each one, identify:

a) what type of mobility is being shown

b) whether it is long range or short range.

Juliet's first job – bartender in hotel
↓
second job – holiday representative
↓
third job – senior lecturer in Travel and Tourism

Grandfather's job – miner
↓
Father's job – mechanic
↓
Daughter's job – architect

Glossary terms: intergenerational social mobility   intra-generational social mobility

Social mobility, origins and destinations

WRITTEN ACTIVITY

In a socially mobile society, there is a weak link between family background (origins) and a person's destination in life. This means, for example, that a child born to unemployed parents with little education would have the same chance of a later professional career as a child who is born to professional parents. The opposite of social mobility is social reproduction. In a socially reproductive society, children tend to copy the educational and occupational paths of their parents.

Source: adapted from Gorard (2008)

In a socially mobile society:

a) How strong is the link between an individual's family background and the occupation they end up in?

b) Are the chances of ending up in a professional career distributed evenly or unevenly?

Social mobility and meritocracy are linked together. Where selection is based on merit, education overcomes social origins and disadvantage. In this case, a child's achievements at school do not depend on their social class background. In merit selection, there should be:

- a weak link between social class origin and educational success
- a strong link between educational success and social destination (Gorard, 2008).

Routes to mobility include:

- educational achievements and credentials
- marriage – although most people marry partners who have similar educational and occupational profiles to themselves
- windfalls such as an inheritance or a huge win on the National Lottery – these may lead to changes in lifestyle, but an individual may choose to remain in their current occupation
- changes in the occupational structure – a growth in white-collar work and a reduction in manual work may mean that there are more chances of upward mobility and fewer chances of downward mobility.

Barriers to upward social mobility include: discrimination based on ethnicity or gender; lack of skills and educational credentials.

STRETCH AND CHALLENGE ACTIVITY

Explain the difference between social mobility and social reproduction.

CHECK YOUR UNDERSTANDING

1 What do sociologists mean by the term 'social mobility'?

2 Why is social mobility of interest to politicians and policy makers?

3 Explain one difference between intergenerational and intra-generational social mobility.

KEY POINTS

Social mobility refers to people's movement up or down between society's strata. High rates of social mobility can be seen as evidence of a meritocratic society in which status is achieved and opportunities are offered to all.

TOPIC 16 How much social mobility is there in Britain?

OBJECTIVES

Discuss how much social mobility there is in contemporary Britain
Identify problems in measuring social mobility

Social mobility in contemporary Britain

Mobility research has indicated that a working-class child's chances of getting a professional or managerial job are a quarter of those of a child from the professional class. Goldthorpe's 1972–74 mobility study, for example, showed that although working-class children could and did end up in middle-class occupations, they were much less likely than middle-class children to do so. The relative chances of working-class and middle-class children getting professional jobs had changed very little.

Goldthorpe's mobility study

WRITTEN ACTIVITY

Goldthorpe's 1972–74 study of social mobility suggested that a considerable amount of long-range mobility had occurred. For example, 28.5 per cent of those in class I in the 1972 survey were from class VI and VII backgrounds. However, Goldthorpe argued that these results did not show that Britain had become a more 'open' society. This was because there were marked, and persistent, differences in the relative chances of men of different social backgrounds moving into higher-level occupations.

Source: adapted from Crompton (2008)

1 How much long-range social mobility did Goldthorpe find?

2 On what grounds did Goldthorpe conclude that Britain had not become a more open society?

Evidence suggests that social mobility fell towards the end of the 20th century in the UK. Children born into manual working-class families in 1958 had a better chance of moving into higher occupations than children born into similar families in the 1970s. Crompton (2008) notes that in Britain, social mobility is in decline. This is partly a result of changes in the occupational structure. Skilled manual jobs have declined and the growth in professional and managerial jobs has slowed down.

Research on social mobility has focused on how far education determines people's chances of upward and downward mobility. One question is whether people with higher educational qualifications achieve higher social class positions.

Eye on the exam

The second question in CHECK YOUR UNDERSTANDING asks you to 'discuss how far'. This signals that you need to debate an issue and evaluate a viewpoint by arguing for and against it. Remember also that you need to reach a balanced conclusion on 'how far'.

Class matters

Education does not appear to matter very much when it comes to determining occupational success and improvements in income. Overall, it seems that class structures are self-reproducing. This means that the chances of a person rising or falling in the social hierarchy depends on their class background far more than it does on their individual educational achievement. Class shows a weaker influence than in the past, but it remains the strongest influence. Those in the higher classes have a far better chance of securing the opportunities for upward mobility and for avoiding downward mobility.

Source: adapted from Scott (2005)

1 How significant is education in influencing occupational success?

2 Does mobility depend more on an individual's educational achievements or their social origins?

What do Scott's conclusions tell us about social class influences on people's life chances in terms of their destinations or outcomes in life?

What problems do sociologists face in studying social mobility?

Some studies of intergenerational mobility focus only on males. In doing so, they include families with fathers and sons but exclude those with no sons or no known fathers. In this case, women and most lone-parent families would be excluded from the study and the results would tell us nothing about their mobility experiences.

Studies that ask participants to recall their earlier employment, or that of their parents, are likely to be based on unreliable data.

Do we include temporary jobs when measuring mobility?

Mobility studies record movement at two (or more) points in time. Researchers have to decide which age and point in a person's career to measure mobility from. There are potential problems associated with such decisions. A young person, for example, might be in a temporary job (such as in a call centre) while waiting for a suitable opening in a city bank, or they might not have reached their final class destination. An older person might have moved into semi-retirement.

1 Explain two problems in measuring social mobility.

2 Discuss how far sociologists would agree that social mobility has increased in Britain since the 1960s.

Although long-range mobility has occurred, children from working-class backgrounds have less chance of moving into professional occupations than children who are from professional backgrounds. Mobility chances may still depend on class background rather than on educational achievement. There are problems in measuring mobility.

TOPIC 17 What is poverty?

OBJECTIVES

Explain what the terms 'absolute poverty' and 'relative poverty' mean

Explain why the definition of poverty used by governments is important

Poverty is a controversial issue and there is no single agreed way of defining it. As a result, different researchers work with different definitions of poverty.

Poverty is... ❖ DISCUSSION ACTIVITY

...having no money left after the weekend

...starving

...existing rather than living

...buying second-hand clothes

...homeless people sleeping on the street

...destitution or extreme hardship

...not being able to afford a healthy diet

...having no money for a social life

1 In a small group, discuss these statements and decide which two are the most satisfactory and which two are the least satisfactory examples of poverty.

2 Write your own group definition of poverty.

Absolute and relative poverty

There are two broad approaches to defining poverty – the absolute and relative approaches. People experience absolute poverty when their income is insufficient to obtain the minimum they need to survive. People in absolute poverty do not have access to even the basic necessities of life such as food, clean water, shelter, heating and clothes. Their income is so low that they can barely survive.

The absolute definition is useful in that it allows researchers to measure trends over time. It is criticized, however, because in practice it is very difficult to determine what the 'minimum needed to survive' is. For example, is the minimum dietary requirement just bread and water, or should we include fresh fruit and vegetables?

Absolute poverty and relative poverty.

People experience relative poverty when they cannot afford to meet the general standard of living of most other people in their society. The income of people in relative poverty is much less than the average for society as a whole, so they are poor compared with others in their society. In relatively affluent or rich societies such as Britain and the USA, even those experiencing poverty are well off compared with people in many other societies. Most researchers in Britain today agree that the relative definition of poverty should be used.

What is considered to be poverty differs from time to time and from society to society. Using the relative approach means that we will always find poverty in a society in so far as we will find some people who have much less than the average income, unless incomes are distributed almost equally.

Glossary terms: absolute poverty   relative poverty

Even though defining poverty has proved difficult, the issue of how we define it is important. This is because our definition will influence how we measure poverty, the number of people said to be in poverty and the extent to which it is said to exist. Our definition will also influence our views on how poverty should be tackled.

Walker and Walker (1997) argue that the definition of poverty chosen by the state is crucial. This is because it determines to what extent the government accepts that poverty exists, what policies are adopted to tackle poverty and how those experiencing poverty will be treated. If an absolute definition of poverty is used, the role of government and the amount of resources needed to address it will be much more limited than if a relative definition is used.

The Child Poverty Action Group sees poverty not simply in terms of being short of money, clothing or food. Poverty is also not being able to join a sports club, go out socially or send one's children on a school trip. Poverty is experienced in terms of having limited access to decent services such as education, housing and health services.

Defining poverty

WRITTEN ACTIVITY

Groups such as the Child Poverty Action Group use Peter Townsend's influential definition of poverty. Read through this definition and answer the question that follows.

> Individuals, families and groups in the population can be said to be in poverty when they lack the resources to obtain the types of diet, participate in the activities and have the living conditions and amenities which are customary, or at least widely encouraged or approved, in the societies to which they belong. Their resources are so seriously below those commanded by the average individual or family that they are, in effect, excluded from ordinary living patterns and activities.

Source: Townsend (1979) p. 31

Does this provide us with an absolute or a relative definition of poverty? Explain your answer.

The European Union defines people as poor where 'their material, cultural and social resources are so limited as to exclude them from the minimum acceptable way of life in the member state in which they live.' This definition recognizes that poverty is not simply about income. It is also about the exclusion of people living in poverty from ordinary activities and customs (see Topic 22).

CHECK YOUR UNDERSTANDING

1 What do sociologists mean by the terms 'absolute poverty' and 'relative poverty'?
2 Why is the issue of how the government defines poverty an important one?

KEY POINTS

Poverty has been defined in absolute and relative terms. It has also been defined in terms of exclusion from everyday activities and customs. The definition adopted is important because it influences the extent to which poverty is said to exist, the numbers counted as in poverty and the government policies adopted to address it.

TOPIC 18   How do we measure poverty?

OBJECTIVES
Explain the different ways of measuring poverty
Identify reasons why poverty and inequality have increased

There are several different ways of measuring poverty. The main official UK government way of measuring poverty is in terms of low incomes. The low-income threshold is fixed at 60 per cent of the median (midpoint) income of the population after housing costs (which vary between regions). In other words, low incomes are those below three-fifths of the income of a family right in the middle of the income distribution (Hills, 2006). Twenty-two per cent, almost a quarter of the population, is below the UK government's poverty level (Piachaud, 2009).

The national Poverty and Social Exclusion (PSE) survey examined the extent of poverty and social exclusion in Britain at the turn of the century. The 2000 PSE survey used several different measures of poverty including:

- income levels
- lack of items seen as necessities by the majority of the population
- subjective measures, where people consider themselves to be living in poverty.

The 2000 PSE survey asked respondents to identify which items and activities from a list they considered necessities. Necessities are items and activities that all adults should be able to afford and not have to do without. Some may, of course, choose to do without some of these items even though they can afford them. This would not count as being in poverty.

The 2000 PSE Survey

Items/activities	% who saw the items as necessities	% who lacked & could not afford items
Access to the internet	6	16
An outfit for social occasions	51	4
Beds and bedding for everyone	95	1
Celebrations on special occasions such as Christmas	83	2
Friends of family round for a meal	64	6
Hobby or leisure activity	78	7
Insurance of contents of dwelling	79	8
Regular savings (of £10 per month) for rainy days or retirement	66	25
Satellite television	5	7
Telephone	71	1
Television	56	1
Two meals a day	91	1
Visits to friends or family	84	2
Warm, waterproof coat	85	4

Source: adapted from Gordon et al (2000)

Items and activities seen as necessities

The table shows results for some of the items listed in the survey. It gives the percentage of respondents identifying different adult items and activities as necessities. For example, 78 per cent saw having a hobby or leisure activity as a necessity.

The researchers classed as necessities the items and activities that more than 50 per cent of respondents believed all adults should be able to afford and not do without.

1   What percentage of respondents saw having a telephone as a necessity?

2   Identify two items or activities that the researchers classed as necessities and two that they did not class as necessities.

Lacking items seen as necessities

Having established what items were seen as necessities by the majority of the population, the researchers went on to find out what items people both lacked and could not afford. The table shows the items that respondents did not have and could not afford.

1   Which measure of poverty are the researchers using here?

2   Which item did the biggest proportion of respondents lack because they could not afford it?

The PSE survey found that 26 per cent of the British population were living in poverty, that is they were unable to afford two or more necessities. The survey also found that poverty rates had risen sharply. In 1983, 14 per cent of households lacked three or more necessities because they could not afford them. By 1999, the proportion stood at 24 per cent. However, while poverty rose dramatically during this period, the majority of British people became richer.

When poverty grows among some groups while other people become richer, this results in greater inequality. Butler and Watt (2007) identify several factors that explain the increase in poverty and inequality. These include:

- An increase in the proportion of workless households in which there is no earner. Unemployment peaked at over 3 million in 1986 and again at just under 3 million in 1993.
- An increase in the pay gap between low-skilled and high-skilled workers.
- Changes in taxation, such as reductions in the rate of income tax, which have benefited the better off.
- Demographic changes which have resulted in an increase in groups with low incomes. Examples include pensioners and lone-parent families.

CHECK YOUR UNDERSTANDING

1   Identify and explain two ways in which poverty can be measured.

2   Identify two reasons for the increase in poverty and inequality over the last 25 years.

KEY POINTS

There are several ways of measuring poverty. The official UK government measure is incomes below 60 per cent of the median income of the population. Other measures include lack of items seen as necessities and subjective measures. Research suggests that poverty and inequality have increased.

TOPIC 19   Who is likely to experience poverty?

OBJECTIVES

Identify the different social groups that are likely to experience poverty
Explain why women and some minority ethnic groups are at risk of poverty

People from some social groups are more likely to experience poverty than others. The PSE survey found that the proportion of people in poverty is higher among groups such as:

- lone-parent households
- households with no paid workers
- families with a child under 11
- adults living in one-person households, including single pensioners
- children and young people
- those who left school aged 16 or under
- women.

The distribution of income by family type

WRITTEN ACTIVITY

Income is not distributed evenly across the UK population (see page 303). The chart provides a breakdown of the people in low-income and high-income families in 2005/06.

In which family type were people most likely to be in the:

a) bottom income group?

b) top income group?

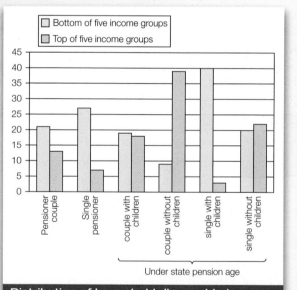

Distribution of household disposable income by family type 2005/06, UK.

Source: adapted from *Social Trends* (2008)

Ethnicity and poverty

People who live in UK households headed by someone from a minority ethnic group are at risk of living in low-income households. This is particularly the case for people of Pakistani or Bangladeshi heritage. Lister (2004) notes that most explanations for these patterns of poverty identify racism and discrimination as key factors. Minority ethnic groups, for example, are

Glossary terms: gender pay gap

generally disadvantaged in terms of unemployment, pay and the quality of their jobs. They also tend to be disadvantaged within the welfare state through, for example, low take-up of state assistance.

WRITTEN ACTIVITY

Distribution of income for individuals by ethnicity of head of household (before housing costs) 2006/07

According to this information, 19 per cent of all white people are in the bottom income group and 21 per cent are in the top income group.

1 Which ethnic group had the highest percentage in the bottom income group?

2 What percentage of all people in the mixed ethnic group is in the top income group?

UK Percentage of individuals

Ethnic group	Bottom of five income groups	Top of five income groups
White	19	21
Mixed	27	23
Asian or Asian British	37	13
Indian	23	21
Pakistani or Bangladeshi	54	4
Black or black British	31	12
Black Caribbean	27	13
Black non-Caribbean	35	10
Chinese or other ethnic group	27	22

Source: adapted from DWP (2008)

Gender and poverty

Evidence from the EU and USA shows that women face a greater risk of poverty than men (Lister, 2004). Millar (1997) points out that the two groups with the highest risk and the longest durations of poverty comprise females: lone mothers and older women living alone.

- Women have longer life expectancy than men, so there are more older female pensioners living alone (see page 70) than males. They are less likely than men to have income from an occupational pension.

- Women are more likely than men to head lone-parent families. Over 50 per cent of lone-parent households in the UK have low incomes.

- Women in paid work earn, on average, less than men (see page 291). In 2006, women's average hourly earnings working full time in the UK were £10.24 and men's were £11.71 (the gender pay gap).

- Women are more likely than men to work part time.

CHECK YOUR UNDERSTANDING

1 Identify two groups who are at risk of poverty.

2 Identify and explain two reasons why women are more likely than men to experience poverty in the UK.

KEY POINTS

The chances of experiencing poverty are not distributed equally. Women and people from some minority ethnic groups are more likely to experience poverty than some other groups.

TOPIC 20 **Which other groups are likely to experience poverty?**

OBJECTIVES

Identify other groups at risk of poverty

Describe how the life cycle of poverty operates

Groups at risk of poverty

In 2005/06, children were particularly vulnerable to poverty if they were living in a family:

- with four or more children
- where the head of the household was a lone parent
- where the head of the household was from a minority ethnic group
- that was workless.

Poverty is seen as having a negative impact on children's life chances, including their life expectancy, health, housing, educational attainments and job prospects.

End Child Poverty coalition.

End Child Poverty ✿ DISCUSSION ACTIVITY

In 1999, the Labour government set a target to halve child poverty by 2010 and eradicate (end) it by 2020. Poverty is measured as living in a household with an income below 60 per cent of the average (median).

> Our historic aim will be for ours to be the first generation to end child poverty, and it will take a generation. It is a 20-year mission but I believe it can be done.
>
> Tony Blair, 1999

End Child Poverty coalition was set up to eradicate child poverty in the UK. It is made up of over 150 organizations, including children's charities and faith groups. Its aims include:
- informing the public about the causes and effects of child poverty
- promoting the case for ending child poverty by 2020 with the present and future governments.

End Child Poverty demands that government invests the necessary resources and makes policy changes to deliver on its promise to end child poverty in the UK by 2020.

Source: adapted from http://www.endchildpoverty.org.uk/our-campaign/what-we-do

1 In a small group, discuss the possible reasons why the government has pledged to end child poverty in particular rather than poverty in general. Make a note of your reasons.
2 End Child Poverty coalition wants the government to invest resources and make the necessary policy changes to end child poverty in the UK by 2020. Discuss and note down what policy changes might help to end child poverty.

Glossary terms: life cycle of poverty

As a group, pensioners are likely to have to live on a low income over time. There are, however, differences between older people in their risk of experiencing poverty. People who retire with an occupational pension are likely to enjoy a relatively good standard of living. Those who rely on the state retirement pension are more vulnerable to poverty.

Older people's vulnerability to poverty is also linked to their social class, gender and ethnicity. Middle-class men, for example, are more likely than other groups to have built up an occupational pension.

People with disabilities are at risk of poverty. Lister (2008) argues that the additional needs associated with many forms of disability create extra expenses that other people on low incomes do not face. Such extra costs include, for example, special diet, equipment and transport costs. People with disabilities may also have relatively low incomes because they are at a disadvantage in the labour market. For example, they are more likely to be unemployed or to work in low-paid jobs.

The life cycle of poverty

Official statistics provide us with snapshots of the proportion of households below average income at a particular point in time. The idea of the life cycle of poverty is important because it provides more of a moving picture over time. It highlights movement into and out of poverty over a lifetime and suggests that people may move into and out of poverty at different stages during the course of their lives.

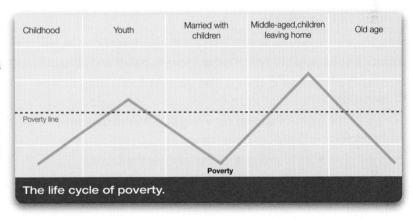

The life cycle of poverty.

Is poverty history?

1 Some politicians have suggested that poverty no longer really exists in the UK. Discuss the possible arguments and evidence for and against this view. To what extent do you agree with this view?

2 Make a note of your conclusion with your reasons.

CHECK YOUR UNDERSTANDING

1 Identify two reasons why people with disabilities may experience poverty.

2 Explain two ways in which poverty may affect children's life chances.

3 Explain briefly what is meant by 'the life cycle of poverty'.

KEY POINTS

The chances of experiencing poverty are linked to age – children and pensioners are more at risk of poverty than other age groups. This is expressed in the idea of the life cycle of poverty. People with disabilities are also more at risk.

TOPIC 21   How do we explain poverty?

OBJECTIVE

Understand the culture of poverty and the cycle of deprivation as explanations of poverty

There are several explanations of poverty. Some explanations focus on individuals and others focus on the structures of society. Individual accounts tend to focus on 'the poor' themselves. They highlight the behaviour of individuals or groups who experience poverty, and imply that they are responsible for their position in some way. Structural accounts focus on how economic, social and political structures create and perpetuate poverty (Lister, 2004).

The culture of poverty

During the 1950s and 1960s, the persistence of poverty among some groups was explained in terms of their culture or way of life. According to this view, people from the poorest section of society were socialized within the subculture of poverty. As a result, they were unable to take up opportunities to break free from poverty.

Individuals in poverty developed a way of life and a set of values to cope with their position, including the following beliefs and attitudes:

- people can do little to change their situation so they may as well accept it
- live for the moment and do not worry about what tomorrow may bring
- there is no point in saving up or planning for the future.

WRITTEN ACTIVITY

The culture of poverty

Does the culture of poverty explanation tend to focus on individuals or on the structure of society?
Briefly explain your answer.

These values, which those in poverty developed to help them adapt to their situation, also prevented them from escaping poverty by, for example, staying on at school or saving up money for the future.

Through socialization within families, such values were passed on from parents to their children. In this way, poverty persisted over time from generation to generation and locked people into a cycle of deprivation. According to the culture of poverty explanation, the policy to remove poverty would consist of educating and training children to compensate for their home values.

This explanation of poverty is an example of one that focuses on individuals. It can be criticized as follows:

- It shows how people might adapt to poverty but it does not explain what actually causes poverty in the first place.
- By focusing on individuals and their culture, it blames those in poverty for their situation. It ignores structural factors such as unemployment levels.

The cycle of deprivation

Supporters of the culture of poverty approach argued that poverty persisted from one generation to the next, locking people into a cycle of deprivation. During the 1970s, several versions of the cycle of deprivation were developed in the UK to explain the persistence of poverty between generations. More recently, the

Labour government has identified the need to break the intergenerational cycle of deprivation.

Financial or material deprivation involves having insufficient money to be able to afford goods and services. As a result of this, people may not be able to afford a balanced diet. Poverty may result in ill health during childhood.

Cultural deprivation means that the children's backgrounds do not provide them with the resources to perform well at school. They have less parental encouragement and a poorer educational experience than children from more affluent (well-off) backgrounds.

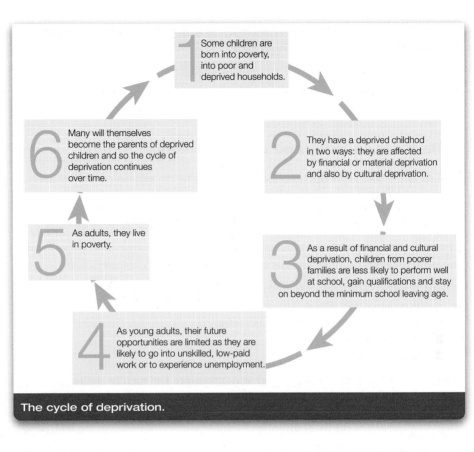

1 Some children are born into poverty, into poor and deprived households.

2 They have a deprived childhod in two ways: they are affected by financial or material deprivation and also by cultural deprivation.

3 As a result of financial and cultural deprivation, children from poorer families are less likely to perform well at school, gain qualifications and stay on beyond the minimum school leaving age.

4 As young adults, their future opportunities are limited as they are likely to go into unskilled, low-paid work or to experience unemployment.

5 As adults, they live in poverty.

6 Many will themselves become the parents of deprived children and so the cycle of deprivation continues over time.

The cycle of deprivation.

To remove poverty according to this explanation, the policy was to employ social workers and to use local authority provisions to help children to break out of the cycle of deprivation. More recently, programmes such as Sure Start (see page 94) have been introduced as an attempt to break the cycle of deprivation.

Critics, however, argue that while this explanation may describe how poverty persists between generations, it fails to explain why some groups actually fall into poverty. They also argue that poverty should be treated as a structural phenomenon, due to the way society is structured and organized. It should not be treated as an individual or family phenomenon.

WRITTEN ACTIVITY

The cycle of deprivation

Explain in your own words how the cycle of deprivation works.

CHECK YOUR UNDERSTANDING

1 To what extent does the culture of poverty explain the causes of poverty?

2 Describe one feature of material deprivation and one feature of cultural deprivation.

KEY POINTS

The culture of poverty shows that the way people adapt to poverty (particularly in their subcultural values) can keep them in poverty. The cycle of deprivation shows how poverty is passed between the generations of a family.

TOPIC 22 What other explanations of poverty are there?

OBJECTIVE

Understand welfare dependency and social exclusion as explanations of poverty

Welfare dependency and the 'underclass'

More recently, New Right approaches have attempted to explain poverty in ways similar to the culture of poverty and cycle of deprivation. In the 1980s and 1990s, New Right approaches identified the emergence in Britain of an 'underclass', a group whose attitudes and values are different from those of mainstream society. In general terms, the concept of an underclass describes people who experience long-term poverty and who are unable, for whatever reason, to gain a living.

Charles Murray (1996) focused on the behaviour of individuals who he saw as the 'undeserving poor'. Reflecting upon his own childhood experiences in the USA, Murray described the underclass as follows:

> Their homes were littered and unkempt. The men in the family were unable to hold a job for more than a few weeks at a time. Drunkenness was common. The children grew up ill-schooled and ill-behaved and contributed a disproportionate share of the local juvenile delinquents.

Source: Murray (1996)

Murray focused on three symptoms of the underclass: crime, extramarital births and economic inactivity among men of working age. He argued that welfare reform encouraged crime, single parenthood and unemployment and took away the incentive to work.

According to New Right approaches, the 'undeserving poor' remain in poverty because the welfare state encourages them to depend on state provision. State provision is too generous and makes the problem of poverty worse by creating 'welfare dependency' and the development of an underclass.

The concept of the underclass, and the use of this term, is highly controversial. Some critics reject the notion that an underclass actually exists. Others argue that the term was developed not to describe a phenomenon that exists but as a label that 'blames the victims' for their misfortunes (Crompton, 2008). Labels such as the underclass stigmatize some people and distance them from the rest of society.

Social exclusion

During the 1980s and 1990s, a distinction was drawn between poverty and social exclusion. Poverty refers to a lack of material resources, particularly income. Social exclusion is a broader concept which refers to being shut out or excluded from participation in society's social, economic, political and cultural life. Socially excluded people are those who would like to participate but who are prevented from doing so by factors beyond their control.

Burchardt et al (2002) define social exclusion in terms of being unable to participate in key activities in society, such as:

- consumption – purchasing goods and services
- production – participating in socially or economically valuable activity
- political engagement – participating in local or national decision making
- social interaction – with family, friends and communities.

WRITTEN ACTIVITY

The Social Exclusion Task Force

The Labour government's Social Exclusion Task Force coordinates the government's work against exclusion.

> Social exclusion is about more than income poverty. It is a short-hand term for what can happen when people or areas have a combination of linked problems, such as unemployment, discrimination, poor skills, low incomes, poor housing, high crime and family breakdown. These problems are linked and mutually reinforcing. Social exclusion is an extreme consequence of what happens when people don't get a fair deal throughout their lives, often because of disadvantage they face at birth, and this disadvantage can be transmitted from one generation to the next.

Source: http://www.cabinetoffice.gov.uk/social_exclusion_task_force/context.aspx

1 How far does this account of social exclusion appear to focus on individuals' behaviour?

2 What problems does social exclusion arise from?

The use of terms such as underclass and poverty can encourage the practice of blaming the individual victims. The term social exclusion, however, stresses the role of society in excluding certain people from full participation. Social exclusion is seen as a more useful concept than poverty because it highlights that social problems have many causes. However, critics argue that the concept includes too many different things, ranging from unemployment to crime, to be useful.

STRETCH AND CHALLENGE ACTIVITY

Identify one way in which this account of social exclusion appears similar to earlier accounts of the cycle of deprivation.

DISCUSSION ACTIVITY

At risk of social exclusion

In a small group, discuss why young people who are not in employment, education or training (NEETs) are seen as being at risk of long-term social exclusion.

CHECK YOUR UNDERSTANDING

1 How might the idea of welfare dependency be used to explain poverty?

2 Explain what the term 'social exclusion' means.

KEY POINTS

New Right approaches argue that welfare state provision is too generous and makes the problem of poverty worse by creating 'welfare dependency' and the development of an underclass. Social exclusion refers to being shut out or excluded from participation in society's social, economic, political and cultural life.

TOPIC 23 What do structural explanations of poverty involve?

OBJECTIVES

Explain the Marxist approach to understanding poverty

Describe how unemployment and welfare state inadequacies may be linked to poverty

As explained in Topic 21, some explanations of poverty focus on what are seen as the individual's inadequacies or the problems faced by people, such as material or cultural deprivation. Structural approaches, however, reject the focus on individuals and groups in explaining poverty. Instead, they examine the way in which society itself is structured or organized.

The Marxist approach

According to this view (see page 282), poverty results from the class-based inequalities which are built into capitalist society. The Marxist approach argues that capitalism as an economic system generates extreme wealth for the capitalist class. It also produces poverty among sections of the working class. However, while poverty is generally seen as a social problem, wealth is not recognized as a problem in capitalist society.

Wealth as a social problem?

Through the work of groups such as Oxfam and activities linked to Comic Relief, we are familiar with the idea that poverty is a social problem that needs tackling. However, the view that wealth is also a problem gets less publicity.

1 In a small group, discuss what commentators mean by the idea that wealth is a social problem. How far do you agree with the view that wealth is a problem?

2 Make a note of three points arising from your discussion.

DISCUSSION ACTIVITY

While poverty is seen as a social problem, wealth is not seen as such.

Poverty is seen as a product of the way capitalist society works. In a class society that is based on inequalities of wealth, a minority group makes a profit out of the rest of the population. It is therefore inevitable that some people will be poor.

Marxist explanations argue that poverty works to the advantage of the employers or bourgeoisie (the capitalist class). For example, if people in paid employment demand higher wages then employers can threaten to replace them with workers from among the unemployed. In this way, the fear of poverty can be used to discipline the workers and keep wages down.

According to the Marxist approach, the only way to remove poverty is to have revolutionary change in society, and to replace capitalism as an economic system with communal ownership of factories, land and capital (in other words, they are owned by everyone rather than just a few people). This would ensure that nobody was exploited and it would end poverty. Critics argue, however, that if we examine societies that went through such social change, we would still find poverty, inequality and differences in the distribution of income and wealth.

Unemployment and the inadequacies of the welfare state

Piachaud (2009) sees unemployment as a central issue in understanding the causes of poverty. For example, if an economic recession occurs and unemployment increases then poverty also increases, through no fault of the unemployed people themselves.

Some sociologists believe that the social security system often fails to meet people's needs. For example, many people who are entitled to benefits do not claim them.

One viewpoint is that benefits are simply too low. It is argued that the solution to ending poverty is to provide people in poverty with more money (Shaw, 2002) by increasing the value of pensions and welfare benefits.

> **Eye on the exam**
>
> Try to include the relevant terms (such as material deprivation, cultural deprivation, inequality and wealth) in your answers.

Reaching the people — DISCUSSION ACTIVITY

Discuss the possible reasons why some people who are entitled to benefits do not claim them.

Explanations of poverty — WRITTEN ACTIVITY

Copy out and complete the following table by summarizing each explanation and providing at least one criticism of it.

Culture of poverty	Cycle of deprivation	New Right approaches	Marxist approaches
Main causes of poverty Criticism	Main causes of poverty Criticism	Main causes of poverty Criticism	Main causes of poverty Criticism

STRETCH AND CHALLENGE ACTIVITY

Explain which of the various explanations of poverty you find most satisfactory and why.

CHECK YOUR UNDERSTANDING

1 Identify one difference between individual and structural explanations of poverty.

2 To what extent would sociologists agree with the view that children who are born into poor families will go on to experience poverty over the course of their lives?

KEY POINTS

Marxist approaches see poverty as an outcome of class-based divisions in capitalist society. Other structural approaches explain poverty in terms of unemployment or inadequacies of the welfare state.

TOPIC 24   Does social class still matter?

OBJECTIVE
Examine the view that social class is less relevant today than in the past

In recent years, there have been hot debates within sociology about whether 'class' is still a useful concept. One view is that social class has become less relevant in contemporary Britain. Some commentators argue that class divisions and identities are no longer of great significance. Others suggest that we now live in a classless society or that class is dead.

Them and us!   ❖ DISCUSSION ACTIVITY

One view is that social class divisions are less clear cut compared with the 1950s.

> Class was a staple part of the British way of life. Each class had unique characteristics. The upper class had stately homes, aristocratic backgrounds and posh accents; the middle class, semi-detached houses, suits and bowler hats; the working class, common accents, fish and chips and council flats. This produced a society divided between 'Us' (the workers) and 'Them' (the rich and the bosses). Pubs always had a public bar and a lounge. Even railway carriages were divided into First, Second and Third class compartments.

Source: McDonough (2002)

Discuss how far social class divisions have changed, and note down three changes.

It is argued that the working class has shrunk in size as a result of changes in the occupational structure, and a decline in manufacturing industries and major industries such as mining and shipbuilding. Such changes in working-class employment are linked to a decline in working-class communities centred on heavy industry, coal mining and shipbuilding. There has also been a sharp decline in trade union membership since the 1970s.

A related view argues that social class identities have weakened. In the period following the Second World War, surveys indicated that most people in England saw themselves as either working class or middle class. Most manual workers identified themselves as working class and most non-manual workers (professionals, managers and clerical workers) identified themselves as middle class (Butler and Watt, 2007).

During the last 20 years, however, class identity has become less straightforward. It is argued, for example, that class has become less important as a social identity. Class is now only one social identity among many others, including gender and ethnicity, which we might pick and choose from (see page 204).

Saunders (1996) argues that class origins are not very important in shaping outcomes in modern Britain. He suggests that the supposed advantages (such as private education) enjoyed by children born to relatively affluent (financially well-off) parents are not particularly significant in shaping outcomes.

Young people and social class

In the following extract, Furlong and his colleagues outline a version of the view that social class is declining. This focuses on class in young people's lives.

> Young people's experiences in education and work were once stratified in visible ways and were predictable on the basis of social class. More privileged young people from higher social classes often went on to university and tended to enter the more prestigious sectors of the labour market fairly rapidly. In contrast, young people from working-class families tended to leave school at a relatively early stage and move into manual or routine white-collar work.
>
> The majority of young people in Britain now experience further education and soon one in two will enter higher education. They combine education and work and take longer to establish their careers. As a result, their work contexts are more likely to be socially mixed. In call centres, for example, students often work, temporarily, next to same-age peers who lack advanced qualifications and who are likely to spend a large part of their lives in routine employment.

Source: adapted from Furlong et al (2006)

1 How did the educational experiences of young people from different social classes differ in the past?

2 Identify two ways in which the experiences of young people from different social classes are becoming more blurred.

In Saunders' view, social background and social identities can have an influence on where people end up in the occupational hierarchy. He argues that the following social factors all count for something:

- parents (their social class, level of education and interest in their children's schooling)
- gender
- type of school attended (private education helps)
- conditions at home (overcrowding hinders success).

However, Saunders emphasizes the importance of an individual's ability and motivation rather than their social class origins on the occupation they achieve. The key factors influencing occupational class destinations are mental ability, motivation to succeed and qualifications. Furthermore, Britain is, to a large extent, a meritocracy in which people are allocated to occupational class positions mainly on the basis of ability and effort.

STRETCH AND CHALLENGE ACTIVITY

Does this account suggest that processes of social reproduction are becoming more or less clear cut?

CHECK YOUR UNDERSTANDING

Identify and explain two reasons why class may have declined in importance over the last 50 years.

KEY POINTS

Some sociologists argue that class is becoming less important as a social division. For example, the occupational structure has changed, people no longer strongly identify themselves as belonging to a particular class, young people's experiences are becoming increasingly similar in important respects regardless of their class backgrounds, and Britain largely operates as a meritocracy in allocating individuals to jobs.

TOPIC 25 # What other views are there on the changing significance of social class?

OBJECTIVES

Describe the view that other divisions are now more important than class

Examine arguments that social class remains significant

Divisions based on gender, age and ethnicity

We have examined several arguments suggesting that class is no longer of major significance as a cause of social division in Britain today. An alternative version of the 'decline of class' view argues that divisions based on gender, age and ethnicity are now more important. For example:

- In the 1950s, a higher proportion of the workforce was male. As more women are now in paid employment, this has highlighted the significance of gender inequalities at work.

- Although the gender pay gap is narrowing, it still exists.

- Men from some minority ethnic groups earn significantly less than their white male peers.

- Income is distributed unequally. Some minority ethnic groups are over-represented among low-income households.

- Gender, ethnicity and age are becoming more important than class as sources of social identity.

- Women, children, older people and some minority ethnic groups are more at risk of poverty than other groups.

- Power is distributed unequally in society. Women and members of some minority ethnic groups are under-represented in powerful positions, for example in Parliament and the judiciary (see page 244).

- Women and some minority ethnic groups are under-represented in the professions. However, if we take age into account, we get a different picture. For example, there are now more or less equal numbers of male and female doctors aged under 40 but many more male doctors aged over 50. This is because it takes time for changes to work through the occupational and class systems.

- Despite equality legislation, women, members of some ethnic minority groups and older people may experience discrimination in daily life.

Other sociologists, however, do not focus on whether one form of inequality is a more important cause of social division than another. Instead, they argue that inequalities associated with class, gender, ethnicity and age are all important. Furthermore, class, gender, ethnicity and age are seen as interrelated or linked aspects of inequality rather than completely separate aspects. So an individual will have several overlapping social positions. White middle-class men, for example, may experience advantages while black working-class women experience disadvantages based on class, gender and ethnicity.

> ### DISCUSSION ACTIVITY
>
> **The importance of gender, ethnicity, age and class**
>
> Inequalities based on class, gender, ethnicity and age may generate social divisions.
>
> 1 In a small group, discuss whether one is more significant than the others.
>
> 2 Make a note of your conclusions.

The continuing significance of class in the 21st century

Despite social changes, it is argued that class remains a central concept in sociology because social class continues to impact on people's daily lives. Class-based inequalities in life chances (related, for example, to income, housing, education, social mobility, life expectancy and health) persist into the 21st century.

Many sociologists argue that our experiences are still broadly predictable on the basis of social factors such as class. Roberts (2001) argues that social class still matters in contemporary Britain. While class may be changing, we should not confuse this with decline. However, this does not mean that divisions such as ethnicity and gender are less important. Roberts argues that it is possible for inequalities based on class, gender and ethnicity to exist together in one society.

Class matters in higher education.

Furlong et al (2006) agree that social class still matters. Class continues to impact on young people's lives. In higher education, for instance, young people from privileged backgrounds overwhelmingly attend elite institutions such as Oxford and Cambridge and study more prestigious courses such as law and international relations. They are also more likely to have stable careers afterwards. In contrast, those from less privileged backgrounds are more likely to attend 'new' universities, less likely to complete their degrees (often for financial reasons) and less likely to get graduate jobs afterwards.

Curtice and Heath (2009) note that, compared with the 1960s, a smaller proportion of people today identify themselves as working class and a bigger proportion identify themselves as middle class. However, they argue that this is not surprising given that more people today are employed in white-collar jobs. Curtice and Heath argue that overall, people are as likely to identify with a class today as they were in the 1960s. They reject the idea that class identities have declined.

> ✎ WRITTEN ACTIVITY
>
> ### The continuing significance of class
>
> Roberts, Furlong et al and Curtice and Heath argue that class is still significant in modern Britain. Summarize each of their arguments.

> 💡 STRETCH AND CHALLENGE ACTIVITY
>
> How do you think Marxist and feminist approaches might address the question of whether class or gender inequality is more significant today?

> CHECK YOUR UNDERSTANDING
>
> 1   Identify two ways in which each of the following can be seen as an important source of social division: a) age, b) ethnicity.
>
> 2   To what extent would sociologists agree that gender inequality is the most significant cause of division in contemporary British society?

> KEY POINTS
>
> One version of the 'decline of class' view argues that social inequalities linked to gender, ethnicity and age are now more significant sources of social divisions than class. However, it may be useful to see class, gender, ethnicity and age as interrelated aspects of inequality rather than as separate aspects. Many sociologists accept that class has changed but reject the ideas that it has declined.

9 Examination practice and preparation

Examination practice

Studying Society

The following answers were written under examination conditions by Jatinder.

As a sociologist, you have been asked to investigate truancy among secondary school pupils.

(i) Identify and explain one ethical issue that could arise during the course of your research. (4 marks)

An examiner comments

An appropriate issue is identified but it is not explained.

One ethical issue is that this topic on truancy could be sensitive in some schools. So you'd have to make sure that no one else saw the questionnaires once they'd been filled in by the pupils, even if they don't write down names. (2/4)

An examiner comments

The answer suggests a solution; this is not asked for. However, the answer implies that the candidate understands the idea of anonymity.

(ii) Identify one secondary source you would use and explain why this source would help you. (4 marks)

The secondary source I'd use is official statistics on absences because they give statistics on the different absences including truancy. (2/4)

An examiner comments

An appropriate secondary source is identified but the explanation is weak.

(iii) Identify one primary method of research you would use and explain why this method would be better than another possible primary method for getting the information you require. (6 marks)

One primary method of research I'd use is a questionnaire.

I'd use a questionnaire to ask pupils a list of questions about their views on truanting and whether they've done it and who with. I would then compare boys and girls and different year groups in different schools.

An examiner comments

This is a good choice of a primary method and a good description of how it would be used.

An examiner comments

However, the explanation of why it would be better than interviews is very short.

This would be better than using interviews because no one would ever admit truanting in an interview. 4/6

Total: 8/14

Families

The following answer was written under examination conditions by Nicole.

Discuss how far sociologists would agree that the roles of men and women in the family have changed since the 1970s. (12 marks)

The roles of men and women in the family and in society have changed since the 1970s. Thirty years ago, men and women had different roles in the family compared to today.

A lot of research has been done on conjugal roles. Young and Willmott studied the family and argued that the symmetrical family was now typical. In this type of family, the male and female made an equal contribution to the overall running of the family home. Today, housework and childcare are more likely to be shared by men and women.

An examiner comments

By citing Young and Willmott (1973), the candidate is saying that the roles have not changed, i.e. they were equal then and are still equal now.

There are now dual worker families in which the husband and wife both go out to work. There are now laws to make discrimination illegal in employment.

An examiner comments

The examples of equality are good.

Sociologists would agree that the roles of men and women in the family have changed since the 1970s. 5/12

An examiner comments

The conclusion does not follow from the rest of the answer.

Education

The following answer was written under examination conditions by Nabeel.

> Discuss how far sociologists would agree that material factors are the most important influence on a child's educational achievement. (12 marks)

An examiner comments

A good start, with two examples that show the candidate understands 'material factors'.

Material factors can include things like the house you live in and the amount of money available for education.

It is argued that working-class children are more likely to suffer from material deprivation.

An examiner comments

The Douglas reference is reasonably accurate but the candidate should recognize that the evidence is 50 years old.

Douglas said that if people live in overcrowded houses they won't have enough space to study quietly and to concentrate.

Their house may also be damp and so they may miss school a lot because of illness. This will mean they miss out on work and explanations for things in lessons. Later on in their education, working-class children may not go to college or university as they may not be able to afford to not work.

Although, EMA payments brought in by New Labour may have made this less of a problem for some children now.

An examiner comments

The candidate describes two alternative influences, both with good examples, though at least one reference would have been welcome.

On the other hand, some sociologists might say that cultural deprivation is more important.

Middle-class students do well because their parents encourage them more by things like attending parents' evenings more often. But working-class parents may be unable to attend due to working hours so they may still be very interested in their child's education but can't go.

Another argument is that schools can also influence achievement.

Labelling and the self-fulfilling prophecy, where pupils act out the label teachers give them can mean that a child's achievement is affected by how the teacher sees them. For example, teachers may now see girls as better pupils and so ignore boys needs more and so they don't do so well.

An examiner comments

This is a clear and confident conclusion that responds directly to the 'how far' aspect of the question.

In conclusion, all of these factors, and not just material ones, may influence a child's achievement. For example, for some middle-class Asian children, material factors may have little effect but teachers' attitudes may be very influential. 10/12

An examiner comments

The answer scores in the top band but not the maximum: 10 or 11 marks out of 12.

Crime and Deviance

The following answer was written under examination conditions by Ben.

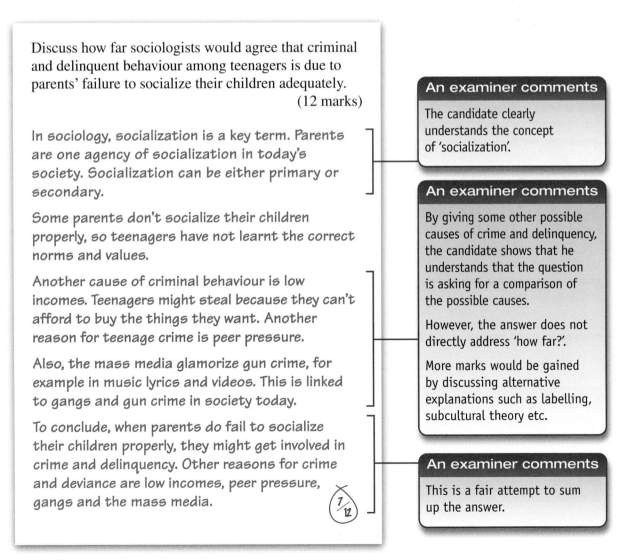

Discuss how far sociologists would agree that criminal and delinquent behaviour among teenagers is due to parents' failure to socialize their children adequately.
(12 marks)

In sociology, socialization is a key term. Parents are one agency of socialization in today's society. Socialization can be either primary or secondary.

Some parents don't socialize their children properly, so teenagers have not learnt the correct norms and values.

Another cause of criminal behaviour is low incomes. Teenagers might steal because they can't afford to buy the things they want. Another reason for teenage crime is peer pressure.

Also, the mass media glamorize gun crime, for example in music lyrics and videos. This is linked to gangs and gun crime in society today.

To conclude, when parents do fail to socialize their children properly, they might get involved in crime and delinquency. Other reasons for crime and deviance are low incomes, peer pressure, gangs and the mass media. 7/12

An examiner comments

The candidate clearly understands the concept of 'socialization'.

An examiner comments

By giving some other possible causes of crime and delinquency, the candidate shows that he understands that the question is asking for a comparison of the possible causes.

However, the answer does not directly address 'how far?'.

More marks would be gained by discussing alternative explanations such as labelling, subcultural theory etc.

An examiner comments

This is a fair attempt to sum up the answer.

Mass Media

The following answer was written under examination conditions by Kristin.

An examiner comments

Examiners are told to award full marks to an answer that is the best that can be reasonably expected from a 16-year-old writing under exam conditions.

This answer is probably even better than that and so scores full marks.

An examiner comments

These are excellent definitions of the key concepts in the question.

An examiner comments

The approach of comparing stereotyping over time is clever and is carried through very well.

An examiner comments

All the examples are good.

An examiner comments

Accurate reference.

An examiner comments

Good contemporary example.

An examiner comments

Good summary.

Discuss how far sociologists would agree that the mass media present a stereotypical rather than realistic image of people from minority ethnic groups.

(12 marks)

A stereotypical image means an exaggerated and distorted representation of individuals such as women or groups such as minority ethnic groups. The mass media refer to forms of communication that reach large audiences, for example TV and films.

One view is that, up until the 1970s, the media did present a stereotypical image of minority ethnic groups. During this time, black people did not appear much in British TV drama productions. When they did appear, they were usually presented as negative stereotypes such as criminals or in narrow roles such as singers, dancers and athletes. Sociologists argue that during the 1970s, news reports focused on stories such as famine and poverty in African countries.

During the 1990s, the images changed and the media presented more realistic and less stereotyped views of minority ethic groups. Abercrombie is a sociologist who argued that black actors were now playing ordinary, realistic characters – rather than stereotyped roles.

Things seem to have come full circle in the 2000s because sociologists now argue that media images of British Asian communities are stereotyped and distorted rather than realistic. Images are negative and the media tend to focus mainly on stories about forced marriage and refusal to fit in.

Media images of different minority ethnic groups have changed over time. Today, sociologists would agree that the media present stereotypical images particularly of British Asians.

12/12

Power

The following answer was written under examination conditions by Luke.

Discuss how far sociologists would agree with the view that pressure group activity in Britain helps to ensure that power is distributed equally throughout society.

(12 marks)

There are different types of pressure groups, such as insider, outsider and promotional groups. Examples of pressure groups in Britain include the RSPB, which has a very big membership, and the NUT. Environmental groups (e.g. Greenpeace) are becoming more well known. They have encouraged consumers to think about what they buy.

An examiner comments

These are correct types and examples of pressure groups, but there is no definition of 'pressure group'.

Some pressure groups are more successful than others. Groups with a lot of resources such as staffing and money are usually more successful in getting their views across.

Some groups organise activities such as big protests (e.g. at Heathrow Airport) to get publicity in the media and to try to change public opinion.

An examiner comments

This shows more knowledge about pressure groups and begins to link, though indirectly, to the question about the distribution of power in Britain.

Sociologists study power and how power is distributed among the different groups in society. One view is that power is spread widely among the many interests and groups. Another view is that power is concentrated in only a few hands. The pluralist and conflict approaches have different ideas about pressure groups and their power.

An examiner comments

This paragraph is accurate but is not linked to the question.

To sum up, pressure groups play an important role in society today. They help people to participate in politics. Other ways of participating include voting in elections or joining a political party.

An examiner comments

The conclusion is not a response to the question. The necessary links have not been made.

7/12

Social Inequality

The following answer was written under examination conditions by Joseph.

> Discuss how far sociologists would agree with the view that children who are born into poor families will themselves grow up to be poor.
>
> (12 marks)
>
> The life cycle of poverty shows how people start off in poverty but move out during their lives. If you are born into a poor family, you can get richer as you get older. (For example, some people become millionaires by winning the lottery or by being top footballers or models.) But, according to the life cycle of poverty, you will become poor again as you get older, e.g. if you have to live off just a pension without any savings or wealth.

4/12

An examiner comments

The candidate has correctly identified that the question is about the cycle of poverty, and gives a reasonable explanation of it. However, no alternative explanations are offered and there is no discussion.

Doing research

During the course of studying sociology, you may be asked by your tutor to undertake a small-scale research project. By doing this, you will be able to put your knowledge of the different research methods into practice. You will also gain a better understanding of the research process (see Chapter 2) and the sorts of issues and difficulties that sociologists face when undertaking their fieldwork. This will help you to answer the examination question on Studying Society.

Preparing for the exam

Before beginning your revision, it is important to do some preparation work.

Be clear on the areas you have to revise for the examination

This will depend on whether you are doing the Short Course or the Full Course. If you are not sure about this, your teacher will be able to tell you.

* If you are doing the AQA short course in sociology, you will study Unit 1 of the AQA specifications (see page 1). The Unit 1 examination consists of a written paper which lasts for 1 hour and 30 minutes. This paper is divided into three sections (Studying Society, Education and Families) and you are required to answer all of the questions in each of the three sections. Each question is marked out of 30.

* If you are doing the AQA full course in Sociology, you will cover Unit 2 as well as Unit 1 (see page 1). The Unit 2 examination consists of a written paper lasting 1 hour and 30 minutes. This paper is divided into four sections (Crime

and Deviance, Mass Media, Power and Social Inequality). You are required to choose three out of the four sections and to answer all of the questions from the three chosen sections. Each question is marked out of 30.

Identify the different topics and ideas to be covered in each area

You will need to be clear about the main themes or issues, terms, concepts, sociological approaches and research findings in each area of the specification. You might consider this to be your 'tool kit' for the area. By using this tool kit, you should be able to deal with any questions that the examiners may ask you.

Your revision tool kit

✎ WRITTEN ACTIVITY

Select an area that you want to revise, such as Mass Media. Next, decide which particular topic you are going to revise. The topic might be the effects of the mass media on their audiences. Now, use the following headings to help you structure your revision for this topic:

- main themes/issues
- sociological approaches
- terms/concepts
- research findings.

You could produce your plan as a summary on one side of A4 paper in order to make it as concise and easy to revise from as possible. It might begin as follows:

Area: Mass media

Topic: Effects of mass media on their audience

Main themes/issues:
The power of the media and its effects on audiences
How far the media can influence political attitudes and behaviour
How far screen violence leads to real-life violence

Terms/concepts:
Mass media, audience, power

Sociological approaches:
1) The hypodermic syringe approach — the audience receives daily injections of messages, e.g. from the press. These messages work like a drug & have a powerful effect on behaviour & attitudes.
Criticisms:
Problem in measuring any effects.
Consumers do actually question what the media tell them.
2) Uses and gratifications — focuses on how the audience use the media and what needs the media meet. Needs include information, personal identity, relationships & entertainment.
3) Decoding approach — the contents of a TV programme (e.g. the news) has several meanings so it could be interpreted in different ways. Different groups (e.g. women, trade union members) decode the contents differently according to their social & cultural backgrounds.

Your revision tool kit

It is also a good idea to develop a revision checklist for each area of the specification. This will involve listing each topic within a particular area, checking whether or not you have got all the notes and whether you understand them. If you identify anything that you are not sure about then you need to discuss this with your teacher. Once you have revised a topic, you can then tick it off your list. This will help you to keep track of where you are up to in your revision.

You could set out your revision checklist in three columns as shown below. Note down the topic in the first column. Note down anything you are unsure about in the second column and then check your queries with your teacher. Once you have fully revised the topic, you can tick it off in the third column.

The mass media: revision checklist

Topic	I need to check the following points with my teacher.	Revised
Definition of mass media	(Note down queries.)	✓
The difference between traditional & new media		✓
The difference between the press, broadcasting & electronic media		

Ensure that you understand what skills you will be assessed on

It is important to appreciate that the examination is not simply a test of your knowledge of the subject content. It is also about what you do with what you know. Make sure that you are clear about what skills will be assessed in the examination – for example, your skills of interpretation and evaluation. If you do not feel confident with these, then you should check them with your teacher.

Gather together the materials you will be using

You will need your notes for each area and topic, presented in a clear and logical order, and your textbook. If you can get hold of past examination papers or questions, these are useful as a check to see how your revision is progressing. Another useful source of help might be the examiners' reports which are published each year. These include the examiners' feedback on how questions were tackled. Check with your teacher about getting copies of these. Once you have done the preparation, you are ready to start revising.

Revision techniques

Revising by doing

While everyone has their own way of revising, it is important to try to be active in your revision. For example, this could involve making notes from notes. Refer to the section on note-taking techniques on page 4 of Chapter 1 for guidance on this. Summarizing your notes will help you to reduce them to a manageable length. It is also a way of checking that you understand everything.

Practising skills

You should also try to make time in your revision to practise your sociological skills. For example, you might select a method of research and then try to identify its uses, strengths and limitations. Alternatively, you might take a particular view or issue and list arguments for and against it. This will help you to develop your skills of evaluation.

Your list might look something like this:

ISSUE: SOCIAL CLASS IS LESS RELEVANT TODAY THAN IN THE PAST

Arguments for	Arguments against
• Social class is less important as a source of identity. •	• Class-based inequalities in life chances and opportunities still exist today. •

As you work through your revision notes, try to identify links between the different areas of the specification that you have studied. You could do this by putting together diagrams on key concepts such as socialization.

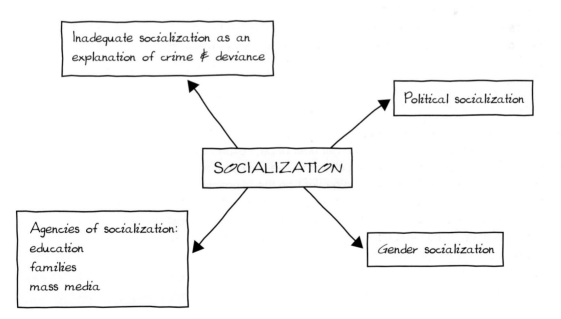

Practise answering exam questions

Before an examination, you may feel a bit nervous. One way of trying to minimize these feelings is to know what to expect. By getting as much practice as possible at answering examination questions, you will be in a better position to know what to expect in the examination. It is a good idea to try answering questions under timed conditions as this will help you to think about your use of time during the examination.

Revision timetable

To get the most from your revision, it is better to plan it out in advance rather than leaving it until the last minute. One way to plan your revision is to set yourself a revision timetable. Use a calendar or a wall planner to work out how many weeks you have left before the exam begins. You can then assess how much time is available to spend on each of the areas that you need to revise. You could set out your weekly revision timetable in a format similar to your time management plan described in Chapter 1.

Examination techniques

It is important to get as much practice with examination questions as possible. However, it is also important to identify good examination practice. What follows is a range of tips based on good practice to improve your examination technique.

1 The examination instructions

Read the instructions carefully. This will help you to avoid answering too few or too many questions.

2 Read the questions carefully

Taking time to read a question carefully can prevent you from misinterpreting it and so losing marks.

3 Look for key words

Questions will include cue words which act as a prompt or instruction to tell you what to do. It might be helpful to underline these key words. Examples include:

- *From Item A*
- *Outline*
- *Explain what is meant by*
- *Identify*
- *Describe*
- *Discuss how far*

These key words help you to recognize which sociological skill you are being assessed on in a particular question. For example:

- If a question directs you to an item (as in 'From Item A…'), it is asking you to examine that item of information and to interpret or make sense of the information contained in it. An item could consist of a table of statistics or a short extract from a book or newspaper article.

- If a question asks you to 'Explain what is meant by…' or 'Explain how…' then it is asking for an explanation. This may seem obvious! However, it is important to be clear that a question asking for an explanation of something is different from one asking for a description. An explanation requires more depth than a description.

- If a question asks you to 'Discuss how far…' then it is asking you to evaluate a particular view or approach. In other words, you will need to assess, argue for and against or present alternative approaches and views. You will also need to reach a clear conclusion regarding 'how far'.

- Some questions ask you to do two things. For example, 'Identify and explain…' or 'Describe and explain…'. In this case, remember to address both of these cue words in your answer.

4 Question instructions

Follow the question instructions carefully. If a question asks you to provide 'two reasons for' then you need to give two separate (and accurate) reasons in order to get full marks. If a question asks you to answer **either** part (i) **or** part (ii) then ensure that you follow this instruction and do not answer both.

5 Time frame

Some questions refer to a particular time frame, such as 'since the 1970s' or 'during the last 20 years' or 'today'. In this case, you must focus your answer on this time frame.

6 Terminology

Make sure you understand what is meant by terms such as 'trend', 'change' and 'rate'.

7 Data in the items

- As discussed in Chapter 1 (see pages 4–5), when you are examining statistical items provided in the question, be careful to check what units the statistics are presented in. For example, they may be in percentages, or in thousands, and so on.

- Draw on relevant information from the items when you are asked to do so, but do not simply copy out chunks of material. This wastes time and will not get you any extra marks.

- Where one mark is on offer, a brief but accurate response is all that is required.

8 Allocation of time

Be careful to give yourself enough time to answer all of the required questions. Do not spend too much time on questions worth one or two marks. Try to divide your time according to the marks allocated to a question. The marks for each question are clearly shown in brackets. If a question is worth 12 marks then you need to spend the appropriate amount of time on it. Bear in mind that reading the questions and studying the items will also take up time.

9 Re-read your answers

It is easy to make a mistake that could be spotted and amended by simply reading through your answer in the last few minutes of an examination.

Glossary

Chapter 2

Agencies of socialization: the social groups or institutions responsible for undertaking socialization, such as families, peer groups, schools, workplaces, religions and the mass media.

Analysis: the process of examining data, highlighting significant findings and results.

Anonymity of research participants: when individuals participating in research are not required to provide their name or, if they give their name, it will not appear in any reports arising from the research.

Closed questions: fixed-choice questions which require the respondent to choose between a number of given answers.

Cohort: a group of people with a characteristic in common, such as age.

Covert participant observation: when the researcher joins a group, observes and participates in its activities in order to study it, but without informing its members about his or her research activities.

Culture: the whole way of life of a particular society or social group. Culture includes the values, norms, customs, beliefs, knowledge, skills and language of the society or group.

Ethics: these relate to morals and, in the context of sociological research, raise questions about how to conduct morally acceptable research which protects the rights of research participants and safeguards their wellbeing.

Ethnic group: a social group whose members share an identity based on their cultural traditions or cultural characteristics, such as religion or language. Britain is home to a wide range of minority ethnic groups including those of Irish, Polish, Greek Cypriot, Indian and African-Caribbean heritage.

Ethos: the climate or character of an organization, for example the ethos of a school will include its policies on homework, uniform and discipline.

Gender: this relates to social or cultural (rather than biological) differences between men and women, which are associated with masculinity and femininity.

Generalizations: general statements and conclusions that apply not only to the sample studied but also to the broader population.

Hypothesis: a supposition, hunch or informed guess, usually written as a statement that can be tested and then either supported by the evidence or proved wrong.

Institutional racism: this occurs when an organization (such as a police force or hospital) fails to provide an appropriate service to people because of their ethnic origin, culture or colour. Institutional racism can be seen in organizational attitudes or behaviour that discriminates, even when individuals themselves act without intending this.

Interview bias: also known as the 'interview effect', this occurs when the interview situation itself influences interviewees' responses. Interviewees may give answers which they think are socially acceptable or which show them in a positive light.

Interview schedule: the pre-set list of questions delivered by an interviewer in a structured interview.

Interviewer bias: also known as the 'interviewer effect', this occurs when the interviewer influences the interviewee's responses. It may be linked to the interviewer's style of interviewing (for example, asking leading questions), dress, age, gender, ethnicity, appearance or accent.

Longitudinal studies: studies of the same group of people conducted over a period of time. After the initial survey or interview has taken place, follow-up surveys or interviews are carried out at intervals over a number of years.

Mass media: forms of communication (media) that reach large (mass) audiences, including newspapers, magazines, books, television, cinema and the internet.

Negative sanctions: sanctions that punish those who do not conform to the group's expectations, for example by ignoring them.

Norms: these define appropriate and expected behaviour in particular social contexts such as classrooms, cinemas, restaurants or aeroplanes.

Observer effect: in a study based on observation, this occurs when the researcher's known presence influences and changes the behaviour of the group under study.

Official statistics: existing sources of quantitative data compiled by government agencies such as the Home Office.

Open-ended questions: questions that allow respondents to put forward their own answers rather than choose a response from several pre-set answers.

Overt participant observation: in a study based on overt PO, the researcher informs participants that they are being observed as part of a research study.

Peer group: a group of people who share a similar status and position in society, such as people of a similar age, outlook or occupation.

Pilot study: a small-scale trial run carried out before the main research.

Population: the particular group under study. The population may consist of people such as higher education students, or institutions such as schools, depending on the aims of the research.

Positive sanctions: sanctions that reward those who behave according to the group's expectations, for example through praise.

Poverty: there are two broad approaches to defining poverty: absolute and relative poverty. People experience absolute poverty when their income is insufficient to obtain the minimum needed to survive. People experience relative poverty when they cannot afford to meet the general standard of living of most other people in their society.

Prejudice: a prejudgement in favour of, or against, a person, group or issue. Prejudice involves opinions and beliefs rather than action.

Primary data: information that is generated and collected first hand by doing research using techniques such as questionnaires, interviews or observation.

Primary socialization: the process of early childhood learning, usually within families, during which babies and infants acquire the basic behaviour patterns, language and skills needed in later life.

Probability (or random) sample: a sample (subgroup) in which each member of the population has a known chance of being selected for inclusion in the sample.

Qualitative data: information presented in visual or verbal form, for example as words or quotations rather than numbers.

Quantitative data: information presented in numerical form, for example as graphs or tables of statistics.

Race: the term 'race' has been used in different ways. It has been used to refer to the idea that humankind could be divided up into different 'racial groups' on the basis of natural, physical characteristics. More recent scientific evidence, however, rejects the idea of different biological races. Sociologists point to the socially constructed division of social groups according to their race. Like gender differences, racial differences are created by society.

Racism: also known as 'racial discrimination', occurs when people are treated differently and less favourably on the basis of their ethnicity.

Reliability: this refers to consistency. Research findings are reliable if the same or consistent results are obtained a second time using the same methods.

Replication: standardized methods such as questionnaires can be replicated or repeated by other researchers to check the reliability of the research findings. Getting the same or similar results a second time round confirms reliability.

Representative sample: a sample is a subgroup of the wider population. A representative sample is one that reflects the characteristics of its population. It is just like the population but a smaller version of it.

Research design: the combination of techniques and sources (such as individual interviews, observation, questionnaires and official statistics) used in a particular study.

Research process: the process of carrying out sociological research involving the following broad stages: research aims or hypotheses; pilot study; sample selection; data collection; data analysis; evaluation.

Research techniques: systematic methods of collecting data, such as questionnaires, interviews and observation.

Respondent: the person from whom information is sought, for example, the person who fills in a questionnaire.

Response rate: the number of replies received in proportion to the total number of questionnaires distributed.

Sample: a subgroup of the population selected for study.

Sampling frame: a complete list of all members of the population from which a sample is drawn. Examples include membership lists, school registers and the Royal Mail's list of postcode addresses.

Sampling procedures: the techniques used to obtain a sample. Probability (or random) sampling includes simple random and stratified random sampling. Non-probability sampling includes snowball and quota sampling.

Secondary data: information that already exists and has previously been generated or collected by other people. Sources of secondary data include official statistics, the mass media, autobiographies and studies by other sociologists.

Secondary socialization: during secondary socialization, which begins during later childhood and continues throughout our adult lives, we learn society's norms and values. Agencies of secondary socialization (the social groups or institutions which contribute to this process) include peer groups, schools, workplaces, religions and the mass media.

Social issues: issues that affect communities, groups and people's lives. Contemporary social issues relating to families, for example, include the quality of parenting, relationships between adults and teenagers, care of the elderly, arranged and forced marriages. Issues related to the mass media include the question of whether exposure to the media (for example, watching violent films) encourages copycat violent behaviour. Often, social issues are also considered to be social problems.

Social policies: sets of plans and actions put into place by governments, local authorities or other organizations in order to address particular social problems in the fields, for example, of welfare, criminal justice and education.

Social problems: problems facing society, such as racism, discrimination, teenage crime, poverty, unemployment and domestic violence. Social problems are seen as damaging or harmful to society and, therefore, require tackling or solving through social policies.

Social processes: processes in society that involve interaction between individuals, groups and institutions. Socialization, for example, is a social process through which we learn the culture of a society or group. It involves interaction between individuals, groups (such as families) and institutions (such as schools).

Social structures: the institutions that make up society, such as the family, education and stratification systems.

Socialization: the process through which we learn the culture and appropriate behaviour (the norms and values) of the particular group or society we are born into. The socialization process also prepares us for the roles we will play in society. A role refers to the pattern of expected and acceptable behaviour of people who occupy a particular social position. The role of 'teacher', for instance, defines how we expect a teacher to behave during the working day.

Stratification: the way society is structured or divided into hierarchical strata – or layers – with the most privileged at the top and the least favoured at the bottom. Social class is an example of a stratification system.

Subcultures: social groups which differ from the dominant or main culture in terms of their members' values, beliefs, customs, language, dress or diet and so on. Examples include travellers who have a nomadic way of life and youth subcultures such as Goths.

Taboo: describes behaviour that is not usually allowed according to custom or tradition.

Transcript: a written copy of the full contents of an interview.

Validity: this refers to truth or authenticity. Findings are valid if they provide a true or authentic picture of what is being studied.

Values: values such as privacy and respect for life provide general guidelines for conduct. A value is a belief or idea about what is desirable and worth striving for.

Welfare state: a system in which the state takes responsibility for protecting the health and welfare of its citizens and meeting their social needs. The state does this through provision, for example, of free schooling, state benefits, the National Health Service and council housing.

Chapter 3

Ageing population: in an ageing population, the proportion of the population over retirement age is gradually increasing.

Agencies of social control: the groups and organizations in society that control or constrain people's behaviour and actions.

Beanpole families: multigenerational families that are long and thin in shape.

Birth rate: the number of live births per 1000 of the population per year.

Civil partnership: a relationship between two people of the same sex who register as civil partners and thereby have their relationship legally recognized.

Cohabitation: living with a partner outside marriage or civil partnership.

Conjugal roles: the domestic roles of married or cohabiting partners.

Cultural diversity: culturally based differences between people in a society in terms of religion, ethnicity, social class and so on.

Death rate: the number of deaths per 1000 of the population per year.

Democratic relationships: relationships between, for example, married partners or parents and children, based on equality.

Demography: the systematic study of human populations, including their size, age and gender structures, birth and death rates and life expectancy.

Division of domestic labour: the division of tasks such as housework, childcare and DIY between men and women within the home.

Divorce rate: the number of divorces per 1000 married people per year.

Dual-earner household: a household in which two adults work in paid employment.

Dual-worker families: families in which both adult partners work in paid employment.

Extended family: a group of relatives extending beyond the nuclear family. The classic extended family contains three generations who either live under the same roof or nearby. This type of extension is known as vertical extension. In modified extended families, members live apart geographically but maintain regular contact and provide support.

Ethnic group: *see* Chapter 2 glossary.

Feminism: a sociological approach which examines the ways gender operates within social structures such as families or education systems. Feminists are committed to bringing about equality in the status and power of women and men in society.

Fertility: the average number of children born to women of childbearing age (usually 15–44) in a particular society.

Fertility rate: the number of live births per 1000 women of childbearing age (usually 15–44) in a given year.

Functionalism: a sociological approach which examines society's structures (such as the family, the education system and religion) in terms of the functions they perform for the continuation of society and for individuals.

Gay or lesbian family: a family in which a same-sex couple live together with their child or children.

Gender: gender relates to socially constructed or cultural (rather than biological) differences between men and women, which are associated with masculinity and femininity.

Geographical mobility: moving house from one area to live in another area, region or country.

Household: a household comprises either one person who lives alone or a group of people who live at the same address and who share at least one meal a day or facilities such as a living room.

Infant mortality: the death of infants in the first year of life.

Infant mortality rate: the number of infant deaths (aged under one year) per 1000 live births per year.

Joint conjugal roles: this term describes domestic roles of married or cohabiting partners, which are divided or shared in an equal way.

Kinship relationships: relationships between people based on ties of blood, marriage or adoption.

Life expectancy at birth: the average number of years a newborn baby may be expected to live.

Lone-parent family: a family consisting of one parent and a child or children who live together.

Male-breadwinner household: a household in which the adult male works in paid employment and earns the bulk of the household income.

Marriage rate: the number of marriages per 1000 people per year.

Marxism: a sociological approach which draws on the ideas of Karl Marx and applies them to modern societies.

Monogamy: the practice of being married to only one person at a time.

Migration: the movement of people either nationally, from one region of a country to another, or internationally from one country to another.

New man: a caring, sharing man.

Nuclear family: a family containing a father, mother and their child or children. It contains two generations and family members live together in the same household. The parents may be married or cohabiting outside marriage.

Patriarchy: male power and dominance over women.

Pivot generation: the generation that is sandwiched between younger family generations (the pivot generation's children and grandchildren) and older generations (the pivot generation's parents). People in the pivot generation may provide care not only for their parents but also for their grandchildren.

Power: in social relationships between individuals (for example, between spouses or parents and children) or groups, power usually refers to the dominance and control of one individual or group over others.

Role: the pattern of expected and acceptable behaviour of people who occupy a particular social position. The role of 'teacher', for instance, defines how we expect a teacher to behave during the working day.

Secularization: the process whereby the influence of religion in a society declines.

Segregated conjugal roles: this term describes domestic roles of married or cohabiting partners which are separated out or divided in an unequal way.

Serial monogamy: the practice of divorcing, remarrying, divorcing, remarrying and so on.

Social construction: this term is often used in relation to age, gender and race and reflects the idea that, rather than being rooted in biology or nature, these are created by society or culture.

Spouse: a husband or wife.

Stepfamily: a reconstituted family in which one or both partners have a child or children from a previous relationship living with them. Most stepfamilies comprise a stepfather, a biological mother and her child or children, but they can combine biological and social parenting in more complex ways.

Symmetrical family: a family form in which spouses carry out different tasks but each makes a similar contribution within the home.

Welfare state provisions: benefits and services provided through government departments to ensure that people's wellbeing is taken care of.

Chapter 4

Academy: a failed school, taken over by central government, in partnership with private sponsors such as businesses or churches. The aim of their creation was to raise achievement.

Agency of social control: *see* 'Agencies of social control' in Chapter 3 glossary.

Beacon school: a school or college recognized as centres of excellence, part of whose role is to share its expertise with other schools and colleges.

Comprehensive system: introduced from 1965, this is a non-selective education system. All children attend the same type of secondary school regardless of ability.

Counter-school subculture: a group within a school that rejects the values and norms of the school and replaces them with anti-school values and norms.

Cultural deprivation: a theory that suggests that working-class and ethnic minority students lack the 'correct' values and attitudes from socialization to succeed in education.

Hidden curriculum: things learnt in school that are not formally taught, such as valuing punctuality or conformity and obedience.

Home education: also called home schooling or home learning, this refers to teaching children at home rather than at school, usually by parents or private tutors.

Independent sector: this is made up of schools that charge fees and/or are not subject to the same rules as the state sector.

Labelling: the process of attaching a characteristic or definition to an individual or group.

Marketisation: the policy of bringing market forces (such as competition, supply and demand) into education and other areas.

Material deprivation: a lack of resources related to financial situation or poverty. In education this might include poor housing or an inability to afford educational aids.

Meritocracy (or meritocratic system): a system in which everyone is seen as having an equal opportunity to succeed. Success is based on ability and effort, not on social class, gender or ethnicity.

Nature: the idea that intelligence is inherited or genetic. Educational success is thus determined by the abilities we are born with.

Nurture: the idea that educational success is linked to the social environment and factors such as social class, gender, ethnicity and peer groups.

Official curriculum: the formal learning that takes place in schools. This includes subjects and courses studied.

Private schools: schools that charge fees.

Power: *see* Chapter 7 glossary.

Public school: the older and more famous independent schools, such as Eton and Harrow.

Self-fulfilling prophecy: where teachers may make a prediction about a student that comes true. Treating a student according to the prediction may lead the student to come to accept the teacher's view of them and so the prediction comes true.

Social exclusion: *see* Chapter 8 glossary.

Social mobility: where people change position or status in a stratification system, moving up or down between the layers.

Socialization: *see* Chapter 2 glossary.

Specialist schools: centres of excellence in particular subject areas, such as languages or technology. They are intended to raise standards of teaching and learning in these areas.

Streaming: where students are separated into different ability groups and then taught in these separate groups for all of their subjects.

Tri-partite system: created by the 1944 Education Act, this system used the 11-plus test to identify students' ability levels. Students were then allocated to one of three types of school based on their tested abilities (Grammar, Secondary Modern or Technical).

Vocational education: work or career-related education.

11-plus exam: a national IQ test introduced by the 1944 Education Act to be used as a method of allocating students to one of three types of school in the tri-partite system.

Chapter 5

Agencies of social control: *see* Chapter 3 glossary.

Antisocial behaviour: behaviour that causes harassment, distress or alarm to other people.

Corporate crime: crimes committed by employees on behalf of the company or organization they work for. Examples include the manufacture and sale of unsafe products.

Crime: an illegal act (such as shoplifting or murder) which is punishable by law.

Deviance: behaviour which does not confirm to society's norms and values and, if detected, is likely to lead to negative sanctions. Deviance can be – but is not necessarily – illegal.

Folk devil: a group that is defined as a threat to society's values.

Formal and informal rules: formal rules are written down in the form, for example, of laws or codes of conduct. They have official status and, if we are caught breaking them, some sort of punishment, penalty or negative sanction usually follows. Informal rules are taken for granted rather than written down. They provide guidelines on how we are expected to behave in particular social settings.

Formal social control: control of people's behaviour based on written laws and rules. Formal social control is usually associated with the ways the state regulates and controls our behaviour. The agencies of formal social control include the police force, the courts and prisons.

Informal social control: control of people's behaviour based on social processes such as the approval and disapproval of others. Informal social control is enforced via social pressure. The agencies of informal social control include peer groups and families.

Negative sanctions: in the processes of social control and socialization, negative sanctions punish those who do not conform to the group's expectations, for example by ignoring them or using argument to try to get them to change their behaviour.

Moral panic: a media-fuelled over-reaction to social groups (such as 'hoodies'). This process involves the media exaggerating the extent and significance of a social problem. A particular group is cast as a folk devil and becomes defined as a threat to society's values.

Positive sanctions: *see* Chapter 2 glossary.

Racist victimization: individuals are targeted and victimized because of their race, ethnicity or religion.

Relative deprivation: this occurs when individuals or groups feel that they are unfairly disadvantaged in relation to other similar people.

Repeat victimization: being a victim of the same type of crime regularly over time.

Scapegoating: the process of blaming an individual or group for something that is not their fault.

Self-report studies: household surveys which ask respondents whether they have committed particular offences during a specified time period such as the last year. They provide information on offenders and offences that are not necessarily dealt with by the police or courts.

Social control methods: the processes by which individuals are encouraged or persuaded to conform to the rules, and the ways in which social groups or societies deal with behaviour that breaks these rules. Social control methods may involve sanctions or other social reactions to deviance that aim to limit or reduce the frequency of deviant acts.

Social order: social order occurs when society is stable, ordered and runs smoothly without continual disruption.

Social problems: *see* Chapter 2 glossary.

Stereotypes: fixed, standardized and distorted views of the characteristics of particular groups such as women. Stereotypes are often based on prejudice.

Victim surveys: household-based studies which ask respondents about their experiences of crime, whether they have been victims of particular offences during a specified time period such as the last year and, if so, whether they reported the crimes to the police.

White-collar crime: this refers broadly to crimes committed by people in relatively high-status positions, such as accountants, doctors or solicitors, during their work. Examples include tax evasion and 'fiddling' expense accounts at work.

Chapter 6

Agenda setting: the ability of the media to focus public attention on particular topics and thereby direct public discussion and debate onto these topics.

Amplification of deviance: the process whereby the social reaction to deviance from the mass media and public leads to an increase in – or amplifies – the deviance by provoking more of the same behaviour.

Conglomerate: a huge corporation or company formed by the merging of different firms. Media conglomerates have stakes across a range of media such as newspapers, films and digital television services. They operate on a global rather than a national scale.

Convergence: when the technologies of the media, telecommunications and computing come together – or converge – in one product. For example, some digital television services allow us to access the internet as well as text, e-mail, shop and bank through our television sets.

Democracy: government by the people.

Digital divide: a division or gap between those who have access to new media technology and those who do not.

Folk devil: *see* Chapter 5 glossary.

Gatekeepers: the programme controllers, editors, journalists and owners who decide what to cover and how to present it.

Globalization: the growing interconnections between different countries, regions and people as the same consumer goods, brands and economic interests stretch across the globe.

Identity: how we see ourselves and how others *see* us.

Interactivity: the consumer's ability to interact with a media product. For example, we can interact with reality television programmes by texting to vote for a contestant.

Mass media: *see* Chapter 2 glossary.

Moral panic: *see* Chapter 5 glossary.

News values: media professionals' values about what issues and personalities are considered newsworthy, topical or important.

Norm referencing: the ability of the media to present some behaviour, views and groups positively and others negatively, thereby shaping public opinion on these groups.

Pluralism: an approach which argues that a range of views and opinions exists in society and this range is reflected in the varied media products available to consumers.

Political socialization: the process via which we acquire our political values, beliefs and preferences.

Power: an individual's or group's ability to get what they want, despite opposition from others.

Pressure group: a group of people who try to persuade the government to adopt a particular policy or to influence public opinion on an issue.

Sexuality: in broad terms, sexuality refers to the way an individual expresses themselves and behaves as a sexual being. It also refers to sexual orientation and preference (for example, being heterosexual, lesbian, gay or bisexual).

Stratification: *see* Chapter 2 glossary.

Chapter 7

All-women shortlist: a list of female-only, selected candidates from which the final choice is made.

Apartheid: *see* Chapter 8 glossary.

Apathy: lack of interest.

Authority: the exercise of power based on consent or agreement.

Charismatic authority: obedience based on an individual's charisma or extraordinary personal qualities.

Citizens: members of a state who have full legal rights (e.g. to vote in elections) and responsibilities (e.g. to respect the law).

Citizenship: this can refer either to the political and legal status associated with membership of a particular state such as the UK, or to active involvement in public life and the political process.

Class dealignment: the weakening of the links between social class and voting behaviour.

Coercion: obedience based on the use of force.

Constituency: a specific area in which the constituents elect an MP to represent them in Parliament.

Constituents: the voters who live in a particular constituency.

Contributory benefits: benefits which require the claimant to have paid sufficient contributions into the national insurance (NI) scheme in order to qualify for them.

Democracy: *see* Chapter 6 glossary.

Dependency culture: some people who rely on state benefits are seen as developing a way of life in which they become so dependent on benefits that they lose all motivation to work.

Direct democracy: a democratic political system in which citizens participate directly in the decision-making process.

Discrimination: less favourable or unfair treatment based, for example, on an individual's gender, ethnicity or age.

Economically inactive: people who are neither in work nor actively seeking it.

Electorate: those eligible to vote in elections.

Insider groups: pressure groups such as the CBI which operate inside government networks.

Legal rational authority: a type of authority in which obedience is based on an individual or group's position in an organisation.

Local benefits: benefits, such as housing benefit, that are the responsibility of local councils.

Mandate: after a general election, the winning party can claim that it has a mandate (or the authority) to carry out its policies, based on the wishes of the electorate.

Manifesto: a statement of policy proposals issued, for example, by a political party before an election.

Means test: a test to establish need before financial help from public funds is given.

National benefits: benefits, including national insurance (NI) benefits, which are the responsibility of central government.

Non-contributory benefits: benefits, such as Income Support, that are designed for people in financial need who have not paid enough NI contributions to qualify for NI benefits.

Outsider groups: pressure groups that are not consulted automatically by government.

Poverty: *see* Chapter 2 glossary.

Power: an individual or group's ability to get what they want, despite opposition from others.

Pressure group: a group of people who try to persuade the government to adopt a particular policy or to influence public opinion on an issue.

Promotional group: a pressure group such as Amnesty International that seeks to promote a particular cause or campaign on a specific issue.

Protective group: a pressure group, such as a trade union, that seeks to protect or defend its members' common interests.

Representative democracy: a democratic political system in which citizens elect representatives (such as MPs) who make political decisions on their behalf.

State: the various institutions (such as the civil service and the courts) that organise and regulate society by making, implementing and enforcing laws.

Trade union: an association of employees (such as the National Union of Teachers) that protects its members' rights in the workplace.

Traditional authority: a type of authority in which obedience is based on custom and tradition.

Turnout: the proportion of eligible voters who actually turn out to vote in an election.

Unemployment rate: the percentage of economically active people (those aged 16 and over who are either in work or actively seeking work) who are unemployed at a given time.

Welfare state: a system in which the state takes responsibility for protecting its citizens' health and welfare by providing services (e.g. the NHS) and benefits (e.g. Income Support).

Chapter 8

Absolute poverty: *see* 'Poverty' in Chapter 2 glossary.

Achieved status: social positions that are earned on the basis of personal talents or merit.

Apartheid: in South Africa (1948–94), a government policy of racial segregation (known as Apartheid) was used as the basis for stratification.

Ascribed status: social positions that are fixed at birth and unchanging over time, including a hereditary title linked to family background (Princess or Lord, for example).

Caste: an example of a stratification system linked to Hinduism, which that operated in India. People were born into a particular caste or stratum and their social position was ascribed at birth.

Cycle of deprivation: the idea that deprivation and poverty are passed on from parents to their children.

Deprivation: the lack of material resources.

Gender pay gap: the difference between men's and women's hourly earnings.

Glass ceiling: an invisible barrier to promotion faced by some groups, including women.

Income: the flow of resources which individuals and households receive over a specific period of time. Income may be received in cash (for example from earnings) or in kind (for instance a petrol allowance).

Inequalities: differences in the distribution of resources (such as income) or outcomes (such as educational achievement).

Inter-generational social mobility: movement up or down between the layers as measured between the generations of a family.

Intra-generational social mobility: movement of an individual over the course of their life up or down from one occupational classification to another.

Life chances: an individual's chances of achieving positive or negative outcomes (relating, for example, to health, education, housing) as they progress through life.

Life cycle of poverty: movement into and out of poverty at different stages during the course of a person's life.

Meritocracy: *see* Chapter 4 glossary.

Poverty: *see* Chapter 2 glossary.

Relative poverty: *see* 'Poverty' in Chapter 2 glossary.

Social exclusion: being shut out or excluded from participation in society's social, economic, political and cultural life.

Social inequality: the uneven distribution of resources such as money and power, or of opportunities and outcomes related to, for example, education and health related to education and health.

Social mobility: *see* Chapter 4 glossary.

Social stratification: *see* 'Stratification' in Chapter 2 glossary.

Underclass: this term has been used in different ways. It can refer to a group whose attitudes and values are different from those of mainstream society. It can also refer to people who experience long-term poverty and who are unable to obtain a living.

Vertical segregation: within the same occupation, women and men tend to be found in jobs at different levels.

Wealth: ownership of assets such as property, land and works of art, as well as money held in savings accounts and shares in companies.

Welfare dependency: the idea that some groups remain in poverty because the welfare state encourages them to depend on overly generous state provision.

Bibliography

Chapter 2

Bagguley, P. and Hussain, Y. (2007) *The Role of Higher Education in Providing Opportunities for South Asian Women*, Polity Press.

Bagguley, P. and Hussain, Y. (2008) *Riotous Citizens: Ethnic Conflict in Multicultural Britain,* Ashgate.

Ball, S. J., Maguire, M. and Macrae, S. (2000) *Choice, Pathways and Transitions Post-16: New youth, new economies in the global city*. RoutledgeFalmer.

Baracco, L. (2007) 'Using interviews in sociological research', *Sociology Review*, 16 (4), 18–21.

Barker, E. (1994) *The Making of a Moonie: Brainwashing or Choice?* Blackwell Publishers.

BSA (2002) *Statement of Ethical Practice,* www.britsoc.co.uk.

Burman, M. (2004) 'A view from the girls: challenging conceptions of violence', *Sociology Review*, 13 (4), 2–5.

Charles, N., Aull Davies, C. and Harris, C. (2008) *Families in Transition: Social Change, Family Formation and Kin Relationships*, Policy Press.

Day, A. (2007) 'A sociology of belief', *Sociology Review*, 16 (4), 25–27.

Eden, K. and Roker, D. (2002) *'… Doing Something': Young People as Social Actors,* National Youth Agency.

Gauntlett, D. (2008) *Media, Gender and Identity: An Introduction*, Routledge.

Gomm, R. (2008) *Social Research Methodology*, Palgrave Macmillan.

Hatterton, P. and Hollands, R. (2003) *Urban Nightscapes: youth cultures, pleasure spaces and corporate power*, Routledge.

Heath, S. and Cleaver, E. (2003) *Young, Free and Single? Twenty-Somethings and Household Change*, Palgrave Macmillan.

Maclean, C. (1979) *The Wolf Children: Fact or Fantasy?* Penguin.

May, T. (2001) *Social Research: Issues, methods and process*, Open University Press.

McNeill, P. and Chapman, S. (2005) *Research Methods*, Routledge.

ONS (2004) Census 2001 Definitions, TSO.

ONS (2005) Census 2001 Quality Report for England and Wales, Palgrave Macmillan.

ONS (2008) *Social Trends No 38*, Palgrave Macmillan.

O'Reilly, K. (2000) *The British on the Costa del Sol: Transnational Identities and Local Communities*, Routledge.

Pilcher, J. (2004) 'The uses of sociology', *Sociology Review* 14(1), 2–4.

Reay, D., David, M. E. and Ball, S. (2005) *Degrees of Choice: Social Class, Race and Gender in Higher Education*, Trentham Books.

Robertson, D. (2008) 'Clothes giant plans female only store in Saudi Arabia', *Timesonline*, May 19.

Robson, E. (2001) 'The routes project: disadvantaged young people interviewing their peers' in J. Clark et al. *Young People as Researchers: Possibilities, Problems and Politics*, National Youth Agency.

Roseneil, S. and Budgeon, S. (2006) 'Beyond "the family": personal life and social change', *Sociology Review*, 16 (1), 14–16.

Sapsford, R. (2007) *Survey Research*, Sage Publications Ltd.

Shildrick, T. (2002) 'Young people, illicit drug use and the question of normalization', *Journal of Youth Studies*, 5(1), 35–48.

Taylor, C. F. (1996) *Native American Life*, Salamander Books.

Ward, J. (2008) 'Researching drug sellers: an "experiential" account from "the field"', *Sociological Research Online*, 13(1).

Winlow, S. and Hall, S. (2006) *Violent Night: Urban Leisure and Contemporary Culture*, Berg.

Chapter 3

Allan, G. and Crow, G. (2001) *Families, Households and Society*, Palgrave.

Anderson, M. (1971) *Family Structure in Nineteenth-Century Lancashire*, Cambridge University Press.

Aries, P. (1973) *Centuries of Childhood*, Peregrine.

Bernard, J. (1982) *The Future of Marriage*, Yale University Press.

Brannen, J. (2003) 'The age of beanpole families', *Sociology Review*, 13 (1), 6–9.

Charles, N., Davies, C. and Harris, C. (2008a) 'The family: continuity and change', *Sociology Review*, 18(2), 2–5.

Charles, N., Aull Davies, C. and Harris, C. (2008b) *Families in Transition: Social Change, Family Formation and Kin Relationships*. Policy Press.

Charter, D. (2007) 'You won't see New Man for dust when the cleaning needs doing', *The Times*, 17 March.

Clarke, J. (1997) 'Domestic violence revisited', *Sociology Review*, 6 (4), 32–33.

Coleman, D. and Salt, J. (eds) (1996) *Ethnicity in the 1991 Census. Volume one,* HMSO.

Crompton, R. and Lyonette, C. (2008) 'Who does the housework? The division of labour within the home' in *British Social Attitudes: the 24th Report*, Sage Publications Ltd.

Denscombe, M. (1997) *Sociology Update,* Olympus Books.

DES, (2006) *Children Looked After in England (including adoption and care leavers) 200–06. Statistical First Release*. SFR 44/2006, ONS.

Duncan, S. (2006) 'What's the problem with teenage parents?' *Sociology Review*, 16 (1), 2–5.

Duncan, S. and Phillips, M. (2008) 'New families? Tradition and change in modern relationships' in *British Social Attitudes: the 24th Report*, Sage Publications Ltd.

Evandrou, M. (2005) 'Health and Social Care' in Soule, A., Babb, P., Evandrou, M., Balchin, S. and Zealey, L. (eds) *Focus on Older People*, ONS.

Garrod, J. (2005a) 'Campaigns for fathers' rights', *Sociology Review*, 14(3), 17–19.

Garrod, J. (2005b) 'Forced marriages', *Sociology Review*, 14(4), 14–15.

Garrod, J. (2008) 'Childhood', *Sociology Review*, 18 (1), 14–16.

Gatrell, C. (2008) 'Involved fatherhood?' *Sociology Review*, 18 (1), 2–5.

Halsey, A. H. (1992) in N. Dennis and G. Erdos, *Families Without Fatherhood*, The IEA Health and Welfare Unit.

Jewson, N. (1994) 'Family values and relationships', *Sociology Review*, 3 (3),

Laslett, P. K. (1965) *The World We Have Lost*, Methuen.

Meikle, J. (2008) 'Grown-up offspring cost parents £21,500' in *The Guardian*, 5 September.

Morris, N. (2008) 'Fattest children to be taken away from their parents' in *The Independent*, 16 Augugust.

Munro, R. and Rigsby, J. (1996) *Death By Default*, Human Rights Watch.

Oakley A. (1974) *The Sociology of Housework*, Martin Robertson.

ONS (2006) *Focus on Ethnicity and Religion*, Palgrave Macmillan.

ONS (2007) *Social Trends No 37*, Palgrave Macmillan.

ONS (2008) *Social Trends No 38*, Palgrave Macmillan.

Pahl, J. (1989) *Money and Marriage*, Macmillan.

Peach, C. (ed.) (1996) *Ethnicity in the 1991 Census. Volume two*, HMSO.

Pryor, J. and Trinder, L. (2004) 'Children, families, and divorce' in J. Scott, J. Treas and M. Richards (eds) *The Blackwell Companion to the Sociology of Families*, Blackwell Publishing.

Roseneil, S. and Budgeon, S. (2006) 'Beyond "the family": personal life and social change', *Sociology Review*, 16 (1), 14–16.

Sardar, Z. (2008) 'First person' in *The Guardian*, 13 September.

Scott, J. (2004) 'Children's families' in J. Scott, J. Treas and M. Richards (eds) *The Blackwell Companion to the Sociology of Families*, Blackwell Publishing.

Smith, J. (2008) 'Domestic violence is a crime society ignores' in *The Independent*.

Soule, A., Babb, P., Evandrou, M., Balchin, S. and Zealey, L. (2005) (eds) *Focus on Older People*, ONS.

Westwood, S. and Bhachu, P. (1988) 'Images and Reality', *New Society*, 6 May.

Williams, J. (2008) in 'Focus: Households', *Sociology Review*, 18 (1), 34.

Winstanley, M. (ed) (1995) *Working Children in Nineteenth-Century Lancashire*, Lancashire County Books.

Young, M. and Willmott, P. (1957) *Family and Kinship in East London*. Routledge and Kegan Paul.

Young, M. and Willmott, P. (1973) *The Symmetrical Family*. Routledge and Kegan Paul.

Chapter 4

Asthana, A. (2006), 'Single-sex schools no benefit for girls' in *The Observer*, 25 June.

Ball, S. (2003), 'It's not what you know – education and social capital', *Sociology Review*, 13 (2),

Bernstein, B. (1960) 'Social class and linguistic development – a theory of social learning' in Halsey, Flood and Anderson (1961), *Education, Economy and Society*, Free Press.

Bhatti, G. (1999), *Asian Children at Home and at School*, Routledge.

Burgess-Macey, C. (1992) 'Tackling racism in the classroom' in Gill, Mayor, Blair (eds) *Racism and Education – Structures and strategies*, Sage Publications Ltd.

Clarke, J. (1997), 'Ethnicity and education revisited', *Sociology Review*, 7 (2),

Davies, C. and Born, M. (2000), 'Girl power leaves lads lagging behind' in *The Telegraph*, 18 August.

Department for Education and Skills (2006), 'Ethnicity and education: the evidence on minority ethnic pupils aged 5–16'. Research paper.

Department for Children, Schools and Families (2008), education and training statistics.

Douglas, J. W. B. et al (1967) *The Home and the School*, Panther.

Fleming, S. (1993) 'Schooling, sport and ethnicity', *Sociology Review*, 3 (1),

Garner, R. (2007) 'Private schools still best route to the top job, survey shows' in *The Independent*, 28 June.

Gewirtz, S. et al (1995) *Markets, Choice and Equity in Education*, Open University Press.

Gillborn, D. and Youdell, D. (2000) *Rationing Education: policy, practice, reform and equity*, Open University Press.

Halsey, Heath and Ridge (1980) *Origins and Destinations*, Clarenden Press.

Hargreaves, D. (1967) *Social Relations in a Secondary School*, Routledge and Kegan Paul.

Harris, S. et al. (1993) 'Schoolwork, homework and gender' in *Gender and Education*, 5 (1),

Katz, C. (1993) 'Growing Girls' in Katz, C. et al (eds) *Full Circles*, Routledge.

Kelly, A. (1981) *The Missing Half: Girls and Science Education*, Manchester University Press.

Lacey, D. (1970) *Hightown Grammar: The School as a Social System*, Manchester University Press.

MacBeath, J. and Mortimore, P. (2001) *Improving School Effectiveness*, Open University Press.

Mac an Ghaill, M. (1992) 'Coming of age in 1980s England', in Gill, Mayor and Blair (eds), *Racism and Education – Structures and Strategies*, Sage Publications Ltd.

Mason, D. (2000) *Race and Ethnicity in Modern Britain*, Open University Press.

Mirza, Heidi Safia (1997) *Black British Feminism*, Routledge.

Mitsos, E. and Browne, K. (1998), 'Gender and Education', *Sociology Review*, September.

Modood, T. (1997), *Ethnic Minorities in Britain*, PSI.

Moir, A. and Moir, B. (1998) *Why men don't iron: the real science of gender studies*, HarperCollins.

Murphy, P. and Elwood, J. (1998) 'Gendered learning outside and inside school', in Epstein, D. et al (ed) *Failing Boys?* Open University Press.

Pryce, K. (1979) *Endless Pressure*, Penguin.

Reid, I. (1996) 'Education and Inequality', *Sociology Review,* 6 (2),

Rose, Sir David (2008) *Independent Review of the Primary Curriculum,* December 2008.

Rutter, M. et al (1979) *Fifteen Thousand Hours*, Open Books.

Smith, D. and Tomlinson, S. (1989) *The School Effect: A Study of Multi-Racial Comprehensives*, Policy Studies Institute.

Sutton Trust (2008) *The Educational Background of Vice Chancellors*.

Wilkinson, H. (1994) 'No Turning Back: Generations and Genderquake', *Weekend Guardian,* October.

Williams, J. (2003) 'Schooling and educational performance', *Sociology Review,* 13 (2),

Wragg, T. (2003) 'Education – bouncing back', *Sociology Review,* 13 (2),

Wright, C. (1992) 'Multi-racial primary school classrooms', in Gill, Mayor and Blair (eds), *Racism and Education – Structures and Strategies,* Sage Publications Ltd.

Youth Cohort Study (2008)

Chapter 5

Budd, T, Sharp, C, Weir, G, Wilson, D and Owen, N. (2005) 'Young People and Crime: Findings from the 2004 Offending, Crime and Justice Survey', *Home Office Statistical Bulletin 20/05*, Home Office.

Cicourel, A. V. (1976) *The Social Organisation of Juvenile Justice,* Heinemann.

Clinard, M. B. and Meier, R. F. (2001) *Sociology of Deviant Behaviour*, Harcourt College Publishers.

Cohen, A. K. (1955) *Delinquent Boys: The Culture of the Gang*, Free Press.

Downes, D. and Rock. P. (2007) *Understanding Deviance*, Oxford University Press.

Garrod, J. (2007) 'Women in Prison', *Sociology Review*, 16(3), 26–27.

Goode, E. (2008) 'Introduction: the significance of extreme deviance' in E. Goode and D. A. Vail *Extreme Deviance*, Sage Publications Ltd.

Hough, M. and Mayhew, P. (2006) 'What is happening to crime?' *Sociology Review*, 15(4), 6–9.

Hoyle, C. and Zedner, L. (2007) 'Victims, victimization and criminal justice' in M. Maguire, R. Morgan and R. Reiner (eds), *The Oxford Handbook of Criminology*, Oxford University Press.

Jansson, K. (2006) 'Black and Minority Ethnic Groups' Experiences and Perceptions of Crime, Racially Motivated Crime and the Police: Findings from the 2004/05 British Crime Survey.' *Home Office Online Report 25/06*, Home Office.

Jansson, K, Robb, P, Higgins, N. and Babb, P. (2008) 'Extent and trends' in C. Kershaw, S. Nicholas and A. Walker (eds) 'Crime in England and Wales 2007/08. Findings from the British Crime Survey and police recorded crime.' *Home Office Statistical Bulletin 07/08*, Home Office.

Maguire, M. (2007) 'Crime data and statistics' in M. Maguire, R. Morgan and R. Reiner (eds) *The Oxford Handbook of Criminology,* Oxford University Press.

Marsh, I. (2006) (ed.) *Theories of Crime*, Routledge.

Ministry of Justice (2007) *Criminal Statistics 2006 England and Wales*. A Ministry of Justice Publication under Section 95 of the Criminal Justice Act 1991.

Ministry of Justice (2008) *Statistics on Race and the Criminal Justice System – 2006/7*. A Ministry of Justice Publication under Section 95 of the Criminal Justice Act 1991.

Nelken, D. (2007) 'White-collar and corporate crime' in M. Maguire, R. Morgan and R. Reiner (eds) *The Oxford Handbook of Criminology*, Oxford University Press.

Newburn, T. (2007) 'Youth crime and youth culture' in M. Maguire, R. Morgan and R. Reiner (eds) *The Oxford Handbook of Criminology*, Oxford University Press.

ONS (2008) *Social Trends No 38*, Palgrave Macmillan.

Phillips, C. and Bowling, B. (2007) 'Ethnicities, racism, crime and criminal justice' in M. Maguire, R. Morgan and R. Reiner (eds) *The Oxford Handbook of Criminology*, Oxford University Press.

Pitts, J. (2005) 'New Labour, the media and youth justice', *Sociology Review* 14(3), 8–10.

Ray, L. and Smith, D. (2002) 'Hate crime, violence and cultures of racism' in P. Iganski (ed.) *The Hate Debate – Should Hate Crime be Punished as a Crime,* Profile Books.

Salisbury, H. and Upson, A. (2004) *Ethnicity, Victimization and Worry about Crime: Findings from the 2001/2002 and 2002/2003 British Crime Survey, Findings 237*, Home Office.

Sapsted, D. (2005) 'Shopping centre outlaws "hoodies"', *Telegraph online*, 12 May.

Slack, J. (2007) 'Girl gangs muscling in on street violence', *Mail Online*, 22 August.

Tombs, S. (2005) 'Corporate crime', *Sociology Review* 14(4), 2–5.

Townsley, M. and Marshall, B. (2006) 'Is policing fair?' *Sociology Review* 16(2), 19–21.

Walklate, S. (2007) *Imagining the Victim of Crime*, Open University Press.

Williams, B. (2005) *Victims of Crime and Community Justice*, Jessica Kingsley Publishers.

Williams, J. (2008) 'The victims of crime', *Sociology Review* 17(4), 30–32.

Williams, T. (1989) *The Cocaine Kids*, Addison-Wesley.

Willis, P. (1977) *Learning to Labour: How Working-class Kids Get Working-class Jobs*. Saxon House.

Young, M. A., Herman, S., Davis, R. C. and Lurigio, A. J. (2007) 'Introduction to Victims of Crime: The interaction of research and practice' in R. C. Davis, A. J. Lurigio and S. Herman (eds) *Victims of Crime*, Sage Publications.

Chapter 6

Abercrombie, N. (1996) *Television and Society*, Polity Press.

Alexander, C. (2004) 'Writing race: ethnography and the imagination of the Asian gang' in M. Bulmer and J. Solomons (2004) (eds) *Researching Race and Racism*, Routledge.

Bagguley, P. and Hussain, Y. (2008) *Riotous Citizens: Ethnic Conflict in Multicultural Britain*, Ashgate.

Baker, C. E. (2007) *Media Concentration and Democracy: Why Ownership Matters*, Cambridge University Press.

Ball, S. J., Maguire, M. and Macrae, S. (2000) *Choice, Pathways and Transitions Post-16: New youth, new economies in the global city*, RoutledgeFalmer.

Barker, M. and Petley, J. (eds) (2001) *Ill Effects: The Media/Violence Debate*, Routledge.

Boyle, R. (2005) 'Press the red button now: television and technology', *Sociology Review* 15(2), 27–29.

Branston, G. and Stafford, R. (2006) *The Media Student's Book*. London: Routledge.

Broadcasting Standards Council report (1990) *Sexual Stereotyping in Advertising.*

Burton, G. (2005) *Media and Society: Critical Perspectives*, Open University Press.

Cohen, S. (2002) *Folk Devils and Moral Panics* (3rd edition), Routledge.

Cottle, S. (1994) 'The news media and "race" – a case of intended and unintended outcomes' in *Social Science Teacher*, 23(2).

Curran, J. and Seaton, J. (2003) *Power Without Responsibility: The press, broadcasting and new media in Britain*, Routledge.

Curran, J. and Gurevitch, M. (2005) *Mass Media and Society*, Hodder Education.

Curtice, J. and Mair, A. (2008) 'Where have all the readers gone? Popular newspapers and Britain's political health' in *British Social Attitudes: the 24th Report*, Sage Publications Ltd.

Gauntlett, D. (2001) 'The worrying influence of 'media effects' studies' in M. Barker and J. Petley (eds) *Ill Effects: The Media/Violence Debate*, Routledge.

Gauntlett, D. (2008) *Media, Gender and Identity: An Introduction*, Routledge.

Gunter, B. (2008) 'Why study media content?' *Sociology Review* 18(2), 6–9.

Hallsworth, S. (1994) 'Understanding new social movements', *Sociology Review*, 4(1).

Livingstone, S. (2005) 'Critical debates in internet studies: reflections on an emerging field' in J. Curran and M. Gurevitch. (eds) *Mass Media and Society*, Hodder Arnold.

McQuail, D. (1987) *Mass Communication Theory* (2nd edition), Sage Publications Ltd.

McQuail, D. (2003) *Media Accountability and Freedom of Publication*, Oxford University Press.

Murdock. G and Golding, P. (2005) 'Culture, communications and political economy' in J. Curran and M. Gurevitch (eds) *Mass Media and Society,* Hodder Arnold.

Oates, S. (2008) *Introduction to Media and Politics*, Sage Publications Ltd.

ONS (2007) *Focus on the Digital Age*, Palgrave Macmillan.

ONS (2008) *Social Trends No 38*, Palgrave Macmillan.

Peak, S. and Fisher, P. (1996) *The Media Guide 1997*, Fourth Estate.

Robertson, J. W, Blain, N. and Cowan, P. (2006) 'Mum or Eminem? Media influences on today's teenagers', *Sociology Review* 26(1), 8–11.

Sharpe, S. (1994) *Just Like a Girl*, Penguin.

The UK Media Ownership Guide 2007 (2007), London: Brad Insight.

Williams, J. (1997) 'Support for all?' in *When Saturday Comes*, No. 121 (March).

Williams, J. (2004) 'Media wars', *Sociology Review* 13(4), 17–19.

Chapter 7

Alcock, P. (2008) 'Poverty and social exclusion' in P. Alcock, M. May and K. Rowlingson (eds) *The Student's Companion to Social Policy*, Blackwell.

Beetham, D, Byrne, I, Ngan, P. and Weir, S. (2002) *Democracy under Blair: A democratic audit of the United Kingdom*, Politico's.

Beetham, D, Blick, A, Margetts, H. and Weir, S. (2008) *Power and Participation in Modern Britain. A Literature Review by Democratic Audit*, Carnegie UK Trust.

Billinghurst, A. (2001) 'General election 2001: findings from the British Election Study', *Sociology Review*, 11(2), 16–19.

Brown, G. (2008) *Foreword: Raising expectations and increasing support. Easy read summary,* DWP.

Cameron, D. (2008), *Foreword: Responsibility Agenda Policy Green Paper No. 3*, Work for Welfare.

Childs, S. and Campbell, R. (2007) 'Women in Parliament', *Sociology Review*, 17(2), 8–11.

Cole, M. (2006) *Democracy in Britain*, Edinburgh University Press.

Crawford, A. and Lister, S. (2007) *The use and impact of dispersal orders: Sticking plasters and wake-up calls*, The Policy Press.

Cunningham, H. (2007) 'Social constructions of childhood', *Sociology Review,* 17(1), 12–15

Curtice, J. and Seyd, B. (2003) 'Is there a crisis of political participation?' *British Social Attitudes. The 20th Report.* Sage Publications Ltd.

Curtice, J. (2005) 'Historic triumph or rebuff? UK general election', *Politics Review*, 15(1), 2–7.

Czerniawski, G. (2005) 'Pressure Groups', *Sociology Review,* 14(4), 22–24.

Davies, T. (2002) 'Can sociology shape social policy?' *Sociology Review*, 12(1), 20–23.

Deacon, A. (2008) 'Employment' in P. Alcock, M. May and K. Rowlingson (eds) *The Student's Companion to Social Policy*, Blackwell.

Deacon, D, Golding, P. and Billig, M. (2002) 'Politics and the media: the 2001 British general election', *Sociology Review*, 12(2), 2–4.

Denver, D. (2002), 'Who voted in 2001? '*Sociology Review*. 12(2), 20–23.

Denver, D. (2006) 'A matter of duty? Turnout patterns in the 2005 general election', *Sociology Review*, 15(4), 2–4.

Denver, D. (2008) 'Valence and volatility: Explaining party choice in the twenty-first century', *Politics Review*, 18(2), 28–30.

Eden, K. and Roker, D. (2002), '...doing something': young people as social actors, National Youth Agency.

Equal Opportunities Commission (2004), Advising ethnic minority women about discrimination at work.

Equality and Human Rights Commission (2008) Who we are and what we do.

Fact File (2005), 'Equal votes?' Politics Review, 15 (1).

Fahmy, E. (2004) 'Young people and politics', Sociology Review, 14(2), 19–22.

Fraser, D. (1984) The Evolution of the British Welfare State, Macmillan.

Garnett, M. (2005) 'Groups and democracy', Politics Review, 15(2), 31–33.

Giddens, A. (2006) Sociology, Polity Press.

Ginn, J. (2008) 'Poverty and financial inequality in later life', in T. Ridge and S. Wright (eds) Understanding Inequality, Poverty and Wealth: Policies and Prospects, Policy Press.

Grant, W. (2000) Pressure Groups and British Politics, Macmillan.

Hoffman, J. (2003), 'Direct and representative democracy', Politics Review. 13(1), 11.

Home Office (2007) Life in the United Kingdom. A Journey to Citizenship.

Kavanagh, D. and Butler, D. (2005) The British General Election of 2005, Palgrave Macmillan.

Kimberlee, R.H. (2002) 'Why don't British young people vote at general elections?' Journal of Youth Studies, 5(1), 85–98.

Kitchen, S., Michaelson, J., Wood, N. and John, P. (2006) 2005 Citizenship Survey: Active communities topic report, Department for Communities and Local Government.

Lister, R. (2008) 'Citizenship and access to welfare', in P. Alcock, M. May and K. Rowlingson (eds) The Student's Companion to Social Policy, Blackwell.

Maloney, W. (2007) 'Interests groups in Britain', Politics Review, 16(4), 26–29.

McGarvey, N. and Cairney, P. (2008) Scottish Politics: An Introduction, Palgrave Macmillan.

Morgan, I. (2005) Power and Politics, Hodder & Stoughton.

Norris. P. and Wlezien, C. (2005) Britain Votes 2005, Oxford University Press.

ONS (2004), Focus on Social Inequality 2004, Palgrave Macmillan.

ONS (2007), Social Trends No 37, Palgrave Macmillan.

Power to the People (2006) The report of Power: An Independent Inquiry into Britain's Democracy, The Power Inquiry.

Rallings, C. and Thrasher, M. (1997) 'Can Labour win? Voting and general elections', Sociology Review, 6(4).

Rowe, M. (2002), The changing politics of race and ethnicity, Politics Review, 12(1), 32–33.

Rowe, M. (2005), 'The 2005 UK general election in focus', Politics Review, 15(1), 34.

Sanders, D, Clarke, H, Stewart, M. and Whiteley, P. (2005) The 2005 General Election in Great Britain: Report for the Electoral Commission.

Scammell, M. and Harrop, M. (2005) 'The Press: Still for Labour despite Blair', in Kavanagh and Butler (2005)

Sutton Trust (2005), Sutton Trust Briefing Note: The educational backgrounds of the UK's top solicitors, barristers and judges.

Walker, A. and Maltby, T. (2008), 'Older people', in P. Alcock, M. May and K. Rowlingson (eds) The Student's Companion to Social Policy, Blackwell.

Whiteley, P. (2006), 'The state of participation in Britain', Sociology Review, 16(1), 18–21.

Williams, J (1995) 'In focus: power and politics', Sociology Review, 5(1).

Chapter 8

Aries, P. (1962) Centuries of Childhood, Jonathan Cape.

Bland, A. (2008) 'The Big Question: Who are the elders, and can they do anything to resolve world crises?' The Independent, 25 November (accessed online).

Burchardt, T., Le Grand, J. and Piachaud, D. (2002), 'Degrees of exclusion: Developing a dynamic, multidimensional measure', in J. Hills, J. Le Grand and D. Piachaud. Understanding Social Exclusion, Oxford University Press.

Butler, T. and Watt, P. (2007) Understanding Social Inequality, Sage Publications Ltd.

Chapman, S. (2008) 'Is social class still important?' Sociology Review 18 (2), 30–33.

Crompton, R. (2008) Class and Stratification, Polity Press.

Curtice, J. and Heath, A. (2009), 'Have we lost our sense of identity?' Sociology Review, 18(3), 12–16.

DWP (2008) Households Below Average Income: An analysis of the income distribution 1994/95–2006/07.

Dodd, V. (2009) 'Police failing us still – Doreen Lawrence', The Guardian, 21 February.

Dunscombe, J. and Marsden, D. (1995) 'Women's "triple shift": paid employment, domestic labour and "emotion work"', Sociology Review, 4 (4).

Furlong, A., Cartmel, F., Biggart, A., Sweeting, H. and West, P. (2006) 'Social class in an "individualised" society', Sociology Review, 15(4), 28–32.

Gorard, S. (2008), 'Researching Social Mobility', Sociology Review, 18(1), 26–28.

Gordon, D., Levitas, R., Pantazis et al. (2000) Poverty and Social Exclusion in the UK, Joseph Rowntree Foundation.

Hills, J. (2006) 'Why isn't poverty history? Stratification and inequality', Sociology Review, 15(3), 8–11.

Holmes, M. (2009) Gender and Everyday Life, Routledge.

Kober, C. (2008) 'The poverty premium' in J. Strelitz and R. Lister (eds) Why Money Matters: Family Income, Poverty and Children's Lives, Save the Children.

Leach, B. (2008) 'Age discrimination claims triple in a year', Telegraph online.

Li, Y., Devine, F. and Heath, A. (2008) Equality Group Inequalities in Education, Employment and Earnings, Equality and Human Rights Commission.

Lister, R. (2004) Poverty, Polity Press.

Lister, R. (2008), in J. Strelitz and R. Lister (eds) *Why Money Matters: Family Income, Poverty and Children's Lives,* Save the Children.

McDonough, F. (2002), Class and politics, in M. Storry and P Childs (Eds) British Cultural Identities. London: Routledge, 175–207.

Millar, J. (1997) Gender, in A. Walker and C. Walker (eds) *Britain Divided*, Child Poverty Action Group.

Mizen, P. (2002) 'Putting the politics back into youth studies: Keynesianism, monetarism and the changing state of youth', *Journal of Youth Studies*, 5(1), 5–20.

Murray, C. (1996), 'The emerging British underclass', in R. Lister (ed.) *Charles Murray and the Underclass: the developing debate*, IEA.

ONS. (2004), *Social Trends No 34*, Palgrave Macmillan.

ONS (2006) *Focus on Ethnicity and Religion, 2006 Edition*, Palgrave Macmillan.

ONS (2008), *Social Trends No 38*, Palgrave Macmillan.

Piachaud, D. (2009) 'Making poverty history in the UK?' *Sociology Review*, 18(3), 2–5.

Pilcher, J. (1995) 'Growing up and growing older: The sociology of age', *Sociology Review,* 5(1), 8–13

Richards, A. (1982) *Chisunga: A Girl's Initiation Ceremony Among the Bemba of Zambia,* Tavistock.

Roberts, K. (2001) *Class in Modern Britain*, Palgrave.

Robertson, D. (2008) 'Clothes giant plans female-only store in Saudi Arabia,' *Timesonline*, May 19.

Saunders, P. (1996) *Unequal but Fair? A Study of Class Barriers in Britain*, IEA.

Savage, M. (2005), 'Class and stratification: current problems and revival prospects', in C. Calhoun, C. Rojek, and B. Turner (eds), *The SAGE Handbook of Sociology*, Sage Publications Ltd.

Scott, J. (2005) 'Social mobility: Occupational snakes and ladders', *Sociology Review*, 15(2), 18–21.

Shaw, M. (2002), A matter of life and death: How can we reduce inequalities in health?, *Sociology Review*, 11(4), 10–13.

Shaw, M, Wheeler, B, Dorling, D. and Mitchell, R. (2006). Divided Britain: Inequalities in health and healthcare', *Sociology Review* 15(3), 18–20.

Townsend, P. (1979) *Poverty in the United Kingdom*, Penguin Books.

Vincent, J. (2001) 'The life course and old age', *Sociology Review,* Nov 2001.

Walker, C. and Walker, A. (1997) 'Poverty and Social Exclusion', *Developments in Sociology*, *Volume 13*, Causeway Press.

West, J. (1997) 'Gender and work: continuity and change in the sexual division of labour' in *Developments in Sociology, Volume 13*, Causeway Press.

Index

Acknowledgements

The authors and publisher would like to thank the following for permission to reproduce photographs, pictures and artwork in this book.

Alamy (7/Images-USA); Alamy (22/B.R.Bratby); Getty Images (27/David Hume Kennerly); Getty Images (28/Frank Schwere/Stone+); Corbis (30/Ezio Petersen/Bettmann); iStockphoto (31/dwphotos); Photolibrary.com (34/Banana Stock); Alamy (37/Jo Ann Snover); Getty Images (38/Matt Cardy); Rex Features (45); Rex Features (46/© 20thC.Fox/Everett); Punchstock (48/Valueline); iStockphoto (49/aldomurillo); Photos.com (57l); iStockphoto (57r/skodonnell); Getty Images (58/George Marks/Retrofile/Hulton Archive); Photos.com (63); Getty Images (64/Daniel Berehulak); Mary Evans Picture Library (66); Alamy (68/Peter Cavanagh); Photos.com (75); NHS (80); Alamy (84/Jacky Chapman/Janine Wiedel Photolibrary); Alamy (89/Pictorial Press Ltd); Rex Features (90); Getty Images (93/EyesWideOpen); Getty Images (98l/ColorBlind Images); Alamy (98cl/Sally and Richard Greenhill); iStockphoto (98cr/track5); Alamy (98r/UpperCut Images); Alamy (100/Martin Mayer); Alamy (101/Ace Stock Ltd); Mary Evans Picture Library (102); Alamy (104/Maggie Murray/Photofusion Picture Library); Alamy (107/James Dobson); Alamy (108t/LondonPhotos - Homer Sykes); Alamy (108b/Philip Gordon/Imagestate Media Partners Limited - Impact Photos); Corbis (110/Corbis Yellow/Value RF); Courtesy of Sands School (111); Alamy (113/Jacky Chapman/Janine Wiedel Photolibrary); John Walmsley Education Photos (115); Alamy (116/Tetra Images); Alamy (118/The Photolibrary Wales); Corbis (119/Construction Photography); Alamy (122/Dan Atkin); Alamy (123/JUPITERIMAGES/BananaStock); Alamy (128/plainpicture GmbH & Co. KG); Alamy (131/apply pictures, German Images); Rex Features (134/ITV); Alamy (137/Jim West); Rex Features (145/David Fisher); iStockphoto (147/LeggNet); Getty Images (151/Peter Dazeley/Photographer's Choice RF); Wikimedia (152l); Norbert Hamann/Panoramio (152cl); Rex Features (152cr/Peter Brooker); iStockphoto (152r/ChrisSteer); Alamy (158/Nic Cleave Photography); Alamy (161/ Ace Stock Ltd); Alamy (164/Alastair Balderstone); iStockphoto (179/narvikk); Courtesy of CheethambellJWT and The Department for Work and Pensions (183); Getty Images (188b/Luc Beziat/Taxi); Alamy (188t/vario images GmbH & Co.KG); Alamy (189/keith morris); Rex Features (191/Alex Segre); Alamy (192t/Eyre); Alamy (192b/Alex Segre); iStockphoto (198/alexsl); Getty Images (200/Fox Photos/Hulton Archive); Rex Features (201/Ken McKay); Rex Features (202/Ken McKay); Rex Features (205l/Francis Dean); Rex Features (205c/Denkou Images); Getty Images (205r/Gulfimages); Rex Features (213/David Fisher); Alamy (215l/Stockbroker/MBI); PA Photos (215r/Johnny Green); Rex Features (216/Debra L. Rothenberg); BBC Photo Library (218/EastEnders : 2006 : Picture shows: (l-r) Diane Parish as Denise Fox, Rudolph Walker as Patrick Trueman, Tiana Benjamin as Chelsea Fox and Belinda Owusu as Libby); PA Photos (223/Andy Zakeli); Getty Images (224/Haynes Archive/Popperfoto); Picturedesk/The Kobal Collection (226/Relativity/Spyglass/Universal); Getty Images (229t/Pablo Martinez Monsivais-Pool); Getty Images (229b/Alexander Joe/AFP); House of Commons (230); Rex Features (232); Alamy (236/Lightworks Media); Alamy (246/David Crausby); Rex Features (248); PA Photos (251/Dave Thompson); PA Photos (259/John Birdsall); Alamy (261/By Ian Miles-Flashpoint Pictures); Rex Features (262/Ray Tang); Rex Features (263/Nils Jorgensen); Getty Images (266/Shaun Curry/AFP); Alamy (268/Brenda Prince/Photofusion Picture Library); Alamy (276l/Stockbroker/MBI); Alamy (276r/John Sturrock); Getty Images (281/Rolls Press/Popperfoto); Alamy (283/Tim Graham); Getty Images (285l/Ron Levine/The Image Bank); Getty Images (285c/Dave M. Benett); Alamy (285r/Peter Titmuss); Alamy (286/David Hoffman Photo Library); Getty Images (288l/James Keyser/Time Life Pictures); Rex Features (288r); Getty Images (293r/Ben Stansall); PA Photos (293l/Martin Rickett); Rex Features (297/Alison Wright/Robert Harding); Getty Images (299/Keystone Features/Hulton Archive); Alamy (300/i love images / Beauty and Wellbeing); iStockphoto (307/quavondo); Rex Features (308l/Sipa Press); Alamy (308r/Libby Welsh/Janine Wiedel Photolibrary); PA Photos (314/Geoff Caddick); Rex Features (320/Jonathan Hordle); Alamy (325/Peter Barritt)

The authors and publishers are grateful to the copyright holders for permission to use the following quoted materials.

p. 8: extract from www.sheffield.ac.uk; p. 10: extract from Taylor, C. F. (1996) *Native American Life* London: Salamander Books; p. 11 extract from Maclean, C. (1979) *The Wolf Children: Fact or Fantasy?* Harmondsworth: Penguin; pp. 13 & 40: extracts adapted from *The British on the Costa del Sol: Transitional Identities and Local Communities* by K. O'Reilly, Routledge 2000, reprinted with permission of Taylor and Francis Books UK; p. 25: extract adapted from Winlow, S. and Hall, S. (2006) *Violent Night: Urban Leisure and Contemporary Culture*, Oxford: BERG; extract from Robson E., 2001 'The routes project: disadvantaged young people interviewing their peers' in J. Clark et al *Young People as Researchers: Possibilities, Problems and Politics* Leicester National Youth Agency (www.nya.org.uk); p. 27: extract adapted from *Young, Free and Single: Twenty-Somethings and Household Change* by S. Heath and E. Cleaver, Palgrave Macmillan, 2003. Reprinted with permission of Palgrave Macmillan; p. 31: extract adapted from Ward, J. (2008) 'Researching drug sellers: an experimental account from the field' SOCIOLOGICAL RESEARCH ONLINE 13 (1); p. 40: extract adapted from Charles, N., Aull Davies, C., and Harris, C. (2008) *Families in Transition: Social Change, Family Formation and Kin Relationships*, Policy Press; p. 42: an adaptation of the BSA (2002) *Statement of Ethical Practice*, reproduced by permission of The British Sociological Association. The British Sociological Association is both a Registered Charity (no. 1080235) and a Company Limited by Guarantee (no. 3890729); p. 45: extract adapted from 'The uses of Sociology' by J. Pilcher, *Sociology Review*, 14 (1), p. 204 (2004), reprinted by permission of Philip Allan Updates; p. 47: extract adapted from *Families, Households and Society* by G. Allan and G. Crow, Palgrave Macmillan, 2001. Reprinted with permission of Palgrave Macmillan; p. 55: extract adapted from Halsey, A. H. (1992) in N. Dennis and G. Erdos, *Families Without Fatherhood*. London: The IEA Health and Welfare Unit; pp. 61 & 62: tables adapted from Table 3.1 'Attitudes to women's employment, by sex, 1989–2006' (p. 55), from Crompton, R. and Lyonette, C. (2008) 'Who does the housework? The division of labour within the home' in *British Social Attitudes: the 24th Report*. London, Sage Publications (material adapted); p. 65: extract adapted from 'Domestic violence is a crime society ignores' by Joan Smith, *The Independent*, 18 July 2008; p. 69: extract adapted from 'Grown-up offspring cost parents £21,500' by James Meikle, *The Guardian*, 5 September 2008. © Guardian News & Media Ltd, 2008; pp. 70–71: two diagrams adapted from 'The age of beanpole families' by J. Brannen, *Sociology Review*, 13 (1) pp. 6–9, 2003. Reprinted with permission of Philip Allan Updates; p. 85: Ginn and Arber Resource Triangle (adapted) from 'Gender and resources in later life' by J. Ginn and S. Arber, *Sociology Review*, 2 (2) 1992. Reprinted by permission of Philip Allan Updates; p. 92: two extracts adapted from 'Forced Marriages' by J. Garrod, *Sociology Review*, 14 (4) pp. 14–15, 2005. Reprinted by permission of Philip Allan Updates; p. 93: extract adapted from 'First person: Arranged marriages fascinate people in the UK, like watching horror films' by Ziauddin Sardar, *The Guardian*, 13 September 2008. © Guardian News & Media Ltd 2008; p. 95: extract adapted from 'Fattest children to be taken away from their parents' by N. Morris, *The Independent*, 16 August 2008; p. 109: table adapted from *The Educational Background of Vice Chancellors*, November 2008, produced by The Sutton Trust. Reprinted with permission of The Sutton Trust; p. 111: extract about Sands School (and photo), www.sands-school.co.uk. Reprinted with kind permission; pp. 112 & 114: extracts adapted from Gewirtz, S. et al (1995) *Markets, Choice and Equity in Education*. Oxford: Open University Press; p. 113: extract from 'Education – bouncing back' by T. Wragg, *Sociology Review*, 13 (2), 2003. Reproduced by permission of Philip Allan Updates; p116: extract adapted from Gillborn, D. and Youdell, D. (2000) *Rationing Education: policy, practice, reform and equity*. Oxford: Open University Press; p. 123: extract from 'Schooling and educational performance' by J. Williams, *Sociology Review*, 13 (2), 2003. Reproduced with permission of Philip Allan Updates; p. 125: extract from 'It's not what you know – education and social capital' by S. Ball, *Sociology Review*, 13 (2), 2003. Reproduced with permission of Philip Allan Updates; p. 132: extract adapted from 'Single-sex schools, no benefit for girls' by Anushka Asthana, *The Observer*, 25 June 2006. Copyright © Guardian News & Media Ltd 2006. Reprinted with permission; p. 154: extract adapted from *Theories of Crime*, edited by I. Marsh, Routledge, 2006. Reprinted with permission of Taylor & Francis Books UK; p. 155: extract adapted from 'Do your genes make you a criminal?' by Steve Connor, *The Independent*, February 12 1996; 9. 157: extract from *The Cocaine Kids* by Terry Williams, Addison Wesley. Reprinted by permission of Perseus Books Group; p. 161: extract adapted from 'Shopping centre outlaws "hoodies" ' by David Sapsted, *The Telegraph*, 12 May 2005; p. 172: extract adapted from 'Girl gangs muscling in on street violence' by J. Slack, *The Daily Mail*, 22 August 2007; p. 177: extract adapted from 'Is policing fair?' by M. Townsley and B. Marshall, *Sociology Review*, 16 (2) pp. 19–21, 2006. Reprinted by permission of Philip Allan Updates; p. 180

Crimeshare: The Unequal Impact of Crime by M. Dixon et al, IPPR, 2006 quoted in Walklate (2007); p. 190: table adapted from The *Media Student's Book* 4th edition, by G. Branston and R. Stafford, Routledge, 2006. Reprinted with permission of Taylor & Francis Books UK; pp. 194, 196,197, 208 & 209: extracts from *The Brad UK Media Ownership Guide 2007*; p. 195: adapted Table 8.1 'Trends in newspaper readership, 1983–2006' (p. 163) from Curtice, J. and Mair, A. (2008) 'Where have all the readers gone? Popular newspapers and Britain's political health' in *British Social Attitudes: the 24th Report*. London: Sage Publications (material adapted); p. 201: extract from 'Why study media content?' by B. Gunter, *Sociology Review*, 18 (2) pp 6–9, 2008. Reprinted by permission of Philip Allan Updates; p. 202: extract from *Television and Society* by N. Abercrombie, Polity Press, 1996; p. 205: extract adapted from *Media, Gender and Identity: An Introduction* by D. Gauntlett, Routledge 2008. Reprinted with permission of Taylor & Francis Books UK; pp. 207 & 240: tables adapted from Kavanagh and Butler, *The British General Election of 2005*. Reproduced with permission of Palgrave Macmillan; p. 219: extract adapted from Alexander C. (2004) 'Writing race: Ethnography and the Imagination of the Asian Gang' in M. Bulmer and J. Solomons, eds (2004) *Researching Race and Racism*, pp. 134–9, Routledge. Reprinted with permission of Taylor & Francis Books UK; p. 220: extract from Broadcasting Standards Council report (1990) *Sexual Stereotyping in Advertising*, Reprinted with permission of Ofcom (www.ofcom.org.uk); p. 221: extract adapted from 'Phwoar-ty Love' by Charlie Wyett, *The Sun*, 29 May 2003. © NI Syndications; p. 223: bullet points from Oates, S. (2008) Introduction to Media and Politics, London: Sage Publications (material adapted); p. 224: extract from *Fold Devils and Moral Panics* by S. Cohen, Routledge 2002, 3rd edition. Reprinted with permission of Taylor & Francis Books UK; p. 225: extract adapted from *Media Accountability and Freedom of Publication* by McQuail, D. (2003), p. 6, Oxford University Press; p. 227: extract adapted from *Ill Effects: The Media Violence Debate* edited by M. Barker and J. Petley, Routledge 2001. Reprinted with permission of Taylor & Francis Books UK; p. 233: table adapted from Sutton Trust 2005, *Sutton Briefing Note: The educational backgrounds of the UK's top solicitors, barristers and judges*; p. 235: 2 pie charts drawn with figures taken from 'Fact File 2005, Equal Votes?' *Political Review*, 15 (1) 2005. Reprinted with permission of Philip Allan Updates; p. 237: table adapted from Curtice, J. and Seyd, B. (2003) 'Is there a crisis of political participation?' in Park, A., Curtice, J., Thomson, K., Jarvis, L. and Bromley, C. (eds) *British Social Attitudes. The 20th Report*. London: Sage. Reprinted with permission of National Centre for Social Research; chart drawn from figures from Sanders, D., Clarke, H., Stewart, M. and Whiteley, P. (2005) *The 2005 General Election in Great Britain: Report for the Electoral Commission*. Reprinted with permission of the authors; p. 244: table adapted from *Democracy in Britain* by Matthew Cole, published by Edinburgh University Press, 2006 p. 7. Reprinted with permission of Edinburgh University Press; p. 247: extract adapted from 'Interests Groups in Britain' by W. Maloney, *Politics Review*, 16 (4) pp. 26–29, 2007. Reproduced with permission of Philip Allan Updates; p. 248: table adapted from *Power and Participation in Modern Britain* by Beetham, D., Blick, A., Margetts, H. and Weir, S., published by Democratic Audit (www.democraticaudit.com); p. 251: extract adapted from

'Pressure Groups' by G. Czerniawkski, *Sociology Review*, 14 (4) pp. 22–24, 2005. Reproduced with permission of Philip Allan Updates; p. 258: extract adapted from …*doing something: young people as social actors* by K. Eden and D. Roker, The National Youth Agency, 2002; p. 259: extract adapted from 'Young People and Politics' by E. Fahmy, *Sociology Review*, 14 (2) pp. 19–22. Reproduced with permission of Philip Allan Updates; p. 264: extract adapted from Alcock, P. 2008 'Poverty and social exclusion' in P. Alcock, M. May and K. Rowlingson (eds) *The Student's Companion to Social Policy*, pp. 131–8, Oxford: Blackwell; p. 266: extract adapted from Deacon, A. (2008) 'Employment' in P. Alcock, M. May and K. Rowlingson (eds) *The Student's Companion to Social Policy*, pp. 311–17, Oxford: Blackwell; p. 268: text adapted from Equality and Human Rights Commission (2008) *Who we are and what we do*; p. 269: text adapted from Equal Opportunities Commission. (2004) *Advising ethnic minority women about discrimination at work*; p. 273: extract adapted from www.schoolcouncils.org/front-page/News/pupils-get-a-real-voice-what-to-do-now; p. 274: extract adapted from Crawford, A. and Lister, S. (2007) *The use and impact of dispersal orders: Sticking plasters and wake-up calls*. Bristol: The Policy Press; p. 277: extract adapted from *Class in Modern Britain* by K. Roberts, Palgrave, 2001. Reprinted with permission of Palgrave Macmillan; p. 279: extract adapted from Shaw, M. 'A matter of life and death: How can we reduce inequalities in health?' *Sociology Review*, 11(4), pp. 10–13, 2002. Reproduced with permission of Philip Allan Updates; p. 289: extract adapted from *Gender and Everyday Life* by M. Holmes, Routledge, 2009. Reprinted with permission of Taylor & Francis Books UK; extract adapted from 'Clothes giant plans female-only-store in Saudi Arabia' by D. Robertson, *The Times*, May 19 2008. © NI Syndications; p. 295: table adapted from Li, Y., Devine, F. and Heath, A. (2008) *Group Inequalities in Education, Employment and Earnings*, Equality and Human Rights Commission; p. 298: table adapted from 'Putting the Politics back into youth studies: Keynesianism, Monetarism and the Changing State of Youth' by Phillip Mizen, *Journal of Youth Studies*, 5 (1) January 3 2002. Reprinted with permission of Taylor & Francis Journals via Rightslink; p. 299, 300: extracts adapted from Pilcher, J. (1995) 'Growing up and growing older: The sociology of age', *Sociology Review*, 5 (1), pp. 8–13. Reprinted by permission of Philip Allan Updates; p. 301: extract adapted from 'Age discrimination claims triple in a year' by Ben Leach, *The Telegraph*, 7 December 2008. Reprinted with permission; p. 303: extract from *The Sunday Times Rich List*, 2008 © NI Syndication Reprinted with permission; p. 305: extract adapted from Gorard, S. (2008), 'Researching Social Mobility', *Sociology Review*, 18(1), pp. 26–28. Reprinted by permission of Philip Allan Updates; p. 306: extract adapted from *Class and Stratification* by R. Crompton, Polity Press, 2008. Reprinted with permission of Polity Press; p. 307: extract adapted from Scott, J. (2005) 'Social mobility: Occupational snakes and ladders', *Sociology Review*, 15(2), 1pp. 8–21. Reprinted with permission of Philip Allan Updates; p. 308: extract from *Poverty in the United Kingdom* by Peter Townsend (Penguin, 1979) Copyright © Peter Townsend 1979. Reprinted with permission of Penguin Books UK; p. 310, table adapted from *Poverty and Social Exclusion in the UK* by D. Gordon, R. Levitas, Pantazis, published in 2000 by The Joseph Rowntree Foundation. Reproduced with permission of The Joseph Rowntree Foundation; p. 314: extract adapted from www.ecpc.org.uk; p. 318: extract from Murray, C. (1996), 'The emerging British underclass', in R. Lister (ed.) *Charles Murray and the Underclass: the developing debate*, IEA; p. 322: extract from 'Class and politics' by F. McDonough, in *British Cultural Identities* by M. Storry and P. Childs (eds) published by Routledge 2002. Reprinted with permission of Taylor & Francis Books UK; p. 323: extract adapted from Furlong, A., Cartmel, F., Biggart, A., Sweeting, H. and West, P. (2006) 'Social class in an "individualised" society', *Sociology Review*, 15(4), pp. 28–32. Reprinted by permission of Philip Allan Updates.

All Crown Copyright Material is reproduced with permission of the Controller, Office of Public Sector Information (OPSI).

Every effort has been made to contact copyright holders, but if any have been inadvertently overlooked, the publishers will be pleased to make the necessary arrangements at the first opportunity.